FACETS OF
INDIAN CIVILIZATION

— Recent Perspectives —

(*Essays in Honour of Prof. B.B. Lal*)

Chief Editor
Jagat Pati Joshi

Editors
D.K. Sinha, S.C. Saran, C.B. Mishra and G.S. Gaur

Volume II

HISTORICAL ARCHAEOLOGY, ART and ARCHITECTURE,
BEYOND INDIAN FRONTIERS

Aryan Books International
New Delhi

These volumes are being reprinted to celebrate
the centenary of Prof. B.B. Lal
(born 2nd May, 1921)

FACETS OF INDIAN CIVILIZATION

ISBN: 978-81-7305-085-5 (Vol. II)
978-81-7305-087-9 (Set)

First Published: 1997

Reprinted: 2021

Responsibility for statements made and visuals provided in the various papers rests solely with the contributors. The views expressed by individual authors are not necessarily those of the editors or of the publisher.

Published by:

Aryan Books International
Pooja Apartments, 4B, Ansari Road, New Delhi-110 002 (India)
Tel.: 23287589, 23255799; Fax: 91-11-23270385
E-mail: aryanbooks@gmail.com
www.aryanbooks.com

Printed in India

CONTENTS

TRIBUTES

(In Vol. I)

Vol. I

Section A–Prehistory & Rock Art

Section B–Protohistory

Vol. II

Section C–Historical Archaeology

Section D–Art & Architecture

Section E–Beyond Indian Frontiers

Vol. III

Section F–Epigraphy & Numismatics

Section G–Heritage Conservation

Section H–Religion & Philosophy

Section I–Museology

Section J–Underwater Archaeology

Section K–Ethno-Archaeology, Archaeo-Botany & Archaeo-Zoology

Section L–Allied Aspects

LIST OF ILLUSTRATIONS

VOL. I

VOL. II

VOL. III

LIST OF CONTRIBUTORS

A. Sundara
Director, Karnataka University P.G. Centre, Sholapur Road, Bijapur-586 103.

A.K. Sharma
Superintending Archaeologist (Retd.), ASI, Prehistory Branch, Nagpur.

A.K. Singh
Deptt. of A.I.H.C. & Archaeology, Jiwaji University, Gwalior-474 011.

Abhay Kumar Singh
Deptt. of Ancient History & Culture, Rohilkhand University, Bareilly.

Ahmed Ali
D-11, Shastri Nagar, Bhadbhada Road, Bhopal, M.P.

Ajay Mitra Shastri
23, Vidya Vihar, Rana Pratap Nagar, Nagpur-440 022.

Alok Tripathi
Mama Ka Bazar, Lashkar, Gwalior, M.P.-474 001.

Anirudh Singh Gaur
Marine Archaeology Centre, National Institute of Oceanography, Dona Paula, Goa.

Arun Kesarwani
Deptt. of Ancient Indian History & Archaeology, Kurukshetra University, Kurukshetra.

Ashwani Asthana
Venus Apatments, Rohtak Road, New Delhi.

A. Jha
Asstt. Superintending Archaeologist, ASI, Guwahati.

Anil K.S. Pokharia
Birbal Sahni Institute of Palaeobotany, Lucknow.

B.K. Sinha
Superintending Archaeologist (Retd.), Bhubaneswar.

B.K. Thapar
Director General (Retd.), 342, SFS, DDA, Hauz Khas, New Delhi.

B.L. Nagarch
Director (Retd.), ASI, New Delhi.

B.M. Pande
Director (Retd.), ASI, New Delhi.

B.N. Tandon
Jt. Director General (Retd.), ASI, New Delhi.

B.P. Sinha
Professor (Retd.), Deptt. of A.I.H.C. & Archaeology, Patna University, Patna.

B.R. Mani
Superintending Archaeologist, Excavation Branch, ASI, Purana Qila, New Delhi.

B.S. Verma
J-124, Kankar Bagh Colony, Patna-800 020.

Bansi Lal Malla
I.G.N.C.A., Janpath, New Delhi.

Baldev Singh Negi
Assistant Superintending Archaeologist, ASI, New Delhi.

Bharat Jhunjhunwala
C/o Shri Krishna Deva, C-121, D.D.A. Flats, Saket, N. Delhi-110017.

Bhupendra Pal Singh
Deptt. of A.I.H.C. & Archaeology, B.H.U., Varanasi-221 005.

Binoy Kumar Sahay
National Museum, Janpath, New Delhi-110 011.

Birendra Kumar Sinha
Research Officer, Revenue & L.R. Deptt., Patna.

Bhagwan Singh
136, Maharana Pratap Enclave, Delhi-110034.

C.B. Trivedi
Superintending Archaeologist (Retd.), ASI, Bhopal.

C.S. Mahadevan
International Society for the Investigation of Ancient Civilization, 102, Mount Road, Guindy, Madras-600 032.

C.S. Vasudavan
No. 2, Krishnaraja, Boulevard Road, Chamaraja Puram, Mysore-570 004.

Chandrashekhar Gupta
Head, Deptt. of A.I.H.C. & Archaeology, Nagpur University, Nagpur.

Channabassapa S. Patil
Deputy Director, Directorate of Archaeology & Museums, The Palace Complex, Mysore-570 001.

C. Margabandhu
Director (Retd.), ASI, New Delhi.

C. Dorje
Superintending Archaeologist, ASI, New Delhi.

D.K. Sinha
Superintending Archaeologist (Retd.), Venus Apartments, Delhi-110 041.

D.P. Agrawal
Physical Research Laboratory, Ahmedabad-380 009.

D.P. Sharma
Keeper, National Museum, New Delhi.

Devendra Handa
Deptt. of A.I.H.C. & Archaeology, Punjabi University, Chandigarh-160 014.

Debala Mitra
Director General (Retd.), A.S.I., New Delhi.

Farooq A. Lone
Botany Department, Kashmir University, Srinagar-190 006.

G. Stacul
University Di Trieste, Trieste.

G.M. Bongard-Levin
Moscow University Institute of South Asian & African Studies, Moscow.

G.M. Buth
Botany Department, Kashmir University, Srinagar-190 006.

Gayatri Chaturvedi
Deptt. of Ancient Indian History, Culture & Archaeology, Banaras Hindu University, Varanasi-221-005.

Gregory L. Possehl
The University Museum, University of Pennsylvania, Philadelphia, PA 19104-6324.

Gyanendra Nath Srivastava
ASI, Agra Circle, Agra-282 001.

G.S. Gaur
Asstt. Superintending Archaeologist, Archaeological Museum, Sanchi.

H.A. Phadke
Deptt. of History, Kurukshetra University, Kurukeshtra.

H.N. Singh
Director (Retd.), ASI, Lucknow.

H.L. Raina
Asstt. Superintending Engineer, ASI, Delhi

Hem Chandra Pande
Centre of Russian Studies, Jawaharlal Nehru University, New Delhi-110 067.

I.K. Sarma
Director, Salarjung Museum, Hyderabad.

J.S. Nigam
Superintending Archaeologist (Retd.), Nijam Bagh, Lucknow.

Jagat Pati Joshi
Director General (Retd.), ASI, New Delhi.

Jitendra Nath
National Museum, New Delhi.

J.S. Khatri
Deptt. of Archaeology and Museums, Govt. of Haryana, Chandigarh.

Jose Pereira
Deptt. of Theology, Fordhan University, New York 10705 (U.S.A.).

K.D. Bajpai
HIG-15, Padmakar Nagar, Sagar (M.P.)-470 004.

K.K. Raman
President, Indus Valley Script Study Society, Elavumthitta, Kerala.

K.M. Srivastava
Director (Retd.), ASI, New Delhi.

K.M. Suresh
Director of Museum, Kannada University, Hampi, Kamalpur, Bellary-583 221.

K.P. Padhy
Assistant Superintending Archaeologist, Ratnagiri Museum, Ratnagiri, Orissa.

K.P. Poonacha
Superintending Archaeologist, ASI, Bangalore Circle, Bangalore.

Kalyan Kumar Sarkar
University of Windsor, Canada.

Kiran Kumar Thaplyal
Professor, Lucknow University, Lucknow.

Krishna Deva
Director (Retd.), ASI, New Delhi.

Krishna Kumar
Asstt. Superintending Archaeologist (Retd.), ASI, Singhpur Palace, Chanderi (M.P.).

K.S. Saraswat
Birbal Sahni Institute of Palaeobotany, Lucknow.

Lallanji Gopal
9, Gurudham Colony, Varanasi-221 010.

Lokesh Chandra
J-22, Hauz Khas Enclave, New Delhi-110 016.

M.D. Sampath
Chief Epigraphist, ASI, Epigraphy Branch, Mysore-570 005.

M.S. Mate
Deccan College, Pune.

M.V. Visweswara
ASI, Bangalore Circle, Bangalore.

Madhuri Sharma
National Museum, New Delhi-110 001.

Malati J. Shendge
1603, Sadashiv Peth, Pune-411 030.

Manju Pant
Chemist, Pt. G.B. Pant Govt. Museum, Almora.

Maqsooda Khan
Botany Department, Kashmir University, Srinagar-190 006.

Monira Khatun
Superintending Archaeologist (Retd.), Venus Apartments, Rohtak Road, Delhi-110 041.

Maruti Nandan Prasad Tiwari
Reader & Head, Deptt. of History of Art, B.H.U., Varanasi-221 005.

M. Acharya
Deptt. of Archaeology and Museums, Govt. of Haryana, Chandigarh.

Madhu Bala
Deputy Director, Institute of Archaeology, ASI, Delhi.

N.C. Ghosh
Professor (Retd.), Visva-Bharati, Santiniketan.

N.L. Batra
Superintending Engineer, ASI, New Delhi.

Nisar Ahmed
Deptt. of A.I.H.C. & Archaeology, Banaras Hindu University, Varanasi.

O.P. Jaiswal
Deptt. of A.I.H.C. & Archaeology, Banaras Hindu University, Varanasi.

P.K. Trivedi
Professor, Deptt. of A.I.H.C. & Archaeology, Patna University, Patna.

Parmeshwari Lal Gupta
Indian Institute of Research in Numismatic Studies, Anjaneri, Nasik-422 213.

Pranabanand Jash
Visva Bharati, P.O. Santiniketan (W. Bengal) 731235.

Prithvi Kumar Agrawala
Reader, Deptt. of A.I.H.C. & Archaeology, B.H.U., Varanasi-221 005.

R. Morton Smith
Professor Emeritus, Deptt. of East Asian Studies, University of Toronto, Toronto, Canada-M5S 1A5.

R. Nagaswamy
22nd Cross Street, Besant Nagar, Madras-600 090.

R. Sengupta
40/78, Chitranjan Park, New Delhi-110 019.

R.C. Agrawal
Director, ASI, New Delhi.

R.C. Agrawala
Ex-Director of Museums, 8/192, Malaviya Nagar, Jaipur-302 017.

R.C. Gaur
A/10, Kela Nagar, Morris Road Extension, Aligarh-202 001.

R.C. Sharma
Director General (Retd.), National Museum, New Delhi-110 001.

R.N. Mehta
8, Shreyas Society, Race Course, Vadodara-390 007, Gujarat.

R.P. Pandey
Deptt. of A.I.H.C. & Archaeology, Jiwaji University, Gwalior, M.P.

R.S. Fonia
Superintending Archaeologist, ASI, Jammu.

Radha Kant Verma
Prof. & Head, Deptt. of A.I.H.C. & Arch., APS University, Rewa.

Ram Vallabh Somani
53A, Satya Nagar, Jhotawara, Jaipur.

R.S. Bisht
Director, Institute of Archaeology, New Delhi.

S.A. Sali
Superintending Archaeologist (Retd.), ASI, Aurangabad.

S.L. Shali
Dy. Superintending Archaeologist, ASI, Srinagar.

S.S. Biswas
Director-General, National Museum, New Delhi.

S. Swaminathan
Senior Epigraphical Asstt., ASI, Epigraphy Branch, Mysore-570 005.

S.C. Saran
Deputy Superintending Archaeologist, Museum Branch, Lal Qila, Delhi.

S.K. Dubey
Exploration Assistant, Regional Archaeological Unit, Almora.

S.P. Gupta
148, Vigyan Vihar, Delhi-110 092.

S.R. Goyal
Professor, Deptt. of History, University of Jodhpur, Jodhpur-342 001.

S.S. Gupta
ASI, Prehistory Branch, Nagpur.

Shankar Goyal
Asstt. Professor, Jai Narain Vyas University, Jodhpur.

Shashi Asthana
National Museum, Janpath, New Delhi.

Shiva Kant Dwivedi
Indira Kala Sangit University, Khairagarh, M.P.

Sila Tripathi
Marine Archaeology Centre, National Institute of Oceanography, Dona-Paula, Goa-403 004.

Sudha Malaiya
Deptt. of A.I.H.C. & A., H.S. Gaur University, Sagar (H.P.).

Sumita Chakravarty
Visva-Bharati, Santiniketan.

Susmita Pandey
Prachya Niketan, Bhopal.

Sunil Kumar Patnaik
Deptt. of History, Berhampur University, Orissa-760 007.

Tobdan
Sai Kunj, North Oak, Sanjauli, Simla-171006.

T.M. Kesava
ASI, Bangalore Circle, Bangalore.

Umesh Chandra Dwivedi
Curator, Ranchi Museum, Ranchi.

Upendra Thakur
33/247, Road No. 10 E, Rajendra Nagar, Patna-800 016.

V.C. Srivastava
Prof. & Head, Department of A.I.H.C. & Archaeology, B.H.U., Varanasi-5.

V.H. Sonawane
Deptt. of Archaeology, M.S. University of Baroda, Vadodara, Gujarat.

V.R. Mitragotri
Daulat Building, Archaeology Unit, St. Inez, Panaji, Goa.

Vidula Jayaswal
B-30/72A, Nagwa, Varanasi-221 005.

Vidyanand Saraswati
D-14/16, Model Town, Delhi-110007.

Vijay Kumar Thakur
Deptt. of History, Patna University, Patna.

Walter A. Fairservis, Jr.
Vassar College, Poughkeepsie, New York.

Z.A. Desai
Director (Retd.), ASI (Epigraphy Branch), Mysore.

Section C

Historical Archaeology

33
THE CHALUKYAS OF CENTRAL INDIA

AHMED ALI

A New Light

During the early mediaeval period, due to the absence of single supreme sovereign, central India became a political chessboard. Many Rajput chiefs like the Gurjara Pratīhāras, Paramāras, Chandellas, Kalachuris and the Kachchapaghātas played their roles to establish their sovereignty.

Some of these chiefs could outshine because of the jealous rulers who could influence over larger regions politically and culturally but the others were bound to their limited regions and for comparatively shorter period of time.

The inscriptions discovered from Maser (District Vidisha) and Bilhari (District Jabalpur) have brought the names of Salki (Chalukya) rulers in this region. In these epigraphic records the origin of the dynasty has been traced from Brahmā and his legendary son Bharadvāja,[1] but the lists of the rulers differ from one inscription to other. Thus, for example, the Bilhari inscription of the Kalachuri ruler Yuvarājadeva-I mentions the names of Salki rulers like Siṁhavarmana, Shadhanva and Avantivarmana and his daughter Nohla who was the wife of Yuvarājadeva[2] while the Maser inscription mentions the names of Narasiṁha and his son Kesarin. Scholars like Mirashi and Venkataramayya are of the opinion that these rulers are the offspring of same stock.[3] Mirashi has further advanced his views by adding the names of Avantivarmana of Rannod inscriptions with the list of the rulers of this dynasty;[4] and he has prepared a genealogical table of this dynasty. According to it, the period of Avantivarmana is A.D. 825. He was succeeded by Siṁhavarmana sometime in A.D. 850. His son Shadhanva succeeded him in A.D. 875 while Shadhanva was followed by his son Avantivarmana in A.D. 900 who was the father of Nohla. Most probably, Narasiṁha ruled before A.D. 950 and his son Kesarin ruled after it.[5]

The correlation of the families mentioned in both the inscriptions as of progeny of the same stock seems to be quite possible but they can not be closely related because Maser inscription mentions the permanent abode of Narasiṁha at Kūṭagrāma known as Golahath Chanaki situated near Etapura; and, later on, they established themselves at Vida-dvadasa.[6] Venkataramayya has identified Golahatti-Chanaki with Gola and Chanegaon and Etapura with modern Ellora (District Aurangabad, Maharashtra). If this identification is correct, then Narasiṁha and his ancestors might have migrated from Gola and Chanegaon while Avantivarmana had already established his capital at Mattamayūra in the beginning of ninth century A.D.[7] His successors Siṁhavarmana, Shadhanva and Avantivarmana might have ruled from Mattamayūra. This fact is also substantiated by the names of the *āchāryas* of Pāśupata sect of Mattamayūra clan who were invited by the Kalachuri rulers.

In this context, we may, however, consider the historical facts of the Maser inscription which mentions that Narasiṁha and his son Kesarin were the feudatories of Kṛṣṇa. Mirashi has identified him as the younger brother of Dhaṅga (A.D. 950-1005) whose minister Vāchaspati of *Kaundinya-gotra* killed a Sabara chief Siṁha and placed the chief of Ralamaṇḍala and Rādapani.[8] If we agree with the views of Mirashi, then we shall have to consider a conflict between the Chandellas and the Kachchhapaghatas as the conflict between Kesarin—the feudatory of Kṛṣṇa—and joint army of Laṭeśa and Kachchhawaha is mentioned in the Maser inscription.

The Kachchhawahas are no other than the Kachchhapaghatas of Gwalior region but no such evidence has, so far, been found as both had been the feudatories of the Pratihāras. In due course, the Kachchhapaghata chief Vairadamana snatched Gwalior Fort from the Pratihāras on behalf of the Chandella king Dhaṅga.[9]

Thus, in our opinion, Kṛṣṇa of Maser inscription may be identified with the Rashtrakuta ruler Kṛṣṇa III (A.D. 939-67) who invaded north India twice as proved by his Karhad plate and Jura stone inscription.[10] Perhaps his first battle against the Kalachuris was fought by his feudatory Narasiṁha as Maser inscription informs that Narasiṁha destroyed the Kalachuris and forced their wives to live as widows.[11]

Similar information is available in the Karhada plate where Kṛṣṇa claims his victory over the Kalachuri *sahashrārjuna.* Thus the battle fought by Narasiṁha against the Kalachuri must be accepted for his master Kṛṣṇa III which must have taken place between A.D. 934 and 939.

Further, the preceding lines of the inscription seem to be more important as it mentions the conflict between Kesarin and the joint army of Laṭeśa and Kachchhawaha. The Kachchhawaha were the Kachchhapaghatas while the Laṭeśa of this inscription is, probably, the Chalukya ruler Barappa who captured the Lāṭa area after the first invasion of Kṛṣṇa III; and assumed the title of Laṭeśa. Most probably, this encroachment by Barappa was made at the instigation of the Pratihāras - the lord of Barappa. It was due to this, when Kesarin marched against Barappa, on behalf of Kṛṣṇa III, the Kachchhapaghatas assisted the army of Barappa as both were the feudatories of the Pratihāras.[12] In this expedition, probably, Kesarin was assisted by the Paramāra ruler Siyaka as both were the feudatories of the Rashtrakutas in central India.

The inscription further mentions about a battle between the rulers of the family of Vakpati and the Rashtrakuta ruler Khaṭṭigadeva at Khalighāta (Khalaghata, District Dhar) on the bank of Narmadā and informs us about the death of a hero who fought in favour of Siyaka.[13] Similar information is supplied in Arthuna inscription of Chāmuṇḍarāja.[14] This event must have taken place in *circa* A.D. 927-73. In this battle though Khattigadeva was strongly opposed by the Paramāras, it however seems that he marched towards north victoriously and thus it is mentioned in Maser inscription.

Thus, the inscription eulogises the victory of the Rashtrakutas and their feudatories. However, we have concrete evidence that soon after this battle they were uprooted by the Paramāras from central India.

The Maser inscription further mentions the conflict between Kesarin and Hūṇas at Paṭṭanaka. Venkataramayya has tried to identify the Paṭṭanaka with Anahilawāda-Paṭṭana. If it is so, then Kesarin might have fought against the Chalukya Mūlaraja and his Hūṇa vassal of Lalikya.

Thus, it is clear that the Chalukyas of central India were the feudatories of the Rashtrakutas for a considerable period during tenth century A.D. Now, our problem is that, who were these Chalukyas (Salkis) and where was their capital ? In this connection, the Maser inscription mentioning the names of Narasiṁha and Kesarin informs us about their permanent abode at Golahatti-Chanaki (modern Gola and Chanegaon) as discussed above, while the earlier inscription of Bilhari does not mention their place. We have seen that Avantivarmana was the first ruler of the Chalukya family of central India and his capital was at Mattamayūra. His successors Siṁhavarmana, Shadhanva and Avantivarmana were ruling at least up to the first decade of tenth century A.D.

Thus, it is quite clear that Narasiṁha and Kesarin of Maser inscription cannot be closely related with Siṁhavarmana, Shadhanva and Avantivarmana.

The answers to above questions can only be obtained if their relations are sought in the Chalukya family of Badami, who later on, ruled in Karnataka and Gujarat. Mirashi has sought their relation with the Chalukya family of Gujarat.[15] But, in our opinion, the Chalukyas of central India were offspring of the Chalukya family of Badami. As we have seen, the king Avantivarmana ruled in ninth century A.D. and hence his ancestors might have settled in that region.

Further, we are also informed from inscriptions that during the last decade of the sixth century A.D., the Kalachuris were ruling from Māhishmati (modern Maheśvara). The Kalachuri ruler Budharaja—son of Lakshmana, was ruling over Malwa and a part of Gujarat. The Jaina temple inscription from Aihole as well as other records mention that Maṅgaleśa - the Chalukya ruler of Badami, defeated Budharaja in A.D. 01-602; since then Malwa region went under the sway of Chalukyas of Badami.[16]

The Aihole inscription further mentions the victory of Pulakesin II over Harsha as well as the ruler of Malwa and Gujarat.

It is quite possible that during the zenith of the Chalukya rule, some members of the family settled in Malwa under the umbrella of Maṅgaleśa and Pulakeshin-II, but in *circa* eighth century, *i.e.*, after a rise of the Pratīhāras, when they became the supreme power in north India, the rulers of Salki (Chalukya) family accepted the hegemony of Gurjara-Pratīhāras.

The integrated relations of the Chalukyas of central India and Badami may also be proved by the names of the founder of Chalukya family. The traditional origin of the Chalukyas of central India is similar to the accounts given in the inscriptions of the Chalukyas of Badami as all the Chalukya inscriptions claim their origin from Brahmā. However, dissimilarity is found in the names of the descendents of Brahmā and the historic persons of the Chalukya family. The Kalyana grant mentions the origin of the Chalukyas from Brahmā and his descendents Svayambhu Manu, Mānavya, Hariti and lastly Chuluka, the real founder of the Chalukya family of Badami[17] while Bilhari and Maser inscriptions described their origin from Brahmā and his legendary son Bharadvāja who was born from the handful water of Brahmā.

Goyal has further cited that the first man of the Chalukya family was 'Chaluka' and even in the time of Panini, a *risi* named Chuluka and his descendent were well known. Thus, the Chalukyas and the Chulukas may be their descendents. Later, when they forgot their real ancestors, the writers of the Chalukya grants described their origin from Brahmā and his later descendents Panchasikhi, Hariti and his son Chuluka.[18] Similarly, when the Chalukya members settled in central India and they forgot their traditional origin from Hariti and Chuluka, the writers of Bilhari and Maser inscriptions described their origin from Bhārdvāja, i.e., the son of Brahmā.

NOTES AND REFERENCES

1. Maser Inscription, (Ed.) M. Venktaramayya, *Epigraphica Indica,* Vol. XXIX, pp. 18-28, and Bilhari Stone Inscription of the Rulers of Chedi, (Ed.) Kielhorn, *Epigraphia India,* Vol. I, pp. 251-70, also *Corpus Inscriptionum Indicarum,* Vol. IV, Part II, pp. 204-24.
2. Bilhari Stone Inscription of the Rulers of Chedi (Ed.) Kielhorn, *Epigraphica Indica,* Vol. I, pp. 251-70, also *Corpus Inscriptionum Indicarum,* Vol. IV, Part I, pp. 204-24.
3. Maser Inscription, *op. cit.*
4. *Corpus Inscriptionum Indicarum,* Vol. IV, Part I, p. civ.
5. *Ibid.*
6. Maser Inscription, *op. cit.*
7. Rannod Inscription, *Epigraphia Indica,* Vol. I, pp. 351ff and *Corpus Inscriptionum Indicarum,* Vol. IV, Part I, p. clv. Mirashi has identified the Mattamayūra with modern Kadwaha (Distt. Guna, MP), see *Epigraphia Indica,* Vol. XXXVII, pp. 118-19 ff.
8. Maser Inscription, *op. cit.,* also see its footnote No. 1, p. 21.
9. 'The Conquest of *Gopādri* by the Kachchhapaghatas', *Indian Historical Quarterly,* Vol. XXIX, pp. 983, 988-93.
10. Karhad Plate Inscription, *Epigraphia Indica,* Vol. IV, pp. 278-90, and Jura Inscription, *Epigraphia Indica,* Vol. XIX, pp. 287-88.
11. Maser Inscription, *op. cit.*
12. Kachhawahas of this inscription are no other than the Kachchhapaghatas of Gwalior region who ruled in three branches, *i.e.,* Gwalior Branch, Dubkuṇḍa and Narwar Branch. At the time of this war probably, Lakshmaṇa was their chief, see Maser Inscription, *op. cit.*
13. Maser Inscription, *op. cit.*

14. Arthuna Inscription of the Paramara Chamundaraja, V.S. 1136, (Ed.) Lionel D. Barnett, *Epigraphia Indica*, Vol. XIV. pp. 295-310.
15. *Corpus Inscriptionum Indicarum*, Vol. IV, Part I, p. clvi.
16. Aihole Inscription of Pulkeshin-II, *Abhilekha mata, Vidya Bhavana Sanskrit Lekhamala* No. 79 (Eds.), Jha, R.K. and Jha, H., Varanasi, 1962, pp. 106-28.
17. Goyal, S.R., *Maukhari, Pusya Bhukti and Chalukya Yugin Abhilekha*, Meerut, 1987, First Part, pp. 38-41.
18. *Ibid.*

34
RECALLED FROM OBLIVION

B.K. SINHA

Civilizations have always been known from the architecture they have left behind. From nomadic food gathering to the birth of civilization man's journey has been a tortuous one, but at each step his footprints, left behind, throw light on his physical, social, cultural, economic, spiritual as well as aesthetic progress and achievements. From the crude stone tools to the great monuments, that he has built, man's onward march and quest for perfection has been slow and steady.

But unfortunately, parallel with the will to create and excel have run the currents of jealousy, greed and desire to subjugate fellow human beings. These parallel currents have resulted in not only the destruction of human beings but also their achievements, *i.e.*, treasures of art, architectural edifices, and precious pieces of literature. Egoistic beliefs in the supremacy of one race, religion or class have resulted in innumerable sufferings to human beings by way of being brutally killed, burnt alive, incapacitated or condemned to oblivion. Duma's Edmond Dante and Dicken's Alexendre Manette are fictional examples of such abominable behaviour. Religious zealots have, to a great extent, been responsible for the destruction of man's greatest creations in our country. Intolerance and bias towards other faiths have resulted in the disappearance of some of our precious temples, which lie either below the mosques of later period or in heaps of rubble and await the spade of the archaeologist to be recalled from oblivion.

Excavations at Barabati Fort, Cuttack in Orissa (Pl. 34.1) have brought back to view an early medieval temple, destroyed by the Sultan of Delhi, Fīrūz S̱ẖāh Tug̱ẖlaq, in the year A.D. 1361.

According to tradition, embodied in *Mādalapañji*, Chronicle of the Puri temple, the city of Cuttack owes its origin to Somavaṁśī king Nirupkesarī in A.D. 989. This date has been a hotbed of controversy, but all opinions agree that king Anaṅgabhimadeva-III, A.D. 1211-38, of the Gaṅga dynasty, was the first king who shifted his capital from Chowdwar, situated across the river

Mahanadi, to a strategically much safer place, which was named as Abhinava Vārāṇasī Kaṭaka. Situated between rivers Mahanadi and Kathjuri, Kaṭaka provided the Gaṅga ruler with a safe and easily defensible stronghold.

The Nagari copperplates, issued from Abhinava Vārāṇasī Kaṭaka, constitute the first royal decree issued from this new capital. Anaṅgabhimadeva-III calling himself 'Purushottama-putra', installed Lord Purushottama at Abhinava Vārāṇasī Kaṭaka. According to the accounts in the *Mādalapañji*, king Anaṅgabhimadeva-III built a fort and a temple of Lord Purushottama Jagannātha, in the village of Barabati. The date of establishment of Lord Purushottama comes to A.D. 1230. The reign of Anaṅgabhimadeva-III ended in A.D. 1238 when his son Narasiṁhadeva, who is accredited with the building of the great Sun Temple at Koṇārka, succeeded him.

In A.D. 1361, Fīrūz Shāh Tughlaq, the Sultan of Delhi, invaded and captured Cuttack after the Gaṅga ruler Bhānudeva-III had fled. Afīf, who has chronicled the conquest of Cuttack in *Tārikh-e-Fīrūz Shāhi*, says that the temple was destroyed, the idol of Purushottama disgraced, perforated and carried off to Delhi. An inscription found recently at Khambad in Gujarat refers to the victorious campaign of Fīrūz Shāh Tughlaq and carrying off some idols to Delhi.

The Gaṅga rule lasted till A.D. 1434 and was succeeded by the Gajpatis who ruled till A.D. 1540. After the fall of the Gajpatis, there was a short rule of Bhoi dynasty till A.D. 1560, and then came the rule of Mukunda Deva Harichandan, who died fighting the forces of Sulṭan Karanani of Bengal in A.D. 1568. Abul Faẓal mentions of a nine *āshiāna* palace, built by Raja Mukunda Deva at Barabati, in his *Āin-e-Akbarī*. In A.D. 1569, the citadel of Barabati fell into the hands of the Sulṭans of Bengal.

Emperor Akbar, an ally of the late Raja Mukunda Deva, captured Cuttack in A.D. 1595. Cuttack remained in the hands of the Mughals till A.D. 1751, when the Mahrattas captured it. The British captured Cuttack in A.D. 1804 and after demolishing the fort and buildings inside it, sold the retrieved stones to the locals. Cuttack, its pride shattered, its magnificence and glory, referred to by foreign visitors as the court of Malacandy or that bearing resemblance with the western side of Windsor Castle, destroyed, now passed into the hands of British rulers. The British occupiers did not even spare its ruins.

In the aftermath of that devastation and destruction, nothing remained in the memory of the people of Cuttack about the temple of Lord Purushottama, built by a Gaṅga ruler. Since then much water has flown down the Mahanadi and hundreds of years have rolled by. The only source that remained to stir the memory of the people was a tradition, in the form of the texts of *Mādalapañji*.

The texts of *Mādalapañji*, Chronicle of the Puri temple, were recorded sometime in the late medieval period and hence lack historical authenticity. In the year 1950 a set of 5 copperplates was found at village Nagari near Cuttack. These copperplates came into the hands of the great historian and former Chief Minister of Orissa, Dr. H.K. Mahatab, who published them. These copperplate inscriptions turned to be a decree referring to the donation of land to a Brahmin and the establishment of Lord Purushottama at Abhinava Vārāṇasī Kaṭaka, issued by the Gaṅga ruler Anaṅgabhīmadeva-III from his new capital.

Gradually by now the evidence was accumulating and by A.D. 1950 there existed at least three evidences, which suggested that there once existed in the town of Abhinava Vārāṇasī Kaṭaka a temple built by the Gaṅga ruler, Anaṅgabhīmadeva-III. Added to these was the discovery of a headless image of Vishṇu, belonging to Gaṅga period from a tank in Cuttack city, now housed in Bhubaneswar Museum.

On the basis of these evidences, some scholars probed about the possible location of the lost temple. It is important to mention here that in Cuttack city, till recently, there was no monument assignable to the Gaṅga period, and hence the search must have started in right earnest leading to some definite results. But, instead, the search ended with some probabilities here and there.

Belief amongst most of the historians was that the temple, possibly, existed in a locality of Cuttack town known as "Deul Shahi". Although a large number of architectural fragments belonging to temples were reported from the area inside Barabati Fort, but sadly, no one paid any attention or gave them any significance.

During the construction of J.L. Nehru Indoor Stadium, inside Barabati Fort, sometime in A.D. 1984, about 33 architectural pieces and sculptures were found. The state government collected the finest among them and handed these over to the State Museum at Bhubaneswar and there the matter ended.

In early eighties an inscription was discovered at Khambad, Gujarat State, which referred to the victorious campaign of Fīrūz Tug͟hlaq against Jajnagar (Muslim historians have mentioned Orissa by that name) and the carrying away of some idols from Cuttack to Delhi. This epigraphical corroboration of Afīf's account, in *Tārīk͟h-e-Fīrūz S͟hāhī,* practically remained unnoticed to Orissa and its historians.

The search of the temple was destined to the spade of an archaeologist, and the honour went to the Archaeological Survey of India, the premier institution of the country. Though the Archaeological Survey of India pioneered the search and the ultimate discovery, due credit must be given to the elders of the city of Cuttack.

The elders of the city of Cuttack took initiative and approached the Director General, Archaeological Survey of India, for excavation of a mound, situated inside Barabati Fort at Cuttack. Cuttack was celebrating in December 1989 one thousand years of its existence, and the celebrations were to start from 1st December 1989. Respecting the wishes of the city elders, the Archaeological Survey of India started excavations at Barabati on that date so as to coincide with the start of the millennium celebrations.

When excavations started at the high mound, inside Barabati Fort, precious little was known about the mound. Local tradition pointed that the mound contained the ruins of Navtala Prasada, nine-storeyed palace of Rājā Mukundadeva, who by virtue of having died in the battlefield fighting a Muslim invader, had attained the status of a martyr in the eyes of the people of Cuttack.

The high mound inside Barabati Fort covering an area of 18 acres, presented to the visitor a strange or a rather curious appearance. From the surrounding plain, a steep rise of about 7 metres led to an area which had a flat appearance at the top, barring the ravines created by downrushing rain waters. In the south-western corner of this flat area, there, again, was a steep rise from three sides, *i.e.*, east, west and south of about 10 metres, while on the northern side there existed a gentle slope, suggestive of a ramp leading to the highest point wherein sat a bench-mark recording 40.6 metres above M.S.L.

To start with, trenches were taken on the southern and south-western slopes of the mound. Trenches were also taken on the highest point adjacent to the bench-mark, and these trenches showed the existence of loose filling, which at places was stabilized by boulders, up to a depth of about 5 metres. On top of this filling was found a circular structure made of stone blocks with a hole in the centre, obviously intended for a flagstaff. Below the filling was noticed a square structure, 20 metres on the side, profusely pointed in lime mortar. On the northern side was found a ramp built of dressed stone blocks and available up to a length of 25 metres.

In the construction of this square structure and the ramp, huge blocks of khondalite stones, architectural fragments and sculptural panels, extracted from some destroyed temple, were used. In the filling, cleared from over the structure, two mutilated heads of female deities and some other small and big architectural fragments, numbering about one hundred, were found.

Excavations undertaken on the eastern and southern sides of the mound revealed the existence of a citadel wall, having a width of about 4.25 metres with an entrance on the eastern side. Although the material used in the citadel wall was laterite, a few architectural fragments belonging to some temples, were also seen reused.

The use of a large number of dressed khondalite stone blocks, showing dowel marks over them, was suggestive of the time when use of dry masonry was the order of the day. Use of architectural fragments and sculptural panes in the citadel wall, the square structure and the connecting ramp, amply pointed towards the fact that some destroyed temple, whose material was reused in these structures, was located somewhere in neighbourhood.

Trenches taken at the centre of the mound revealed a filling of sand and *malba* under which were buried the remains of an earlier period. In this filling were found 9 pillars, made of laterite blocks, forming a palace complex, accompanied with a courtyard.

The pillars on plan showed a central hall having a width of 10 m north-south and length of over 20 m east-west. The central hall had seven openings in its flanks on the northern and southern sides while there were three each in the eastern and western wings, thus a total of 20 openings leading into the central hall. On eastern, southern and western sides were pillared corridors, while a plastered wall formed a verandah on the northern side. To the south of the pillared corridor was found a small courtyard. There was evidence of thorough stone robbing as a result of which the available height of the pillars varied. Some pillars, when excavated to the lowest course, showed a total of 29 laterite courses, standing up to a height of about 8 metres.

Excavations in the eastern corridor showed that the pillars on this side were resting on a solid platform made of laterite blocks. The stones of this platform seemed to have been robbed thoroughly, but the platform at places stood to a height of about 3.5 m. Over the top of this platform in a small area was noticed lime plaster of good quality, having a thickness of around 12 cm. The plaster was destroyed near the pillars which indicated that the plaster was earlier to the pillars of the palace and foundation trenches dug in order to build the pillars were the cause of the damage to the plaster.

In the northern area, the platform was found buried under a heap of debris consisting of pieces and dressed blocks of white sandstone. This debris could not be cleared for some time due to other preoccupations but 3rd March 1991, the day the debris was removed, will always remain inscribed not only in the memory of the excavation team, but also in the annals of Cuttack's history. Below the debris were found the remains of what once was a temple. The remains consisted of the base of a temple made of whitish sandstone over a foundation of laterite blocks. Three mouldings of the base of the temple (*pishṭa* portion) were identifiable and were initially seen passing between the two pillars on the eastern side which were 4.25 m apart. The mouldings, though badly damaged, were observed going in between the rows of pillars of the eastern corridor on both sides. Excavations, across the row of pillars, on the eastern side, revealed the further continuation of the laterite platform as well as the moulding of white sandstone of the temple.

The mouldings of the base were traced to a total length of 11.5 metres, after which these were found destroyed. The platform of laterite blocks, though very much robbed, was found right up to its eastern extremity and was available up to a length of 35 m. The platform and the mouldings appear to continue westwards and were lying buried under the central hall of the palace. North-south, the platform is available up to a length of about 25 m. after which it is buried under the fillings on the southern side.

These mouldings of whitish sandstone are on the edge of the platform and thus the platform, in reality, represents the inner core of the temple base upon which a paved floor of whitish sandstone was provided. A small portion of this sandstone flooring on the eastern side, near this area was found what appeared as the base of a pillar, the pillar seeming to have been completely cleared out.

Beautiful sculptures representing erotic couples, musicians, female heads showing ornaments and different hairstyles, lotus pedestals with broken images, architectural fragments, and elephant friezes, akin to those used in the Sun Temple at Konarka, were recovered from among the debris. (Pls. 34.2–34.4)

The most important sculptural find came from the area near the pillar base, mentioned above. It was a 1.5 metre high image made in greenish chlorite stone.The image showed in its lower part the complete base mouldings of an Orissan temple while in the upper half are shown two female *chawrī*-bearers, standing back to back. In the one hand they are holding a bunch of grapes and in the other *chawrīs*. The two images, standing back to back, are almost identical but with one difference, *i.e.*, one female holds the *chawrī* straight to her shoulder while its counterpart holds it obliquely against her chest. (Pl. 34.5) The image has tenons at both ends, the upper one slightly shorter on one side. The image was used as a bracket figure with a slightly oblique display. The image, a fine specimen and showing southern influence, can be dated to 12th-13th c. A.D.

Excavations have revealed that the temple was thoroughly destroyed up to its *pishṭa* and at places right up to its foundations. After destruction it looked as a heap of debris, over which Kapilendradeva, the Gajapati king, laid the foundation of his grand palace more than a century later.

The temple, buried under the royal palace, got lost from the memory of the people of Cuttack as year after year, decade after decade and century after century passed by. "Out of sight, out of mind" proved absolutely true in this case. But that was not the end of this glorious 13th century edifice. Fate had willed otherwise and destiny recalled it six hundred and thirty years after it was condemned to oblivion.

35

NEW LIGHT ON ERICH, DISTRICT JHANSI (UTTAR PRADESH)

H.N. SINGH

Endowed with the local tradition of being the birthplace of Bhakta Prahalāda, the illustrious son of the legendary king Hiraṇyakashyapa, the ancient site of Erich (lat. 25° 47' N; long. 79° 7' E) is situated on the right (eastern) bank of the river Betwa (ancient Vetravati) in the Garautha tahsil of District Jhansi (U.P.). Located at a distance of about 64 km from its district headquarters of Jhansi, it is approachable from the latter place via Poonchh on Jhansi-Kanpur National Highway. However, during rainy season one has to take a circuitous route via Mau-Ranipur as the pontoon bridge across the river Betwa is removed. Since a pucca bridge under construction is nearing completion, the seasonal functioning of the pontoon bridge shall be discontinued permanently.

The Betwa, like the other rivers of the area, i.e., Dhasan, Pahuj and Jamini, follows the general slope of the countryside and is flowing towards the north and north-east. It may be put on record that the Betwa for the most part flows in a rocky bed and forms a series of deep pools and picturesque cataracts. It is nowhere navigable and owing to the rocky nature of its bed and steep banks it is fordable only at a few points.[1]

As stated above, the site of Erich is traditionally associated with the story of Bhakta Prahlāda. The narration is found in the *Vishṇu Purāṇa*. Popular traditions, however, assert some interesting anecdotes. It is said that Hiraṇyakaśipu (Hirankus) had secured the blessings of Brahmā denying him death either in the night or in the day, either within a house or without. Moved by his cruelty in trying to cause the death of his son, Bhakta Prahlāda, Vishṇu is said to have assumed the form of Narasiṁha (neither man nor animal) to destroy him and emerging out of a pillar in the hall, he fought with Hirankus till it was evening (i.e., neither day nor night), when having dragged him to the threshold of his palace (neither within nor without), he killed him.[2]

Before proceeding to make an appraisal of the new evidences throwing fresh light on the ancient site of Erich (Pl. 35.1), it is worthwhile to recapitulate the various historical events associated with the site which are attributable to the Sultanate and Mughal periods respectively.

Historical Background

The available historical records indicate that Erich first came under the control and governance of the Khiljis (A.D. 1290-1325), when it was transformed into an important and leading Sultanate settlement.[3] A large number of famous religious persons, who hailed from this place, are mentioned by the author of *Gulẓār-i-Abrār*. It seems that during the reign of Muḥammad bin Tughluq (A.D. 1325-51), Erich was governed from Chanderi which at that time had become the headquarters of a large province. Erich appears to have remained a part of the Delhi Sultanate during the reign of Fīruz Tughluq (A.D. 1351-88).[4]

During 1389-90, Erich passed into the hands of Sulṭān Nasīr-ud-dīn of Kalpi, who had by then set himself up as an independent ruler. Soon Sulṭān Nasīr-ud-dīn lost control of Erich, which, after witnessing brief vicissitude, however, again came under the direct governance of Sulṭān Nasīr-ud-dīn. After some time, Sulṭān Nasīr-ud-dīn conferred the territory of Erich on his own brother Āzam Humāyun Junaid Khān.[5]

Assuming the title of Qādir Shāh, his son succeeded him in A.D. 1410-11. Ibrāhim Shāh Sharqī of Jaunpur eyed intensely to occupy Erich. Around A.D. 1419 in a hotly contested battle the Faujdār of the fort of Erich Bhiamad Khān was defeated, whereafter the charge of the fort was handed over to Malik Jafar (a brother of Sulaimān Khān).[6] However, no sooner had the Jaunpur forces left Erich and Kalpi than Qādir Shāh made a successful bid to recover Erich from Malik Jafar, who was eventually murdered by Qādir Shāh's slaves. Thereupon, Erich was recaptured and Qādir Shāh conferred it on his *vizir*, Daulat Khān.[7]

After Qādir Shāh's death in A.D. 1431-32, a war of succession ensued amongst his three sons, particularly between his eldest son Naṣīr Khan and second son Jalāl Khān. Eventually Jalāl Khān won the war of succession. Subsequently, Jalāl Khān's vizir Mubārak Khān entrenched himself at Erich which was his hereditary *iqta* and within a couple of years had made himself practically independent. He accepted the overlordship of Ibrāhim Shāh Sharqī of Jaunpur, who confirmed him in the possession of *iqta* of Erich.[8]

In A.D. 1434-35, Rai Dungar of Gwalior attacked Erich but retired after acquiring much booty and receiving presents from Mubārak Khān.[9] In A.D. 1443-44, Maḥmūd Shāh Sharqī and Naṣīr Khān came into conflict and the opposing armies encamped near Erich. The prolonged and indecisive battle ended in the form of a peace-treaty, according to which Maḥmūd Shāh promised to restore the territory of Erich to Naṣīr Khān.[10]

Bābur's invasion of the territories of Bundelkhand was stubbornly resisted by Chanderi, which was ruled by Medinī Rāi, a powerful vassal of Rāṇā Saṅgrām. In order to capture Chanderi, Bābur arrived at Erich on January 10, 1528, where he halted for the night. At this time, the fort of Erich was garrisoned by Mullā Afaq, one of Bābur's servants. On his return journey to Bhander he again passed through Erich.[11]

During the period of conflict between the Mughals and Afghans, the territory of Erich, besides others, came under the possession of the Bundelas of Orchha. Madhukar Sāha succeeded Bharat Chand in A.D. 1554. After his death in A.D. 1591-92, he was succeeded by the eldest of his eight sons, Rām Chand, who was confirmed in his possession by Akbar. However, Bīr Singh Dev (a brother of Rām Chand) with two brothers, Indrajīt and Pratāp Rāo, seized a number of *jāgīrs* including Erich (which was in the possession of a Mughal officer). In A.D. 1592, when Akbar made attempts to arrest him, Bīr Singh Deo was compelled to vacate Erich. During the days of Akbar, Erich was a *sirkar* in the *subah* of Agra.[12]

During the time of Mughal Emperor Jahāngīr, it is said to have been in the possession of Bīr Singh Deo whose descendant lost it to the Bundelas from whom it was retrieved and reoccupied by the Muslims. It was devastated by Chhatrasāl towards the end of the seventeenth century. In 1712, along with some other places in Bundelkhand, Farrukh Siyar conferred it on Moḥammad Khān Bangesh. He, however, lost it to Chhatrasāl whose descendant Har Dās could not retain it for long and it became part of the Maratha territory at the beginning of the latter half of the eighteenth century. Ultimately, it passed to the British in 1853 with the lapse of the Jhansi state. It was also the headquarters of the Piṇḍārīs under Amīr Khān (A.D. 1803).[13] In 1817, Lord Hastings had encamped at Erich on his way to Gwalior with a view to liquidating the Piṇḍārīs.[14]

Of the various monuments of Erich, mention may be made of old fort which stands in ruins on the banks of the Betwa.[15] Inside the fort there is a mosque, which is locally known as Jama Masjid. It is reputed to have been built in A.D. 1413 by Ghāzī Ziā-ud-dīn, a portion of the mosque being constructed during the time of Mughal emperor Aurangzeb.[16]

During the early medieval times Erich, like Dudhai, Madanpur and Lalitpur, was also an important centre of trade and commerce.[17] Erich was an equally important centre of learning, too. It is noticed that in the fourteenth and fifteenth centuries Erich had grown into a flourishing centre of Islamic learning. According to the illustrious author of *Tārīkh-i-Muḥammadi*, Muḥammad Bihamad Khān, numerous leading saints and scholars had flourished at Erich during this period.[18] For instance, Yusuf bin Muḥammad (also known as Yusuf Budh) was a celebrated saint of Erich and is widely known for his translation of Ghizali's *Minhaj-ul-Afifin*.[19] His disciple Muḥammad Bihamad Khān (author of *Tārīkh-i-Muḥammadi*) wrote a general history of the Muslim rulers in India and outside from the time of the Prophet Muḥammad down to 1438-39 and of the Muslim dynasty of Kalpi in particular (which held sway over Erich) for the period from A.D. 1354 to 1439.[20] Maḥmūd of Erich recorded in writing the discourses of his master, Shaikh Ahmad Kahtu, also known as Aḥmad Maghribi (A.D. 1338-1446).[21] Again, it was at Erich that around thirteenth century A.D. the Unani system of medicine was introduced by the Muslims when they settled down in this part of the country.[22]

It was at Erich again that the celebrated Hindi poet Sadharu, who was a Jain, wrote his *Pradyumna-Charit* in A.D. 1354.[23]

This in brief is the chequered history of Erich during the Sultanate, Mughal and post-Mughal times. Moreover, besides Erich, there are a couple of other ancient sites which, too, had flourished on the banks of the Betwa river, e.g., Bhojpur, near Bhopal (M.P.), Orchha (M.P.), Deogarh (District Lalitpur, U.P.). Viewed in this context, it was considered worthwhile to excavate the Quila mound of Erich with a view to unfolding the chronology as well as to knowing the sequence of cultures, particularly the history of the site during the ancient period.

Excavation

In the recent past the mound was explored by W.H. Siddiqui and Indu Prakash in the year 1987, which had brought to light thick occupational deposit, besides the discovery of N.B.P. Ware.[24] The exposed sections of the deposit formed in the rain-gullies reflected an accumulation of about 10 m thickness. Considering the immense potentiality of the site trial-digs were conducted by the Lucknow Circle[25] of the Archaeological Survey of India from 15 February 1989 to 14 Mach 1989. Two trial trenches, namely B3-4 and XF-1 were laid on the southern and western slopes of the mound respectively. Excavation in Trench B3-4 was suspended as a brick structure was encountered at a depth of 5.60 m (Pl. 35.5). However, in Trench XF-1 the digging could be carried unhindered till the natural soil was reached (Pl. 35.6).

On the strength of our trial-excavations in Tr. B3-4 and Tr. XF-1, it is seen that the total cultural deposit is 9.65 m. On the basis of the associated finds like brick-structures, potteries, coins, seals and other antiquities etc., the chronology of the site may tentatively be worked out as under:

Period I : Distinguished by black-and-red ware (BRW).
: *Circa* 800 B.C. to *c.* 600 B.C.

Period II : Characterised by Northern Black Polished Ware (NBPW).
: *Circa* 600 B.C. to the beginning of the Christian era.

Period III : Kushan Period.
: Beginning of the Christian era to *c.* A.D. 350.

Period IV : Gupta Period.
: *Circa* A.D. 350 to *c.* A.D. 700.

Period V : Post-Gupta : Pre-Sultanate.
: *Circa* A.D. 700 to A.D. 1200.

Period VI : Sultanate and Mughal Periods.
: *Circa* A.D. 1200 to A.D. 1707.

The salient features of the aforestated periods reflecting the sequence of cultures at Erich may be delineated as under.

Period I

Characterized chiefly by the incidence of the plain black-and-red ware, the total cultural deposit, which is resting over the virgin soil of Period I is ranging between 25 cm to 45 cm. It may be recalled that at Atranjikhera (District Etah, U.P.), too, like Erich, the BRW deposit is very meagre, *i.e.*, 15 cm to 50 cm thick.[26] Wheel-made and plain, the BRW of Erich is bereft of painting. The shapes comprise dishes with incurved rim and bowls with their variants. While no antiquity could be retrieved from the regular deposit, a couple of objects were found in a pit, which was cut into the virgin soil. In this pit, besides the sherds of the BRW, lumps of copper, a bone point and a *ghaṭa*-shaped terracotta bead were found. Use of fire is attested to by the discovery of the remains of charcoal and ash deposits in the pit. The latter is sealed by the layers of Period I.

It may be recalled that like Period I of Erich, at Jakhera (District Etah, U.P.), too, the beginning of Period I is distinguished by the incidence of BRW.[27]

Period II

While BRW is persisting in Period II, too, it is, however, the emergence and proliferation of the NBPW which distinguishes it comprehensively from the preceding Period I. On the strength of absence or presence of burnt brick structures, Period II is further divisible into two sub-periods, viz., sub-period II-A and sub-period II-B, which may be discussed in detail as under.

Sub-Period II-A

During sub-period II-A, there is a total absence of burnt bricks. That the rickety houses were largely made of bamboo or reed plastered with mud is testified to by the discovery of mud-clods bearing the impressions of bamboo or reed over them.

Further, the spadework yielded NBPW with the classical lustre specially in black and steel-grey colours. Comprising utilitarian shapes, the other associated wares are the BRW and black-sliped ware (BSW) as well as the common red ware. In the lower layers the frequency of the BRW and BSW is more but gradually the incidence of the NBPW increases. Special mention may be made of the discovery of orange coloured pottery with fine fabric, the shapes of which are chiefly the dishes and bowls. Besides the potteries, the occupational deposit of the sub-period II-A also yielded a couple of antiquities, *e.g.*, a hexagonal biconical bead in crystal stone; glass bangle piece; stone ball; terracotta disc, hop-scotch, *ghaṭa*-shaped bead and pendant; bone point or stylus and numerous iron objects including nails with square section, etc.

The total occupational deposit of the sub-period II-A is approximately 1.35 m.

Sub-Period II-B

Unlike the preceding sub-period II-A, the sub-period II-B is distinguished by the introduction of burnt bricks. The structural vestiges (Pl. 35.4) consist of a brick-lined drain in this phase. Close-by, the remains of terracotta rings were also retrieved in the excavations, which denote the use of terracotta ring-wells for soakage by the people of this sub-period. The use of terracotta tiles for roofing is also discernible because several fragments of such tiles were unearthed during the course of excavations. Amongst the potteries, mention may be made of the NBPW, BRW, BSW and the common red ware with their typical shapes and forms. The principal ware of the sub-period II-B is undoubtedly NBPW, the incidence of which, however, marginally decreases in the upper layers.

The minor antiquities are as follows: a soapstone object with hole for suspension and showing engraved design for moulding on either sides; terracotta disc, dabber, hop-scotch, skin-rubber (triangular), fragmentary mother-goddess (Mauryan), and miscellaneous iron objects.

The total habitational accumulation of the sub-period II-B is approximately 1.25 m.

Period III

The ceramic contents of this Period consist of red ware pottery with typical Kushan shapes such as sprinkler, inkpot, lamp, knife-edged bowl, carinated *hāṇḍī* and other utilitarian shapes. The structural activity (Pl. 35.3) is represented in the form of the ruins of a wall built of burnt bricks, the measurement being 48x27x6 cm. The most notable discovery is that of a terracotta seal inscribed in positive in typical Kushan Brāhmī characters reading "*Saṁghasya*". The assortment of minor antiquities includes the following: an ivory bangle-piece, miniature terracotta bull, bone stylus, copper antimony rod and iron objects, etc.

The total cultural deposit of this period is approximately 1.50 m in thickness.

Period IV

It is ascribable to the Gupta period. A brick structure of this period has been noticed in Tr. B3 (Pl. 35.2), which is seen raised by re-utilising the fragmentary burnt-bricks of the preceding Kushan period, besides a floor with brick-on-edge paving. Associated with it was also recovered a small much-corroded copper coin. In the Tr. XF-1 a huge pit cut deep in the habitational deposit of this period deprived us substantially from retrieving the cultural vestiges of this period; still the pit yielded a couple of terracottas displaying male figurines with elaborated hairstyle typical of the Gupta period. The other antiquities which were exhumed from the regular layers include, besides a small much-corroded copper coin, an ivory vase (miniature); terracotta ear-stud, pendant and arecanut-shaped bead; shell bangle pieces and numerous iron objects, etc.

Period V

The upper levels of the site are found to be too much disturbed owing to large scale brick robbing in the past. The robbing of the bricks has been found to be so comprehensive that even to-day majority of the houses of the township are seen raised by re-utilising the brickbats robbed from the ancient mound of Erich.

Period VI

This period denotes the occupation of the site by an entirely new set of peoples who introduced their own cultural ethos including new material components like glazed pottery, coinage, metal objects and artifacts, building materials and architecture, etc. Of this period the cultural vestiges, however, are found to be too scarce owing chiefly to disturbed stratigraphy caused by extensive diggings of pits with a view to rob the buried bricks. It is the Muslim glazed pottery only of which a couple of stray sherds are retrieved from the debris devoid of stratigraphical context. The common red ware persisted in this period too.

The foregoing delineation reflects the reconstruction of the history of Erich from *circa* 800 B.C. to A.D. 1853. In other words, it may be stated that the site is now noted for the continuity of the occupation from *circa* 800 B.C. onwards uninterruptedly till date. It may, however, be recalled that hitherto the site was known for a couple of historical events of the Sultanate, Mughal and British periods only but its pre-Sultanate history had remained largely unknown to the people. It is this hidden history as tacitly manifested in the cultural deposits of the site which has been brought to light for the first time through brief but fruitful spadework, which has now pushed back the antiquity of the site of Erich to *circa* 800 B.C.

Acknowledgement

Copyright of the photographs and drawings rests with the Director General, Archaeological Survey of India, New Delhi. I am grateful to D.G., AS.I. for permitting me to publish them.

NOTES AND REFERENCES

1. E.B. Joshi (Ed.), *Jhansi District Gazetteer,* Lucknow, 1965, p. 174.
2. A. Cunninghum, *Archaeological Survey of India, Report for the years 1871-72 and 1873-74,* Calcutta, 1878, Vol. VII, p. 36.
3. Joshi, *op. cit.*, p. 37.
4. *Ibid.*, p. 38.
5. *Ibid.*
6. *Ibid.*, p. 39.
7. *Ibid.*
8. *Ibid.*
9. *Ibid.*
10. *Ibid.*, p. 40.
11. *Ibid.*, p. 41.
12. *Ibid.*, pp. 42-43.
13. *Ibid.*, pp. 46-50 and 339.
14. *Ibid.*, p. 50.
15. *Ibid.*, p. 340; Cunninghum, *op. cit.*, pp. 34-35.
16. Joshi, *op. cit.*, pp. 280 and 340; Cunninghum, *op. cit.*, pp. 32-34.
17. Joshi, *op. cit.*, p. 155.
18. *Ibid.*, p. 267.
19. *Ibid.*, p. 285.

20. *Ibid.*
21. *Ibid.*
22. *Ibid.*
23. *Ibid.*, p. 282.
24. Information from Dr. W.H. Siddiqui, Director (Retd.) and Sri Indu Prakash, Asstt. Archaeologist, Archaeological Survey of India.
25. The excavation team comprised the following: Dr. H.N. Singh, Dr. Arun Kumar, Sri R. Pathak, Sri Indu Prakash, Sri S.B. Shukla, Sri Dinesh Goswami and Sri K.M. Saxena.
26. R.C. Gaur, *Excavations at Atranjikhera*, Delhi, 1983, p. 76.
27. *Ibid.*, p. 76, fn. 1; H.N. Singh, *History and Archaeology of Black-and-Red Ware*, Delhi, 1982, p. 475, Appendix-A.

36

ARTIFICIAL WATER SYSTEMS IN ANCIENT AND MEDIEVAL INDIA

I.K. SARMA

The earliest food-producing village cultures, as well as the earliest civilization in India revealed the existence of artificial canals and channels for irrigation and trade. At the Harappan site of Lothal an inlet channel[1] of 7 m width was found connecting a massive dockyard. Its embankment walls measuring 212 m at the west, 209.3 m. on the east, 34.7 m south and 36.4 m on the north are first of its kind establishing the seaborne trade of the Harappans.

Specific evidence for artificial moulding of water through reservoirs is forthcoming in the Indus Civilisation, and almost certainly the Harappan economy, like the Egyptian and Babylonian, rested on irrigation farming. Recent evidence[2] from Dholavira, district Kutch, in Gujarat revealed the existence of a unique example of a tank serving as a reservoir of water for the use of the city dwellers. The geographical set-up itself is such that two seasonal torrents namely Mansar and Manhar emanate from the hills in north-east and carry a heavy volume of water after downpour in the catchment area but they dry up quickly. The source of water is only from the artificial tanks and ponds which depended solely on the monsoon. The masonry tank measured more than 100 metres long, 13 metres wide in the central zone of the citadel, and has revealed a fine network of inlet monsoon channels for collecting the rain water. The drains were covered with a hole for desiltation. At another place, on the defence wall, a stone platform was caused to collect the rain water and therefrom it flowed to a deep chamber through a polished stone water chute. R.S. Bisht also recovered mother-goddess figures from one of the deep water channels and such figures are rare in the Harappan contexts in the sites beyond the Indus Valley zone.

In the excavations at Inamgaon[3] (Maharashtra) an artificial irrigation channel, 4 m wide and 3.50 m deep was reported from an early Jorwe Culture (1400-1000 BC) level. An embankment wall of rubble set in mud-mortar was found to a length of 240 m and 2.2 m width.

This formed part of a tank which was provided with a feeder channel connected to the close by river.

Literary and Inscriptional References

Ṛgveda and *Atharvaveda*[4] refer to *kulya* (canals) and *Khanitrima* (artificial channels) *Dharmapada*, a Pali work (400 BC), speaks of *nettika* meaning builders of canals and aqueducts. Manu ordains capital punishment for those who damage or spoil the channels and tanks. Various terms like *praṇāla, parivāha, kulya, vāhika, tilāmaka, nadīvāha* and *nadimatrakas* connote the different channels and canals. The *Arthaśāstra* refers to a tax system on irrigation works provided by the state and the administrative network to inspect the sluices, branch canals etc. Hathigumpha *praśasti*[5] (1st century BC) narrates the history of an irrigation canal which was originally caused by the Magadhan ruler Nanda (296 BC) and extended up to the capital of Kaliṅganagara through Tanasauli road by king Khāravela during his 5th regnal year.

The inscription further states the construction of embankments to several deep and cool tanks, restoration of gardens etc. in the very first year of Khāravela's accession.[6] Girnar rock inscription provides a graphic account of the great *Sudarśana taḍāka*[7] (lake with charming looks), which was caused by Rāshṭriya Pushyagupta with earthen and stone embankments during the reign of Chandragupta Maurya (324-300 BC). It became *Durdarśana* (ugly looking due to a devastating storm) but perfected and made beautiful for ever, *Sudarśanatara* by Mahākshatrapa Rudradāman (AD 150). A Kanheri record (2nd century AD) refers to the construction of a reservoir by one *seṭhī puṇaka.*[8]

Sarasi or *saraṁsi* which meant 'tank' or 'reservoir' (or lake) often occurs in *Yajurveda*. The *Dharmaśāstras* mention *setus* (dams or aqueducts). *Kuṇāla Jātaka* narrates a story of Sakiya and Koliya tribes fighting for the distribution of water from the dam across the river Rohiṇi. The *Arthaśāstra* refers to the breaking of dams to halt the enemy. A tax of one-fourth of the produce was levied and licencing for fishing in rivers, dams, etc., was necessary. These measures indicate a large network of artificial water sources during the Nanda-Maurya times. Construction of tanks and their proper maintenance was one of the great seven meritorious acts (*Saptasanthāna*).

This vivid epigraphical information is amply corroborated by the archaeological excavations at the important early historical sites like Besnagar, Kumrahar, Ujjain and Nagarjunakonda, to cite only a few examples.

In peninsular India much of the irrigation, right from neolithic period, was through rain water ponds, tanks and water-reservoirs; while in the north the stress was more on 'Regulation Canals', linked to the rivers, which were largely perennial but also perilous.

In south India one notices a sudden emergence, without traces of antecedent cultures of such traits as megalithic buildings, tank irrigation, Brāhmī writing, etc., transforming the tribal society. The farming systems crystallised in the north during Nanda-Maurya period descended deep into the south and set a model for the early rulers like the Chera-Chōḷa, Pāṇḍya, Pallava-Kadamba, not to speak of the imperial Sātavāhanas.

Archaeological Evidences

At Besnagar, District Vidisha, D.R. Bhandarkar[9] traced a storage canal 2.13 m wide, 1.67 m high and 56 m length with masonry brick walls serving as embankments and a flight of descents at one point. The brick wall was given a batter inwardly and plastered with super strong lime mortar. At Kumrahar,[10] District Patna, the canal had a width of 13 m. and 3 m. deep, located by the side of a spacious wooden pillared hall of the Mauryan period. Altekar records that it was connected to the river Gaṅgā and used to wet the huge pillars from the Chunar quarries to the door of the hall. So here it served as a transport channel. A sunk brick-lined channel from Ujjain is also noteworthy. It was found to a length of 45 m and 11 m wide and 2.59 m deep.[11]

S.R. Rao unearthed[12] at Kaveripumpattnam excavations a water reservoir at the site known as Vanagiri in the levels dated to 2nd century A.D. This had an inlet channel connected from the river Kaveri. An I'-shaped massive brick building, built of unusually large baked-bricks 60 x 20 x 12 cm was unearthed which was identified as a wharf. The wooden poles planted within the structure were meant for anchorage of cargo-boats. This wharf is dated *circa* 200 BC and the Sangam classic *Paṭṭinapaḷai* confirms this flourishing seaborne trade.

Evidence from Śriṅgaverapurā, District Allahabad (U.P.)

Deemed as a notable contribution to the early historical archaeology of the country, the joint tank exposed at Śriṅgaverapurā, measuring approximately 250 metres long and about 23 to 13 metres wide is a monumental structure dated to 1st century BC -AD.

As rightly described by B.B. Lal,[13] this *Bharata Kunda* is a unique example of ancient Indian hydraulic engineering of which the country can be justifiably proud.

In addition to the technical devices, the ancient engineers allowed for what is today technically known as 'horizontal and vertical warping'. The structural units are three in number and interlinked. Tank-A, which received the water first, becomes wider as the distance from inlet channel increases. This made the water spread out without bringing undue pressure on the side walls. They are not vertical but slope back at an angle of about 11° to the vertical, reducing further the force of the incoming water. This tank measures 34 metres in length, 13 metres in width and 4 metres in depth like the two chambers already referred to. It also seems to have been used primarily for siltation. From its upper level, fully cleaned water passed into Tank-B, through a channel about 5.30 metres long and 1.35 metres wide. Here, too, the water cascaded over a series of steps to reach the bottom, where again the remains of a brick-pavement have been found. Tank-B is much larger than Tank-A, the overall width at the top being nearly 23 metres and the depth 7 metres. It has three successively higher retaining walls, each one being constructed about 2 metres outwards from the one below it. All three are inclined to be vertical at angles varying from 10° to 13°. The lowest retaining wall alone has as many as 49 courses, reaching a height of 3.20 metres.

It would appear that Tank-B was the main one, for in it we have discovered three separate staircases each leading down to the water-level. At another place two flights of facing steps were found; these descend to a level where a ramp, built of bricks set on their edges, continues to the bottom of the tank.

Besides meeting the prime need of water-supply Tank-B seems to have been used for religious purposes as well. Many terracotta figurines of a goddess holding a child in her arms, probably Hāritī or her equivalent have been found in it. These figurines appear to have been ceremoniously immersed.

Tank-B discharges its water into another adjoining circular Tank-C (14.50 metres diameter) and from there the overspilling water merges with the Gaṅgā. From Tank-C, terracotta figurines datable to 1st-2nd century AD have been found from the alluvial deposit.

One final fact remains to be noted: the main Tank-B was not only carried down to sub-soil water-level but in its bed several wells were also sunk to allow sub-soil water to rise more easily. This arrangement of interlinking the stored water with sub-soil water was obviously made to ensure an adequate water supply even during the dry summer months.

Evidence of a Canal from Nāgārjunakoṇḍa

The large scale excavations at Nāgārjunakoṇḍa brought to light a multipurpose canal[14] (dated to 3rd-4th centuries AD) to a length of 800 metres with the flow indicating east-west and with an average width of 15-25 m and 2 m deep. Its bed and embankments were made of rubble and gravel rammed in hard lime to withstand the gush of water. Further its northern embankment was strengthened by a random rubble wall 1.37 m wide, to prevent the erosion from the hillside. This was primarily like the Kumrahar example, a transport canal, and perhaps served well for minor horticultural operations around the sprawling Vihāra units.

Other Evidences

In the south the construction of tanks, canals and channels, their administrative control and upkeep alike, during the early as well as later historical periods, followed the well-established Maurya-Sātavāhana pattern. Some reputed irrigation channels deserve to be noted here.

Construction of tanks was common during *Kadamba*[15] and Pallava periods. Kadamba king Ravivarman built a tank in the village Varijaka, whereas Kākusthavarman excavated a reservoir (*taḍākāni*) at Talagunda. Chāḷukya and Rāshtrakūṭa records refer to several *taṭākas* and feeder-channels in the Karṇataka territory. The Mahendrataḍāka caused by Mahendravarman I (AD 580-630), the Paramēśvara *taḍāka* in the Kurram village, District Chingleput by Paramēśvara Varman I (AD 672-700), the Teneri reservoir of the Nandivarman's time, the Vairamega Taṭāka in Chitramerur, are noteworthy examples serving till date in Tamilnadu.

Similarly the Uyyakōṇḍa irrigation channels in district Tiruchirapalli constructed by Rāja Rāja I (AD 985-1013) are extant examples even now. Tiruvalangadu plates of Rājendra Chōḷa (I) provide interesting data on the irrigation canals during AD 1012-44.

A large network of canals (*kāluvas*), and sluices (*tumu*), like the *kollipaka (Vaṁśavardhana Kāluva)*, Lempaka (*Rāya Sahasramalla Kāluva*) were caused by the Kākatīya rulers. Among the powers of Deccan, the Kākatīyas (11th-12th centuries AD) like Chōḷas in the south, created a large and efficient network of irrigation tanks which are in use even today. Notable examples such as the *Chāvuṇḍa Samudram, Kesarītaṭākam, Śivapura taṭākam* (Hanumakoṇḍa), Pakhal, Ghanpur and Rāmappa lakes with high embankments and sluices are object lessons to the modern engineers[16] and still serve the irrigational and drinking needs of the society.

Sūrajkuṇḍ (Delhi)

The Tomar Rajputs originally feudatories of the Pratīhāra rulers from the closing years of 10th century AD occupied the regions of south Delhi bordering Haryana. Sūraj Pāḷ of this dynasty is stated to be the builder of a large reservoir known as Sūrajkuṇḍ.[17] There is a dam ascribed to Anaṅgapāla of the same dynasty over a kilometre to its south in the village of the same name Anaṅgpur. Anaṅgapāla is also known as the builder of the Lal-koṭ, the first known defence work in Delhi. Sūrajkuṇḍ consists of an embankment on a semicircular plan collecting rain waters from near the hills. This reservoir is believed to be part of a temple for the Sun god and a small tank called *Siddhakuṇḍ* about 600 m south of Sūrajkuṇḍ attracts a large number of pilgrims on certain holy days. The vast lake formed by the waters imparts a very impressive look during rainy months. The sluice openings in the dam allow the water to flow through a ravine and the fields nearby get irrigated.

Vijayanagara Water Architecture

Water channels for irrigating the fields as well as filling the masonry tanks and bath houses are many in the vast Vijayanagara city. The extensive lines of cut-stone troughs witness the complex hydraulic system. The largest aqueduct is to the north of Virūpāksha temple extending across the Tungabhadra river. Here the massive stone piers hold the water channel high above the river. Several baths with water channels and stone aqueduct lines are noteworthy exposures in the large scale excavations at Hampi, particularly in the Royal Enclosure area. Apart from rearing fish, 'the smaller tanks in the Royal area of the Metropolis were meant for *Jalakrīḍās* of the palace women and men'.[18] The king himself partook in these festivities like *holī* and enjoyed the sight of beautiful courtesans taking bath in the tanks.

Tanks, for religious purpose, were also known and the example unearthed between Queen's Palace and the shrine is one such outstanding example. This stepped tank 22 metres square and 7 metres deep was covered with basaltic blocks. It has five landings, each projecting to a width of 1.05 m. These landings of the tank made four inner squares varying in measurement from the maximum 19.80 m to 6.10 m minimum and each square displayed ornamented steps. The central pit of the tank measured 2.45 metres. Mason marks in Telugu-Kannada on each of the veneer stones clearly indicated its well planned layout. The antiquities unearthed from the clearance of the tank are, mostly ritual figures — Veṇugopāla, Śaktī, Gaṇēśa, Vīrabhadra, crystal liṅgas and so on. The Koregal channel from the river Tungabhadra and the Basavana channel caused by the great Vijayanagara monarch Śrī Krishṇa Devarāya are live ones. These examples are mostly feeder and irrigational ones with sluices, their maintenance and administration alike vested with hydraulic engineers known as *Jalasūtradas*.

NOTES AND REFERENCES

1. S.R. Rao, *Lothal and Indus Civilization* (1973), pp. 58-59, 70-71, fig. 18, Pls. XII, XIII, XXV.
2. R.S. Bisht, 'Dholavira: New Horizons of the Indus Civilization', *Purātattva*, no. 20 (1989-90), pp. 80-81 and Amarnath Khanna, *Archaeology of India* (New Delhi, 1992), p. 112.
3. *Purātattva*, no. 8 (1978), pp. 47-48, fig. 1.
4. *Vedic Index*, I, pp. 173-214.
5. D.C. Sircar, *Select Inscriptions*, Vol. I (Calcutta, 1965), p. 218, line 6.
6. *Ibid.*, p. 214, line 3.
7. D.C. Sircar, *op. cit.*, pp. 176-80. Also R.N. Mehta, 'Sudarasana Lake', *Journal of Oriental Institute* (Baroda, 1968), XVIII, pp. 20-28.
8. D.C. Sircar, *Inscriptions of Aśoka* (New Delhi, 1957), p. 27.
9. *ASIAR*, 1914-1915, pp. 69-71, Pl. XLIX A.
10. A.S. Altekar and V. Mishra, *Kumrahar Excavations* (Patna, 1959), p. 30, Fig. 5.
11. *Indian Archaeology, 1957-58; A Review* (hereafter *IAR*), p. 38, Pl. XLIII A.
12. *Transactions of the Archaeological Society of South India* (Madras, 1964-65), pp. 164-65; *Ibid.*, 1966-68, pp. 193-95.
13. B.B. Lal, 'The giant tank of Śriṅgaverpurā', *Purātattva*, no. 10 (1978-79), pp. 1-7 (1981). Also 'Historicity of the Mahābhārata and the Rāmāyaṇa: What has Archaeology to say in the matter', *International Seminar, ICHR* (New Delhi, 15-17 Dec. 1988), A.N. Khanna, *Archaeology of India* (New Delhi, 1992), pp. 183-84, Figs. 50-51.
14. *IAR, 1958-59*, p. 8, Pl. XII A; I.K. Sarma, 'Ancient Canals', *Journal of Indian History*, Vol. XL, pt. II (Aug. 1962), pp. 301-12, Pl. 1, Fig. 2.
15. K.V. Ramesh (ed.), *Studies in Indian Epigraphy, JESI* (Mysore, 1974) I, pp. 50-52.
16. G. Yazdani (ed.), *The Early History of Deccan* Part-II (London, 1980), pp. 679-80.
17. Y.D. Sharma, *Delhi and its Neighbourhood* (New Delhi, 1990), pp. 12-13, 100-101.
18. *Splendours of Vijayanagara Empire, Hampi, Marg* (1981), pp. 64-65; *IAR*, 1984-85, pp. 27-28; B. Narasimhaiah, *Metropolis Vijayanagara* (New Delhi, 1992), pp. 67, 72, 87-88, Pl. XXV A.

37
CONTRIBUTION OF KALINGA TO INDIAN CULTURE

K.D. BAJPAI

In ancient times the popular name of Orissa was Kaliṅga. This name often occurs in the *Mahābhārata*, the Purāṇas and in several classical Sanskrit works, besides the Buddhist and Jaina literature. Kālidāsa, the great Sanskrit poet, in his *Raghuvaṁśa*, places the capital of Kaliṅga on the seacoast. He refers to Mahendra, the famous mountainous range of Orissa, its seacoast and the commercial activities of Orissa with the *dvīpāntaras*.

In connection with the *Indumatī-svayaṁvara*, the poet eulogises the power of the Kaliṅga ruler and the beautiful land ruled over by him.[1]

In the same work *Raghuvaṁśa*, in the context of Raghu's *Digvijaya*,[2] Kālidāsa describes the victory of Raghu over the Vaṅga country. The Vaṅga had a strong fleet of boats. Thereafter the people of Utkala helped Raghu in entering the mainland of Kaliṅga, covered with the Mahendra mountain ranges:

Sa tīrttvā Kapiśāṁ sainair-baddha dvirada-setubhiḥ,

Utkalā-darśita pathaḥ, Kaliṅgābhimukhuṁ yayau

(*Raghu.*, IV, 38)

The Mahendra mountain was counted among the eight chief mountains of the country (*Kulaparvatas*). The ruler of Kaliṅga gave a stiff resistance to Raghu, but was eventually overpowered. The victor, after establishing his symbolic supremacy over Kaliṅga, gave it back to the ruler as a gesture of friendship and goodwill :

gṛhīta-pratimuktasya sa dharma-vijayī nṛpah;

śriyaṁ Mahendra-nāthasya jahāra na tu medinīm

(*Raghu.*, IV, 43)

This *digvijaya* of Raghu is reminiscent of the victory of Samudragupta over the Kaliṅgas in the fourth century A.D.

In this connection it would be worthwhile to compare the symbolic victory of the Gupta ruler with the war on Kaliṅga, waged by the Maurya king Aśoka in the third century B.C. Aśoka in his wild pursuit of uprooting his contemporary ruler of Kaliṅga adhered to the ruthless ways of imperial expansion. The people of Kaliṅga, who had enjoyed a long tradition of independence till then, could not tolerate any external domination. They were aware of the imperial policies of the previous Magadhan monarchs and hence were not prepared to yield to the machination of Aśoka.

It seems that Aśoka was probably ill-advised by his warmonger and greedy generals. They might have compelled him to wage the disastrous war to occupy the fertile region of Kaliṅga, having considerable trade potentiality due to its long seacoast. The consequences of that war are well known. Aśoka could succeed in Kaliṅga only after an unprecedented bloodshed and upheaval.

The Mauryan domination could not last long in Kaliṅga. Soon after the demise of Aśoka, Kaliṅga declared its independence. A family of rulers, known as the Mahāmegha-vāhanas, came into power after the downfall of the Mauryas. This new ruling dynasty of Kaliṅga seems to have had close relations with the Chedi region. This can be inferred from the name 'Chedi' occurring in the records of the Mahāmegha-vāhana family of the Kaliṅga region.

The Chedi region had become a centre of the Aryan culture from the early Vedic times. The worship of god Indra, one of whose epithets was *Mahāmegha-vāhana* was quite popular in that region. King Vasu, one of the early Vedic rulers of Chedi, was appropriately designated as *Chaidya uparichara* (ruler of Chedi *janapada*). The Chedis probably migrated from their original land to the Kaliṅga region during the late Maurya period. They may have found there a congenial atmosphere for the growth of their power. Soon they established themselves as the ruling dynasty of the main Kaliṅga region. Khāravela, of the well-known Hathigumpha inscription, had his hegemony felt beyond the limits of Kaliṅga. Khāravela and his successors made their kingdom politically strong. They also followed a broad-based policy of religious toleration. The chief Indian religions and various folk-cults flourished in Kaliṅga side by side.

The Greek writers Megasthenes, Pliny and Ptolemy have described the main Kaliṅga region (*Macco-Calingae*) and its important towns, such as Katak, Konarka (Konnagara) and Purī.

The names Utkala and Oḍra (for parts of the present Orissa), were not so popular as the name Kaliṅga. The available evidences indicate that at least from about the beginning of the Christian era, the people of Kaliṅga used to travel through the Bay of Bengal towards China in the north-east and to Indo-China and Indonesia in the south-east. The name 'Kaliṅga' became well known outside India in the regions with which Orissan people came into contact.

The discovery of Roman and Chinese coins in several parts of Orissa and the occasional references to Kaliṅga in the Chinese and Indonesian literature furnish eloquent testimony to the maritime activities of the people of this area and their cultural and trade-relations with far-off lands.[3]

During its palmy days in the early historical period, the boundaries of Kalinga extended from Sumha (south-western part of Bengal) to river Godavari in the south. Its western limit was Amarakantak in the Shahdol district of Madhya Pradesh. The Bay of Bengal (*Mahodadhi*) marked its eastern boundary.

From the *Periplus* (first century A.D.) we learn that Kaliṅga was also known as Dosarene (Sanskrit *Daśārṇa*).[4] We know that the region of eastern Malwa was famous as Daśārṇa. It was watered by river Daśārṇa (present Dhasān). The similarity in the name Daśārṇa of both the areas is striking indeed. The *Periplus* says that the region of Orissa yielded ivory, which was known as *Dosarenic*.[5] The Orissan ivory has long been famous and is mentioned in early and medieval literature as a major item of industry and export.

Kaliṅgapattanaṁ on the seacoast was an important port. Ptolemy has referred to Palur, another important town of Kaliṅga, which has been identified with Dantapura. The ship-building industry in the coastal area was given a fillip by the ruling dynasties of Orissa. The rulers of the Bhaumakara and Gaṅga dynasties paid special attention to the internal and external trade-routes. This was necessary for developing the economic condition of the country.

It is interesting to note that names of several rivers and towns of ancient Orissa became popular in south-east Asia. Apart from some other names, the name of Siṁhapura might have given its name to the present city of Singapore.

The sea-route trade-relations of Orissa and the Coromandel coast with the eastern and south-eastern foreign countries were favourable to India. Hence an impetus in this direction was given during the Gupta and post-Gupta periods by the contemporary ruling dynasties. This is borne out by the literary and archaeological evidences. The contribution of Orissa to cultural and commercial relations with foreign lands and the resultant economic advancement of India became a recognized fact in the past.[6]

In the field of religion, literature, architecture, sculpture and performing arts, Ḳaliṅga played no less significant role. The Vedic-Purāṇic religions, Buddhism, Jainism and several folk cults (*loka-dharmas*) found in Orissa an encouraging atmosphere for their simultaneous growth. The ancient ruling dynasties of Orissa—the Chedis, the Bhaumakaras, the Somavaṁśīs, the Gaṅgas and others—never tried to impose on the people their own religion as the State religion. On the other hand, they patronized all the popular religious faiths. They had particular regard for the social customs and religious leanings of tribal people.

Ancient Orissa occupies a prestigious position in regard to the development of Sanskrit literature of different categories. Probably it was there that works like the *Bhāgavata Purāṇa* and the *Pañchatantra* were composed. The tradition continued during the medieval period also.

The development of architecture and sculpture, particularly related to the Vedic-Purāṇic faiths and Buddhism continued in Orissa. From the second century B.C. to the thirteenth century A.D. there were close contacts of Orissa with the art-centres of Sanchī, Mathurā, Sirpur, Malhār, Sarnath, Nalanda and Kurkihar. When we compare the art of Bhubaneswar, Udaigiri-Khandagiri, Lalitgiri and Ratnagiri with that of the other art-centres mentioned above, we notice close mutual contacts among them. Orissa became the centre of several art-traits and became a connecting link between the north and south. It was through Kaliṅga that several Indian themes and art-devices reached Thailand, Cambodia and Indonesia.

NOTES AND REFERENCES

1. *Raghuvaṁśa*, VI, 53-8.
2. *Ibid., ch. IV.*
3. See K.D. Bajpai, *Prāchīna Bhārata Kā Videshon Se Saṁbandha* (Indore, 1973), pp. 104-8, 115-28.
4. See W.H. Schoff, *The Periplus of the Erythraean Sea,* 2nd ed. (Delhi, 1974), pp. 47 and 253.
5. *Ibid.*, p. 47 and notes.
6. For details see Motichandra, *Sārthavāha* (Patna, 1966), pp. 106-32.

38
THE DATE OF BHAṬṬOTPALA : A RE-EXAMINATION

LALLANJI GOPAL

Bhaṭṭotpala and his commentaries[1] enjoy a place of unique importance in the study of Varāhamihira.[2] It is significant that Al-Bīrūnī, in his account of Indian astrology-astronomy, gives a high importance to Bhaṭṭotpala, referring to him and his views in details.[3] Bhaṭṭotpala's commentaries easily rank among the outstanding commentaries in Sanskrit literature. In the field of astronomy-astrology they are without much competition. They contributed to the prestige of the scientific treatises written by Varāhamihira. They very effectively serve their basic purpose of explaining words and phrases in the original work, and also help us understand the texts better. They elaborate the information by giving more details. At places Varāhamihira summarily refers to earlier authorities. Bhaṭṭotpala reproduces actual quotations from them to substantiate the references in Varāhamihira. Sometimes he quotes parallel passages from similar authoritative texts. Bhaṭṭotpala leaves no doubt that there were earlier commentaries[4] which seem to have been overshadowed by Bhaṭṭotpala's commentaries and hence were pushed into oblivion. Thus, Bhaṭṭotpala offers a valuable compendium of quotations from many texts which are no longer available. Even in the case of Varāhamihira himself we find that his own *Samāsasaṁhitā*, though lost in its original form, has been quoted by Bhaṭṭotpala so profusely that we can get some idea of its original form by piecing together the quotations.[5]

We are on a sure ground about the times of Bhaṭṭotpala. He himself mentions the precise date on which he completed his commentaries on Varāhamihira's *Bṛhajjātaka* and *Bṛhatsaṁhitā*. He says that he completed his commentary on the *Bṛhajjātaka* on Thursday, the fifth day of the bright half of the month of Caitra in the Śaka year 888 (*vasvaṣṭāṣṭamita śāke*),[6] which has been calculated to be equivalent to Thursday, the 9th of March in A.D. 965.[7] Likewise, Bhaṭṭotpala records that his commentary on the *Bṛhatsaṃhitā* was completed on Thursday, the second day of the dark half of Phālguna in the Śaka year 888 (*vasvaṣṭāṣṭamite śāke*),[8] which is calculated to have fallen on Thursday, the 11th of January in A.D. 966.[9] Thus, A.D. 965 and 966 are recorded to have been the creative years in the career of Bhaṭṭotpala. On this basis one can, with reasonable certainty, place Bhaṭṭotpala in the second to the fourth quarter of the ninth century.

Earlier, these dates were accepted without any serious doubts about their authenticity.[10] But, after the reference in Arab writer Abu Ma'shar's work was brought out by Otto Naugebaurer,[11] the validity of the dates has been questioned and alternative explanations have been offered to reconcile the apparent contradictions. This necessitates a review of the existing views and available evidence.

The dates in the commentaries on the *Bṛhajjātaka* and *Bṛhatsaṁhitā* receive valuable confirmation from the tradition circulating among the astronomers of Ujjayinī. Hunter obtained in Ujjayinī a list of astronomers which assigns to Bhaṭṭotpala the Śaka year 890.[12] This approximates very closely to the dates mentioned by Bhaṭṭotpala, with a negligible difference of only two years. The difference can be easily expected, because the two sources do not refer to the same point in the life of Bhaṭṭotpala.

Al-Bīrūnī and Varuṇabhaṭṭa also provide support for these dates. None of these later authorities pointedly refer to the date of Bhaṭṭotpala, but both know him well; hence their own dates serve as the lower limit for the date of Bhaṭṭotpala. As we have pointed out above, Al-Bīrūnī had a clear knowledge of Bhaṭṭotpala and his writings. Likewise, Varuṇabhaṭṭa in his commentary on Brahmagupta's *Khaṇḍakhādyakakaraṇa* shows a similar knowledge about Bhaṭṭotpala.[13] Now, Al-Bīrūnī composed his work on India in A.D. 1030 and Varuṇabhaṭṭa seems to have flourished around the date Śaka 962 (= AD. 1040).[14] Hence for Bhaṭṭotpala a date in the middle of the tenth century will not be beyond the limits of probability.

Raghunandana in his *Jyotiṣtattva* quotes from the *Yuddha-jayārṇava*, which may be the same as the *Yuddha-jayārṇavatantra* attributed to Bhaṭṭotpala.[15] Raghunandana is said to have composed his works during A.D. 1550-75. We are not discussing this and other later references to Bhaṭṭotpala,[16] because they cannot make improvements over the dates suggested by Al-Bīrūnī and Varuṇabhaṭṭa.

The upper limit for the date of Bhaṭṭotpala is provided by the dates of the astronomers on whose works he wrote commentaries. Varāhamihira's texts on which his commentaries are available are the *Bṛhajjātaka*, *Bṛhatsaṁhitā*, *Laghujātaka*, *Yogayātrā* and *Vivāhapaṭala*.[17] A manuscript copy of his commentary on *Ṣaṭpañcāśikā* (or *Praśnamahodadhi*) attributed to Pṛthuyaśas, the son of Varāhamihira, is mentioned by S.B. Dikshit.[18] Bhaṭṭotpala[f] himself mentions his own commentary on the *Khaṇḍakhādyaka* and reproduces two verses from it. His commentary on Brahmagupta's *Khaṇḍakhādyaka* is available in manuscript form.[20] He wrote a commentary entitled *Cintāmaṇi* on the *Bādarāyaṇa-praśna* and its manuscripts have been noticed.[21] Al-Bīrūnī[22] mentions his commentary on a text named the great *Mānas* (*Bṛhanmānasa*) composed by Manu. Besides these commentaries Bhaṭṭotpala is known to have completed Kalyāṇavarman's *Sārāvalī*, which is said to have remained incomplete for a long time.

Bhaṭṭotpala has to be placed after the astronomers mentioned above. But we do not know anything about the *Bṛhanmānasa* of Manu[23] and the *Bādarāyaṇapraśna* to determine their dates. Hence we can only say that Bhaṭṭotpala was later than Varāhamihira, his son Pṛthuyaśas,

Brahmagupta and Kalyāṇavaraman. Varāhamihira is generally placed in the sixth century. Elsewhere we have argued to place his birth and death respectively in A.D. 505 and 587.[24] The date of Pṛthuyaśas[25] is not known independently and has to be inferred from that of Varāhamihira. In the case of Brahmagupta we are fortunate to have definite dates. According to his *Brāhmasphuṭasiddhānta*,[26] he wrote this work in Śaka 550 (= A.D. 628) at the age of thirty, which gives Śaka 520 (= A.D. 598) as the year of his birth. His another text, the *Khaṇḍakhādyakaraṇa* has the date Śaka 587 (= A.D. 665). The precise date of Kalyāṇavarman is not known and hence has been variously determined as being A.D. 628 (S. Dvivedi), A.D. 650 (S.L. Katre), A.D. 650-725 (A.M. Shastri), A.D. 750 (D.C. Bhattacharya) and A.D. 899 (S.B. Dikshit).[27]

The concluding verse in some manuscripts of Kalyāṇavarman's *Sārāvalī* refers to a gap of hundreds of years (*Varṣaśatānāṁ madhye*) between its original composition by Kalyāṇavarman and its completion later by Bhaṭṭotpala.[28] S.L. Katre[29] took the plural form of the expression *varṣaśatānāṁ* too literally to suggest that the gap was at least about three hundred years. A.M. Shastri objects to it on the ground that it would require us to place Kalyāṇavarman not later than A.D. 530, which clashes with his own reference to Brahmagupta, who wrote his *Brāhmasphuṭasiddhānta* in A.D. 628. But the chronological impasse is created only because Shastri takes Śaka 888 mentioned by Bhaṭṭotpala as the date of the composition of his commentaries to be actually Vikrama 888. Shastri, however, is justified in not taking *varṣaśatānāṁ* too literally. The expression meaning 'hundreds of years' is used to refer in a general way to a long period, without implying a specific number of years. It may be added that if *varṣaśatānāṁ* is taken to signify the minimum period of three hundred years, Kalyāṇavarmana's date will be around Śaka 588 (= A.D. 666), which does not involve any chronological absurdity. The date of Kalyāṇavarman being not known for certain, the present reference cannot help us in calculating the date of Bhaṭṭotpala; it is the date of Kalyāṇavarman which can be roughly calculated back from the date of Bhaṭṭotpala on the basis of the approximate indication in the verse.

The likely dates for Varāhamihira (A.D. 505-78), his son Pṛthuyaśas, Brahmagupta (A.D. 598-665) and Kalyāṇavarman will give the upper bracket of roughly A.D. 700.[30]

Thus, we can infer that Bhaṭṭotpala is to be placed sometime after A.D. 700 but before A.D. 1000. This time-bracket does not conflict with the known date Śaka 888 = A.D. 965-66.

One evidence which goes against this date is the occurrence of quotations from the *Bhāskarasiddhānta* in Bhaṭṭotpala's commentary on the *Bṛhajjātaka*. There are two sets of quotations: four verses are quoted in the introductory part of the commentary and one in the commentary on *Bṛhajjātaka* I.1. Of these, the first set of verses is found in the *Siddhānta-śiromaṇi*[31] of Bhāskarācārya. Bhāskara himself records that he was born in Śaka 1036 and composed his work *Siddhānta-śiromaṇi* at the age of thirty-six.[32] Thus, the date of the composition of the text will be Śaka 1072 (= A.D. 1150). This creates a chronologically impossible position. An author belonging to the ninth or tenth century cannot quote from a text which was composed in the twelfth century.

Those who rely on the evidence of the *Siddhānta-śiromaṇi* verses being quoted by Bhaṭṭotpala, dismiss the date (Śaka 888) occurring in his commentaries and opt for later dates. But this view is to be rejected, because it goes against the unassailable testimony of Al-Bīrūnī (A.D. 1030) mentioning Bhaṭṭotpala and his writings and quoting from them. Hence we have to offer a plausible explanation of the quotations from *Siddhānta-śiromaṇi*. Kane[33] has suggested two alternative explanations. The first is that before Bhāskarācārya, the author of the *Siddhānta-śiromaṇi*, there was an earlier astronomer of the name of Bhāskara in whose work *Bhāskara-siddhānta* the five verses quoted by Bhaṭṭotpala actually occurred. It is not unlikely that Bhāskarācārya used four of these verses in his *Siddhāntaśiromaṇi*. P.C. Sengupta[34] mentions an earlier Bhāskara, a direct disciple of Āryabhaṭa. He is credited with two texts, the *Mahā-Bhāskarīya* and the *Laghu-Bhāskarīya*, though they are no longer available.[35] The other possibility is that at a certain stage the verses in question were scribbled as marginal notes to Bhaṭṭotpala's commentary on the *Bṛhajjātaka*, which a subsequent copyist incorporated in the text of the commentary. The likelihood of this possibility is strengthened by the fact that some manuscripts of the commentary do not contain these verses.

Some scholars, who do not accept the date (Śaka 888) mentioned by Bhaṭṭotpala in his commentaries on the *Bṛhajjātaka* and *Bṛhatsaṁhitā*, suggest different readings for the expression *vasvaṣṭāṣṭamite* mentioning the date. Sitaram Jha proposes the reading *vasvaṣṭāṣṭimite* (1688) to accommodate the difficulty raised by the quotations from Bhāskarācārya.[36] But it is not realised that the difficulty is not genuine; it is an artificial creation on account of a mistake at some stage in the history of the copying of Bhaṭṭotpala's commentary. Jha does not take cognisance of one of the basic realities in the discussion of the date of Bhaṭṭotpala that he preceded Al-Bīrūnī and Bhaṭṭavaruṇa. Moreover, there is no manuscript sanction for the amendment proposed by Sitaram Jha.

Another variant reading, proposed by D.C. Bhattacharya, is *vasvaśvāśvamite* (778) for *vasvaṣṭāṣṭamite*,[37] because, according to his calculations, the details of the date of the completion of the commentary fall on the 28th of February, A.D. 966, which was a Wednesday and not a Thursday. But the objection based on astronomical calculation is not valid. The calculation, quoted above, as done by A.M. Shastri, perfectly tallies with the details given in the original quotation, including its being a Thursday. The emended date stands exposed to all those objections which are levelled against the date contained in the original reading (Śaka 888). No doubt the conflict with the reference in the writing of Abu Mashar appears to be partially resolved. But this is only on paper and would not have worked in reality. It is difficult to believe that a commentary completed in A.D. 856 (Śaka 778) gained such a wide currency as to have reached the Arab astronomer Abu Mashar, who died in A.D. 886. The basic mistake in Bhattacharya's emendment also is the absence of this reading in any one manuscript at least.

The variant reading *vasvaṣṭāśvamite* (Śaka 788) is found only in one manuscript noticed by R.L. Mitra.[38] There is absolutely no reason why this reading occurring in a single manuscript should get preference over the reading supported by a large number of manuscripts. The objections raised against the emended date (Śaka 778) are applicable to this data (Śaka 788) as well. In this case the gap between the date of the composition of Bhaṭṭotpala's commentaries and death of Abu Mashar (A.D. 886) is further reduced from A.D. 856-86 to A.D. 866-86 and is made more improbable.

In calculating the date of the composition of Bhaṭṭotpala's commentary some scholars do not agree with the common view that the Śaka era mentioned here is not the one which began in A.D. 78. They identify this Śaka era with the so-called Cyrus era. But there is no unanimity about the epoch of this Cyrus era and the event commemorated by it. Some fix the commencement of the Cyrus era in 551-50 B.C. marking the foundation of the Achaemenid empire by Cyrus or his incursions into India.[39] According to Rangarajan, this Śaka era commenced in 523-522 B.C. commemorating the appointment of the first viceroy for the Indian province of the Achaemenid empire.[40] Calculating on the basis of the suggested identification of the Śaka era mentioned in Bhaṭṭotpala's commentary with the Cyrus era, we arrive at 551/550 B.C. - 888 = A.D. 337/338[41] and 523/522 B.C. - 888 = A.D. 365/366 as the date of the composition of the commentaries by Bhaṭṭotpala. These dates create serious chronological problems in respect of the known correlation of Bhaṭṭotpala with Varāhamihira, Āryabhaṭa, Brahmagupta, Kalyāṇavarman and Muñjāla. A more serious objection of a basic nature is that the so-called Cyrus era has only a hypothetical existence. We do not have any evidence for its creation by Cyrus or for its circulation in the country of its supposed origin. In India also we have no evidence for the use of such an era. As is well known, the ancient sources in India in their long span do not reveal even the haziest memory of the Achaemenid occupation of a part of India. Even if we grant the foundation of an era commemorating an event in the life and career of Cyrus, we will not succeed in explaining how it came to be designated as Śaka-kāla. Again, it has been pointed out that the calculation of the details of the date of the composition of the commentaries do not admit a Thursday in A.D. 388 or 339.[42]

Recently A.M. Shastri[43] has argued in support of the possibility that the dates mentioned in Bhaṭṭotpala's two commentaries are to be referred to the Vikrama era commencing in 58 B.C. and not the Śaka era of A.D. 78. J.F. Fleet[44] had mooted the suggestion, but had hesitated to stick to it, because he could not work out the requirement of a Thursday falling on the date calculated for the years A.D. 830 and 831. But the calculations made by A.M. Shastri show that even the dates A.D. 830 and 831 fulfil the requirement of the week-day being a Thursday.[45]

A.M. Shastri argues that the word Śaka was also used in the sense of time-reckoning in general and sometimes denoted the Vikram era. His main argument is that according to Bhaṭṭotpala himself *śakendrakāla* begins with the time of the murder of the Śaka king and explains it by adding that that time (*kāla*) is known as Śaka when the kings of the barbarian people named the Śakas were killed by king Vikramāditya.[46]

In earlier inscriptions, supposed to use the Śaka era of A.D. 78, the name Śaka does not appear. It is only in inscriptions beginning with the year Śaka 500 (= A.D. 578) that the name Śaka occurs. The expressions used mean 'the era of the Śakas' (*Śaka-saṁvat, Śaka-varṣa* or *Śaka-kāla*), 'the era of the Śaka king (or kings)' (*Śakanṛpatisaṁvatsara, Śaka-nṛpa-saṁvatsara* or *Śaka-nṛpa-kāla*) or 'the era of the coronation of the Śaka king' (*Śaka-nṛpati-rājyābhiṣeka-saṁvatsara*).[47] The use of the term *śaka* for time-reckoning in general or for Vikrama era is not evidenced for earlier periods. It is found in inscriptions which are of a very late period. The

Jyotirvidābharaṇa, referred to in this connection, though attributed to Kālidāsa, is definitely of a late date A.D. 1242-43. It is quite likely that by these late dates the origin of the Śaka era had been obscured and people imagined a story about it. It is to be noted that Brahmagupta (A.D. 598-665), though mentioning it in terms of the years after the end of the Śakas (*Śakānte'bdāḥ*), still retains A.D. 78 as the epoch of the era.[48] Likewise, Bhāskarācārya (A.D. 1150) also, while mentioning that the era marks the end of the Śaka king, calculates on the basis of A.D. 78 being its epoch.[49] There is no reason why Bhaṭṭotpala is to be placed in a different category. It will be in the logic of things to hold that he also, like Brahmagupta of an earlier date and Bhāskarācārya of a later date, while advancing the view that the era marked the death of a Śaka king, calculates by retaining the epoch of the era as A.D. 78. There is no reason why we should make an exception and interpret the Śaka era mentioned by him to be Vikrama era. There is no indication in Bhaṭṭotpala's commentary to suggest that he takes the epoch of this era to be 58 B.C.

The observations of Al-Bīrūnī clear the confusion. He very distinctly differentiates between the two eras pointing out the gap of 135 years between their epochs. He records the current tradition and as a critical rational scientist, mentions the absurdity involved. The Śaka era could not have marked the killing of the Śaka king by Vikramāditya, with whose name the Vikrama era of 58 B.C. is associated, and hence the Śaka era is not to be mixed up with the Vikrama era of 58 B.C. We quote the relevant passage in Al-Bīrūnī's account.[50] "The epoch of the era of Śaka or Śakakāla falls 135 years later than that of Vikramāditya. The here-mentioned Śaka tyrannised over their country between the river Sindh and the ocean, after he had made Āryāvarta in the midst of their realm his dwelling place. He interdicted the Hindus from considering and representing themselves as anything but Śakas... . The Hindus had much to suffer from him, till at last they received help from the east, when Vikramāditya marched against him, put him to fight and killed him in the region of Karūr, between Multan and the castle of Lūnī. Now this date became famous, as people rejoiced in the news of the death of the tyrant, and was used as the epoch of an era, especially by the astronomers.... Since there is a long interval between the era which is called the era of Vikramāditya from whom the era has got its name is not identical with that one who killed Śaka, but only a namesake of his."

In ancient India the traditions about the epoch of an era and its name were faithfully preserved and handed down because of their continued use, but the stories about their actual origin were not always recorded. In the absence of an effective system for recording details of political history the fading out of the memories of the facts about their origin in course of time was a strong possibility. In the present case we notice this eventuality arising first some five hundred years after the commencement of the era.

We have a parallel case of confusion about the origin of an era, though there is no confusion about its epoch. Al-Bīrūnī takes the era of Valabha and the Guptakāla to be identical. He says: "The era of Valabha is called so from Valabha, the ruler of the town Valabhī. The epoch of this era falls 241 years later than the epoch of the Śaka era.... As regards Guptakāla, people say that the Guptas were wicked powerful people, and that when they ceased to exist this date was used as the epoch of an era. It seems that Valabha was the last of them, because the epoch of the era of the Guptas falls, like that of the Valabha era, 241 years later than the Śaka-kāla."[51] Al-Bīrūnī, who depended on Indian sources for his information, is perfectly correct about the epoch of the Valabha-Gupta era (241 + 78 = A.D. 319). But, within four hundred years of the distintegration of the Gupta empire people had forgotten the real origin of the era and filled up the gap by a fanciful account. It was said that the era was floated after the end of the Gupta dynasty and that Valabha was the last king of the dynasty. We need not discuss the criticism of the Guptas as wicked people. The epigraphical evidence disproves the account about the origin of the era. It is well known that the Gupta era was in use since very early times, as is evidenced by the Mathura inscription of the reign of Chandragupta II dated in the year 61. We have a long continuous series of inscriptions during the times of the Guptas employing the era, and the practice continued even during the period they were politically ineffective and later when their rule had ended. The narrative about the use of the appellation Valabha for the era is equally incorrect. History does not confirm the existence of any king of the name of Valabha in the Gupta family. Evidently, the use of the Gupta era persisted in the Valabhi area with the result that, after the disappearance of the Guptas, people in the area forgot the Gupta origin of the era and came to designate it as the Valabhi era, which Al-Bīrūnī mentions as the era of Valabha.

Thus, on the analogy of the account about the origin of Valabha-Gupta era by Al-Bīrūnī and the testimony of Brahmagupta and Bhāskarācārya about the Śaka-kāla we can maintain the natural interpretation of the Śaka-kāla mentioned by Bhaṭṭotpala as being the Śaka era with A.D. 78 as its epoch, dismissing the fanciful suggestion about its origin.

A.M. Shastri does not mention any intrinsic inaccuracy and contradiction in the reference made by Bhaṭṭotpala which force him to interpret the Śakakāla as being the Vikrama era of 58 B.C. We find that he has noted the references to dates in the Śaka era given by Varāhamihira[52] and has critically discussed in detail the various suggestions about the identification of the Śaka era of Varāhamihira with the Cyrus era, Buddha Nirvāṇa era and the Vikrama era.[53] The identification with the Vikrama era has been suggested by G.S. Gai and S. Sankaranarayanan.[54] Shastri maintains that the Śaka-kāla mentioned by Varāhamihira is the Śālivāhana-Śaka era commencing in A.D. 78. He finds the reference to the year 427 of the Śaka-kāla in the *Pañcasiddhāntikā* to be decisive. In the natural course A.M. Shastri should have applied to the commentator Bhaṭṭotpala the same interpretation about the epoch of the Śaka era which he convincingly proves for the original author Varāhamihira. If he deviates from this, he must have very strong arguments and independent evidence in support of his view. We know that Bhaṭṭotpala had a very intimate knowledge of the texts of Varāhamihira and also earlier commentaries on his works. We do not have any convincing argument in favour of the view differentiating between the epochs of the Śaka era as calculated by Varāhamihira and Bhaṭṭotpala.

A.M. Shastri's compulsion for seeking the equation of the Śaka-kāla of Bhaṭṭotpala with the Vikrama era of 57 B.C. arises from the difficulty supposed to be created by a reference in another source. The reference has been traced in the work of the Arab writer Abu Mashar. Otto Naugebaurer[55] has pointed out that Abu Mashar cites a passage about the third *decan* of Aries which belongs to Bhaṭṭotpala's commentary on Chapter 27 of the *Bṛhajjātaka*. Abu Ma'shar died in A.D. 886, hence the composition of Bhaṭṭotpala's commentary on the *Bṛhajjātaka* must belong to a date before A.D. 886.

This cannot be reconciled with the fact that Bhaṭṭotpala himself mentions the date of its composition as being Śaka 888, which is equivalent to A.D. 965. Unable to offer any plausible reconciliation of the two conflicting pieces of evidence, P.V. Kane[56] rejects the authenticity of the date mentioned by Bhaṭṭotpala and infers that Bhaṭṭotpala belonged to a date not later than A.D. 850. A.M. Shastri, however, upholds the authenticity of the manuscripts of the commentaries mentioning the date Śaka 888 and, hence, to reconcile their evidence with the reference in the work of Abu Ma'shar, suggests that the Śaka year 888 has to be calculated as being in the Vikrama era. He has tried to cut the Gordian knot, but the chronological tangle is not satisfactorily resolved. Abu Ma'shar died in A.D. 866, but the composition of his work has to be dated many years before this date. Converted into the Vikrama era the year Śaka 888 will be equivalent to A.D. 831, after which we have to postulate sufficient number of years for the circulation of Bhaṭṭotpala's commentary and its academic acceptance for its travelling to Abu Ma'shar. The narrow span of thirty-five years, though not so short as to find it incredibly impossible to accommodate all this, will definitely be improbably congested and short.

The applicability of the Abu Ma'shar evidence is not so definitive as it is taken to be. Abu Ma'shar does not quote the passage in question as being from Bhaṭṭotpala's commentary on the *Bṛhajjātaka*. In cases where the original source is not specifically mentioned, its identification can be attempted on the basis of a comparison of the actual expression used in the two texts. But, in the present case, in the translation of Abu Ma'shar's work we can never be sure about the actual Sanskrit words quoted from the original commentary. It is not a question of ideas and views, it is the actual expression which matters. The same view can be expressed by different writers in different expressions. We know that there were earlier commentaries on the works of Varāhamihira. Bhaṭṭotpala in some cases refers to them. Some of these views may occur in other texts and commentaries. We learn from Al-Bīrūnī that Bhaṭṭotpala had borrowed from Muñjāla, the author of the *Laghumānasa*, a theory about the real solstice preceding the solstice used by astronomers for calculation. The *Laghumānasa* was an epitome of the *Bṛhanmānas* ascribed to Manu, on which Bhaṭṭotpala had written a commentary. Thus, Bhaṭṭotpala did not necessarily confine himself to the works of Varāhamihira. It is clear from his commentaries that Bhaṭṭotpala consulted a large number of writings, both before and after Varāhamihira, and drew upon their views. Hence it is quite likely that the view which O. Naugebaurer attributes to Bhaṭṭotpala occurred in some other earlier work also, which possibly served as the source for Abu Ma'shar. As the evidence stands, the reference in Abu Ma'shar cannot be taken to establish that Bhaṭṭotpala preceded Abu Mashar. Hence we need not reject the natural calculation of the year Śaka 888 in terms of the Śaka era commencing in A.D. 78 and attempt a patently incorrect identification of the Śaka era with the Vikrama era commencing in 57 B.C.

In fine, we can maintain, on the basis of Bhaṭṭotpala's own statements in his commentaries on the *Bṛhajjātaka* and *Bṛhatsaṁhitā*, that he composed these commentaries in the Śaka year 888 on dates which fall respectively in A.D. 965 and 966.

NOTES AND REFERENCES

1. On *Bṛhajjātaka, Bṛhatsaṁhitā, Laghujātaka, Yogayātrā* and *Vivāhapaṭala*. He wrote commentaries also on Pṛthuyaśas's *Ṣaṭpañcāśikā*, Brahmagupta's *Khaṇḍakhādyaka, Bṛhanmānasa* attributed to Manu, and the

Bādarāyaṇa-praśna. He is credited with the authorship of some independent works, such as *Āryasaptati* and *Yuddhajayārṇavatantra*, besides the four mentioned by Al-Bīrūnī, but now not available. See A.M. Shastri, *Varāhamihira and his times*, Jodhpur, 1991, p. 205-7.

2. *Ibid.*, p. 206.

3. Sachau, *Alberuni's India*, I, pp. 157-58, 298, 334, 336-37, 361, 367.

4. A.M. Shastri, *op. cit.*, p. 207.

5. *Ibid.*, pp. 62-76.

6. चैत्रमासस्य पंचम्यां सितायां गुरुवासरे ।
   वस्वष्टाष्टामिते शाके कृतायां विवृतिर्मया ।।

   See A.M. Shastri, *op. cit.*, p. 201, f.n. 2.

7. A.M. Shastri, *op. cit.*, p. 202 H. Kern, *Bṛhatsaṁhitā*, Preface, pp. 6ff considers the fact that the details of the date require Thursday as the week day, which works out in the case of the years A.D. 965 and 966 to be a strong reason for identifying Bhaṭṭotpala's Śaka era with the one having A.D. 78 as its epoch.

8. फाल्गुनस्य द्वितीयायामसितायां गुरोर्दिने ।
   वस्वष्टाष्टामिते शाके कृतेयं विवृतिर्मया ।।

   See A.M. Shastri, *op. cit.*, p. 201, f. n. 4.

9. A.M. Shastri, *op. cit.*, p. 202.

10. S.B. Dikshit, *Bhāratīya Jyotiṣa* (Hindi translation by Sevanath Jharkhandi), 2nd edn., 1961, Lucknow, pp. 326-27; Baladeva Upadhyay, Foreword to A.V. Tripathi, *Bṛhatsaṁhitā of Varāhamihira*, Part I (Varanasi, 1968), pp. 8-9; G.V. Devasthali in the *Age of Imperial Kanauj* (eds. R.C. Majumdar and A.D. Pusalkar), p. 199.

11. 'Variants to the Greek translation of Abu Ma'shar's version of the Paranatellonta of Varahamihira and Tenkros', *Bulletin of the Royal Academy of Belgium*, 1957-58, pp. 133-40. P.V. Kane, 'Date of Utpala, Commentator of Varāhamihira's *Bṛhajjātaka* and other works', *Journal of the Asiatic Society*, Bombay, Vol. XXXIII (1958), pp. 147-49.

12. H.T. Colebroke, *Miscellaneous Essays*, II, pp. 461-63.

13. S.B. Dikshit, *op. cit.*, p. 328.

14. *Ibid.*, p. 331.

15. *Manuscripts from Indian Collections*, National Museum, New Delhi, 1964, pp. 9-10.

16. S.B. Dikshit, *op. cit.*, pp. 327-28 points out that two works composed in Kashmir, a commentary (dated Śaka 1564 = A.D. 1642) on the *Khaṇḍakhādyaka*, and the *Pañcāṅgakautuka* (dated Śaka 1567 = A.D. 1645) refer to his commentary.

17. A.M. Shastri, *op. cit.*, p. 206.

18. *Op. cit.*, p. 327.

19. On *Bṛhatsaṁhitā* V. 19. He introduces his verses as *Tathā ca Khaṇḍakhādyakaraṇa'smadīyavacanam.*

20. S.B. Dikshit, *op. cit.*

21. A.M. Shastri, *op. cit.*, p. 211, f.n. 63.

22. Sachau, *Alberuni's India*, I, p. 157.

23. G.V. Devasthali (*op. cit.*,) places it in the last quarter of the ninth century. Al-Bīrūnī (*op. cit.*, I, p. 157) mentions an epitome of the *Bṛhanmānasa* by Puñcala (?) or Puñgala, which he later names as the *Small Mānasa* (*ibid.*, p. 366). Puñjala is evidently a mistake for Muñjāla whose *Laghumānasa* in 60 verses is mentioned by Sudhakara Dvivedi, *Gaṇakataraṅgiṇi*. Munīśvara (b. A.D. 1603) in his commentary *Marīci*

quotes four verses of Muñjāla. Al-Bīrūnī (*op. cit.*, pp. 366-67) associates Śakakāla 854 (= A.D. 932) with Puñjala. S. Dvivedi also gives Śaka 854 as the date of the text. The list of astronomers compiled by Ujjain astronomers also places Muñjāla in Śaka 854 - Colebrooke, *Miscellaneous Essays*, Vol. II, p. 461. See S.B. Dikshit, *op. cit.*, pp. 319-20. On this basis Dikshit (*ibid.*, p. 318) infers that *circa* Śaka 800 (= A.D. 878) was the date of *Bṛhanmānasa*. Al-Bīrūnī later (*op. cit.*, I, p. 367) says that Utpala took the theory about the real solstice and the solstice of the astronomers for calculation being different from Puñjāla (or Muñjāla). This would imply that Bhaṭṭotpala belonged to a period after Muñjāla.

24. Our article on "The Date Varāhamihira" is to be published in Prof. S.B. Deo Felicitation Volume.

25. By mistake Sir John Williams, *Asiatic Researches*, Vol. II, p. 390 mentions Bhaṭṭotpala as the son of Varāhamihira. H.T. Colebrooke, *Miscellaneous Essays*, II, p. 479 criticised it. Williams possibly followed blindly some manuscript. A manuscript of *Praśnajñāna* (A. Banerji-Sastri, *Catalogue of Sanskrit Manuscripts in Mithila*, Vol. III, p. 213, No. 184) in its colophon mentions Bhaṭṭotpala as the son of Varāhamihira (*Śrī Varāhamihirātmaja-Bhaṭṭotpalana*). Likewise, Pṛthuyaśas is mentioned as a son of Bhaṭṭotpala in the colophon of some manuscripts of *Ṣaṭpañcāśikā* (or Praśnamahodadhi) - Kuppuswamy, *Descriptive Catalogue of Sanskrit Manuscripts in Government Oriental Manuscripts Library*, Nos. 13954, 13957 and 13959.

26. Verses 7-8.

27. For fuller references see A.M. Shastri, *op. cit.*, pp. 195-98.

28. The first line of the verse shows minor variants. See A.M. Shastri, *op. cit.*, pp. 198, 200 (f. n. 17).

29. *Indian Culture*, Vol. XI (1944), pp. 1-9.

30. If, as mentioned by Al-Bīrūnī, Bhaṭṭotpala is taken to have borrowed a theory from Muñjāla his date will be after A.D. 934, otherwise he will be placed after the *Bṛhanmānasa*, whose date, as suggested by S.B. Dikshit, is c. A.D. 878. This will narrow down the upper time-bracket for Bhaṭṭotpala.

31. I. 9-12.

32. *Golādhyāya*, 58. Bhāskarācārya's date is confirmed by epigraphic records also. See S.B. Dikshit, *op. cit.*, pp. 342-44.

33. *Journal of the Bombay Branch of the Royal Asiatic Society*, 1948-49, pp. 30-31.

34. *Khaṇḍakhādyaka*, Preface, pp. XIII-XIV.

35. The non-availability of one verse attributed to the *Bhāskarasiddhānta* in the *Siddhānta-śiromaṇi* and the difference in the titles of the two texts can be explained away and are not sufficient reasons for rejecting their suggested identification.

36. *Bṛhajjātaka* with Utpala's gloss (Banaras, 1934). V. Subrahmanya Sastry (*Sārāvalī* of Kalyāṇavarman, Preface, pp. 1-2) places Utpala during the reign of Jehangir (A.D. 1605-27). The suggestion is exposed to all those points of criticism which have been raised above against Sitaram Jha's view. The view, further, does not have the support of any text or tradition.

37. *Indian Culture*, Vol. XII (1945-46), pp. 81-82.

38. *Notices of Sanskrit Manuscripts*, Vol. II (1874), p. 166.

39. K. Venkatachalam, *Journal of the Andhra Historical Research Society*, Vol. XX (1949-50), pp. 39-82; XXI (1950-51), pp. 1-40; V. Thiruvenkatachar, *Journal of Indian History*, Vol. XXVIII (1950), pp. 103-10; G. Rai, *Journal of the Punjab University Historical Society*, Vol. I, pp. 61-73, 123-36.

40. *Proceedings of the Indian History Congress*, 1941 session, p. 164.

41. V. Thiruvenkatachar, *Popular Astronomy* mentions A.D. 340 as the date of Utpala.

42. For a detailed criticism of the view, see A.M. Shastri in *Vidarbha Research Society's Annual*, 1961, pp. 26-46.

43. *Varāhamihira and his times*, pp. 197, 203-4. See also *Indian Historical Quarterly*, Vol. XXXVIII, pp. 247-59.

44. *Indian Antiquary*, Vol. XIX (1890), pp. 41-43.

45. *Op. cit.*

46. On *Bṛhatsaṁhitā* VIII. 20- शक नाम म्लेच्छजातयो राजावस्ते यस्मिन् काले विक्रमादित्यदेवेन व्यापादिताः स कालो लोके शक इति प्रसिद्धः । Similar statements are made by Pṛthūdakasvāmin (c. A.D. 864) and Āmarāja (c. \A.D. 1180) in their commentaries on Brahmagupta's *Khaṇḍakhādyaka*. P.C. Sengupta, *Khaṇḍakhādykakaraṇa* (with Pṛthūdakasvāmin's gloss) Calcutta, 1941, p. 3- शक नाम म्लेच्छा राजानस्ते यस्मिन् काले विक्रमादित्ये व्यापादिताः स कालोऽत्यर्तं प्रसिद्धः ॥ Sengupta, *Khaṇḍakhādkakaraṇa* (with Āmarāja's commentary) Calcutta, 1925, p. 2-शका नाम राजानस्ते यस्मिन् काले विक्रमादित्येन व्यापादिताः स शक-सम्बन्धी कालः शक इत्युच्यते । Evidently, the three commentaries are not independent but derive their information from one common source.

47. A.M. Shastri, *op. cit.*, pp. 204, 209.

48. त्रीणि कृतादीनि कलेर्गौगैकगुणाः शकान्तेरऽब्दाः-

    Brāhmasphuṭasiddhānta q. by A.M. Shastri, *op. cit.*, p. 209, f.n. 29. Also शकनृपाणां पंचाशतसंयुत्तेर्मषशतैः पंचभि 550 रतीतै :-*Brāhmasphuṭasiddhānta*, v. 7 in S.B. Dikshit, *op. cit.*, p. 300.

49. नन्दान्द्रीन्द्रयुणास्तथा शाकनृपस्यान्ते कलेर्वत्सराः :-

    Siddhāntaśiromaṇi q. by A.M. Shastri, *op. cit.*, p. 209, f. n. 30.

50. E. Sachau, *op. cit.*, II, p. 6.

51. *Op. cit.*, II, p. 7.

52. *Pañcasiddhāntikā*, I. 8-10 (*Śaka-kāla*); *Bṛhatsaṁhitā* XIII. 3-4 (*Śaka-kāla*); *ibid.*, VIII. 20 (*Śakendrakāla*), 21 (*Śakabhūpālakāla*).

53. *Op. cit.*, pp. 31-42.

54. *Epigraphia Indica*, Vol. XXXVII, pp. 5-8.

55. *Supra*, f.n. 11.

56. *Op. cit.*

39

THE RISE OF URBANISM IN THE UPPER GAṄGĀ-YAMUNĀ *DOĀB*

R.C. GAUR

The revival of urbanisation after the disappearance of the Harappan civilization has deservedly excited the attention of historians like D.D. Kosambi and of archaeologists like A. Ghosh. The general thesis seems to be that urban culture developed only by 600 B.C. As archaeological evidence has grown with explorations and excavations of new sites in the last decade or so, it may be worthwhile to review this thesis by going once again to the evidence.

We may begin by noting, first, that the late dating of urbanisation does not have very firm roots in the literary evidence, which appears to suggest that states and towns, as the necessary nuclei of power, had arisen much earlier than 600 B.C. Indeed, much before the rise of the sixteen *mahajanapadas* and their capital towns referred to in the early Buddhist texts (*Aṅguttara Nikāya*, II 2), a few states had already emerged in northern India. This might well have occurred around 1200 B.C. when the Aryans became familiar with iron technology. The Aryans were now able to advance from the Drishadvati and Sarasvati region eastwards into the upper Gaṅgā-Yamunā *Doāb* with their horse-drawn chariots and iron weapons. Iron tools must have helped them to colonize the region after clearing the monsoon forests. The *Śatapatha Brāhmaṇa* (XXII.2.2.13) and *Aitareya Brāhmaṇa* (VIII. 1.4) speak of the dense forests of the eastern region. A detailed account of forest clearance with traditional method of burning is given in the *Mahābhārata* (*Khāṇḍavadāha Parva*). The venture was apparently largely peaceful as we come across only a few references to warfare with the *dasyus*, a common phenomenon of the Ṛgvedic period. Perhaps the earlier inhabitants of the eastern zone, represented by the Black-and-Red Ware (B&RW) industry were not in a position to offer effective resistance to check the Aryan advance as they lived in scattered pockets in small groups. Their predecessors, who were using the so-called Ochre Colour Pottery (OCP) and the tools of the copper hoards and were perhaps the earliest settlers in the Upper *Doāb* region, were no more on the scene: it has been argued that their settlements, with a few exceptions had already been washed away in a great natural deluge.[1]

While new Aryan settlements were coming up eastwards, the older settlements in the Saraswati and Drishadvati region also were extended and strengthened signalling the process of urbanism at selected places as administrative centres.[2]

According to the *Taittiriya Āraṇyaka* (I.11),[3] Kurukshetra emerged as powerful state. It was bounded by *Khāṇḍava vana* on the south, the *Turghna* on the north, and the *Pariṇah* on the west. This suggests territory comprising the area around Thanesar and Delhi and the greater part of the upper *Doāb*; the capital was at Asandivata,[4] probably the Hastinapura of the epics and the Purāṇas. The same sources associate the kings of Kurukshetra with the Puru-Bharata family. That the Pauravas had their links with the Kurus is also suggested by the *Ṛgveda*. It is alleged that Janamejaya, the eldest son of Parikshit and grandson of Abhimanyu had conquered Takshaśilā (Taxila) and performed a great snake sacrifice. The possession of Taxila in the extreme north-west implies control over Madras, the homeland of Janamejaya's mother Madravati. It may be recalled here that the princes of the Paurava race ruled in the territory lying between the Jhelum and the Ravi down to the time of Alexander. Another important country was that of the Pañchālas which roughly comprised the Districts of Bareilly, Budaun, Farrukhabad and the adjoining areas of central Doab. The Pañchālas[5] as their name indicates, probably consisted of five clans, viz. the Kṛvi, Turvasu, Keśin, Śṛṇjaya and Somaka. They appear to have been the descendants of those Aryan groups, who were defeated in the 'Battle of the Ten Kings' (*Daśarājña*). The tradition of domestic wars and alliances seems to continue in the later periods also. Since we do not get any mention in the Vedic literature of the Śaurasenas of Mathura, a branch of the Yadu family, it may be supposed that the Śaurasena state emerged out of the Pañchāla kingdom itself, comprising its western part. This assumption is possible because of the fact that in the *Ṛgveda* (I.108.8) the Yadus are shown closely associated with the Turvasu, one of the five founder clans of the Pañchāla country. Just outside the *Doāb* was the Matsya[6] country bounded in the north by the territory of the Kurus and in the east by the country of the Śaurasenas; it thus comprised parts of Alwar, Jaipur and Bharatpur. According to Manu, there were four territories, viz. the lands of the Kurus, Pañchālas, Śaursenas and the Matsyas which the Aryans occupied first when they moved eastward from Brahmāvarta *i.e.* the region between the Sarasvati and Drashadvati.

Extensive exploration of this region, and excavations of a few sites such as Noh and Jodhpura in Rajasthan and Hastinapura, Ahichchatra, Sonkh, Jakhera and Atranjikhera in U.P., have confirmed that the Painted Grey Ware Culture (PGW) had its longest duration at these places. After consolidating their power in Upper *Doāb*, the Aryans moved further eastward (Śatpatha Br. 1.4.10.19; 4.1.1.4.) up to Sadānīrā river (Rapti). This stage seems to correspond with the age of the later Brāhmaṇas and the Upanishads, when the PGW industry was in the process of decline.

The archaeological evidence largely corroborates the literary evidence of the period. By this time agriculture had made great strides. Not only were two harvests being raised in the year, but wheat was being grown which meant that artificial irrigation was being undertaken. Several *kuchcha* (unlined) wells were found outside the habitational area at Atranjikhera offering actual evidence of irrigation from well, a device which still continues in the vicinity.[7]

Agricultural surplus enabled the communities to engage in trade on an appreciable scale. Without trade they could neither have acquired so much metal (iron and copper) nor semi-precious stones for their beads. At Atranjikhera traces of *chir*-wood (*pinus roxburghii*) were found; and this could only have been brought from a distance of some hundreds of kilometres from the Khyber region mainly for its resin probably needed for fire oblation. In addition remie-fibres were used for fishing-nets which again shows contacts between the hill-dwellers and the PGW people of Atranjikhera.[8]

Another significant feature of the PGW settlement was the raising of a mud-bond of considerable thickness primarily to protect the habitation from floods; in later periods such embankments provided base for the fortification of the town during the NBPW period. Available height and length of the bund at Atranjikhera were 1.45 m and 35 m respectively,[9] and at Jakhera, another PGW site in the same district (Etah) the basal width of the bund was 4.80 m and extant height 1.20 m.[10]

Time and again it has been suggested that iron emerged in northern India in developed form with the PGW in the Upper *Doāb* region and the surrounding areas around 1300-1200 B.C. The presence of a large number of iron objects, pieces of slag and tools of blacksmiths at Atranjikhera suggest that not only were the iron goods manufactured at the site but also the smelting of iron ore itself was being carried out. Chemical analysis has conclusively proved that the PGW people at Atranjikhera collected their ore from the Agra-Gwalior range. This range possibly was also the main source of iron for the inhabitants of Hastinapura, Hulas, Alamgirpur and several other sites in the Gaṅgā-Yamunā basin. If the Atranjikhera people could collect their semi-precious stones for their beads from the Ranthambhor region, the PGW people of Jodhpura and other sites in Rajasthan, Haryana, etc. could also surely obtain their ore from the Agra-Gwalior region.[11] With the advent of iron technology multifarious activities in various fields started bringing northern India gradually at the threshold of urbanisation by the middle phase of the PGW period.

The material complex in the early phase of the PGW at Atranjikhera more or less remained the same as in Period II except that PGW, iron and horse were introduced signalling the advent of a new cultural period. Now deforestation started on a large scale and new settlements began to appear. The settlements were now villages having cluster of huts or houses. But as we have mentioned by the middle phase (around 1000-900 B.C.) monarchical states began to emerge. Both archaeological and literary sources attest this fact. During the course of explorations quite a few extensive sites have been located which appear to be the ancient towns. The term '*nagara*' (town) specifically is referred to in the *Taittariya Āraṇyaka* (I.11.18). Now not only agricultural production was accelerated but there was marked improvement and advancement in other professions. Many of these needed skilled craftsmen and artisans. The surplus agriculture yield was now available to sustain a large non-agriculturist population. Several village industries were now advanced industries. The process of urbanisation may be expected to have been slow until the period of the Nandas and Mauryans when brick structures became prolific and towns were fortified.

Professions of the PGW Period

A brief account is given below of some of prominent professions and occupations, which accelerated the process of urbanism from village economy.

Agriculture

A large portion of the population was necessarily involved in this profession. Much land became available for raising two crops in a year, after clearing the dense forest with the help of iron axes. Though agricultural tools have not been found in large numbers, a hoe and sickles have been found at Jakhera.[12] At Atranjikhera, rice (*Oryza satiwa L.*), wheat (Triticism *compaetum Host*) and barley (*Horderem Vulgare* L., hulled six row) have been found. Wheat was introduced for the first time in the Ganga plain during the PGW period, and rice (unhusked) was found in heaps. Professor Chowdhury remarked, "that the production of cereals was then not only enough to meet the requirements of the entire community but there was also some surplus".[13] We have already seen that well irrigation was being practised. Since the PGW people had a large number of cattle herds, their droppings could easily be used as manure. Among the domesticated animals we can enumerate the cow, buffalo, goat, sheep, pig and dog. While the first two animals provided milk from which various milk products could be had, bullocks were used for ploughing and for drawing carts and carrying pack goods. A large number of bones of cattle, buffalo, sheep, goat and pig had cut marks with sharp weapons suggesting that these were slaughtered for food.

Fishing and Hunting

Quite a large number of fishermen were engaged in fishing as most of the settlements were located on river banks. Fish-hooks have been found from Atranjikhera made of both iron and copper. Nets were made of remi-fibres which were collected from the hilly areas. To these nets terracotta sinkers were tied to stretch them properly down deep into the water. Charred bones of bivalve, lissiemys and trionyx were found which suggest that these were consumed.

Among other items of consumption were various kinds of fowl, *Barasingha* and *Nilgai*. Obviously some people had made hunting their profession to supply the meat of these animals to the consumers.

Blacksmiths

As has been stated, iron seems to have been introduced for the first time in India by the PGW people. The main source of iron ore was the hill range lying between Fatehpur Sikri and Gwalior.[14]

Evidence of furnaces had come to light at Atranjikhera suggesting that these were used with the help of bellows to smelt and forge the iron at the site itself. A variety of objects including war weapons, household objects, and agricultural and craft tools were produced. In a comparatively small area at Atranjikhera, 135 iron items of various types have been found (see Chart).

Though at the initial stage not much material could be produced, in the second phase of this culture, the industry got impetus and production increased considerably. This industry thus had become quite professional and required trained hands to produce the various types of iron artifacts.

Coppersmiths

Though copper items were produced in earlier cultural periods also, they were now produced on considerable scale. Instead of preparing war weapons or craft tools, which were now made of iron, the coppersmiths could now manufacture ornaments like bangles, rings, and beads, toilet goods including nail-parer, antimony rods, tooth-pick, hairpin and domestic goods such as needles and other utensils.

Goldsmiths

Though not enough evidence is available from excavation, literary accounts speak of the use of gold and silver. A soapstone mould was found from Atranjikhera, suggesting that a gold ornament was possibly made from it.[15]

Glass Technology

Introduction of glass technology was certainly a major contribution of the PGW people. Excavations[16] have yielded specimens of glass beads and bangles, as well as a glass receptacle. It is noteworthy that though glass (*kācha*) is not mentioned in the *Ṛgveda*, it has been referred to in the later Vedic literature[17] (Śatapatha Br. XIII. 2.6.8).

Bone Technology

It appears that bone technology had become a specialised profession in which several people were engaged. Among the bone items found during the excavations have been arrowheads of various types sometime decorated with incised circles with dots in the centre, knitting needles, points for engraving sockets, combs, pendants and ear-studs. A majority of these items were made of antlers.

Cloth Industry

Though no cloth of any kind has been found in the excavations, there is enough evidence to prove that cloth making had become by then a specialised profession. A few pottery pieces were found with cloth impressions, indicating plain fabric construction. If cotton was not produced, there could have been an ample supply of wool from sheep. Hemp and other fibres could also be used for preparing cloth. Some plain terracotta discs having a perforation in the centre have been found. These were probably used as spindle whorls. A long spacer having a hole at each extremity was found from Jakhera suggesting that such spacers were most probably used in weaving. Needles both of metal and bone have already been referred to, but these were most probably meant to join the pieces of cloth and to weave nets. Perhaps stitched garments were not in use.

Disc Making

PGW is the first cultural period yielding a large number of terracotta discs having various types of decorations or signs. Atranjikhera alone has yielded as many as 240 discs belonging to this period. Some of them have been treated with fine lustrous slips. While most of the discs bear impressed or incised notches around the circumference many have specific symbols or motifs on them including the representations of sun, moon (crescent), stars, fire-altar, chariot, arrows and motif depicting two eye-like designs intersecting each other, etc. Since most of these symbols appear to represent the familiar deities of the Aryans, these discs were presumably made for some religious purpose. Since they were often required, a band of people must have been occupied with this work.

Bead Making

As the Vedic texts tell us, both men and women bedecked themselves with necklaces made of gold, semi-precious stones, copper, glass, bones, stones. Almost all PGW sites have yielded various types of beads made of semi-precious stones such as agate and carnelian. Beads of quartz marble were also made. These were of various shapes including those of biconical triangular barrel, circular, convex, cylindrical, semi-spherical and rectangular shapes. Those made of banded agate look fascinating. Bone beads could also be used as pendants. Beautiful terracotta beads of different shapes were modelled as lay objects and to decorate animals. However, those nicely finished and slipped could be used as ornaments by the poor people. Thus bead making must have become a specialised skill.

Pottery

Pottery played a significant role in the domestic life of the ancient people particularly when not enough metal was available for manufacturing pots and pans. Since various types of pottery was needed in bulk in day-to-day life, more so because of its fragile nature, a large number of people worked as potters during the PGW period. The most distinctive pottery of the period was the PGW - a sophisticated pottery of grey colour with paintings generally in black though occasionally in red, chocolate, yellowish, whitish grey and bichrome. This ware is usually of fine quality having a thin section made of well levigated clay free from impurities. These were generally wheel-thrown. Though a variety of designs are found in this ware, the common patterns were formed by groups of vertical or oblique strokes below the horizontal rim-bands. Among other popular motifs were Swastikas, sigmas, circlets, etc. Side by side with this ware, Black-and-Red and Black-slipped wares have also been found. All these coloured wares were baked under reducing condition in closed kilns. However, the bulk of pottery was produced under oxidization. The excavation at Atranjikhera brought to light on oval shaped kiln, its longer axis measuring 2.35 m, and about a metre deep.

We have already outlined how our literary evidence suggests an eastward advance of the Aryans into monsoon forests of the *Doāb* synchronising with the use of iron. Archaeology confirms this. Though about 650 PGW sites have been explored so far during the last three decades in a wide area extending from dry bed of the Ghaggar or Hakra in the Bahawalpur region in Pakistan in the west to Śravasti and Sohgaura in U.P. in the east and from Thapli[18] on banks of Alaknanda in the District Tehri (U.P.) in north and Ujjain and Kayatha both in M.P. in the south, their maximum concentration remained in the Upper *Doāb* region.These settlements in the early stage were on the banks of rivers but gradually they were also found in the hinterland being far away from any perennial sources of water as by that time irrigational facilities had been developed. However, most of these sites were village settlements having small houses mostly made of wattle and daub. Among the cluster of village houses that of the village headman (*grāmiṇi* - Rv. X. 62.11) probably used to be larger. At least at Bhagwanpura near Kurukshetra, a house had as many as 13 rooms of various sizes with a corridor and a courtyard.[19]

In due course some of these settlements grew in size with the growth of the monarchical states and became their administrative headquarters. Suraj Bhan and Jim Shaffer[20] have explored a PGW site as large as 96,193 sq. metres in Haryana; and likewise Mughal[21] could find a site of 13.7 hectares on Hakra river. The large area of habitation suggests that these were town sites. It appears that towns began to emerge during the middle phase of the PGW period. There is marked improvement in the increase of various items needed in the day-to-day life including sophisticated ornaments and toilet goods. From literary sources of the later Vedic period (*Brāhmaṇas* and *Upanishads*) we learn that there were by then at least four monarchical states such as South Pañchāla, North Pañchāla, Kuru and Śaursena in the Upper *Doāb* region having their capitals at Kāmpilya, Ahichchatra, Asandivat (Hastinapura) and Mathura respectively. There are still quite large mounds of the PGW period at these places in spite of regular annual erosion by the rivers on the banks of which they are situated.

It is possible that these settlements still did not have all necessary characteristics of a real town as these had probably grown out of rural settlements and retained many of the hallmarks of villages. However, there were now large wooden structures representing houses of rich persons: these continue till the time of the Mauryas or even the Śuṅgas.

We may recall that Megasthenes speaks of wooden structures and the sculptures of the Śuṅga period exhibit the existence of such structures. These wooden structures themselves have perished, but their traces remain. Atranjikhera, for example, has yielded twenty-one clamps of iron and also one of copper with one or two holes at either end for nailing. These might have been used to join wooden planks together or fix doors to side posts. Excavations at the same site have also yielded twenty iron nails, not found in earlier periods. (The *Atharvaveda*, IX.3, 1-25 provides us with information about house construction in which bamboo and wooden posts and beams were frequently used.)

The Northern Black Polished Ware (NBPW) has been broadly placed within the time bracket of 600-50 B.C. though, both in its earliest and latest stages the use of the ware was scanty. This embraces the period of the Mahājanpadas, the Nandas, the Mauryas, the Śuṇgas and the Kaṇvas. However, ^{14}C dates from Mathura (PRL 334: 730±105 B.C.), Noh (RF 994: 685±105 B.C.) and Sringverpur push the industry as back as in *c.* 8th-7th B.C. When calibrated[22] the dates from Mathura and Noh are converted into 840±150 B.C., and 810±100 B.C. respectively pushing the industry to 9th century B.C. Though the industry's maximum concentration is in eastern U.P. and Bihar, this does not necessarily mean that it originated in this region. If the magnetic oxide of iron was an essential element of this fine ware, then it is possible that the earliest attempts for its manufacture were made at some PGW sites, like Atranjikhera, Mathura and Noh, where iron technology was well known.

The NBP Ware deposit is generally preceded at its sites either by the deposits of the PGW or by those of the Black-slipped and Black-and-Red Wares. While Atranjikhera, Noh and Hastinapura fall in the first group of sites, Prahladpur, Rajghat, etc., belong to the second. It is significant that where the iron industry was not known earlier, it was introduced along with the NBPW. With deforestation proceeding on a large scale, new towns sprang up, among which were the capitals of the sixteen Mahājanpadas. Obviously, enough surplus production was now needed which could not be possible without proper agricultural iron tools and irrigational facilities. The results of Atranjikhera excavation as well as of other NBPW sites testify to the existence of both these prerequisites. A variety of farmers' tools were found from almost all the levels of the NBPW deposits at Atranjikhera.

The wide distribution of the NBPW suggests inter-regional contacts and, therefore, implies a considerable development of commerce. Almost all the sites, yielding early NBPW, were either important trade centres or located on trade routes. While iron, copper and semi-precious stones were among the major items of trade, timber was also a commercial item. Of the four timbers recovered from the NBPW levels of Atranjikhera, at least two, namely deodar (*Cedrus deodara*) and Himalayan cypress (*Cypressus torulosa*), grow on the high mountains of the north. The presence of these two coniferous timbers indicates that the inhabitants of Atranjikhera had some trade contacts with the people living in the Himalayas. Among other woods found at Atranjikhera are laurel (*Terminalia tomentosa*) and *farash* (*Tamarix articulate*). Except *farash*, which is traditionally used for shelter-belts around cultivated land and as firewood, laurel as well as the two Himalayan timbers were commercial goods.[23]

It seems, therefore, that while the process of urbanisation had already started in the PGW phase, it began in right earnest only in the NBPW period. The Atranjikhera evidence distinctly shows this process of evolution. Though the extent of the inhabited areas at any of the PGW and the NBPW sites has not been established, Atranjikhera evidence is somewhat of interest. At this site while the three proto-historic settlements (OCP, B & RW and PGW) remained confined to the eastern side of the mound facing the present course of the Kali river, the earliest cultural deposit, in the rest of the mound with a few exceptions, belong to the Northern Black Polished Ware phase which lies immediately over the natural soil. It may further be noted that while the total area of the settlement of the PGW here would be approximately about 1,500 sq. metres or slightly more, that of the NBPW occupation would be approximately 850 x 550 metres. Of course, much of the occupation in both the periods has been washed away by the annual flood. However, it is noteworthy that in the first two phases, A (*c.* 600-500 B.C.) and B (*c.* 500-350 B.C.), particularly in the former the material culture more or less remained the same as it was in the last phase of the preceding PGW period. However, some new trends were now visible. For example, farmers' tools like hoe, sickle and spud as well as ring-fastener, socketed clamp and chopping-knife, all made of iron, appear for the first time. Some ornaments like copper anklet were also found for the first time.[24]

Since there is no break of occupation at Atranjikhera between Periods III and IV, the NBPW sherds in Phase A are found along with the PGW though in a very small number. But the position gradually changes in the subsequent phases. Gradually the NBPW sherds become more frequent and are found in different colours with fine fabric, while the PGW slowly declines. Now a few new shapes emerge including carinated vessel ('*handī*') with featureless rim and the well known pear-shaped vase popularly known as Ahichchhatra type 10^{A}. Other typical shapes appear gradually. A similar picture is provided at Noh, but at Hastinapura there is a considerable break between the PGW and the NBPW periods and therefore the picture of evolution there is not clear.

A marked change in the building activity came about in Phase B. Though the wattle-and-daub tradition still continued, structures of mud-bricks and burnt-bricks began to appear. However, burnt-brick structures were still of casual occurrence. In the last two phases, C and D, the building activity increased considerably and burnt-bricks were frequently used. The town was most probably properly fortified for the first time during Phase C.

In spite of the fact that there is a cultural continuity between the PGW period and NBPW period many new developments are noticeable in the latter. The most significant of them is the emergence of a system of coinage. Likewise, the more noteworthy agricultural tools in iron, such as the ploughshare, sickle, etc., are noticed for the first time. So also are human figurines in terracotta. Beginning with a crude anthropomorphic type, these developed with fine specimens of art represented in the last phase by beautiful terracotta plaques. Among other objects of interest in this period are terracotta amulets, design blocks to print cloth, an exquisitely fine bone bird and two copper frogs produced from the same mould.

Cultivation of rice, wheat and barley was already in vogue at Atranjikhera prior to the NBW period. In this period, however, these were produced on an extensive scale; at any rate, the yield of rice seems to have increased considerably. The recovery of a new pulse namely, *urad*, is of significance; it marks an addition to gram and *khesari*, which were known from earlier periods. *Urad* contains a high percentage of calcium in addition to proteins and can easily be grown more than once a year.

The construction of the defences in the NBW period is divisible into four Sub-Phases, beginning some time in the Phase B (*c*. 500-350 B.C.) of the NBP Ware deposit. It appears that the devastating flood which had once washed away considerable part of the occupied area, prompted the people to raise a massive mud-embankment on the eastern side facing the river.

Sub-Phase 1 is marked by the massive clay deposit laid in slope after the great flood on the eastern side of the mound. The filling material was dug from the natural soil and is, therefore, free of sherds and other waste from human habitation. The clay deposit was not over a uniformly flat ground; its height also varied. In spite of excessive soil erosion caused by subsequent floods and rains, its extant width at base is traceable to approximately 30 metres.

It seems that during Sub-Phase 2 the bund was extended to surround the whole town as a rampart. After some time (Sub-Phase 3) earth was dug from the natural soil to strengthen the rampart and raise its height. Now a few mud brick structures were also added to it. This Sub-Phase witnessed a rapid growth in building activity at the site. A circular tower having a diameter of 4.5 metres was also built. Perhaps there were a few more towers but they could not be exposed. The tower had above 25 cm thick mud plaster and a pronounced projection or ledge in the lower part having nine mud-brick courses to form its base. The inner side of the tower was filled with compact rammed earth mixed with broken pieces of mud-bricks. Attached to this tower were remnants of three pavements of mud-brick which might have provided access to the tower. It appears that the rampart remained neglected for some time. But subsequently several measures were taken to strengthen the defences during Sub-Phase 4. Not only its height was raised but parapet walls were constructed over the rampart for the first time.

It appears that while further raising the rampart, the lower part of the tower was also strengthened with mud filling to provide it a stronger base. So far as the brick construction of the parapet wall is concerned, it does not run as a solid mass throughout, but has regular gaps. This conforms with the description of the ideal fort given in the *Arthaśāstra* (II.3).

This sub-phase (2nd-1st century B.C.) was a time of political turmoil with Bactrian-Greeks extending their domination from the north-west. The reinforcement of fortifications at such a time would therefore not seem unreasonable.

Besides Atranjikhera, evidence of ramparts has been noticed at Ahichchhatra[25] and Mathura.[26] While at the former site the mud rampart enclosing the city had a perimeter of almost six kilometres, at Mathura its exact extent could not be determined. However, while the Mathura rampart goes back to the early phase of the NBPW, that at Ahichchhatra was built only around 200 B.C. or a little earlier. Outside the *Doāb* the fortifications at Rājagṛha, Kauśāmbi and Ujjain were older and can be dated to around *c.* 600 B.C.

Outside the town a few small mounds were noticed at Atranjikhera. One of them revealed the remains of an apsidal temple belonging to the earlier levels of Phase D of Period IV. This temple was situated in the east towards the river, almost in alignment with the main passage of the town at a distance of about 130 metres from the toe of the rampart.

As stated earlier in the first two phases of the NBPW period (*c.* 600-350 B.C.) at Atranjikhera the material culture was more or less a continuation of that of the PGW period. No noteworthy departure or improvement was noted at least in building activity except that now more buildings were constructed having mud walls instead of those of wattle and daub. Mud-bricks were also now in use. However, Phase B (*c.* 500-350 B.C.) yielded four new features: first, the strengthening and extension of the earlier mud-bund, which later on was developed into a rampart; second, the use of well-baked terracotta drain pipe having a diameter of 23 cm[27] besides several other ordinary drains; third, the introduction of coins both punch-marked and cast; and, fourth, most fascinating of all, cloth-printing evidenced by an exquisitely modelled terracotta printing block having stylized designs on each side.

It was Phase C in which the main change in building activity came: the use of burnt-brick became common and frequent. At Hastinapura[28] the trapezoidal bricks were used for constructing barns and capping the ring-wells. Here two burnt-brick drains were exposed, sunk 3 ft. deep from the ground level. "The dimension of these drains suggests that they were meant to drain out refuse water from a sizeable part of the town".[29] How much attention was now given to regular water supply and sanitation is evident from the fact that several wells made of terracotta rings were found at Hastinapura and Atranjikhera. One of them at the former site could be traced down to 27 rings, that is to depth of about 13 ft., and the bottom was still not reached. These were draw wells. One such ancient well was in use till recently in the adjoining village Achalpur not far away from the mound of Atranjikhera. Individual houses had their own sewage arrangements. Several long jars were placed vertically, one above the other in a deep pit, and the bottom of every jar was perforated, so that water could pass freely downwards.[30] Now Atranjikhera had all essential elements of a town for the first time having roads across the town. To this phase belonged a granary, storing different kinds of grains in different cells. It is not a mere coincidence that during this very phase a variety of agricultural tools appeared including spud, hoe, sickle, ploughshare and digger. The artisans' toolkits too had now a variety of iron objects including chisel, borer and scraper; and the carpenter was using ring-fastener to keep his wood in a desired position to fashion out desired objects.

The excavations at Atranjikhera have thrown much light on the social life too. Evidence of chess (or a game similar to it) being very popular was attested by the find of beautiful bone-gamesmen. An exquisite beautiful tiny bone-bird is a proof of highly skilled craftsmanship. Various types of ornaments made of semi-precious stones, copper, iron, and bone were used.

Phase D at Atranjikhera represents the period of the Śuṅgas and Kaṇvas. Now still greater urban activity is visible. The mason of this phase was using plump-bobs[31] frequently to keep the brick wall in proper alignment and the carpenter used to fix staple and bolt in the doors of the houses to make the contents of houses safe. Pendants of metals were used having a gold covering decorated with granulated design.

Our detailed survey of archaeological evidence on urbanisation in the Upper *Doāb* enables us to say a few things on a more or less tentative basis. The general assumption that the second urbanisation began in India around *c*. 600 B.C., does not seem to be corroborated by archaeological finds. There is no marked demarcation between the material life of the preceding PGW period and that of the early NBPW period around *c*. 600 or *c*. 500 B.C. This is because at no stage was there a revolutionary change in the settlement pattern until the 4th century B.C. or the time of the Nandas. Only then do we find the use of burnt-bricks on a large scale in buildings and also fortifications around several towns, the use of new agricultural and artisanal tools. But this did not happen suddenly and the process of urbanisation seems to have begun from about the middle phases of the PGW period around *c*. 1000 B.C. Our discussion of evidence above suggests that we may distinguish three stages in the process of urbanisation:

A PGW middle and late phases when production of iron objects became prolific. Hardly 8 pieces of iron out of 135 belonging to PGW phase came from the early phase of PGW at Atranjikhera, while 46 items belong to the middle phase, and 81 to the upper phase (see the distribution chart given below).

B First two early phases of the NBPW period when more stride is seen in the production of various types of items. Building construction becomes more widespread and process of fortification around the towns begins at some places such as at Mathura. A most noteworthy feature is the introduction of coins, both punch-marked and cast coins and seals and sealings in phase B.

C Phase C (*c.* 350 B.C.-200 B.C.) of the NBPW period witnesses urbanisation in the real sense. Now the structures of burnt bricks are common and coins are in use for ordinary transactions. Incidentally, the Aśokan inscriptions belong to this period. Now the towns were fortified having crossroad. The earliest temples also belong to this period.

Chart showing distribution of various types of items from early phase of PGW to the early phase of NBPW at Atranjikhera

(*c.* 1200 B.C. to 500 B.C.)

Items	PGW Lower Phase	PGW Middle Phase	PGW Upper Phase	Early Phase of NBPW
Iron objects	8	46	81	147
Copper objects	3	6	13	13
Terracotta discs	22	72	146	190
Terracotta beads	1	11	14	59
Semi-precious stone beads	2	6	4	27
Bone objects	7	19	45	92
Glass objects		1	1	4

It may be justifiable to say that our study does not discount the existing thesis; rather it seeks largely to refine it. Urban elements, in our view, appeared in the middle PGW phase, or around 1000 B.C.; but the settlements had still not divested themselves of their rural basis. On the other hand, towns in an entirely unqualified sense, with brick buildings, coin-use, etc., belong to the period of the Nandas, Mauryas and Śuṅgas. In other words, the large towns came not before, but after, the rise of Buddhism.

NOTES AND REFERENCES

1. B.B. Lal, 'A deluge? Which deluge? Yet another facet of the problem of the Copper Hoard Culture', *American Anthropologist*, Vol. 70, 1968, No. 5.
2. Hem Chandra Raychaudhuri, *Political History of Ancient India*, University of Calcutta, Calcutta, 1953 (Sixth edition).
3. A.N. Macdonell and A.B. Keith, *Vedic Index*, Vol. I, Delhi, 1958, pp. 169-70.
4. *Ibid.*, Vol. II, p. 79.
5. *Ibid.*, Vol. II, pp. 162, 165.
6. Raychaudhuri, *op. cit.*, p. 66.
7. R.C. Gaur, *Excavations at Atranjikhera Early Civilization of the Upper Gangā Basin*, Delhi, 1983, p. 123.
8. K.A. Chowdhury *et al.*, *Agriculture and Forestry in Northern India*, Bombay, 1977, pp. 64-69.

9. Gaur, *op. cit.*, p. 126.
10. M.D.N. Sahi, 'New light on the life of the Painted Grey Ware people as revealed from excavations at Jakhera', *Man and Environment*, Vol. II, 1978.
11. Gaur, *op. cit.*, p. 500.
12. M.D.N. Sahi, 'Agricultural production during the early Iron Age in northern India', *Proceedings of the Indian History Congress,* Kurukshetra Session, 1982.
13. Chowdhury *et al.*, 1977, p. 63.
14. Gaur, *op. cit.*, p. 500.
15. *Ibid.*, pp. 500-501.
16. B.B. Lal, 'Excavations at Hastinapura and other explorations in the Upper Gaṅgā and Sutlej basins 1950-52', *Ancient India*, Nos. 10 & 11, 1954-55, pp. 90-91; Gaur, *op. cit.*, p. 218.
17. Lal, 1954-55, p. 81.
18. K.P. Nautiyal, 'Pushing back the antiquity of Garhwal: Results of recent explorations and excavations', Paper presented at Seminar on Regional Historical Writings in India with Special Reference to Western Himalayas, Simla.
19. *Indian Archaeology 1975-76—A Review*, pp. 16-17.
20. Suraj Bhan and Jim G. Shaffer, 'New discoveries in Northern Haryana', *Man and Environment*, Vol. II, 1978, pp. 59-68.
21. M. Rafique Mughal, 'New archaeological evidence from Bahawalpur', *Man and Environment*, Vol. IV, 1980, pp. 93-98.
22. R.M. Clark, 'A Calibration Curve for Radiocarbon dates', *Antiquity*, Vol. XLIX, 1975.
23. Chowdhury *et al., op. cit.*
24. Gaur, *op. cit.*, pp. 427-31.
25. A. Ghosh, *The City in Early Historic India*, Simla, 1973, pp. 61 and 69.
26. *Indian Archaeology 1975-76—A Review*, pp. 53-55
27. Gaur, *op. cit.*, p. 248.
28. Lal, *op. cit.* (1954-55), p. 15
29. *Ibid.*
30. *Ibid.*, p. 16
31. Gaur, *op. cit.*

40

STUPAS AND MONASTERIES : A RECENT DISCOVERY FROM SATDHARA, MADHYA PRADESH

R.C. AGRAWAL

1. Historical Background

Buddhist culture has flourished in India since 3rd B.C. in many parts of the country and has produced a variety of monuments.

The earliest Buddhist monuments which cropped up on Indian soil are located in eastern India (Bihar-U.P.), which witnessed the activities of the Master and his life. The life of Buddha itself had a great bearing on the origin of Buddhist edifices. Monasteries, to provide shelter to Buddha and his disciples during the rainy season, had already come into existence probably, during the lifetime of the Buddha.

On his death-bed, Buddha himself had suggested that his mortal remains should not be worshipped but essence of Dhamma be achieved. But his followers erected stupas and worshipped. How the system of worshipping the stupas became popular despite the fact that Buddha himself disapproved the idea of revering him. It appears that the Buddhists followed the popular tradition of revering the great men or any part, fragment of the body or either its detachment from the original form or its transformation continued to maintain inseparable relation with the original personality of person to whom it belonged once.[1] With this popular tradition, the Buddha's mortal remains were deposited and worshipped, dug and re-deposited in stupas for reverence. This popular belief laid the root of the stupa cult which made the worship of corporeal relics enshrined in stupas an essential feature of early Buddhism. Even during his lifetime stupas might have been erected over the remains of some of his leading disciples. Stupas, symbolizing the Master, remained for a long time afterwards the sole object of worship among the Buddhists in the absence of images of Buddha and consequently of shrines to house them.

The places associated with Buddha were many; and some of them gained great renown in subsequent days as leading centres of Buddhism. Of them, the four great places, Lumbini where Buddha was born, Bodh-Gaya which witnessed his Enlightenment, Sarnath where the First Sermon was delivered and Kuśinagara where he passed away continued to be embellished with monuments of varied kinds. These are regarded as sacred even today by the Buddhists all over the world. Four other places, though of a somewhat lesser importance in Buddha's life, namely, Sankisa where he descended from the heaven, Sravasti where he performed miracles in order to confound the six heretical teachers, Rajgir where he tamed Nalagiri and Vaisali where he was offered a bowl of honey by a monkey similarly became the scene of monumental activities through subsequent centuries. These eight important events of Buddha's life (Eight Great Miracles) were often depicted in a condensed form on the stelae of image of Buddha in later period.[2]

With the passage of time, Buddhism overstepped the boundaries of India, its cradle-land, in the extension of the geographical horizon of which Aśoka, the great Maurya emperor (circa 273-236 B.C.), took a leading role. He employed all his resources for the dissemination of the religion. For the edification of the people he inscribed rocks and pillars describing the merits of non-violence, tolerance, justice, charity, purity, truthfulness, etc. According to the Buddhist tradition, he opened seven out of the eight original stupas and took away the major portion of relics for distribution among eighty-four thousand stupas built by him throughout his empire. Though the number is an exaggeration, there can be no doubt about the truth in the tradition itself. The Chinese pilgrims Fa-hien and Hiuen Tsang saw a number of stupas built by Asoka.

The brick stupa inside the stone casing of the Great Stupa at Sanchi was constructed by Aśoka, who also planted a stone pillar in front of it. The inscribed monolithic pillars of Asoka have been found at several places in India.

Aśoka also took active interest in the Sangha and to maintain the integrity of the Sangha, he promulgated edicts against schism. In his edict on the pillar at Sanchi, he ordered that heretical monks and nuns should be compelled to wear white robes in place of the monks' saffron and should be expelled from the Sangha. It was during his reign learned teachers were deputed to proceed in various directions and countries outside India.

The new life which Aśoka infused into the religion of Sakyamuni and the impetus which he gave to the Buddhist building arts were not extinguished when the Maurya empire fell to pieces. The Mauryas were followed by the Sungas (second and first centuries B.C.) and later on by the Kanvas (first century B.C.) in the north and the Satavahanas (first century B.C. to the third century A.D.) in the south. During the regime of these powerful dynasties, though there was no ruler who took up the cause of Buddhism in the manner of Asoka, building activities continued on an accelerated pace due to the piety of an increasing number of lay devotees of means (merchants, traders, household, etc.). The wealth specially of the rich mercantile community, a large percentage of whom formed the class of lay disciples, was utilized in erecting Buddhist edifices. Every pious Buddhist tried to contribute whatever he could; the poor came forward with their offer of skill and labour; and thus grew up a large number of Buddhist monuments including the celebrated stupas at Sanchi and Satdhara in central India and the Mahachaitya at Amaravati in south India. One can say that in no other period of the history of

Indian Buddhism did art and architectural activity reach such a high pitch of popular participation. So long the stupas had been built in brick; the preference was now for stone so that the edifices might be everlasting. People were not satisfied with giving mere permanency; they wanted to embellish the edifices, to make them things of beauty and attraction. At Sanchi and Satdhara they selected sandstone railings and gateways (only at Sanchi) for the purpose, leaving the stupas austere and plain.

The monument at Sanchi by far overshadows others in Madhya Pradesh not only by the number and variety but also by the quality of its architectural and sculptural products. Amongst the vast galaxy of structural monuments of India, Sanchi with its monuments, stands out majestically. It has the singular distinction of having specimens of almost all kinds of Buddhist architectural forms. With its nucleus dating from the third century B.C., the establishment continued to flourish till the twelfth century A.D., despite all political changes due to the rise and fall of many dynasties.

2. Satdhara (Pl. 40.1)

The group of monuments known as the Satdhara stupas are situated on the left bank of the Halali river about 5 km W.S.W. of the small village of Firozpur and about 10 km from the village of Salamatpur.[3] Satdhara means literally the "seven streams", and the place most probably received its name from the number of streams which meet at the confluence of Gora-Pachhar river and Halali river. The hill on which the stupas stand forms a perpendicular cliff, beneath which flows the Halali river through a deep rocky glen.

The largest of the stupas is now a vast ruinous mound of brick work and of stone like the Great Stupa at Sanchi, which it almost rivals in size. The base of the stupa is 34 m in diameter. Its present height is about 12.55 m. The stupa was crowned by a Buddhist railing, of which several pillars have been salvaged recently.

From the available remains it appeared that the stupa was originally built in brick during Mauryan period and in the subsequent centuries it was encased in stone. With the passage of time major portion of the stone veneering fell down exposing the core, and all the railing pillars once supposed to have been on the top of the stupa also fell down. Around the drum of the stupa the remains of a circumambulation platform have also been noticed which measured 1.60 metres wide and the circumference is 107 metres. In the construction of circumbulation big, locally extracted, stones were used. It appears that during 19th century, when Alexander Cunningham excavated the stupa he left the structure uncovered and the rain and growth of vegetation gave a thrust to the outer layer of the stupa and the structure started falling down. To retain the structure in position, with the fallen material buttresses were erected to retain the remaining part of the stupa in position. This fact has also been substantiated by the use of railing pillars and the coping stones in the construction of the retaining pillars.

A. Apsidal Chaitya

The main stupa is built on the slope of the hill by raising a huge platform. The platform is made of coarse rubble stone and the core is filled up with random rubble stones mixed with mud and moorum. By the side of the main stupa, an apsidal chaitya is also built, the traces of which were found in our exploration. The aspidal chaitya measures 11.50 x 5.60 metres. The upper coarses of the chaitya have almost disappeared. This structure is proposed to be excavated.

B. Monasteries

Near the chaitya, the remains of a monastery were also noticed which measured 18.55 x 15.35 metres. The monastery is totally collapsed and it requires excavation. After systematic exposition of the structure, further details can be gathered. Another monastery which is on the south of the stupa and overlooking the Halali river is built on the edge of the cliff. It measures 29.93 x 16.97 metres. From the fallen material and the remnants of the stone beams and columns it appeared that the monastery was built in double storey. The superstructure, probably made of wood, disappeared with the passage of time leaving behind the traces of collapsed structure. The excavation of this monastery may reveal many hidden features.

C. Stupas and Votive Stupas (Pl. 40.2)

At a distance of 230 ft. to the north-west of the Great Stupa was built another stupa. It is 24 ft. in diameter and 8 ft. in height. This stupa was excavated by Alexander Cunningham in 1853 and in the excavations a steatite casket was encountered. The casket contained the relics of Sariputra and Mahamogalyan, the two contemporary disciples of Lord Buddha. The relics were taken to the British Museum in the last century and a fragment of that was brought to India in the year 1956 and was, then, enshrined in the newly constructed Mahabodi temple at Sanchi.

Towards the east of the monastery overlooking Halali river, on a terrace a stupa was built. Cunningham also excavated this stupa in 1853 and salvaged the relics of Buddhist fraternity. The diameter of this stupa is 9.32 metres and the height is 2.33 metres. The core of this stupa is built in random rubble stones and the exterior layers are made in coarse rubble stones. The bonding material appears to be the mud. The traces of the lime also indicated that at some stage lime was also used in the construction of the stupa.

To the north of stupa (Stupa No. 8) on a elevated plain a cluster of stupas was also encountered in a highly ruinous condition. From the fallen portions of the stupas, the dimensions of these structures appeared to be very small and probably were erected in memory of the monks staying at Satdhara. The nature of the construction of these stupas is similar to those described. The core is built with smaller irregular stones and the outer layers with coarse rubble stones. Every stupa was found disturbed from the centre and, probably, the treasure seekers, sometime in the recent past, had disturbed the fabric of these structures. The ravages of time and the wild growth of vegetation around them further disintegrated. Further to these in the north-eastern direction several dilapidated remains of structures were also noticed. The fallen portions of the structures indicated some kind of ancient platforms or enclosures. Between the cluster of these stupas and the monastic complex ancient pathways were also noticed connecting the stupas with the monasteries and leading towards the river. Pathways are made of locally extracted stones arranged in an alignment with uneven stones in between. The remnants of the pathways connected with the establishments indicate that sangha at Satdhara was bigger than Sanchi.

D. Monastic Complex

To the east of this stupa a monastic complex of sixteen monasteries was also located in our recent exploration. In this complex traces of rectangular monasteries were found. Amongst all the monasteries the monastery No. 2 appeared to be fairly well preserved and intact. It measured 15.60 metres long, 5.37 metres wide and 1 metre high. On the north of this an entrance was provided which measured 1 metre. The thickness of the wall of the monastery is 0.70 metre. The cluster of this monastic complex has established that Satdhara had a regular Sangham and the greater number of monks were living here as compared to Sanchi. The construction of these monasteries has also been done with the available material. The facing stones of the wall are coarse rubble and in the core small chips and stones have been filled. The roof was, probably, raised on wooden beams, perlins and twigs with a thick covering of thatched material. With the passage of time the thatched roofs and wooden material have disappeared leaving behind only stone walls in ruinous condition.

E. Painted Buddha and Stupa

In the cliff overlooking the Halali river, in a natural rock shelter, having a small projected natural cantilever, on the flat surface of the rock two very interesting panels of the paintings were also encountered during the course of the exploration. In one panel a figure of Buddha has been painted and in the other a stupa on a base with inscriptions.

The painted Buddha, which is damaged in the lower half is executed on a flat ground of the rock by preparing the ground with a yellowish ochre substance. At the back of the Buddha in its usual appearance a hallow has also painted. The traces of drapery executed in the painting indicate towards the treatment of the classical age.

The panel of the stupa is very interesting. The stupa is painted on a raised base having mouldings and depicting the inscription on the lower recessed mouldings between the lower and upper portion of the Medhi. On the upper moulded projected portion is painted the drum and on the body of the drum an inscription is also painted. The drum is surmounted by the symbolic Harmika structure, over which is painted an umbrella. The interior of the umbrella is delineated with lotus petals. On either side of the stupa two banner cloths are painted having bells on both the ends. The delineation of these banners attached to the umbrella with bells is a unique representation so far encountered in the Malwa region.

The inscription on the base of the stupa is much more obliterated. And of the drum is painted with the usual sutra of Buddhist creed Ye-dharma hetu prabhava... . The letters in the inscription are the usual Gupta type and in writing the inscription, a kind of free hand has been used. In writing the inscription the letters overlap each other. In the size of the characters, the uniformity has not been maintained. The style of the painting and the palaeography of the inscription place the painting in the Gupta tradition or 4th-5th century A.D.

3. Excavations

To the north of the main stupa, traces of heavily eroded brick structures were visible. The area was fully covered with wild growth of vegetation. To trace the extent of the erosion occurring around the structure, the whole area was eradicated of the wild vegetation and put to systematic excavation.

The excavation conducted to the north of main stupa revealed the traces of apsidal chaityas, the core of which was made of rammed earth and stone chips and the side walls with coarse rubble stones. During the excavation pieces of Northern Back Polished Ware and a punch-marked coin were encountered which substantiated that the Satdhara complex emerged during the Mauryan and Sunga periods.

The removal of debris, primarily from the main stupa, yielded railing pillars depicting vivid symbols, crossbars bearing donatory inscriptions, coping stones having auspicious symbols, fragments of umbrella having ribs in the intrados, fragments of historical pottery and a lid of stone belonging to relic chamber/box.

The railing pillars, invariably, have depiction of half lotus in the upper and lower portions. The middle portion also depicts the lotus medallion. The depiction of the middle lotus medallions is unique in its character and delineation. Each medallion is independent in its pattern and design of lotus petals and stamen. Such rich variety of lotus pattern, though small in number, constitutes an important find from Satdhara area.

4. Inscriptions (Pls. 40.3-40.5)

The finds to the donatory inscriptions inscribed on the crossbars of railing of exceptional interest from the point of view of information and palaeography. In all twenty-three donatory inscriptions on crossbars, four on coping stones, seven on stone slabs, probably fixed in circumambulation path and seven on Vedika railing were found. Amongst all the donatory inscriptions appearing on the crossbars and railing pillar, three donatory inscriptions mentioning (1) Budrakhitas Bhichuna samanasa dānaṁ sutatikas—the gift of Sramana Bhikshu Budharakshita and his son?; (2) Budrakhitasa Dānaṁ—the gift of Budharakshita: and (3) Budrakhi...nakiyas—the gift of Budharakshita belonging to some Nikāya(?) are important as these throw further light on the concept of 'Rakshita' and contact with Satdhara of the Rakshita missionaries mentioned in Ceylonese Chronicle. The inscription No. 1 is composed of twenty characters and the inscription No. 2 is consisting of eight characters. The inscription No. 3 consists of eight characters with some missing character in upper line. The palaeography of the inscription is not as perfect as those of Sanchi. The characters of the Satdhara inscriptions appear to be slightly irregular in articulation. In the size of characters uniformity is not maintained.

The alignment in the upper and lower line has not been maintained and the characters of dh, bu, ya are in proportion either smaller or bigger in the composition. This disproportionate articulation of the characters is not noticed in the characters of the inscriptions of Sanchi. This difference indicates an earlier stage of the writing at Satdhara.

The meaning of the 'Rakshita' and its proper application are not exactly clear. The 'Rakshitā' appears to be a suffix to Buddha name or it denotes a 'Saṇgha' (missionary) who had specific objectives before them. Sanchi has yielded three inscriptions mentioning Budharakshitā from stupas No. 1 and No. 2. In stupa No. 2 on the berm rail the inscription refers to a female Budhārakshitā. The three inscriptions of Satdhara also refer to Budharakshita belonging to a sect or a group of missionaries. S.K. Mitra in his recent discovery of an early inscription from Pitalkora caves has noticed in a inscription 'Rakshitā' which he has translated as brother of Rakshitā or monk Rakshitā.[4] The occurrence of the 'Rakshita' name in the Ceylonese Buddhist Chronicle *Mahavamsa* mentions that the Buddhist missionaries were despatched by emperor Asoka to different parts of his kingdom for the propagation of Dhamma. It appears that the Rakshitās who were despatched towards Deccan and other parts of the country must have stayed at Sanchi and Satdhara and made donations. The occurrence of the Buddha Rakshitā further signifies that they had their own class of Sangha (missionaries) who were responsible for the propagation of Buddha-dharma and to maintain an order in the Sangha.

Besides these inscriptions, few more donatory inscriptions were also found at Satdhara. All the inscriptions appeared the label inscription and invariably signify the donations. A few important are transliterated here:

S. No.	Transliteration & Translation
1.	**Nagdatas...** The gift of Nagdutt
2.	**Beluviya Danam...** The gift of Belubhya?
3.	**Sapilasa...** The gift of Sapil
4.	**Jitha Bhetas Danam...** The gift of Jeetbhadra
5.	**Savagutas Danam...** The gift of Sarvagupta
6.	**Maha...Danam...** The gift of Maha...?
7.	**Vajikas Danam...** The gift of Vajik
8.	**Rachakas Danam...** The gift of Rachaka
9.	**Vajiniya a Ni-Ya...** The gift of ... (probably) resident of Vajji (Ujjaini)
10.	**Manetkas Danam...** The gift of Manetak
11.	**Sakiyabhikhuniya Pemutka...** The gift of a female monk.
12.	**Dhutkas Danam...** The gift of Dhutak.

13. **Dhavikatedhamgutas Danam...**
The gift of Dharmagupta

All these inscriptions have come to light for the first time from Satdhara and some of the donatory names occur at Sanchi and Sonari too. The discovery of these inscriptions has substantiated that Satdhara prospered like Sanchi but went in oblivion much earlier.

5. Conservation Measures Taken

From the 13th century onwards Sanchi gradually lost importance and became deserted and desolated. It was rediscovered by General Tailor in 1818.[5]

Like Sanchi Satdhara and other monuments appear to have gone much earlier in oblivion than Sanchi. Located away from the township and in a thick forest these monuments did not attract the attention of the British archaeologists and the erstwhile State. These famous stupas, therefore, remained in a much neglected condition for a much longer period. The Archaeological Survey of India took over these monuments in the year 1988 and since then constantly looks after them. In the year 1992 to restore and repair these monuments attempts were made from an integrated point of view and to locate other scattered monuments in the forest area. Since the group of Satdhara monuments is contemporaneous with Sanchi and other monuments, for its conservation and development a comprehensive scheme has been drawn which is being funded by Japanese Trust Fund under UNESCO Project. The implementation of the project will bring to light many aspects of early Buddhist architecture in central India.

The stupas and other monuments are located on the different contours of Satdhara hill. On the east and west of the main stupa are located votive and other smaller stupas and on the south the monasteries. In the further east are located the monastic complex and other structures, viz. stone platform, apsidal stupas and ancient pathways. Besides these, on the hill slopes facing the river, several big and small platforms are also built which with the passage of time have fallen down at many places. All these structures are constructed in Vindhyan pink stones except the core of stupa No. 1. In the white buff colour sandstone are carved coping stones, suchi stones (crossbars) and the railing pillars. The white buff colour sandstone appears to have been extracted from the Sanchi area as it is found in abundance in the close vicinity of Sanchi. For building the stupas and monasteries the stone was quarried from the hill itself as revealed by the depression encountered on the hill. It is very likely that the depressions were used as water bodies like Sanchi.

The structures, particularly stupas, are made of two types: (i) having brick core and (ii) of stones. The core of the main stupa is in brick and the veneering layers above brick profile are in stone. The rest of the stupas are built in stone blocks—random stones in the core and the cut coarses on the faces. The original binding material was mud mortar. The cut stone casing was done with mud and lime. The backfill of the stone casing was done with random stones and the facing with wedge-shaped stones. The binding medium was mud for the core masonry and on the top of the structure and profile, probably, lime plaster was applied to make the structure durable, watertight and impervious. The other structures, viz. apsidal chaityas and monasteries were made of locally available Vindhyan pink stone.

All these structures suffered the damage in varying degrees in the past. Built on the slope of the hill, the structures were subjected to human vandalism and reckless excavations. Treasure seekers also disturbed the stupas and many structures. In the process the structures were converted into heaps.

The accumulation of water around the structures and the growth of vegetation virtually disintegrated the edifices. The efforts made in the past resurrected many structures from further decay which constitute today the nucleus of Satdhara complex. The growth of wild vegetation and washing away of soil made boulders and large blocks to roll down causing serious threat to the stability of the structure. The percolation of rain water into the main stupa loosened the masonry and gave thrust to the outer layers, which with the successive rains disintegrated.

To conserve and preserve these monuments, the available structures have been surveyed and efforts are afoot to further locate the structures in the thick forest. Precariously hanging parts of the structures have been supported and heaps accumulated around the structures have been cleared to trace out the outlet of the structures. The excavation of the monastic complex and the apsidal structures is likely to reveal many more features of Satdhara complex.

NOTES AND REFERENCES

1. Joshi, M.C. Early Representations of Buddha and Buddhist Traditions in Asokavadana, *Puratattva,* No. 21, 1991, p. 1.
2. Mitra, D. *Buddhist Monuments,* Calcutta, 1971.
3. Cunningham, A. *Bhilsa Topes,* Varanasi, 1966, pp. 207-10.
4. Mitra, S.K. Discovery of an early inscription from Pitalkora, *Puratattva,* No. 21, 1991, pp. 84-85.
5. Burgess, J. The great stupa at Sanchi, Kanakhedia, J.*R.A.S.*, Jan. 1902, pp. 29-45.

41

EXCAVATIONS AT SANGHOL, DISTRICT LUDHIANA, PUNJAB : 1985-90—A NOTE ON THE SETTLEMENT PATTERN AND CULTURAL SEQUENCE

C. MARGABANDHU

Sanghol (30°47' N and 76°23' 30" E) is situated in Tehsil Samrala, District Ludhiana at a distance of 45 km west of Chandigarh on Chandigarh-Ludhiana State Highway. It is approachable by road leading to the village otherwise familiarly known as Uchapind. The nearest railway station is Morinda on Sirhind-Nangal loop-line which is about 10 km from the village.

On the basis of surface indications and traces of dried up old channels, it may be inferred that the ancient site was located on the banks of Sutlej or one of its now defunct tributaries. Extensive explorations of the area and discovery of sites and distributional pattern have revealed that the region had been settled from early Harappan times continuously up to late historic period.

Though the site has been explored way back in 1933 by Shri M.S. Vats (former Director General, Archaeological Survey of India) regular excavation was undertaken by Shri R.S. Bisht (1969-73) and subsequently by Shri G.B. Sharma (1978-83), both from the Department of Archaeology, Punjab Government. Their work revealed that the site had been settled since the chalcolithic times and subsequently developed into a substantial town during the Kushana period.

It required further excavation in order to know the planning and settlement pattern, the culture and material content including the stages of technological development at various periods, more so that the site has not been deserted from the earliest times to the late historical period.

Hence excavations were resumed in 1986 jointly by the Excavation Branch of the Archaeological Survey of India, New Delhi and the Department of Archaeology and Museums, Government of Punjab and continued up to 1990. This resulted in the exposition of the rich material and cultural content and various architectural features of the settlement datable from the record millennium B.C. to the late medieval times.

The site consists of an artificial mound 18 m thick average habitational deposit over more than 1.5 km or so with several separate extensions of the settlement in different periods of time. However the main habitation of the chalcolithic period was limited to the south and south-western side of the present village with a little expansion to the west of the citadel complex. Extension of the settlement to the east takes place in the succeeding period. Only from the early first century A.D. during the Kushana times, there is expansion of the settlement and a large township was planned consisting of a fortified citadel, dwelling houses and a well laid out town complex.

About 500 m away to the north-east was built an extensive Buddhist establishment consisting of stupas, monasteries and other buildings of religious nature on a solid platform of bricks, which continued to exist up to the end of the second century A.D.

The excavations carried out at Sanghol could be divided into the following periods:

1. Late Harappan culture with dominant Bara (ceramic) elements;
2. An "Overlap" phase characterised by late Harappan (Bara ceramic) and painted grey ware and black slipped ware;
3. Early Historic;
4. Kushana period;
5. Historical (Gupta and post-Gupta) period; and
6. Medieval.

The characteristic features of the various periods at Sanghol are briefly narrated with an emphasis on chronology wherever supporting evidence is available.

The earliest settlement and occupation of the site, though of small dimensions, consist of more or less a small but compact village traced on the south-eastern side of the present township. The total thickness of the cultural deposit of more than 4 m or so indicates a long period of occupation. The early settlers could be termed as "Barans" on the basis of the type site at Bara, situated nearby with earlier antecedents substantially well-documented. So far six phases of structural activity have been traced at Sanghol with semblance of planning at various levels.

The early house plans are of simple nature consisting of walls of packed clay and mud lumps (Pl. 41.1). There is also use of sun-dried bricks in the next phase and the bricks measure 40-50 x 30-35 x 10 cm, and 40 x 30 x 10 cm. In the subsequent phases houses were built of packed earth, clay lumps including use of mud bricks. Post-holes were also traced out indicating possible posts erected for thatched roof. A characteristic feature is the room had neatly laid floors made of soft yellow clay, sometime well rammed and solidly thick in composition. A number of large circular and rectangular corn-bins and small to big storage jars were found placed or embedded in the floors by digging pits. Numerous hearths or *chullahs* were also found, both on the floor and also prepared with side bottom.

So far as general planning is concerned, the orientation of the houses has not been changed viz., north-south, east-west. Moreover habitation layers are quite undisturbed running horizontally.

A few interesting features could be mentioned as found during the excavations. On the mud floor of a house has been traced a burnt terracotta object placed *in situ* of an indistinct shape. It has a long tapering outline with two bifurcated curved terminals, at the upper portion, but damaged on the edge; signs of burning in the form of left-over ash indicate that it was fixed in position on the floor adjacent to a side wall of the room. Similar evidence is also known from other sites such as Bara, Banawali, Hulas etc.

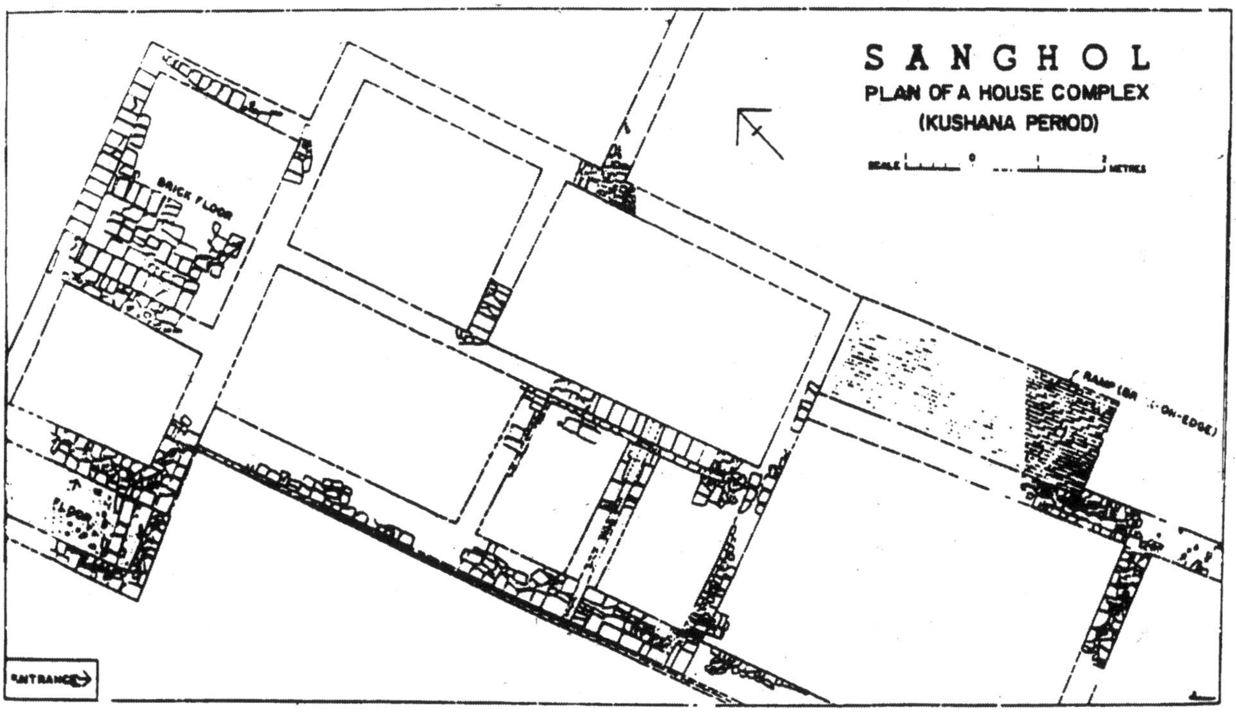

Fig. 1.

In another room, a different feature was observed, though in the same phase a long cylindrical clay object (10-11 cm) was placed on the floor. A small vas was found covered by a stone lid, well ground and polished. These were found in the living room with walls traced up to a height of 50 cm or so. One medium sized storage jar was found embedded in the floor nearby—all of which indicate, these were meant for a specific purpose and use.

The ceramics of the earliest settlers have close affinity in many aspects of shape and types, including fabrics and other features with those known from Bara wherein the culture has been well observed and documented. In other words, the distinct features are so similar that the ceramics at both places occur in 'pure' form.

The pottery shape includes storage jars of various shapes and sizes with collared, beaded or beaked rim and splayed mouth squat dish-on-stand, jars with ring base, large lota-shaped vases, large cooking vessels with roughened up bottoms, bowl-like lid, miniature pots, terracotta cakes etc. An interesting feature is that many vessels bear exterior incised markings below the carination up to the base made on roughened up surfaces. Incisions mostly consist of wavy, parallel and curved lines in two or three bands or rows including many nondescript patterns; decorations and paintings include black bands round neck and shoulder mostly found in small vessels and some geometric patterns. Notable antiquities include terracotta wheels and balls, rings and bangles of faience, bone styluses, terracotta figurines, copper objects, beads of agate, carnelian steatite, faience and terracotta.

On the present showing, the earliest culture at Sanghol, keeping in view the availability of 14C dates, "the reasonable span of Bara culture would be 1900-1500 B.C.; on the whole this means that compared with the site of Bara Sanghol might have had a slightly later start and a later finish."

The next period at Sanghol has been characterised by a consistent occurrence of many ceramics quite dominant such as the Bara or (late Harappan) pottery, painted and plain grey ware, black slipped ware and associated red ware pottery so much so that an 'overlap' of many cultural elements is recorded and hence difficult to assess any individual trait. However, in cultural horizon of painted grey ware, proportion of black slipped ware increases considerably in both type and quantity. So far clear-cut cultural identity for this level is yet to be confirmed. No house plan has been exposed but there is evidence of rammed floors and hearths in undisturbed horizons specially in the cultural stratum of painted grey ware and black slipped ware. It is also to be mentioned that a large number of painted grey ware sherds were found in pits. Some post-holes were also traced in the levels of painted grey ware and black slipped ware.

Apart from ceramics antiquities found include terracotta animal figurines and ear-studs, bangles of faience, beads of agate, jasper, faience and terracotta, copper objects, bone points, ivory styluses, etc.

The next period is designated as "Early Historic Period" mainly for the reason, that there are some plans of houses traced, and some building activity in upper levels. Two structural phases were identified, the earlier characterised by use of large sized mud and burnt bricks and can be designated as pre-Kushana Period. Two house plans were exposed separated by a lane 1.50 m. (Pl. 41.2).

The ceramic is dominated by red ware, while black slipped ware is also found in sizeable number though, in the latter levels, the black slipped ware is absent. Antiquities recovered include terracotta animal figurines, skin rubbers, bone styli, beads of semi-precious stones such as carnelian and crystal and terracotta bangles.

There does not seem to have been any immediate change in habitational features nor any destruction, when the site was settled by the Kushanas. The early first century B.C. remains at Hathiwara which consist of mud and brick-built houses (Pl. 41.3) were replaced by a systematic planning in the form of new extension and fresh building activity which is quite innovative and characteristic of the new settlers. Sufficient open space possibly facing the river to the north and north-east was chosen for this purpose. There is evidence at the town site of large scale levelling wherever such area was available, also those dwellings that are falling and vacant.

Presently, known as Hathiwara, this area represents the major structural remains of the Kushanas, who dominated the scene, for more than a century and a half.

In general, surface features and excavations conducted at Hathiwara and at other places have revealed Kushana remains which consist of the citadel and the buildings inside, the township and the religious complex in the adjacent area around the town.

The citadel and the township have been built on the northern and southern sides respectively. As stated, the citadel was planned and built during the Kushana times whereas the town has been existing comparatively on a higher level than the citadel. The citadel measures 340 m east-west and 210 m north-south approximately. The non-habitational adjacent area, about 500 m away was used for building the religious establishment such as stupas, monasteries and other allied structures.

Excavations carried out extensively in all the three areas viz., the citadel, the township and the religious portion have revealed evidence of stupendous building activity that indicates planning and control centralised by an individual authority. This has been supported by seals and sealings mostly inscribed and numismatic data.

It is difficult to enumerate all the structural findings and hence specific aspects will be brought to focus highlighting the major contributions of Kushanas specially in monumental planning not only in the fortified complex but also their rich cultural traditions by breaking new ground as revealed by the antiquities and ceramics.

The citadel area so far revealed that three major buildings of different identity and purpose are axially situated within the area built in a planned manner. They comprise an administrative building, an Assembly Hall built together on the north, east-west axis, a non-domestic building possibly religious in nature on the east with north-south and east-west orientation and a series of buildings with laid out streets and lanes for dwelling purposes to the south. These represent the core remains (so far exposed) of building activity in the heyday of Kushanas and the citadel remained in regular use for more than a century and half consisting of the Imperial Kushana rulers in this part of Punjab. In other words, Kushana remains at Sanghol would manifest in its planning and structural grandeur to that of Taxila albeit to a limited extent.

The 'palatial' twin building—Assembly Hall and Administrative Complex, built with solid burnt bricks and brick floors and well laid-out platforms possibly stood in a commanding position within the citadel. Both of them seem to have been in use for a long period of time (mostly revealed by coin-finds) and many additions were made in the course of their use.

The Assembly Hall was built in three successive structural phases from the early Kushana to the late Kushana times. These are represented by massive brick laid floors (Pl. 41.4) and numerous post-holes made on floors for wooden poles and raising timber roof (Pl. 41.5).

The entrance of this imposing building was from the southern side ed by a well laid out pathway at the end of which was a raised rectangular brick platform with traces of four post-holes in alignment possibly meant for the seat of the chief functionary or authority (Pl. 41.6). Another such feature was traced to the east built on a raised platform 20 cm high. The post-holes were possibly meant for poles or for some sort of canopy above.

Flanking to the west is the building meant possibly for administrative purposes. It consists of massive brick walls in thickness 0.75-0.90 m uniformly laid and so far (not completely exposed)

20 rooms have been traced out of various sizes provided with thick lime floors which consist of surki, red gravel and lime (Pls. 41.7,8). In one of the rooms were stored 40 terracotta moulds of Kuninda coins of Amoghabuti type; nearby was found a circular furnace built on a brick platform suggesting its use for mint.

The utility of the building also calls for comments, more so there is no supportive evidence forthcoming of its use for domestic purposes. In all likelihood it served as administrative building of the local authority/state as a mint/treasury or allied purposes. It is also closely situated to the entrance gate on the western side facing the town direct.

The religious complex was exposed situated to the south-east portion of Hathiwara. It has been elaborately planned and built over a period of time, mainly during the Kushana period. It has been designated 'religious' mainly for the reason that there is no supportive data found of the use for domestic purposes.

In the beginning the cistern or trough-like rectangular (3.70 x 1.30 m) brick-built structures on solid brick base exposed on clearance of top phase, later turned out to be quite elaborate. The contents (1 m depth) within the cistern consisted of burnt ash, charcoal, loose earth and burnt bones, without any other evidence, suggested to be later configuration of the site or deliberate destruction and subsequent abandonment. When further excavations were undertaken and the area was exposed fully then only the entire features were brought to light with all details.

In its full form, it consists of eleven structures or so, rectangular in shape, solidly brick-built, intact with a depth 1.10-1.30 m (Pl. 41.9). They may be called fire platforms or altars mainly for the reason that the entire contents of the structures consist of layer of black ash, charcoal, burnt bone pieces and some antiquities. The entire complex measures 14.30-17.75 and 13.10-5.30 m on north-south and on east-west axis it measures 10.35-3.25 m.

Some other features exposed include a brick paved floor connecting the complex; remains of a platform with water channels possibly indicate their purpose for performance of some rituals. It is pertinent to add that being situated inside the citadel, it gets more prominence, in spite of the fact that all the religious buildings were planned and built outside much away from the town.

Though not directly connected with the complex was the finding of the skeletal remains of an animal (horse or bull) on the north-eastern side. It stratigraphically belongs to an early level as visualised by the evidence.

In regard to the time-span of its existence, it could be stated that it was in active use during the first century A.D. on the basis of Kushana pottery and copper and gold coins such as of Wema Khadphises, Indo-Parthian rulers viz. Gondapharnes etc..

Another important religious complex is also to be emphasised. Immediately to the north was found a structure built over an extended brick platform consisting of many rooms; close by was situated a ramp and a gate, leading out from the building (Pl. 41.10). Nearby was also exposed the mud fortification, quite solid and rammed, riveted with burnt bricks in various stages of its existence. This is the only clear evidence of an opening out exposed in Hathiwara. (Pl. 41.11)

The entire portion to the south of Hathiwara was also equally well planned for residential use with well laid streets, flanked by closely built houses back-to-back on sides and lanes. As a result of excavations carried out in this area, in revealed that houses were built in blocks closely without break and for every two or four bocks, large courtyards were provided within a central area. This made more secure, since the entrances to the houses faced inward; similar houses are even now built in Sanghol, the present village. -

There is more clear evidence of constructional features in this area which indicate five structural phases of building activity. Of them, the upper or the latest two phases represent repairs, remodelling and reuse of the old material. The lower two phases represent the habitation of the Kushana period which consisted of well laid out and compact houses without encroachment, built with floors, drains, hearths etc. What is more significant, the original planning remained unchanged throughout and only houses were rebuilt by raising floors and building levels.

An evidence of systematic Kushana house planning has been revealed by excavation of a house in all its features more or less intact (Pl. 41.12) on the southern periphery. It consists of a brick built house with a main entrance provided from the main street and the house is approached by brick (on edge) built slopy ramp neatly laid which is still intact. As one enters he directly faces a large sized hall or verandah which leads to the inner room wherein provision is made for entering the bathroom and the kitchen and further to the three living rooms in the interior. Equally there is a side entrance from the lane leading to a small verandah with access direct to the living rooms. An interesting feature is that of a brick built drain (closed type) projecting out of the kitchen and bathrooms clearly revealing that it is connected to the main drain in the service lane. All the rooms have been provided with rammed floor including the kitchen and bath, hence it became easy to clear the area and bring out the features.

Another Kushana house plan was also exposed in the area, a little away to the north but on the same street. It consisted of four rooms with a courtyard and entrance from the lane side. Similar brick drain was also found connected at the service lane.

The planning of Hathiwada with such elaborate buildings clearly reveals the handiwork of a central authority. In order to sustain such a set-up it is necessary to have a stable agricultural and industrial base and a substantial commercial community, not to mention the artistic craftsmen in metal, stone, and other skilled personnel. This is to a certain extent revealed in the town site in the Kushana period.

In the main town, though the area for excavations was very limited owing to the present occupation of the modern village, hence digging could be done only in small areas of mound wherever available. However, a vacant portion on the upper part of the mound was chosen and excavations (25 x 20 m) carried out to the lowest level. The total cultural deposit is about 18 m. or so. It revealed to a great extent the cultural content of the Kushana habitation. Five phases of structural activity have been traced out including floor levels made of rammed clay, brick-laid and in lime. However, there is no consistency or planning followed in building of houses built rather very close almost back-to-back thereby leaving little space for movement. Streets and lanes were also quite narrow. The houses themselves are generally small and rooms built which would have space for only two or three persons at a time. Apart from general nature of such planning in a thickly populated area, at least one fairly extant example of a house complex was exposed indicating better planning in some parts of the town.

This is a double-storeyed building possibly a big one built of burnt bricks with more than five rooms identified. The main wall itself is more than 10 m length partly damaged, with 75 brick courses traced so far. There is a possibility of similar other structure at its back, though heavily damaged due to brick robbing. On the main platform, partly brick floored, was found evidence of a workshop meant for manufacture of seals, sealings, terracotta objects, etc. The open courtyard was used for building a number of circular hearths on a brick-built floor, each separated by 0.50 m. The hearths being clay built have been supported by bricks all round. A large number of seals, sealings, beads and pendants of semi-precious stones, terracotta figurines—human and animal, were found. Further on clearance, the area has also yielded large quantity of burnt grains identified as ber *ziziphus jujube* weighing more than kilo or so mixed with other antiquities from among the debris (Pl. 41.13). The area itself has yielded many valuable antiquities such as Kushana gold coin, inscribed seals in Kharoshthi and Brahmi, and variety of objects of everyday use all of which indicate the affluent nature of the site.

To the north-east of Hathiwara, 500 m away was situated the cluster of establishments religious in nature, identified on surface and clearance undertaken which revealed an extensive complex of stupas, residential monasteries and other buildings. Already in earlier excavations, a major stupa was exposed yielding the famous Kushana sculptures and other votive stupas and the work was extended a little away on the same direction. Excavations undertaken exposed a monastery (27 cells of various sizes), a small stupa of the Dharmachakra pattern and other small structures built over an extensive brick floor. A third stupa was also partly exposed with tiers and spokes but further action could not be taken due to the fact, the area is under private possession. Moreover this part of the site has been levelled off for cultivation purposes.

At Hathiwara, there are indications revealed from excavations that the latest phase of occupation represents reuse of the old building materials such as bricks, and raising the walls of houses and also increasing the levels of floors for habitations. It is also observed when the palatial buildings fall out of use or are abandoned, the site is not completely vacated but the habitation continues in some areas. But one fact has to be emphasised that the debris layers at Hathiwara indicate some sort of burning or destruction and abandonment of site at least for sometime of the area represented by the monumental buildings of the Kushana period. It is difficult to clearly assess the period of abandonment in the absence of cultural and material evidence but the site (Hathiwara) was again inhabited and there is change of cultural milieu replacing the Kushana material remains; at east two structural phases along with floor levels have been observed in the undisturbed areas.

There is also a change in the way of life of the people and their objects of daily use. There are traces of further extension of their living areas specially to the south-east of Hathiwara about 500 m away. There is also continuity of habitation for more than a century or so. In this area excavation conducted reveals at least two groups of houses and the objects found include large and big size terracottas and ivory objects and different types of beads of semi-precious stones and terrocotta and the well-known ceramics such as Red polished ware, stamped pottery, kaolin ware and other associated pottery. Aptly this phase has been called the "Gupta" and post-Gupta period synonymous to the period in Ganga valley sites. The site was abandoned sometime in the sixth century AD and habitation shifts from Sanghol. There is large scale disturbance in the cultural layers which does not indicate presence of habitation nor for that matter any cultural material. This is more clear at Hathiwara which was not inhabited again.

Careful clearance of the main mound of present day Sanghol has also not yielded any cultural material. There are more than 3-metre deposits through represent accumulation of habitation deposits but have failed to yield any cultural data. All these support the view of the shift of habitation for more than seven or eight centuries or so from Sanghol.

Evidence of the remains of early medieval period has been traced from the area to the south of Hathiwara and the main town (present-day Sanghol). Antiquities and ceramics of the period are well represented specially the domestic pottery and other objects of daily use.

There is continuity of habitation of modern Sanghol from late medieval period. Large number of objects specially coins and ceramics of the last two centuries or so testify to the undisturbed occupation of the main mound from eighteenth century onwards.*

NOTES AND REFERENCES

1. Jagat Pati Joshi, Madhubala and Jassu Ram, "The Indus Civilization : A reconsideration on the basis of distribution maps", in (eds.) Lal, B.B. and S.P. Gupta, *Frontiers of the Indus Civilization*, New Delhi, 1984, pp. 511-30.

2. *Indian Archaeology—A Review* (IAR) 1968-69, pp. 25-26; 1969-70, pp. 31-32; 1970-71, pp. 30-31; 1971-72, pp. 39-40; 1972-73, p. 28; 1977-78, pp. 43-44; 1984-85, pp. 62-66; 1985-86, pp. 67-69; 1986-87, pp. 69-71; 1987-88, pp. 95-99; 1988-89, pp. 69-75; 1989-90, pp.; Bisht, R.S., "Transformation of the Harappan culture in Punjab with special reference to the excavations at Sanghol and Chandigarh", in (ed.) Udai Vir Singh, *Archaeological Congress and Seminar Papers*, Kurukshetra, 1976, pp. 16-22; Sharma, Y.D., "Transformation of the Harappan culture in Punjab", *ibid.*, pp. 5-15; Sharma, Y.D. and G.B. Sharma, "Bara culture and its housing remains with special reference to Sanghol", in (ed.) Sharma, R.K., *Indian Archaeology, New perspectives*, Delhi 1982, pp. 71-72; Sharma, Y.D., "The Pre-Harappan in Punjab", *Puratattava*, 11, 1979-80, pp. 32-38; "Harappan complex on the Sutlej", (India), in (ed.) Possehl, Gregory L., *Harappan civilization*, New Delhi, 1983, pp. 141-64; Gupta, S.P. (ed.) *Kushana Sculptures from Sanghol*, New Delhi, 1985; Sharma, G.B., *Coins, seals, and sealings from Sanghol*, Chandigarh,1986, pp. 1-8.

3. Margabandhu, C. and G.S. Gaur, "Some fresh evidence from Sanghol excavations, 1986", *Puratattva*, 16, 1985-86, pp. 73-78; "Sanghol excavations, 1987, Some new evidences", *Puratattva*, 17, 1986-87, pp. 1-4; "Excavations at Sanghol, Dist. Ludhiana, Punjab, 1985-90, Some new evidence on the cultural sequence", in (eds) Nayak, B.U. and N.C. Ghosh, *New trends in Indian Art and Archaeology*, New Delhi, 1992, pp. 183-92.

4. Sharma, *op. cit.*, 1983, p. 161.

5. *Ibid.*, p. 161.

Section D

Art & Architecture

42

PHOO GOMPA—A WINTER SEAT OF LAMAS OF TABO MONASTERY

A. JHA and C. DORJE

Spiti, locally known as Piti or Spyti, constitutes one of the two subdivisional blocks in the District of Lahaul and Spiti. Bounded on the north by Ladakh, on the west by Lahaul and Kullu, on the south by Kinnaur and on the east by Tibet, it comprises the valley of the river Siti and its tributaries. The area is rocky, barren and devoid of vegetation. The surrounding mountain ranges not only render it a difficult region for human beings but also exclude it from the monsoonal clouds. The rainfall is too meagre for the crops and snowfall makes life rather difficult. Despite these factors it is indeed surprising that the local populace has kept their rich cultural heritage in such a wonderful state of preservation. Indeed, it reflects their strong sense of respect and pride for their rich cultural heritage.

The source materials for the history of Spiti are very scanty and limited. Occasional references are available in the annals of the neighbouring states and biographies of the famed Lama travellers *viz.*, Lotsava Rinchen Zango, Rangrik Ras Chen, Lama Go-tsanpa, etc., and travelogues and other administrative reports of the British period. In the twentieth century, important monasteries located at different places of Spiti, attracted the attention of European travellers and scholars particularly A.H. Francke, G. Tucci, D.L. Snellgrove, Shuttleworth, Gerard and others whose findings are useful in understanding the rich cultural heritage of the region. Except a few important shrines/gompas, the identification, documentation, etc. of the other shrines/gompas is yet to be taken up. In the present paper, a less known gompa, a winter seat of the lamas of the Tabo monastery was taken up for detailed study.

Just above the Tabo monastery on the slope of the hill are the remains of numerous caves situated at varying heights. Locally known as *Duphuk,* these caves were used by the lamas of the Tabo monastic establishment during the winter for their periodical meditation (*tsaṁs*) purposes requiring complete seclusion away from the common people and pilgrims coming to pay their offerings at the monastery at Tabo. It is also said that these caves were the earliest Lamaistic establishment of Tabo and were used by the mendicants prior to the establishment of the present Tabo monastic complex.

Whatever be the facts, the traces of ruins of sixteen caves were located, the largest of them being the *Du-wang* or assembly hall (4.30 x 6.50 m) which is partly rock-cut and partly structural.

The *Du-wang*, popularly known as Phoo Gompa, is a single-storeyed flat-roofed mud-structure. It consists of a rectangular hall, a square room (kitchen and dining) and a porch. Entrance to the courtyard is through a small porch which is attached to the *Du-wang* at the south-eastern corner. Towards the west of the courtyard is a square room, used as kitchen and dining room. To the north of the courtyard is a rectangular hall, the roof of which rests on four wooden pillars. This assembly or prayer-hall is entered through a simple wooden door, which is the only opening into this building. This hall was used for prayer as well as assembly purposes and its four walls contain paintings of Buddhist divinities.

The interior wall facing the entrance has the paintings of three deities, the one in the centre is of Buddha, sitting in *padmāsana* on the lotus throne in *bhumisparśa-mudrā*, i.e., touching the earth by right hand. His left hand is placed on the lap, holding on the palm a bowl. The Buddha is flanked by two of his disciples—Sāriputra to the right holding the magic-wand and the bowl full of alms and Maudgalyayāna, to the left, holding the same object as held by Sāriputra. To the right of the Buddha is the figure of Maitreya (*Tibetan*: Byams-pa), the future Buddha, sitting in *padmāsana* on the lotus throne, exhibiting the *dharmachakra-mudrā*, in the usual royal attire with diadems, necklace, armlets and earrings. To the left of Maitreya, on the flower (lotus ?) is kept the vase, the usual cognizance of the deity. The figure to the left of the Buddha is that of Mañjuśrī (*Tibetan*; *Hjam-dpal*), in *dharmachakra-mudra*, and is shown seated in *padmāsana* over a highly ornate lotus seat. On his person can be seen the diadem, necklace, earring and armlets. He is wearing *dhotī* (the style of which reminds us of garments shown in the painted manuscripts of Bengal and Bihar). Both to the right and the left, two lotus flowers rise to the height of the shoulders; the one on the right carries a sword and the left a book, the two symbols of Mañjuśrī.

The western wall contains five deities: the first two figures are damaged due to seepage of rain water and are difficult to identify while the third one is quite interesting. It represents Sitātapatra or *Ekādaśamukha*-Avalokiteśvara or Ārya Pāla, also known as *Samantamukha* (all sided one) or the god who looks in every direction in order to save all creatures. As the name suggests, this deity is shown having eleven heads in different colours placed one above the other in five tiers, the first three tiers having three faces each while the upper two tiers have one face each. The topmost eleventh face, as per Buddhist tradition, is believed to be that of Amitābha, the spiritual sire of the Avalokiteśvara. He is depicted here as having numerous arms (thousand ?), but the main hands are only eight, the principal arms shown in *namaskāra-mudrā*. He holds in the other two right hands the rosary and a wheel and the fourth one is in *varada-mudrā*. Similarly, in the remaining three left hands he holds the lotus flower, bow-arrow and the ewer (*kartri*). A long shawl is draped over his shoulder and a garment resembling *dhotī*, very popular among the Indians, covers the lower part. Next figure in the sequence is that of Tathāgata

Amitābha (Tib. *hod-dpag-med*) in red colour, seated in *padmāsana* in *dhyāna-mudrā* over the lotus throne. *The piṇḍapātra* (alms-bowl) is kept over the palm. To his right is the white-coloured Bodhisattva Padmapāṇi, while to the left is the blue-coloured Lokeśvara Mahāsthānaprāpta, both standing, wearing usual princely ornaments, holding lotus flower and in the preaching gesture. In the background is the depiction of Sukhāvti heaven, the abode of Tathāgata Amitābha. The next figure is of Tsong-kha-pa, sitting in *padmāsana*, wearing usual monk's garments including the conical cap and in teaching gesture. There are two lotus flowers, one each on the right and the left side, rising to the height of the shoulders and supporting a sword and a book. These two symbols are generally associated with Mañjuśrī of whom this monk is believed to be an emanation. By the sides of Tson-kha-pa are shown rGyal-tshab-rje, and mKas-grub-rje, the two principal disciples.

Like the western wall, the eastern wall also contains four panels of paintings most of which are in a bad state of preservation. However, some of the figures which could be identified are that of Bhaishajya-guru (Tib. *Sman-bla*), the god of Medicine, painted in green colour and shown seated in *padmāsana* on the lotus throne. The left hand of the figure is placed on the lap which holds the alms-bowl in which is kept a casket-like object, perhaps medicine-box, while the right is in *varadamudrā*. To his sides are Sūrya Vairochana (Tib-*Rnam-pa-snag-mid-zad*) and Chandra-Vairochana.

Next figure, seated in *padmāsana* over the lotus seat, wearing monk's garb, conical cap and holding manuscript in his left hand while the right hand is in the teaching gesture is very interesting. This figure can be identified to be of Atisa Dipankara, the famous teacher of Vikramashila monastery who went to Tibet on the request of Yes-ses-hod, king of Gu-ge, during the time of Lotsava Rin-Chen-Zan-po to help local people to understand the meaning of Dhamma. On the top register of this panel can be seen Tathāgata Vairochana while Vajrabhairva can be seen at the upper right hand corner.

The paintings of Phoo-Gumpha remind us the paintings of gSer-Khang of the Tabo monastery, particularly in their style of execution. The colours and themes, used at both the gompas, are also the same. The paintings of the gSer-khang have been dated to sixteenth century. The popularity of Tson-kha-pa and Atisa Dipankara spread in the region by fourteenth-fifteenth century. Tabo, which suffered due to the political turmoil of the region regained its lost glory when Senge Namgyal came to power in Ladakh and the adjoining region. On this ground, we can safely place the paintings of Phoo Gumpha to be of the period between the fourteenth-sixteenth centuries, when Atisa Dipankara and Tson-kha-pa became very popular, and the sixteenth century, when Singe Namgyal made Tabo, once again, vibrant and active in its religious pursuit.

NOTES AND REFERENCES

1. Cunningham, Alexander. *Ladak*, London, 1854, (Rep.) Delhi, 1970.
2. Francke, A.H. *Antiquities of Indian Tibet*, in 2 vols. (Rep.) Delhi, 1972.
3. Francke, A.H. *A History of Western Tibet*, London, 1907.
4. Gerard, Alexander. 'Observations on the Spiti Valley and the adjacent countries within the Himalayas', *Asiatic Research*, Vol. XVII, Calcutta, 1833.

5. Holmes, Peter. *Mountains and Monasteries*, London, 1958.
6. Khosla, Romi. *Buddhist Monasteries in the Western Himalayas*, Kathmandu, 1979.
7. Sanyal, B.C. 'Journey to Ḳi and Taboo Monastery in Spiti' in *Roopa Lekha*, Vol. XXXVIII, Nos. 1-2.
8. Shuttleworth, H. Lee. 'Lha Lun temple, Spyiti', *MASI*, Calcutta, 1929.
9. Snellgrove, D.L. *Buddhist Himalaya*, Oxford, 1957.
10. Tucci, Giuseppe. *Indo-Tibetica*, Vol. III, Eng. Version, Delhi, 1988.
11. Tucci, Giuseppe. *Secrets of Tibet*, London, 1935.
12. Tucci, Giuseppe. *Tibetan Painted Scrolls*, 3 vols., Rome, 1949.
13. W[illegible]on, A. *The Abode of Snow*, London, 1875.

43

BANNIKOPPA : THE HIDING PLACE OF THE PĀṆḌAVAS' ASTRAS AND ITS SCULPTURES

A. SUNDARA

Bannikoppa is a small village in Shiggoan Taluka, Dharwad District, Karnataka. Local tradition is that the Pañcha Pāṇḍavas during their incognito exile arrived here and concealed their sacred *astras* and weapons in a Śamī (=Banni in Kannada) tree. The place in course of time therefore came to be known as Bannikoppa[1] (*Koppa*=habitation place of a community. Here the place with Śamī tree inhabited by the Pāṇḍavas) which is thus hallowed.

Temples and Inscriptions

In the locality are three inscriptions[2] and nine ancient temples[3] associated with the names of the Pāṇḍavas, the Dharmarāya, the Bhīma, the Arjuna, the Nakula, the Sahadēva, the Kuntī (the Pāṇḍavas' mother), the Kṛshṇa as well as two other temples: the Kāḷī and Basavaṇṇa (=Nandi). Of the three inscriptions, two are published, the earliest (Pl. 43.6) belonging to the period of Vijayāditya (A.D. 694-733), the Badami Chālukyan king is not only interesting but also relevantly significant. The short inscription speaks of the construction of a temple for the already existing Arjunīśvara; installation of Nandīśvara in the temple in "Banniyūru" ruled by the Mahājanas, by an individual hailing from Uttarāpatha; and land grant to the god Arjunīśvara. It is loosely lying in the open land between two temples of Dharmarāya and Kṛshṇa, nearby. Between the temples is a pillared *maṇḍapa*. The temples and the *maṇḍapa* are late constructions of no standard type and form with the materials of probably the original temples of ninth and twelfth centuries such as pillars *chandraśilā* (Pl. 43.3) etc. In the Dharmarāya temple are : The Dharmarāya *liṅga* in the *garbhagṛha*, the Nakula and the Sahadeva *liṅgas* in the side chambers. In the *garbhagṛha* there is also a sculpture of Durgā (Pl. 43.6). It is in the oblong hall between the *garbhagṛha* and the front hall of the former is an early colossal sculpture of Śrī Rāma but locally known as Arjuna probably because of the mention of Arjunīśvara in the nearby inscription, of the presence of a tall, heavy bow held in the left hand of the figure and of the not readily noticeable *chakra* and *śaṅkha* close to the right shoulder and to the left hand. The other inscription near the Bhīma temple in bricks of A.D. 1130 belonging to the period of Bhūlōkamalladēva *i.e.* Sōmēśvara III (1127-38), the author of the Sanskrit work *Abhilashitārthachintāmaṇi* or *Mānasollāsa*, the Kalyāṇa Chalukyan king, states that Holakēsidēva, the *daṇḍanāyaka* to the king made land grant 55th regnal year of the king Sādhāraṇa Kārtikabahuḷa, Chaturdaśī, saumavāra corresponding to 1st November 1130 to the god Bhīmēśvara already in existence in "Banniyūru Tīrtha" for food offerings and the grant was entrusted to Amṛtarāśi Paṇḍita, a *yati* in charge of the temple. The brick temple[5] as such of the Bhīmēśvara is probably of latter part of ninth century or early part of tenth century. Thus there were at least two temples originally bearing the names of the Pāṇḍavas. The "Bhīmēśvara" and "Arjunīśvara" were in existence prior to eleventh and eighth centuries and Banniyūru was deemed as sacred and therefore described as a *tīrtha* by the ninth century. It would be reasonable therefore to presume that the other temples with the names of the other Pāṇḍavas, Dharmarāya, Nakula, Sahadēva, Kuntī as well as Kṛshṇa, also were in existence although the present architecture of these temples and the identification of icons in one or two temples are respectively neither so old nor correct because of the renovations and replacements in course of time in the subsequent periods. For instance, the icon in the *garbhagṛha* of the so-called "Kṛshṇa" temple is indeed Sūrya of noteworthy type. All these temples were founded at least from about eighth century onwards in the name of the Pāṇḍavas obviously because of the deep-rooted and strong belief in the prevalent tradition: the Pāṇḍavas' stay for a short while here and concealment of their *astras* and weapons in the Śamī tree here. The tradition must have been there at least some two or three centuries before the first foundation of the temples *i.e.* in early centuries of the Christian era.

There are at least sixty and odd inscriptions[6] from Chitradurga-Shimoga-Hassan region mentioning the Pañcha-Pāṇḍavas and many places associated with the *Mahābhārata* personalities in the region. Outside the region there are inscriptions mentioning the names of the Pāṇḍavas and of the personalities of the *Rāmāyaṇa*, but very few scattered afar. The region of Chitradurga-Shimoga-Hassan seems to be focal area connected with the episodes of the two *Mahākāvyas*. Here Magaluru[7] (Chikka-Magalur District), for example, is the place of Sarpayāga performed by Janamējaya. Chandravalli-Chitradurga, about 150 km south-east of Bannikoppa is the ancient Hiḍimbāvana-Kshetra-Paṭṭana as known from the inscriptions[8] at least from eleventh century. Here, again, in Ankali *maṭha* are ten Śiva *liṅgas* of which five are known by the names of the Pañcha-Pāṇḍavas referred to even in an inscription[9] of A.D. 1286 and of Hiḍimbā. I have discussed the archaeology and tradition of this and other places elsewhere.[10] Hangal (Taluk headquarters, Dharwad District), the Pāṁktipura of the early Kadamba period about 50 km south-west of Bannikoppa is believed to be the ancient Virāṭanagara where the Pāṇḍavas lived the last year of their exile in disguise. There is another Virāṭanagara *i.e.* Hagaratgi (Surpur Taluka, Gulbarga District) about 100 km north-east of Bannikoppa where there are eleventh-twelfth century temples known after the names of the Pāṇḍavas, the Dharmarāja, Bhīma etc.[11]. But in the inscriptions of the locality are mentioned the names of temples, some of which are the extant Pāṇḍava temples, but having different names. In course of time therefore people influenced by the prevalent tradition that their place was the ancient Virāṭanagara, began to identify the local temples with the names of the Pāṇḍavas.

It looks as though that the people who had inherited stories about their ancestors' virtuous personalities and achievements poetically described in the *Mahākāvyas* might have been in the course of their movement called the places of their habitation after the names of the places of their ancestors and founded the temples in their memory, *e.g.* Virāṭanagara Pañcha-Pāṇḍava *liṅgas*. This accounts for the occurrence of more than one place with the same name such as Virāṭanagara. Foundation of temples therefore in memory of the celebrated personalities of the two *Mahākāvyas*: the *Rāmāyaṇa* and the *Mahābhārata* in the wake of the deep-rooted influencing traditions left behind by such people in these areas seems to have begun from about the beginning of the Christian era. Bannikoppa therefore is one such site.

The "Arjuna" sculpture (Pls. 43.1, 2)

The so-called "Arjuna" sculpture in the Dharmarāya temple about 2 m high almost in the round placed (apparently not ceremoniously installed) in the right part of the oblong hall depicts a kingly person standing at ease position. In the partially folded right hand is a sturdy arrow with triangular head held obliquely and in the left raised partially up, the mighty bow. On the back on both sides are quivers full of arrows. *Kirīṭamukuṭa, chakra kuṇḍalas*, floral (?) *kēyūras*, four necklaces: two plain, one beaded and the remaining jewelled, plain bangle, jewelled *udarabandha* bedeck the figure. The *kaṭivastra* with loops on the sides is dangling down to the feet. The waist band with a knot at the front centre has its ends hanging with folds over the *ardhōruka*. The long hair are richly spread in curls over the shoulders. The head is slightly tilted to the right. The body with broad chest, strong shoulders, is proportionate and graceful. The serene expression on the countenance adds dignity to the figure.

What is noteworthy is the placement of *chakra* over the right shoulder and elongated *śaṅkha* over the tip of the thumb of left hand and a seated *kapi* in the act of eating fruit close to the lower part of the bow. Its long tail folded in loops is held against the bow. The two features indicate that the figure represents Śrī Rāma and thus symbolically indicate Vishṇu in one of his *avatāras* as an ideal mānava for the mankind.

The anatomical features, particularly the teats with black area around, the absence of leg bangles *nūpura* etc., the characteristic *kiriṭamukuṭa,* necklaces, *yajñopavīta,* the waistband, the bow and arrow and the *śaṅkha-chakra,* suggest that the sculpture is of early Rāshṭrakūṭa period *i.e.* latter part of the eighth century or early part of the ninth century. Incidentally, the sculpture is, therefore, neither Arjunīśvara of the early eighth century inscription of the place referred to above nor Arjuna as told by local people. Arjunāśvara of the inscription, therefore, in all probability, is a Śiva *liṅga* installed in the name of Arjuna, one of the Pañcha-Pāṇḍavas on account of the well-established local tradition, sometime before the eighth century.

Sculptural representation of Śrī Rāma in the narrative panels of the *Rāmāyaṇa* on the walls and pillars of temples of course is very well known at least from the Badami *Chālukyan* period *e.g.* the depiction of the main *Rāmāyaṇa* episodes right from Daśaratha performing "*Putrakāmēshṭhi*" *yaga* to the coronation ceremony of Śrī Rāma with Sītā, is found on the exterior wall of the eighth century Pāpanātha temple in Pattadakal. Episodes from the Araṇya, Sundara and Yuddha kāṇḍas are on the pillars of the *sabhā maṇḍapa* of the Virupāksha and the Mallikārjuna (the Lōkēśvara and Trailōkēśvara) temples got built by the two chief queens of the Chālukya Vikramāditya II. And in the Rāshṭrakūṭa period, Śrī Rāma is depicted as an *avatāra* of Vishṇu in the panels of the *avatāras e.g.* in the rock-excavated/cut temples in Ellora. All these are too well known. But till now a separate individual icon of Śrī Rāma meant for worship or separate Śrī Rāma temple of the pre-Hoysaḷa period is scarcely known in Karnataka. Three temples dedicated to Śrī Rāma of the Hoysaḷa period are known: One in Kōdaṇḍa Rāma in Hire-Magalur[12] (Chikka Magaluru district 1170-1223), the other in Malur[13] (Bangalore district), another in Belgola (Mysore district A.D. 1338) and Dāśarathi Rāma is referred to in an inscription of A.D. 1286 from Kaḍaba (Tumkur district).

The sculpture under discussion is the earliest and the first of its kind known undoubtedly for worship, enshrined in a temple thus pushing back the Rāma cult to the eighth century at least, for the first time in Karnataka. Now we have to look for the evidences leading to the foundation of Rāma temple in the locality. If the locality is also connected with some episode of the *Rāmāyaṇa* as well, it needs to be explored.

The "Kṛshṇa" sculpture (Pls. 43.4,5)

The so-called Kṛshṇa sculpture is actually of Sūrya. The *dvibhuja* figure in *makara tōraṇa*, tall, slender, barefooted is in *samabhaṅga* in the wheeled chariot drawn by the seven horses. The upper part is in the round and the lower part, in bas-relief. *Karaṇḍa mukuṭa, makara (?) kuṇḍalas,* plain and jewelled necklaces, *udarabandha, yajñōpavīta, vaijayanti, mēkhalā* beautifully decorate the figure. The *kaṭivastra* with loops is dangling on the sides down to the feet. The *ardhōruka* is with *mālākāra vastar* over and the vertical *paṭṭikās* of the waistband on it. On the side are the goddesses: Ushā and Pratyushā with bow in the left hand and arrow in the right, stand gracefully in *tribhaṅga* near the pillars of the *makara tōraṇa.* The upper part of the *tōraṇa* is semicircular with the decorative band of *ratna:* The *kirīṭa mukuṭa* of the figure rises a little above the *toraṇa* looking like the circular *maṇḍala* to the god. These features generally are not found in the other sculptures of Sūrya in this part of Karnataka.

The characteristic *vastrālaṁkāra*, the figure, the type of bow in the hands of the goddesses flanking the god, similar to those of the Śrī Rāma sculpture described above, but more delicate the form of the upper part of the *tōraṇa* and the characteristic ornamental band on it suggest that the sculpture is of late ninth century.

The two sculptures from the locality shed welcome light on the religious cults and the history of certain sculptural forms.

Acknowledgements

I am thankful to the people of Bannikoppa village who provided me an opportunity to visit the place and helped in my study of the temples and sculptures there and to Smt. Bhagyalakshmisundara, my wife, who neatly typed the article.

NOTES AND REFERENCES

1. I visited this place as Chief Guest to the 'Teachers' day' celebration on 5th Sept. 1991 and incidentally examined a few of the temple sculptures and inscriptions. Earlier, Dr. S.M. Shadakshraiah, Reader, and Director I/c, Kannada Research Institute, Karnataka University, visited the place in 1990 and noted the sculptures, temples etc.
2. *South Indian Inscriptions* (SII), Vol. XIII, Inscriptions nos. 3 and 135.
3. R.M. Shadakshraiah, 'Dhārwāda Jilleyalli iṭṭichege kaṇḍubanda kelavu mahatvada iṭṭige dēvālayagaḷu', *Karnataka Bharati*, Vol. 23, pt. 1, 1990, Karnataka University, Dharwad.
4. *SII*, Vol. XIII, no. 135.
5. Shadaksharaiah, *op. cit.*, pp. 110-15.
6. *Dharmaraya IV (Mysore),* Ng. 29 *VII (Shimoga)* Sk. 119. *XI (Chitradurga)* cd. 76, Dg. 90.

   Bhima III (Mysore) Md. 50, 121, *IV (Mysore)*, Yd 31; Ng. 94 *V (Hassan)* Bl. 128, 193, 194; dist Cn 198, 209; Ak. 4, 9, 20, 30, 102 (a), 184; H.N. 2, 6, *VI (Chikka Magaluru)* Cm. 160; Tk. 45. *VII (Shimoga dist)*, Sh. 10; Sk. 95, 105, 136, 297; Sk. 118; Hl. 50. *VIII (Shimoga)*, Sb. 138, 152, 262, 277, 384; Sa, 108 (bic),

   Nr. 35, 36, 37, *XI (Chitradurga dist)* Cd. 13, 34, 36, 82, 87; Dg. 25, 43, 44, 70, 87, 115, 121, 129, 163, 171 and 172; Hk. 56; Jl. 30; Mk. 47. *XII (Tumkur dist)*, Tm. 9; Ck. 35; Pg. 47; Tp. 58 and 61.

   Arjuna II (Sravana Belgola), 105, *IV (Mysore dist)*, Ng. 47. *V (Hassan dist)*, Cn. 198 Hn. 57; Bl. 121, 151, 193, 194; Ak. 69, 108, *VI (Chikka Magaluru dist)* Cm. 160, *VII (Shimoga dist)*. Sk. 56, Ci 61, Hl. 8 *VIII (Shimoga dist)* Sb. 47, 203, 502; N. 27, 70. *XI (Chitradurga dist)* Dg. 25, 87. *XII (Tumkur dist)*. Ck. 35, Tm. 9.

   Nakula V(Hassan dist) Bl. 193, 194.

   The above references are from *Epigraphia Carnatica* Vols. Besides there are quite a few references to the temples originally after the names of the Pāṇḍavas as in Bannikoppa under study, in Chitradurga etc.
7. S. Srikantha Sastry, *Hoysala Vāstuśilpa* (HV), University of Mysore, Mysore, 1965.
8. *EC*, Vol. XI, Cd. 6, 13, 14.
9. *EC*, Vol. XI, Cd. 32.
10. A. Sundara, 1990, 'Hampi, the ancient Kiṣkindhā', *Dr. V.S. Pathak Felicitation* Vol.

    ——— 'Prehistoric and Protohistoric Cultures of Dakshina Kannada and Kodagu', *Mangalore University Deccenial Vol.*, Mangalore, 1991.

    ——— 'Jaṭinga Rāmēśvaradalliya Prāgaitihāsika Avaśesagaḷu mattu aitihya', *Itihasa Darśana*, Vol. 6, 1992, Karanataka Itihasa Academy, Bangalore.

    'Hiḍimba Paṭṭana: Ondu Vimarśātmaka ṭippaṇi', *Itihāsa Darśana*, Vol. 7, 1992.
11. A. Sundara, 'Temples and Mātṛka panel from Hagartgi', *Journ. of Karnataka University* (Social Sciences), Vol. XVIII, 1982, Dharwad.
12. *EC*, Vol. IX, Channapattana 110, 111.
13. *Annual Report of the Directorate of Archaeology & Museums (Govt. of Karnataka)for the year 1994*, No. 11.
14. *EC*, Vol. XII, Gb. 19.

44

LATER GUPTA TEMPLES AND ROCK-CUT CAVES AT RAMGARH, DISTRICT VIDISHA (M.P.)

B.L. NAGARCH

The village Ramgarh is located 6 km east of Paṭhari in Vidisha district of Madhya Pradesh. It has three flat-roofed temples which are datable to the later Gupta period (seventh century A.D.).

Temple No. 1

Temple No. 1 stands at the lowest level of the rock. The temple consists on plan of a *triratha* sanctum and a *maṇḍapa* [Pl. 44.1]. At present only a sanctum has survived. The *maṇḍapa* in front of the sanctum has collapsed. The doorway of the sanctum has also collapsed and the door-jambs and door-lintel are kept inside the sanctum.

Both the flanks of the doorway are elaborately carved with four *śākhās*. The first *śākhā* is carved with lotus-scrolls, the second *śākhā* is engraved with rosettes, the third is a *rūpastambha*, and the fourth is carved with a band of diamonds. On the right flank are depicted standing river goddess Gaṅgā and a male attendant [Pl. 44.2], while on the left flank are depicted standing goddess Yamunā on the mount tortoise and a male attendant standing in *tribhaṅga*.

All the *śākhās* of the doorway have been carried over the lintel. The top of the doorway lintel is decorated with a frieze of five *chaitya-gavākshās*. From the door-jambs and the door-lintel it is evident that this is a temple of later Gupta period and belongs to 7th century A.D.

The pillars of the collapsed *maṇḍapa* are also lying at the site. They are decorated with a vase-and-foliage design at the base and in the middle portion with garland loops and a frieze of rosettes. The upper portion of the pillar is also decorated with vase-and-foliage design. In front of the temple is lying a seated Nandī whose head has been chopped off. It belongs to the original temple and shows that this temple was dedicated to Śiva.

The sanctum is *triratha* on plan and is decorated with a *bhadra* niche on the southern, western and northern facades. Each of the *bhadra* niches consists of two rectangular pilasters and is surmounted by the double *chaitya*-pediment. The niches on the southern and western *bhadras* are lying vacant while the niche on the northern *bhadra* contains an image of four-armed Mahishamardinī holding sword, *triśūla, ghaṇṭā* and the tail of the buffalo-demon (Mahishāsura).

In elevation this temple shows from bottom upwards two plain *bhiṭṭas, khura, kumbha, antarpatra* and plain *kapota*. Above this rests the *jaṅghā* which is decorated on each *bhadra* with a niche as already described earlier. The *jaṅghā* is surmounted by *varaṇḍikā* and the flat roof.

The sanctum measures 2 mt sq. The door-jamb measures 35 cm x 1.23 m x 19 cm thick. The lintel of the sanctum-doorway measures 1.39 m x 6 cm x 20 cm. It is made of pink sandstone. Each pillar of the *maṇḍapa* measures 1.92 m high, 24 cm long and 2 cm thick. This is a very important temple of the later Gupta period.

The other two temples which have still survived at the site are as follows.

Temple No. 2

Temple No. 2 consists on plan of a sanctum alone. It measures 1.69 mt. sq. The west wall of the sanctum has collapsed and also the sanctum doorway on the eastern side. The roof of the sanctum is flat. The northern and southern sides of the *jaṅghā* are decorated each with three pilasters. In elevation the temple shows *khura, kumbha, antarpatra* and a plain *kapota*. The height of the sanctum is 1.85 m. The roof of the sanctum is flat. The collapsed members of the temple are lying in front. They show a seated Nandī whose head has been chopped off and who wears a chain of bells. A Śivā-*liṅga*, which was probably enshrined in the sanctum, is lying in front.

Temple No. 3

Temple No. 3 consists on plan of a sanctum alone. It is open on all sides as there are no walls of the sanctum. The flat roof rests on four pillars, each pillar being carved with twc full lotus medallions. From the design of the pillars which have a plain capital, this temple can be dated to 7th century A.D. It measures 1.70 mt. sq. The height of its roof is 1.40 m.

Rock-cut caves

There are two series of rock-cut caves near the temples described earlier. These rock-cut caves are small in size and their front facade is decorated with a frieze of sculptures which are also rock-cut.

Cave No. 1

Cave No. 1 enshrines a Śiva-*liṅga*. The facade of the cave shows from left to right the following sculptures: 1. A male *dvārapāla* standing in *samapāda* and holding a *paraśu* in his left hand. His head has been chopped off. (2) Two-armed Gaṇeśa seated in *lalitāsana*. (3) A female attendant holding a staff by her right hand and standing in *samapāda*. (4) Two-armed Narasiṁha standing in *samapāda*. There is a female devotee seated on his left. (5) Two-armed male attendant standing in *samapāda*. Both of his hands have been chopped off. (6) Mahishamardinī Durgā killing the buffalo-demon and standing in *samapāda*. She is four-armed and holds a *triśūla* and a shield by her upper hands [Pl. 44.3]. (7) A female attendant standing in *samapāda*. (8) A female playing on *vīṇā*. She is comparable to the female playing on *vīṇā* from Pawaya kept in the Gwalior Museum. (9) A female attendant standing in *samapāda*. (10) A male attendant standing in *samapāda*. The rock-cut cave measures 1.36 mt. x 81 cm. Its doorway is 89 cm high.

Cave No. 2

Cave No. 2 enshrines a Śiva-*liṅga* installed on a *yonipaṭṭa* and measures 1.9 m x 2 m broad. Its doorway is 1.13 mt. x 0.54 mt. wide.

Cave No. 3

Cave No. 3 enshrines a Siva-*liṅga* installed on a square *Gaurīpaṭṭa*. It measures 1.90 mt. x 1.80 m. The height of the doorway is 1.08 m and its width is 55 cm.

Cave No. 4

Cave No. 4 also enshrines a *yonipaṭṭa*, but the Śiva-*liṅga* is missing. It was also dedicated to Śiva. The sanctum measures 3.60 m long and 2.30 m broad. Its doorway measures 1.50 m high and 0.82 m wide. The front facades of the caves Nos. 2, 3, 4 are plain.

Cave No. 5

Cave No. 5 is also dedicated to Śiva as it is seen from the Śiva-*liṅga* installed on a square *yonipaṭṭa* kept inside. It measures 1.66 m long and 1.80 cm broad. Its doorway measures 0.97 m high and 50 cm wide. On the front facade of the cave are carved two Vaishṇava *dvārapālas*, each standing in *samapāda* and carrying *chakra* and *gadā* by his lower two hands. Both of them wear a *kiriṭamukuṭa*.

The lower series of caves are as follows.

Cave No. 6

Cave No. 6 is dedicated to Śiva as can be seen from the Śiva-*liṅga* enshrined in it on a square *yonipaṭṭa*. It measures 2.06 m long and 1.94 m broad. Its doorway is 1.3 m high. The front facade of the cave is carved on the right with the sculpture of four-armed Vaishṇava *dvārapāla* standing in *samapāda* and carrying a *gadā* and *chakra* by his lower two hands. His upper right hand has been chopped off, while he holds a *padma* by his upper left hand. On the left flank of this cave are carved the following sculptures [Pl. 44.4]:-

1. Four-armed Narasiṁha standing in *samapāda*. He wears a long *mālā* and is flanked on either side by a male attendant standing in *tribhaṅga*.
2. Eight-armed Trivikrama holding *gadā, chakra, śaṅkha, padma*, a bow and an arrow.
3. Four-armed Vishṇu standing in *samapāda* and holding *abhaya, gadā, chakra* and *śaṅkha*.
4. Anantaśāyī Vishṇu lying on the coils of the *sarpa* Adiśesha.

Cave No. 7

Cave No. 7 is also dedicated to Śiva as can be seen from the Śiva-*liṅga* installed on a square *gauripaṭṭa* kept inside it. It measures 2.07 m sq. Its doorway measures 1.0 m high and 51 cm wide. The sculptures on the facade of the caves are weather-worn. One of the sculptures, *i.e.* of Gaṇeśa is covered with vermilion. This has spoiled the originality of the caves and the sculptures.

I have come to know that the monuments are not under the protection either of the State or Central Government. They deserve to be protected.

Rock-cut sculptures at the foot of the hill

The following rock-cut sculptures are seen at the foot of the hillock:

1. Four-armed Vishṇu holding *gadā* and *padma* by his upper hands.
2. Four-armed Vishṇu carrying *gadā* and *chakra* by his upper hands.
3. Four-armed Vishṇu holding *abhaya, gadā, chakra* and *śaṅkha.*
4. Varāha standing in *ālīḍha.* He is two-armed and carries *kaṭi* and *chakra.*
5. Four-armed Vishṇu standing in *samapāda* and carrying *gadā, chakra* and *śaṅkha.*
6. Two-armed Varāha standing in *ālīḍha* and carrying *kaṭi* and *chakra.*
7. Vishṇu standing in *samapāda* and holding *gadā* and *chakra.*
8. Vishṇu standing in *samapāda* and holding *gadā* and *chakra.*
9. Vishṇu standing in *samapāda* and holding usual attributes.
10. Four-armed Gaṇeśa seated in *lalitāsana.* He carries *triśūla* by his upper right hand.
11. Two-armed Varāha standing in *ālīḍha* and holding *kaṭi* and *chakra.*
12. Four-armed Vishṇu standing in *samapāda* and holding the usual attributes.
13. Two-armed Varāha standing in *ālīḍha* and holding *kaṭi* sand *chakra.* His head has been chopped off.
14. Eight-armed Trivikrama.
15. Four-armed Vishṇu standing in *samapāda* and holding the usual attributes.
16. Four-armed Vishṇu standing in *samapāda* and holding the usual attributes.
17. Four-armed Vishṇu standing in *samapāda* and holding the usual attributes.
18. Eight-armed Trivikrama holding *kaṭi, gadā, chakra, śaṅkha,* bow and arrow.
19. Four-armed Vishṇu standing in *samapāda* and carrying *abhaya, gadā, chakra* and *śaṅkha.*
20. Four-armed Durgā killing the buffalo-demon [Pl. 44.5].
21. Eight-armed Vishṇu standing in *samapāda* and holding *kaṭi, gadā,* arrow, *chakra, chakra, chakra,* bow and *śaṅkha.*

22. Four-armed Narasiṁha standing in *samapāda* and carrying *gadā, chakra, padma* and *śaṅkha*.

23. A male whose head has been chopped off is seated on an elephant.

These sculptures are weather-worn and are ascribable to Gupta period (fifth century). They are similar to the sculptures of Udaigiri caves in the same district.

An image of a *mātṛkā* seated in *pralambapāda* on a pedestal is lying at the foot of the above hillock on the roadside. She wears a *hāra, nūpuras* and a *sārī* fastened by a *mekhalā*. The breasts of *mātṛkā* are very prominently carved. Her head, both the hands and legs have been chopped off. A devotee in *anjalimudrā* is carved on her right. It is made of purple sandstone and belongs to Gupta period *i.e.* 5th cen. A.D. It measures 77 x 50 x 27 cm. This is similar to the sculptures of the *mātṛkās* which have been found at Gajnikheḍi in Ujjain district in Madhya Pradesh.

Ramgarh is thus an important temple site of Vidisha district in Madhya Pradesh. It has yielded not only three sculptural temples but also seven rock-cut caves and a number of rock-cut sculptures of the Gupta and later Gupta period. All the three structural temples and the rock-cut caves from Nos. 1 to 7 were dedicated to Śiva, while the front façade of cave No. 6 and rock-cut sculptures at the foot of the hillock were sacred to Vishṇu. The rock-cut caves and the rock-cut sculptures at Ramgarh bear striking resemblance with the rock-cut caves and rock-cut sculptures at Udaigiri caves in the same district. The sculpture of seated *mātṛkā* from the site is also an important piece of Gupta sculpture. It is thus evident that Ramgarh was equally sacred to the Śaivas, Śāktas and Vaishṇavas who not only built their temples at the site but also got the rock surface of the hillock carved with their sculptures.

While the rock-cut caves and sculptures are earlier in date and belong to fourth-fifth centuries A.D., the three structural temples are later in date and are assignable to seventh century A.D.

Acknowledgements

The author is thankful to the Director General, Archaeological Survey of India, New Delhi for the photographs, the copyright of which lies with the Archaeological Survey of India.

45
THE JAINA ART OF BIHAR (UP TO PRE-PALA PERIOD)

BINOY KUMAR SAHAY

The birth of Mahāvīra in the sixth century B.C. was an event of far reaching consequence. Instrumental in the spread of Jainism in Bihar and beyond its limits, he was born at Kuṇḍagrāma in the suburb of Vaiśālī, situated about 35 km south-west of Muzaffarpur in north Bihar.[1] Vaiśālī, the capital of the Lichchhavīs, was the native town of Mahāvīra. His mother was the sister (or according to another tradition, the daughter) of the Lichchhavī chieftain Cheṭaka. Mahāvīra, in the course of his religious wanderings, had spent a number of rainy seasons at Vaiśālī and the neighbouring Vānijyagrāma, now identified with the village Bania. He had spent six rainy seasons (*varṣāvāsa*) at Mithila, the capital of Videha. Rājagṛha, the capital of Magadha, was also his favourite place. Mahāvīra spent no less than fourteen rainy seasons at Rājagṛha and the neighbouring village of Nalanda. According to the Jaina tradition, the Magadhan king Śreṇika Bimbisāra had married Chellanā, a daughter of the Lichchhavī chieftain Cheṭaka; and, hence, he was related to Mahāvīra. Both Śreṇika Bimbisāra and his son Kuṇika Ajātaśatru were devoted to Mahāvīra. Champā, the capital of Aṅga, was also a favourite resort of Mahāvīra. All these places must have flourished as important centres of Jainism in ancient period.

Jainism continued to receive patronage even after the death of Mahāvīra. Udāyin or Udayabhadra, the successor of Ajātaśatru, was a devout Jaina. He is known to have built a Jaina shrine in the newly founded capital of Pāṭaliputra. Later on, the Nandas were also favourably disposed towards Jainism. The Mauryan monarch Chandragupta Maurya is well known to have become a Jaina in his last days and left his capital Pāṭaliputra along with the Jaina saint Bhadravāhu for the south when a severe famine had overtaken Magadha. At the end of the famine, which is said to have lasted for twelve years, was convened the first Jaina council at Pāṭaliputra to compile the Jaina canon. Aśoka, the grandson of Chandragupta Maurya, in spite of being a Buddhist, did not neglect the Jainas (Nirgranthan). Among his successors, Samprati is stated to have been a devout Jaina ruler, who rendered considerable service to the dissemination of the faith and constructed Jaina edifices.

Religion and art are inseparable from one another, and it is certain that Jainism was as living a faith in this period as Brahmanism and Buddhism were; but unfortunately no specimens of art of such an early period have come to light. The earliest known images from Bihar are those from the oldest Jaina temple of Lohanipur from Patna, from where two nude torsos of the Jaina images were found.[2] They are presently housed in the Patna Museum. One of the torsos, prepared out of sandstone, bears the characteristic Mauryan polish; evidently it belongs to the Mauryan workmanship. Though a large portion of the two arms of the polished torso is missing, the figure was apparently in the *kāyotsarga* pose with arms falling along the thigh, 'a presumption supported not only by the rendering of the extant upper part of the arms and the pose of the body, but by the indication of the fractures left on the thighs where the palms or wrists touched.' The figure undoubtedly represents a Tīrthaṅkara. The modelling of the torso, which is in the round, is fairly naturalistic, bearing the imprint of a master hand. In sculptural qualities, it is on a plane much superior to the other torso from Lohanipur, Patna. The arms of the latter, which are also in the *kāyotsarga* pose, are disproportionately short. Rendered in the tradition of the primitive Yaksha statues, the torso is probably not earlier than the first century B.C.

An over life-size image of Jaina Tīrthaṅkara Pārśvanātha (64 in x 45 in) was discovered on the bank of the Ganga at Mahabirghat in the Gulzarbagh area of Patna city. The image could be easily identified by the presence of the seven-hooded Nāga canopy over the head of the Tīrthaṅkara. The image is now in the Gopikrishna Kanoria collection of Patna city. Pārśvanātha, rendered robeless, stands stiffly erect, with both his hands displayed in the *kāyotsarga* pose. The stiffness of the figure and angular modelling are reminiscent of the late Kushan sculptures. However, the full, fleshy appearance of the thighs, chest, and especially the face with its thick lips and essentially downcast eyes are all Gupta features. The four attendants show similar features, and perhaps even more than the main figure exhibit the rather awkward proportions and angular modelling that recall the late Kushan style. However, as remarked by F.M. Asher,[2a] the obvious reminiscences of the late Kushan style, together with the features that reveal Gupta characteristics, alone would be enough to indicate that the Pārśvānatha is a work of the early Gupta period. The image is assigned to the fourth century A.D.

In 1931 a hoard of eighteen Jaina bronzes was accidentally discovered from a field at Chausa, situated at a distance of about 11 km west of Buxar in the district of Bhojpur. The discovery opens up the possibility of the find of early Jaina monuments at the place or in its neighbourhood. The hoard of eighteen bronzes, presently preserved in the Patna Museum, includes sixteen bronze image of the Tırthaṅkaras, a *dharmachakra* on a post and a *kalpa-vṛksha,* the latter two being undoubtedly of religious significance connected with Jainism. Of the sixteen images of the Tīrthaṅkaras, ten images are represented standing in the *kāyotsarga* pose and the remaining six images are shown seated in *dhyāna-mudrā*. These bronzes have already been published by Hari Kishore Prasad.[3] While H.K. Prasad has placed the *dharmachakra* and the *kalpa-vṛksha* in the Ṣuṅga period,[4] Karl Khandalawala is disposed to suggest a date somewhat later than the Śuṅga period[5] and Debala Mitra has ascribed them to the first century A.D.[6] The ten standing images of the Tīrthaṅkaras, on the basis of their comparison with the Mathura Jaina sculptures, have been assigned by H.K. Prasad to the Kushan period,[7] and Karl Khandalawala, as well, agreeing with him, has suggested that these statues can certainly be ascribed to the Kushan period.[8] But a study of these ten standing images of the Tīrthaṅkaras evidently suggests that they may be placed under two groups. While seven of the figures,[9] as suggested by H.K. Prasad and Karl Khandalawala, may be placed in the Kushan period, the remaining three,[10] on consideration of style, appear to belong to the early Gupta or Gupta period. In this regard the remark of Debala Mitra is significant that the standing images, all robeless, cover a wider period from the pre-Kushan to the Gupta period.[11] As the *lāñchhaṇas* are depicted in none of the standing images, so Ṛṣabhanātha and Pārśvanātha alone can be identified by the locks of hair and the serpent-hood respectively. There are two figures of Ṛṣabhanātha[12] and two figures of Pārśvanātha[13] among the standing images, while the remaining eight may simply be regarded as those of the Jaina Tīrthaṅkaras.

The six seated bronze images of the Tīrthaṅkaras have been placed in the early Gupta or the Gupta period by H.K. Prasad.[14] Karl Khandalawala, however, differing from Prasad, is emphatic in suggesting that the images appear more likely to belong to the end of the Kushan period to the Kushan-Gupta transition style, about the middle of the fourth century A.D., rather than to the phase of the full-fledged Gupta art.[15] It is significant to note that R.N. Mishra has placed these images under the period A.D. 300 to A.D. 600.[16] These seated bronze images are all endowed with simple charm, felicity of expression and dynamism. They have delicacy and refinement in their execution. Different limbs are quite in proportion to the bodies of the figures. Two of the Tīrthaṅkara images are even provided with their specific *lāñchhaṇas* (particular symbols). In view of all these developed features, these seated images, as suggested by H.K. Prasad, may be ascribed to the early Gupta period or to the full-fledged phase of the Gupta art. Among these six seated images, on account of the treatment of the locks of hair, may be identified as those of Ṛṣabhanātha[17] and two images, due to the presence of the crescent in the headdress, may be taken as representing Chandraprabhā,[18] the remaining two being simply the images of the Jaina Tīrthaṅkaras.

Rājagṛha (modern Rajgir) was an important centre of Jainism. The hills girdling the place are dotted with the remains of ancient Jaina temples, besides modern temples adorning them. It is, therefore, natural that Rājagṛha has yielded a number of Jain images representing the Tīrthaṅkaras. One of the earliest images represents Neminātha, the twenty-second Tīrthaṅkara, in the ruined temple on the Vaibhara hill at Rājagṛha.[19] This black basalt image (79 cm x 68 cm) contains a mutiliated inscription recording the name of (Mahārājādhirāja) Chandrangupta II Vikramāditya. The head of the image is badly mutiliated, otherwise it is a perfect specimen of the Gupta art. The Jaina figure is shown seated in the *dhyāna-mudrā* on a *siṁhāsana*. The pedestal bears the figures of rampant lions on its extreme ends and a princely figure standing inside the periphery of an oblong and spoked *chakra*. On his either side are the figures of two Jainas with shaven heads, sitting in the *dhyāna-mudrā*. The princely figure in the *chakra* was identified by R.P. Chandra with Ariṣṭanomī (Neminātha as a young prince),[20] but according to U.P. Shah the figure represents the Chakrapuruṣa.[21]

There are six other Jaina figures of almost similar style carved on the southern wall inside the eastern Soṇbhandār cave of Rājagṛha.[22] Of these six figures, five are carved on the one side of the entrance to the cave, while the sixth one stands in isolation on the other side. The first five figures, represented within panels, are carved in a row. The first two figures represent Padmaprabhā, the sixth Tīrthaṅkara, the third one Pārśvanātha, the twenty-third Tīrthaṅkara and the last two Jaina Mahāvīra, the last twenty-fourth Tīrthaṅkara. They are also accompanied by the attendants, devotees and the flying Gandharvas bearing garlands in their hands. The whole composition highlights a contrast in portraying the static and stereotyped Jaina figures seated or standing juxtaposed to the frolicking figures of attendants caught in various stances of movement.[23] The whole composition is laid out symmetrically; the different Jina figures are properly framed and combine to make a frieze in the form of an extended panel. The symmetry of this panel is, however, broken only by the two diminutive lotuses below the first two figures of Padmanātha; but this does not have any adverse effect on the total artistry of the composition. These reliefs have an almost identical scheme of presentation as regards the accessory details, and the deviation manifests itself only in the presentation of the individual cognizances of the different Jinas. So the Jinas are either standing or seated and in all the cases they are accompanied in tiers from top to bottom by the flying figures on either side, holding garlands or simply folding the hands in adoration, attendant figures standing on each side and holding fly-whisk and two seated Jainas, one each on either side, in the *dhyāna-mudrā*. Between the niched figures of these seated Jainas, below the pedestal carry some more details. The reliefs of Padmaprabha have lotuses, that of Pārśvanātha has two elephants facing in opposite directions and separated by a beautifully carved *Chakra*; Mahāvīra, on the other hand, has lions flanking similar *Chakras*.

The lonely sixth relief on the other side of the entrance is larger in size but badly mutiliated. Even so, it presents the same breadth of style as seen in other figures. It has certain elaborations in that a *kalpa-vṛkṣha* (wish-fulfilling tree) is carved on the top of Jaina's halo. The tree has the distinctive bunches of the Aśoka flower and leaves.

There are three standing sculptures of the Tīrthaṅkaras in the cell containing the Neminātha image of the fifth century A.D. on the Vaibhāra hill already discussed above. They seem to belong to a different tradition. Among these, one image has the depiction of conches flanking a lotus and thus represents Neminātha; the other, though smaller and less articulate in accessory details, is nevertheless similar to the preceding. These two images of the Tīrthaṅkaras exhibit a configuration of oval face, neatly arranged hair in spirals, the *kāyotsarga-mudrā* and an enriched ornamentation of halo throughout the course of its circular sweep. The *parikara* (attendant) of these images has *chaurī* (fly-whisk) and the garland bearing figures in both the sides of the Tīrthaṅkaras. The third image of this group is the smallest and simplest and shows the Tīrthaṅkara standing along with the *chaurī*-bearers under a parasol consisting of triple layers of inverted lotus. This image is corroded and its finer details have disappeared. Yet another image of this class, with the same refrain of style, is now in the Gopikrishna Kanodia collection at Patna city. This image represents Pārśvanātha and in the details of the *parikara* is typically Gupta in style. However, the delineation of the face is at variance in style with the rest of the figure. This might have been due to a re-cutting of the image at some later date. All these images have been assigned to the Gupta period.[24]

There was an image of the favourite Tīrthaṅkara of Rājagṛha, *i.e.* Tīrthaṅkara Neminātha which was found outside the eastern wall of a temple on the Rathagiri hill. Unfortunately, the whereabout of the image is now not known.[25] The massive qualities of the body and rather flaccid flesh of the image seem to have been derived from the rock-cut sculpture of the Son Bhandar cave. The image is decorated with a bolster at the back common to the Buddha images of the time and the canopy over the head which we usually find on the Jaina images of the period and subsequent centuries. Stylistically, the Jaina image seems to recall the Buddha image from Telhara in style. Of approximately the same date, there is a second image of Nemināthа now placed in a niche of the ruined temple of the Vaibhāragiri, the site of the fifth century Nemināthа image already mentioned above. This sculpture is, however, not as refined as the Ratnagiri image. This image generally follows the form of the Ratnagiri Tīrthaṅkara, although flanking the seated figure of Nemināthа are eight miniature panels, four on each side, containing the figures of the deities. Eight such similar deities have been found flanking a pair of much later Pārśvanātha images from sites in the Bankura district of West Bengal.

Champā, the capital of Aṅga, was and still is an important centre of pilgrimage for the Jainas. According to the *Kalpasūtra,* Mahāvira spent three rainy seasons at Champa in course of his religious wanderings. The twelfth Jaina Tīrthaṅkara Vasupūjya is stated to have been born at Champānagar or Champāpurī. There were six images of the Jaina Tīrthaṅkaras in the Jaina Digambara temple at Champāpur. After having been shifted from Champāpur, they are now installed in the Jaina Digambara temple at Nathnagar, about 5 km west of Bhagalpur. Of these images, two images deserve special notice. Both the images are large sized and both of them are representing the Jaina Tīrthaṅkara Ṛṣabhanātha—one of them having been rendered standing, while the other is shown seated. Though said to be of south Indian origin, the standing image is an indigenous product, having been prepared out of pink sandstone. The stocky build and sensitively modelled torso contrasting with the stumpy legs suggest the image to have been contemporary with the standing Nemināthа images of the Vaibhara hill at Rājagṛha datable in *circa* eighth century A.D. It is, however, not so refined an image as the Vaibhāragiri examples.[26] The other image representing Ṛṣabhanātha seated is superbly executed. It is reminiscent of the contemporary image of Ṛṣabhanātha dedicated by the Āchārya Vasantanandi at Rājagṛha, though it is more heavily set than that figure, the artist of which probably got inspiration from the art of nearby Nalanda. The polished surface of this image presents a metallic impression as in the case of the several other images of the period.

It has, however, to be conceded that unlike the image of the Buddhist and the Brahmanical art, the specimens of the Jaina art are scattered and much smaller in number. But at the same time it has also to be mentioned that the Jaina art of Bihar did not receive the attention of the scholars it rightly deserves. If different centres of Jainism in the state are explored and a proper study of the images that are likely to be obtained by way of such explorations is made, much more light may be shed on the development of the art associated with Jainism in Bihar.

NOTES AND REFERENCES

1. According to another Jaina tradition, Lachchhuar, about 6.5 km from Sikandara in Jamui subdivision of Monghyr district is supposed to be the 'janamsthan' (birthplace) of Mahāvira. Bloch, *Annual Report, ASI,* BC, 1903, p. 11; BODG, Monghyr, pp. 210, 228.
2. *JBORS,* Vol. XXIII, 1937, pp. 130-32; Vol. XXVI, 1940, pp. 120-24.

2a. F.M. Asher. *The Art of Eastern India*, 300-800, p. 17.
3. *Shri Mahabir Jaina Vidyalaya Golden Jubilee Volume*, Part i, pp. 275ff.
4. *Ibid.*, p. 277.
5. *Lalit Kala*, no. 14, p. 63.
6. Ghosh, A. (ed). *Jaina Art and Architecture*, 1, p. 72.
7. *Shri Mahabir Jaiṇa Vidyalaya Golden Jubilee Volume*, Part i, p. 278.
8. *Lalit Kala*, No. 14, p. 63.
9. PM Arch. Nos. 6531, 6532, 6534, 6535, 6536, 6537.
10. PM Arch. Nos. 6533, 6538, 6539.
11. Ghosh, A., *op. cit.*, p. 72.
12. PM Arch. Nos. 6538, 6539.
13. PM Arch. Nos. 6531, 6533.
14. *Shri Mahabir Jaina Vidyalaya Golden Jubilee Volume*, Part i, p. 279.
15. *Lalit Kala*, No. 14, p. 63.
16. Ghosh, A., *op. cit.*, p. 125.
17. PM Arch. Nos. 6533, 6554.
18. PM Arch. Nos. 6551, 6552.
19. *ASI AR*, 1925-26, pp. 125-26.
20. *Ibid.*
21. Shah, U.P., *Studies in Jaina Art*, p. 14.
22. Kuraishi and Ghosh, Rajgir, p. 26, pl. VII B.
23. Ghosh, A., *op. cit.*, pp. 123-24.
24. *Ibid.*, pp. 123-24.
25. Asher, F.M., *op. cit.*, p. 51, pl. 80.
26. *Ibid.*, p. 89, pls. 200, 201.

46
ART OF ŚIVA AND PĀRVATĪ ICONS IN NORTH BIHAR

BIRENDRA KUMAR SINHA

Śiva is the most influential member of the orthodox Brahmanical triad, Brahmā, Vishṇu and Maheśa.[1] He is specially associated with the set of *saṁhāra* (destruction) or *plalaga* (absorption). Śiva is worshipped either in the *liṅga* form or in human form. In human form again four of his images are found and they are *Mangalakārī śāntamūrti, Samhāramūrti, Dakshināmūrti* and *Nṛttamūrti.*[2] Besides, some composite images of Śiva are also found, *e.g.* Harihara and Ardhanārīśvarra. His normal *āyudhas* are *triśūla, ḍamaru, kheṭaka* and *paraśu*, etc. Normally he is shown with Pārvatī, Gaṇeśa, Kārttikeya, Nandi bull, etc. and he wears *jāṭā-mukuṭa* on his head or a *sarpamālā* in the neck. He is shown with two, four, eight, ten or thousand heads.[3]

Śiva *liṅgas*, the phallic emblems of Śiva belonging to the Gupta period have been discovered at Vaisali and other parts of north Bihar.[4] Some of the *liṅgas* are plain and simple cylindrical shafts whereas others are *mukhaliṅgas* having one (*ekamukha*) or four faces (*chaturmukha*) supposedly of Śiva superimposed on the sides of the *liṅgas.*

The *chaturmukha liṅga* found from Vaisali shows the four human faces of Śiva, superimposed on the four sides of the cylindrical shafts. One of the images is inscribed. The *chaturmukha liṅga* from the village Kamman Chapra (Vaisali) has the superimposed human faces much blurred but the features are quite distinct suggestive of the faces being adorned with *jaṭāmukuṭa*, beaded necklaces and ear ornaments. Carved out of black basalt, the sculpture locally known as Chaturmukh Mahadeo, belongs stylistically to the Gupta period. A gold coin of Chandragupta II and a Gupta inscription have been found in its vicinity which may also point to the date of the sculpture.

An *ekamukha* Śiva *liṅga* of late Pāla period is also reported from Sikligarh in Purnea district.[5]

Another stone image of Umā Maheśvara, now in the Vaisali Museum (Antiquity no. 7) is a beautiful piece of sculpture. It is made of black basalt and belongs to the early Pāla period. The figures of Śiva and Pārvatī are shown seated on a double lotus throne, their *vāhanas* being lion and bull respectively. Four-armed Śiva has three eyes (one being on forehead) and *Jatāmukta* on his head. Gaṅgā is shown flowing from his *jaṭā*. Out of his four hands the upper right of the lord touches Pārvatī's chin and the lower right hand holds the trident, the upper left hand of the god touches the left breast of the goddess and the lower left hand is invisible. Śiva clad in *bāghāmbara* (tiger's skin) wears bracelets besides earlobes, garland and *yajñopavīta*. Pārvati is sitting on Śiva's left thigh with her right hand kept around the neck of her consort, the left hand missing.[6] Her hairdressing is represented by the coiffure with a raised knot at the centre of the head, *i.e.* in *dhammila* style. She bears mark of vermilion on her forehead and wears ear-ring and beaded garland. A lady attendant is clearly seen seated behind Śiva's bull. The height of the image is about 35.56. cm.

An interesting image of Umā Maheśvara is known from Bhelshi near Raxaul in the district of Champaran.[7] The image is made of schist stone. On the basis of the style of art and material, the image may belong to the Pāla period. Its height is 67.31 cm. Umā is shown seated on the lap of Śiva and her right hand is shown on his shoulder. She holds a mirror with stalk. Then definitely the figure has Buddhist influence because lotus with stalk is the chief characteristic of some of the Buddhist female goddesses such as Tara.[8] Then Śiva carries *dhaturā* flower in the upper right hand, while the lower right hand touches the chin of Umā, his upper left hand touches the left hand and lower left hand touches the left breast of Umā. Their feet are placed on lotus and below that are shown bull and lion, the two vahanas of Umā-Maheśvara. An emaciated human being technically known as Bhṛiṅgī is shown in between the two vehicles of Śiva and Pārvatī. The *Rshi* Bhṛiṅgī is in slightly dancing attitude. This is an unusual feature; not only this, a devotee also with folded hands and in a kneeling posture is shown by the side of the bull. Umā and Maheśvara both are adorned with various types of ornaments which add beauty to the image. Hair dressing of Śiva, technically known as *jaṭāmukuṭa* is just like the hair knot of Maitreya and Avalokitesvara from Vishnupur, Gaya, preserved in the Patna Museum. So this suggests Buddhist influence. Above the figure in the halo two flying Gandharvas are shown and the *kī.ttimukha* is on the top. The other interesting feature of the image we find that Śiva holds trident in his left hand which is quite an unusual feature.[9] Generally we find the trident placed in the right hand of Śiva. Further, Śiva holds in his right hand *dhatūra* flower in place of a trident. So the figure is somewhat uncommon.

Other image of Umā Maheśvara was reported fiom Silour village. near Siwan.[10] In this image Śiva is shown with his consort Pārvatī to his right. Śiva's *jaṭāmukṭa* is held by a peculiar triangular band. Śiva's sons Gaṇeśa and Kārttikeya are shown to his right and left respectively. The top of the stele is damaged. The sculpture is a mixed style of the Chedis and Pālas. It is about 50 cm in height and on stylistic ground this sculpture has been dated to the 10th-11th century A.D.

From Chirand an image of Śiva is reported from the excavation.[11] In this image Śiva is shown with two female faces on either side of his face looking like a *trimūrtti*. Śiva wears a *jaṭāmukuṭa*. The *trinetra* is shown on his forehead. The *kuṇḍalas* in both the ears are carved in such a manner that they serve the purpose of the *kuṇḍalas* of the female figure as well. At Chirand itself, two images of Śiva belonging to the Pāla period were collected from a villager.[12] The first image is of Umā Maheśvara. Umā has been shown sitting on the left thigh of Śiva and her right hand is around the neck of Śiva and in her left hand, she is holding a flower. Her left leg is pendent and right is folded. Śiva's right hand holds a *triśūla* and his left hand encircles the waist of Umā and the fingers touch her left breast. The image is badly damaged. Other image in the collection is an *eka-mukha liṅga* in which a female face is shown carved on its side, who is some other than that of Umā.[13] Both the above-mentioned images are in black basalt and on stylistic ground. They belong to the Pāla period, as is proved by huge ornamentation, treatment of the features of the body, etc.

From Sonpur (Chapra district), was found another image of Śiva in composite form and is known as Harihāra image. This form of Śiva establishes the unity between the Vaishṇava and Śiva pantheons.[14] The left half of the image shows the features of Vishṇu (Hari), whereas in the right Śiva (Hara) is shown. The left half of the crown is a *kirītamukuṭa* and on the right half, there is a *jaṭāmukuṭa*. In Vishṇu's ear, there is a *makarakuṇḍala* whereas in Śiva's ear there is *sarpakundala*. This famous image is carved on a polished black basalt stone, in standing posture; style and material-wise this image is also dated to the 10th-11th century A.D.

From Mithila a unique icon of Śiva-Pārvatī, badly weathered is also noticed.[15] One important feature of this image is that Śiva is represented with his normal two arms instead of four. The *prabhāvalī* is completely round. It is datable to 10th-11th century A.D.

From Bhit Bhagwanpur,[16] a highly decorated image of Śiva-Pārvatī in their usual *āliṅgana* pose has been found. It is datable to circa 11th century A.D.

There is a beautiful image of Pārvatī from Girijasthana[17] representing standing *kamalāsana*. The image has four arms. The upper right hand is holding a Śiva-*liṅga* and the lower one a fruit. The upper left hand has a mirror, whereas the lower one rests on the head of Kārttikeya (or Lakshmī ?). To her right, there is a figure of Gaṇeśa. The deity is decorated with usual ornaments. The *sarī* of the deity has been shown fashionably with the help of ripple-like folds. There is a round decorated *prabhāvalī*. At the bottom of the pedestal is shown the alligator. The workmanship is superior. It is datable to 11th century A.D.

There is Śiva-Pārvatī image in the *āliṅgana mudrā* from Bhuvneswarsthana.[18] Śiva is touching the chin of Pārvatī, with his right upper hand, whereas in his upper left hand, he is holding *triśūla*. Nandi is shown just below Śiva and lion just below Pārvatī. The *prabhāvalī* is beautifully decorated with flying *gandharvas* and *kinnaras* and *gajasārdūla* motifs. In the middle of their *vāhanas*, has been shown the dancing figure of emaciated Bhṛiṅgī. It is datable to *circa* 11th-12th century A.D.

A black stone image of Śiva-Pārvatī is a stela, belonging to the late Pāla period (11th-12th century A.D.). It is housed in the Vaisali Museum.[19] Its height is 25.4 cm. Four-armed seated Śiva is shown with a snake coiled round his neck, Gaṅgā flowing from his *jaṭā* (matted hair), knot of *jaṭā* on the forehead, *jaṭā* being indicated by incision on the head. His upper right hand holds *kamaṇḍalu* and lower right one trident, upper left hand has a stick-like object and the lower one holding *ḍamaru* as well as touching the waist of his consort (Pārvatī) who is seated with folded hands on his left thigh. The raised hood of snake touches the trident from its back. The *vāhanas* of both Śiva and Pārvatī, the bull and the lion respectively, are also depicted.[20]

An image of Hara-Gaurī from Basarh is also enshrined in the Bavana Pokhara-ka-Mandir which belongs to the early Pāla period.

Bronze icons of Śiva and Pārvatī in north Bihar have been found from a very few places such as Belwa in Saran district and Pranpur in Katihar district.[21]

From Belwa in course of excavations, three bronze statuettes, two of them representing Śiva-*liṅgas* and the third perhaps the Buddha under the sacred Buddhist tree[22] were found. One of the Śiva-*liṅga* is of the *chaturmukhi* type provided with four faces superimposed on the four sides of the *liṅga* proper. The other piece is identical to the piece, but in this piece Gaṇeśa is also carved on a separate lotus.[23] Both the pieces are corroded and on stylistic grounds they are dated to the 11th century A.D. Both the phallic emblems of Śiva are placed on high double-tiered drums containing figures of a kneeling devotee in *añjali mudrā*, a couchant bull, the *vāhana* of Śiva and a trident, the special emblem of the God, in relief. The *chaturmukha liṅga* as is usual with such stone *liṅgas*, shows four heads of Śiva, superimposed on the four sides of the *liṅga*, each characterised by knotted lock of hair over the head and mark of the third eye vertically over the forehead. The plain cylindrical *liṅga* shows an additional feature by way of a four-armed figure of Gaṇeśa shown seated in an easy posture on a miniature lotus emerging from the side of the drum itself.

The Pranpur Umā-Maheśvara icon presented Lord Śiva, two-handed and seated in *lalitāsana* on a lotus seat placed over a rectangular pedestal with footed legs. Both Umā and Maheśvara are sitting very close embracing each other. The Devī is seated in *sukhāsana* pose on the left thigh of Śiva with her right leg likewise pendent and resting upon the back of a *makara*-like object. Śiva is shown embracing the goddess and catching her left breast by his left hand while his right hand is pecularily shown in *abhaya mudrā*. Umā is also embracing the lord by her right hand and placing it on his right shoulder. The goddess is holding a round mirror in her left hand. To the left of Umā and Maheśvara, their son Gaṇesa is seated and to the right side of the main deity, Kārttikeya is placed. It measures 11 x 8 cm. A devotee is seated in *añjali mudrā* in the lowermost left corner of the platform. Only three bronzes of Umā-Maheśvara, all from Kurkihar, are known from the Bihar state.[24] But none of them shows similarities with the Pranpur Umā-Maheśvara icon. The round mirror in the left hand of the Devi is conspicuous by its absence in the Bihar bronzes belonging to the ancient period.[25]

Another interesting male figure in the Pranpur hoard was of *Dakshiṇāmūrti* of Śiva. It measured 5.5 x 4.4 cm and was found in good condition. He was seated in *samparyaṅkāsana* pose on a double-petalled lotus flower seat. He was in deep meditation and his third eye, vertical in shape was clearly visible. He was wearing a typical tribal-like flat crown over his head. The sacred thread (*yajñopavīta*) was beautifully arranged in his body. According to Gopinatha Rao,[26] Śiva used to deliver sermon to the gods and saints by seating himself towards south. Due to this very fact this form of Śiva became popular as *Dakshiṇāmūrti*. He classified four types of *Dakshiṇāmūrti* among which the *Vyākhyāna* (*Dakshiṇāmūrti*) is prominent. Hence, the Pranpur Śiva comes under the *Vyākhyana Dakshiṇāmūrti* variety.

After going through the bronzes found in north Bihar, the Pranpur bronze images of Pāla period were more important and significant for the study of art. Stone and bronze sculptures of both Buddhist and Brahmanical deities of the Gupta and Pāla periods have been reported in north Bihar, which are eloquent examples of artistic activities of the region. Among the Brahmanical deities, Śiva and Pārvatī were very significant. These deities were popularly worshipped by the people but are significantly absent during pre-Gupta period in north Bihar.

NOTES AND REFERENCES

1. J.N. Banerjee, *Development of Hindu Iconography*, p. 446.
2. *Ibid.*, p. 446.
3. I. Mishra, *Pratima Vigyana*, 1972, p. 262.
4. B.K. Sinha, *Archaeology of North Bihar*, p. 255.
5. *Indian Archaeology 1974-75—A Review*, p. 10.
6. B.K. Sinha, *op. cit.*, p. 257.
7. Patna Museum, Reg. no. 10889.
8. *JBRS*, Vol. XLIII, Parts 1-2, p. 65.
9. B.K. Sinha. *Archaeology of North Bihar*, p. 258.
10. P.L. Gupta, *P.M.C.*, Sect. I, p. 95. (Reg. No. 6363).
11. Sinha, B.P. & Verma, B.S., *P.U. Journal*, Vol. 23 N.
12. *Bihar District Gazetteer, Saran*, p. 42.
13. Mishra, Y. *History of Videha*, p. 278, and Sinha, *op. cit.*, p. 259
14. *JBRS*, Vol. XLV, 1959, pp. 319-21.
15. Mishra, V. *Mithila Art and Architecture*, p. 37.
16. *Ibid.*, p. 37 and Sinha, B.K., *op. cit.*, p. 281.
17. *Ibid.*, p. 37.
18. Mishra, V., *Mithila Art and Architecture*, p. 37.
19. *Ibid.*, pp. 37-38. & Sinha, *op. cit.*, p. 262.
20. *Homage to Vaisali*, Pl. IV.
21. Sinha, B.K., *Archaeology of North Bihar*, p. 290.
22. Sinha, Kamini, *The Early Bronzes of Bihar*, p. 10.
23. *P.M.C.A.*, p. 162 (Reg. nos. 2767 & 2768).
24. *J.B.P.P.*, Vols. VII & VIII, 1983-84, p. 270.
25. Sinha, B.K., *Archaeology of North Bihar*, p. 303.
26. Gopinatha Rao., *Elements of Hindu Iconography*, Vol. 2, Part-I, p. 273.

47

THE PAÑCHATANTRA SCULPTURES IN THE TRIPURĀNTAKEŚVARA TEMPLE AT BALLIGAVE, KARNATAKA

CHANNABASAPPA S. PATIL

The *Pañchatantra,* written in Sanskrit, is a collection of the most widely known stories in the world. It is a *nīti-śāstra, i.e.* textbook of the wise conduct of life. The original *Pañchatantra* composed by Vishṇusharma in India in 2nd-1st centuries B.C., assumed varied forms in its native India, then travelled in translations, and translations of translations, through Persia, Arabia, Syria, Europe and Near East. There is another tradition of the *Pañchatantra* known as Vasubhagabhaṭṭa's *Pañchatantra.* These two traditions appear to have originated at the same time. The *Pañchatantra* has been translated into several Indian regional languages. The Kannada version of the *Pañchatantra* was composed by Durgasiṁha in A.D. 1031. Sanskrit *Tantropākhyāna*, Tamil *Tantropākhyāna* and *Tantri* are some other versions of the *Pañchatantra.*

The Tripurāntakeśvara temple at Balligave in Shikaripura taluk, Shimoga district was constructed in A.D. 1070 during the period of the Chāḷukyas of Kalyāṇa. This temple has been renovated in later period. The *adhishṭhāna* of this ornate temple is decorated with small sculptures depicting stories from the *Pañchatantra* along with scenes from the *Rāmāyaṇa* and some erotic scenes. This temple has been described by M.H. Krishna and H.R. Raghunatha Bhat. They have identified only three stories from the *Pañchatantra, viz.* (1) The Jackal at the Ram-fight, (2) The Geese and the Tortoise, and (3) The Monkey and the Crocodile.[1] But there are two more panels depicting two more stories, *viz.* (1) Self-Defeating Forethought, and (2) The Brahman and the Crab,[2] which have been identified wrongly by M.H. Krishna as (1) "A man of destiny persecuted by serpents and elephants is venerated by them. His identity is uncertain," and (2) "Serpents shade him while he sleeps and birds bring him food," respectively. Raghunatha Bhat has not identified these two panels. M. Seshadri has identified two more stories, *viz.* "The

Loyal Mongoose" and "The Wedge-Pulling Monkey."[3] The panel containing the story of "The Loyal Mongoose", belonging to this temple, is now preserved in the Government Museum, Shimoga. This stone also contains another panel depicting the story of "The Brahman, the Thief and the Ghost," which has not been identified by Seshadri. Hence this temple contains eight panels depicting the following stories:

1. The Wedge-Pulling Monkey
2. The Jackal at the Ram-fight
3. The Geese and the Tortoise
4. Self-Defeating Forethought
5. The Brahman and the Crab
6. The Brahman, the Thief, and the Ghost
7. The Monkey and the Crocodile
8. The Loyal Mongoose

1. The Wedge-Pulling Monkey

The story of "The Wedge-Pulling Monkey" in Vishṇusharmā's *Pañchatantra* is as follows.[4] A merchant was causing the construction of a temple in a grove nearby a city. One day when the workers had gone to the city for lunch, a troop of monkeys arrived at the site. A carpenter who had begun to split a big wooden log had thrust a wedge into its cleft at the top. The monkeys began their mischievous play upon the tree-top, half built temple and wood-pile. One monkey, whose doom was near, seeing the wedge stuck in an odd place, sat upon the log and started pulling the wedge seizing with both the hands. While it was pulling the wedge its private parts had entered the cleft. When the wedge was removed its private parts were jammed in the cleft and the monkey died. Durgasiṁha's *Pañchatantra* also contains similar story.[5]

Seshadri mentions that a small stone beam containing a sculpture depicting this story was in the sculpture gallery near the *kalyānī* (tank). He does not give the details of the panel. Recently the author visited the site but he could not find this panel either in the Museum or at the site.

2. The Jackal at the Ram-Fight

Vishṇusharmā narrates the story of "The Jackal at the Ram-fight" as follows.[6] There was a herd of rams. Among them two were fighting. These two were angrily drawing apart and dashing together, their slab like foreheads crashing so that blood oozed out. This scene attracted a jackal, which had the carnivorous desire. The jackal stood in between two rams and started licking the blood. Then the rams pulled apart and crashed again. This time the jackal being greedy of licking blood did not move away. It was caught between the crashing heads and was killed. Durgasiṁha also narrates this story similarly.[7]

The sculpture (Pl. 47.1) depicts the fighting rams in the act of pulling backward. Both are standing on four legs. There is sufficient space in between them for the jackal to sneak in. The jackal standing on rear legs has risen high to reach the forehead of the ram on the right. It is licking the blood oozing from the forehead of the ram. The artist has carved the complete profile of all the three animals.

3. The Geese and the Tortoise

The story of "The Geese and the Tortoise" (Shell-neck, Slim and Grim) in Vishṇusharmā's *Pañchatantra* is as follows.[8] In a lake lived a tortoise. He had two geese as his friends. Once there was a long drought for twelve years which made the lake to dry. Then the geese thought of moving to some other lake with water. Before their departure they went to the tortoise to inform their decision and bid farewell. When they did so, the tortoise asked them the reason for bidding him farewell. He was a water-dweller and here he would perish without water, and requested them to rescue him from the jaws of death. Then the geese told him that he was a water-creature without wings and they were unable to take him with them. The tortoise told that there was a possibility, and asked them to bring a stick of wood. They did it immediately. Then the tortoise gripped the middle of the stick between his teeth, and told the geese to hold it with their bills, one on each side, fly up until they discover another lake. But the geese objected this plan because if the tortoise indulged in the smallest conversation, then he would lose hold on the stick and would fall to the ground from a great height. Then the tortoise promised that he took a vow of silence from that moment, which would continue as long as they were in sky. When the geese were carrying the tortoise painfully over a neighbouring city, the people saw the cart-like unusual thing in the sky and talked about that. Then the tortoise asked about what the people were talking. The moment he spoke, he lost his grip and fell to the ground. The people cut him to bits to take the meat.

The story narrated by Durgasiṁha is also similar to that of Vishṇusharmā.[9] The Sanskrit *Tantropākhyana*, Tamil *Tantropākhyāna* and *Tantri* include the incident of two jackals in this story. The jackals laughed at the act of geese carrying tortoise belonging to different category. The tortoise opened its mouth to answer them and fell to the ground.[10] Vasubhagabhaṭṭa's tradition of the *Pañchatantra* mentions that the jackal couple ate the flesh of the fallen tortoise.[11]

This story is carved in four scenes here (Pls. 47.2 & 47.3). The first scene on the right side shows a lake indicated by wavy lines. In it is the tortoise. There are two geese, one picking something with its beak and another looking back at the tortoise (Pl. 47.2). On the bank of the lake is a jackal, also looking at the tortoise. The second scene at the centre shows a goose bringing a creeper holding in its beak (Pl. 47.2). The third scene shows two geese holding the creeper and the tortoise hanging from the centre of the creeper. Below is the fourth scene depicting the jackal eating the fallen tortoise (Pl. 47.3). The tortoise has already been cut by the jackal and is disfigured.

The associatian of the jackal in this panel indicates that the version followed here is similar to that of the Sanskrit *Tantropākhyāna*, the Tamil *Tanropākhyāna* and the *Tantrī*.

4. Self-Defeating Forethought

This story is narrated by Vishṇusharmā as follows.[12] In a certain place lived a hill-man. He went out for hunting. On the way he met a boar. Immediately he drew an arrow as far as his ear and shot the boar. In turn the boar angrily tore the hill-man's stomach with a pointed fang. The man dies. After killing the hunter, the boar also died in pain from the arrow-wound. At this moment a starving jackal came there. When it discovered that the boar and the hunter were dead, he was very happy because the fate had provided that unexpected store of food. Then he thought of eating in such a way that he could live on them for many days. He started eating the sinew wrapped round the bow-tip. When the gut was torn, the bow-tip pierced the roof of its mouth. The jackal died from its pain.

Durgasiṁha's narration of this story is as follows.[13] A man living in the forest was standing after killing an elephant. Then a python came suddenly. The man finding no way to escape, shot the python with a poisoned arrow. In turn the python killed the hunter before it died. A jackal which had no food for several days came there in search of food, and found three dead bodies. It was very happy and thought that the elephant provides food for six months, huge serpent for four months, man for three months and should eat immediately only the string tied to the bow. When it bit and tore the bowstring, the bow became straight and pierced into its skull, killing it immediately.

Near the left end of the panel (Pl. 47.4) is the hunter carrying a stick on his shoulder from which a rabbit is suspended. At the right end is the dead elephant. The hunter is standing beside it. At the centre the hunter is playing flute. Below, he is lying dead on his back. A large snake (python) is carved on the upper side. Again at the left end is the jackal in the act of biting the bowstring. The jackal is partly mutilated.

The above panel contains an elephant not boar. The hunter dies because of the snakebite. The elephant and the snake indicate that the version followed here is similar to that of Durgasiṁha.

5. The Brahman and the Crab

Durgasiṁha describes the story of "The Brahman and the Crab" as follows.[14] Once a Brahman was on his pilgrimage. On the way he saw a crab suffering in a dried up lake. The Brahman lifted it with affection and put in his water vase. He visited several holy places carrying it with him. One day, on his way, he was relaxing under a tree. As he was tired he fell asleep. A crow sitting on the tree expressed to the snake, which was its friend, its desire of eating the Brahman's eyes. The snake came forward to help it to fulfil its desire. It bit the Brahman and injected its poison into his body. The Brahman died. The crab was struck with grief for its master's death. Then the crow flew to fall on the Brahman. Being fickle minded by nature it went to the water vase and put its neck in it for drinking water. Taking advantage of this chance the crab caught hold of its enemy's neck in its claws and started pressing hard. Unable to escape from its grip the crow started crying. Hearing the crow's cry the snake came near the vase, saw the crab cutting its neck and asked about what was happening. Then the crab told that the snake had killed its master and now it was killing snake's friend. If it removed the poison from the body of its master, it would leave snake's friend unhurt. The snake sucked the poison immediately from the Brahman's body. Then the Brahman got his life restored and the crab let the crow go.

Vishṇusharmā's narration of this story differs to some extent. According to him the Brahman's mother gave him a crab to take with him for his company on journey. Crow does not appear in this version. Here crab fought with the snake and killed it.[15]

The story is narrated in a single scene (Pl. 47.5). The Brahman is sleeping under a tree. His umbrella is kept against the tree. The snake with spread out hood is issuing from a hole in the trunk of the tree. The water vase is carved in the upper portion. The crow is sitting on its rim. The crab in the vase is holding the neck of the crow with its claws. Only its claws are seen above the vase.

The above panel indicates that the story followed here is similar to that of Durgasiṁha.

6. The Brahman, the Thief, and the Ghost

The story of "The Brahman, the Thief, and the Ghost" occurs in Vishṇusharmā's *Pañchatantra* as follows.[16] In a certain place lived a Brahman. He lived on presents given by others. Some one gave him two calves. The Brahman fed them with butter, oil and other things which he got in begging. The cows grew plump. Once a thief saw them and thought of stealing them. One night he took a rope and went towards Brahman's house. On the way he saw a ghost and enquired about him. The ghost introduced himself and asked about the thief. The thief introduced himself and told that he was on the way to steal the cows of the Brahman. Then the ghost told him that he was going to eat the same Brahman. So they went together to the Brahman's house. They hid in a safe place in the house and waited for a chance. The ghost went near the Brahman to eat him. Then the thief told him not to proceed further until he takes away the cows. Then the ghost told him that that will disturb the Brahman and hence he would eat him before he wakes up. Then they started pleading that each of them would proceed first. Hearing this heated argument the Brahman woke up and saw them. The thief told the Brahman that the ghost had come to eat him. The ghost told him that the thief had come to steal his cows. Then the Brahman remembered a prayer to his favourite god and saved his life from the ghost, and then took a club and saved the cows from the thief. This story also occurring in Durgasiṁha's *Pañchatantra* is similar.[17]

This story is depicted in a single scene in the panel (Pl. 47.6). On the left side is a cot, over which the Brahman and his wife are sleeping. The wife is in the front and the Brahman is behind her. The lady has lifted up her head a little supporting with the right hand. The Brahman has risen up more, but still supporting his body by keeping his right hand on the bed. His left hand is near his mouth expressing shock over the intruders. The couple, woken up by the disturbance of the intruders are looking at them. The ghost, holding a sword in the left hand and another weapon in uplifted right hand is approaching the couple. The thief is standing near the cow holding a club in the left hand and his raised right hand is pointing towards the ghost telling him not to proceed further.

The thief in this panel is holding a staff but the literature mentions that he carries a rope.

7. The Monkey and the Crocodile

Vishṇusharmā narrates the story of "The Monkey and the Crocodile" as follows.[18] A monkey lived on a great rose-apple tree on the shore of the sea. One day a crocodile came out of the sea, reached the tree and rested in the soft sand. The monkey said to the crocodile that he was his guest, threw him the rose-apples and prayed him to eat them. The fruits were like nectar. The crocodile ate them and enjoyed a long and pleasant conversation with the monkey and returned to his home. The monkey and the crocodile assembled every day under the rose-apple tree and spent the time happily.

One day the crocodile did not eat the rose-apples but took them home and gave them to his wife. His wife asked him from where he was getting such fruits which were like nectar. The crocodile told her that he had a good friend, a monkey, who gave him those fruits. Then she said that if any one ate such nectar fruits every day, his heart must have turned to nectar. She told him to bring the monkey's heart, and she would eat it. Then she would never grow old or sick, and would be a delightful wife for him. The crocodile objected this idea because the monkey was dear to him, like his adopted brother and gave them fruits every day. He cannot kill him. Then she said that he had never refused her before. So she was sure that it was a she-monkey and he loved her and spent whole day with her. That is why he was not giving his wife what she wanted. Unless she ate the heart of the monkey she would starve herself to death. When the crocodile saw how determined his wife was, he went to visit the monkey with the idea of killing him in the mind.

The monkey who had missed his friend asked him why he had not been there that long time, and why he was not speaking cheerfully. The crocodile replied that his wife scolded him saying that he was living daily at a friend's expense and made him no return. He had not invited him to his house. She regarded the monkey as her brother-in-law. So he should take him home and they would make some return for his kindness. If he did not take him home his wife would die. So the crocodile requested the monkey to go to his home, with him. Then the monkey said that monkeys lived on trees and crocodile's home was in the water, how could he go there. The crocodile said that he could climb on his back and travel comfortably without fear. Hearing this the monkey sat on the back of the crocodile and proceeded. When the crocodile was swimming in the deep sea the monkey was terribly frightened. His body was completely drenched by the sea waves. He told the crocodile to go slow. Hearing this the crocodile thought that the monkey was in his power. He should tell him his propose, so that he could pray to his favourite god. He told him that he had deceived him and brought him to his death, because his wife told him to do so. The monkey asked what he had done to him or to her to take such a decision. The crocodile replied that those nectar fruits tasted very sweet, and his wife developed liking to eat his heart. Then the intelligent monkey said that why he did not tell him on the shore. He had kept another sweet heart in a hole in the rose-apple tree. He could have brought it. The heart which he had then with him was not of much use to her. Going to her without sweet heart was in vain. Then the crocodile asked the monkey to give him the other heart and his wife would eat it and give up starving. So he turned back and swam towards the rose-apple tree. When he came to the shore the monkey hopped and jumped farther and climbed up the rose-apple tree and thought that his life was saved. When the crocodile asked for the heart, the monkey scolded him saying that he was a traitor. He asked how could anyone have two hearts. He told him to go home and never come back under the rose-apple tree.

Durgasiṁha's version of this story differs from that of Vishṇusharmā in the following aspects.[19] The wife of the crocodile told him that she was suffering from monkey-disease and it would be cured only by eating monkey's heart. The crocodile persuaded the monkey to go with him by telling that in the midst of the sea was a beautiful island where there were young beautiful unmarried she-monkeys in need of a companion. The fruits in that island were sweet and old were becoming young if they ate those fruits. When the crocodile revealed that it was taking the monkey to its house to give its heart to his wife to eat, the monkey replied that it had kept its heart on a branch in the tree.

This story is depicted in two scenes (Pl. 47.7). The first scene on the right side shows the crocodile with the monkey on its back moving toward its home. Water is indicated by waves and a tortoise. The second scene on the left side shows the crocodile near the tree and the monkey climbing over the tree. The monkey has turned back and opened its mouth in the act of scolding the crocodile.

8. The Loyal Mongoose

The story of "The Loyal Mongoose" is narrated by Vishṇusharmā as follows.[20] In a certain town lived a Brahman. His wife had a son and a mongoose. She treated the mongoose also like a son, but she did not trust it, because it was an animal. One day she covered her son in bed, told her husband to take care of the boy, and went out with a water-jar to bring water. When she had gone, the Brahman also went out to beg food. Then a black snake crawled towards the baby's cradle. The mongoose saw its natural enemy and feared that it would kill its baby brother, and fell upon the vicious serpent. It fought with it and tore it into pieces. It was happy with its own heroism. It ran blood trickling from its mouth, to meet the mother, to show its heroic deed. But when the mother saw its bloody mouth and its excitement, she feared that it must have eaten her baby boy. She got angry and dropped that water-jar upon it, without thinking what had happened. The jar killed the mongoose the moment that it struck it. Then she ran to the cradle and found the baby safe and sound, and pieces of a great black snake near the cradle. Then she started crying because she had killed the mongoose without knowing that it had saved her son's life.

The narration of this story by Durgasiṁha is similar with some variations.[21] Here the Brahman came to know that the king was making donations, tied the mongoose with a long rope near the baby's cradle and went to the king to receive donation. When he returned, he saw the mongoose smeared with blood. He smashed its head. In haste he went inside and saw the child sleeping happily in the cradle and dead serpent in several pieces below. Then he returned to the mongoose, poured water on it and discovered that it was dead.

The panel depicting this story is very long and contains seven scenes (Pl. 47.8). The first scene on the right end shows the cradle suspended from the ceiling. The boy is sitting in the cradle holding a rope. Below is seen the snake torn into pieces and a bamboo fan used for winnowing corn. The second scene at the left end shows the sacrificial fire flanked by two men. The Brahman who has performed the sacrifice is departing from there. He is seen next to them, in walking posture, holding umbrella in the right hand and a water vase in the left hand. The third scene carved in the middle shows two ladies pounding grains in a mortar with pedestal with two long wooden pestles. One of them is the wife of the Brahman. The fourth scene shows her carrying the grain or flour, after pounding, in the basket in the left hand and the pestle in the right hand, and going towards her house. In her front is the mongoose, which she is hitting with the pestle. The fifth scene shows her crying with untied hair, holding left hand over the head and walking towards her house. The last scene shows her holding the mongoose in her hands. This she does after knowing the fact that the mongoose has saved the life of the boy.

The above panel depicts some variations from the versions of Vishṇusharmā and Durgasiṁha. Here the lady goes to pound grain and kills the mongoose with the pestle used for pounding. The Brahman goes out for performing a sacrifice (*yajña*).

NOTES AND REFERENCES

1. M.H. Krishna, 1935. *Annual Report of the Mysore Archaeological Department for the year 1931*, pp. 58-62. H.R. Raghunatha Bhat, 1977, "Balligave: Ondu Samskritika Adhyayana," in *Karnataka Bharati*, Quarterly Journal of the Karnatak University, Dharwad, Vol. 10, Issue 2, pp. 66-79; Balligave—Its History and Antiquities, unpublished thesis submitted to the University of Mysore, Mysore, pp. 541-43.
2. I am thankful to Mr. S.K. Vasudeva, Conservation Assistant, of the Directorate of Archaeology and Museums in Karnataka, for drawing my attention towards these two panels.
3. M. Seshadri, 1970. "Karnataka Silpadalli Panchatantra Kathegalu," in *Savinenapu* (The Late Prof. T.S. Venkannayya Commemoration Volume), edited by Kuvempu, Ta. Vem. Smaraka Granthamale, Mysore, pp. 581-84.
4. Arthur W. Ryder, *The Panchatantra*, Bombay, 1949 (1986 impression), p. 21.
5. N. Anantharangachar, ed. *Durgasimha Virachitam Karnataka Panchatantram*, Sharada Mandira, Mysore, 1973, pp. 25-26.
6. Ryder, *op. cit.*, p. 50.
7. Anantharangachar, *op. cit.*, p. 57.
8. Ryder, *op. cit.*, pp. 116-17.
9. Anantharangachar, *op. cit.*, pp. 112-17.
10. Varadaraja Huilgol, *Durgasimhana Panchatantra Samikshe*, Sahitya Bhandara, Hubli, 1976, p. 161.
11. *Ibid.*, p. 161.
12. Ryder, *op. cit.*, pp. 185-86.
13. Anantharangachar, *op. cit.*, pp. 221-22.
14. *Ibid*, pp. 219-20.
15. Huilgol, *op. cit.*, p. 167.
16. Ryder, *op. cit.*, pp. 273-74.
17. Anantharangachar, *op. cit.*, pp. 181-82.
18. Ryder, *op. cit.*, pp. 303-08.
19. Anantharangachar, *op. cit.*, pp. 203-06.
20. Ryder, *op. cit.*, pp. 341-42.
21. Anantharangachar, *op. cit.*, pp. 135-39.

48
A RARE IMAGE OF DHARAṆENDRA

DEVENDRA HANDA

The *yaksha* of Pārśvanātha, the twenty-third Jaina Tīrthaṅkara, is known as Pārśva and Dharaṇendra in the Śvetāmbara and Digambara traditions respectively. This *yaksha* is one of the most important amongst the members of his class. Both the Śvetāmbara and Digambara books lay down that he should be depicted as having snake-hoods, snake-attribute and a tortoise as his vehicle but differ in details.[1]

Hemachandra describes him as elephant-headed, riding a tortoise, having a canopy of snake-hoods and holding ichneumen, snake, citrus and snake in his four hands:

Tattīrthabhūrabhūt-pārśva-yakshaḥ kūrmarathaṇ śitiḥ /
Gajānanaḥ phaṇiphaṇāchhattra-śobhī chaturbhujaḥ /
Nakulāhī vāma-dorbhyāṁ bījapūroragau punaḥ / /[2]

Sūtradhāra Maṇḍana has only repeated what has been said by Hemachandra—

Pārśvaḥ syāt-Pārśvanāthasya kūrmārūḍho gajānanaḥ /
Bījapūroragaṁ nāgaṁ nakulaṁ śyāmavarṇakaḥ /[3]

While endorsing other features, the *Nirvāṇakalikā* prescribes citrus and snake in the right hands and money-bag and snake in the left—

Pārśvayakshaṁ gajamukhamurga-phaṇa-maṇḍita-śirasaṁ
śyāma-varṇaṁ kūrma-vāhanaṁ chaturbhujaṁ
bījapurakoraga-yute-dakshiṇa-pāṇiṁ nakulāhi-yuta-vāma-pāṇiṁ cheti.[4]

Padmānanda Mahākāvya, however, differs slightly and lays down that the elephant-headed, snake-hooded and the tortoise-marked *yaksha* Pārśva should hold a *mātuliṅga* (citrus) and *gadā* (mace or club) in his right hands and *nakula* (ichneumen) and *sarpa* (snake) in his left hands—

Mātuliṅga-gadā-yuktau bibhrāṇo dakshiṇau karau /
Vāmau nakula-sarpāṅkau kūrmāṅkah kuñjarāṇaḥ / /
Mūrdhni phaṇi-chchhatro yakshaḥ Pārśvośita-dyutiḥ /[5]

Many other Śvetāmbara texts also repeat these prescriptions.[6] The *Aparājitapṛichchhā*, however, enjoins that a devotee desiring peace should depict Pārśva like a serpent holding bow, arrow, *bhṛiṇḍi* (a wavy dagger?), hammer, fruit and *vara* (protection affording pose) in his six hands—

Pārśvo dhanurbāṇa-bhṛiṇḍi-mudgaraścha phalaṁ varaḥ /
sarpa-rūpaḥ śyāma-varṇaḥ kartavyaḥ śāntimichchhitā / /[7]

Pratishṭhāsārasaṅgraha names Pārśva's *yaksha* as Dharaṇa and describes him as black in colour and riding a tortoise— *Pārśvasya Dharaṇo yakshaḥ śyāmāṁgaḥ kūrmavāhanaḥ.*[8] *Pratishṭhāsāroddhāra* lays down that he should hold snakes in his upper two hands and noose and *vara* in the others—

Ūrdhva-dvi-hasta-dhṛita Vāsukirudbhaṭādhaḥ
savyānya-pāṇi-phaṇi-pāśa-vara-praṇantā /
Śrī-Nāgarāja-Kakuda-Dharaṇobhara-nīlaḥ
Kūrmāśrito bhajatu Vāsuki-maulirijyām / /[9]

Quoting T.N. Ramachandran, M.N.P. Tiwari refers to an anonymous south Indian text which prescribes vase, noose, goad and citrus in the four hands of the *yaksha.*[10]

There is no evidence of the independent images of Pārśva or Dharaṇa *yaksha* belonging to a period earlier than the 8th century A.D.[11] Even later images are not many. The hitherto known earliest images are from Osian—one carved on the bracket of a pillar just in front of the door of the *gūḍhamaṇḍapa* of the Mahāvīra Temple[12] and other on the left of the *jaṅghā-karṇa* of the sanctum.[13] The former is seated in *lalitāsana* on a lotus pedestal under the canopy of a three-hooded snake, holding a bow in the left hand and an arrow in the right.[14] The *yaksha* seems to have been seated on a tortoise[15] as prescribed in the texts. The image may be dated to *circa* eighth century A.D. on stylistic grounds. The latter looks like a dwarfish figure wearing a *patrakuṇḍala, ekāvalī, yajñopavīta, kaṭisūtra, nūpuras,* a lower garment and a scarf whose free ends fall near the feet. The right hand seems to have been held in *abhaya*[16] while the left one is completely mutilated. The head is canopied by locks of hair dressed in cork-screw curls simulating a seven-hooded cobra.[17] Slightly later example is known from the northern wall of the *maṇḍapa* of the tenth century Digambara temple of Mālādevī at Gyaraspur in Madhya Pradesh showing the *yaksha* standing on a lotus seat in the triple flexion pose under the five-hooded canopy with his right hand disposed in *abhaya* and the left holding a *kamaṇḍalu.*[18] Pārśva on the southern entrance of the sanctum of the Lunavasahi Temple, Mt. Abu, belonging to early twelfth century A.D., holds in his three extant hands *varadāksha* and snakes.[19]

The Prince of Wales Museum, Bombay, also possesses two independent four-handed images of the *yaksha*. Both are canopied by three hoods. One shows the *yaksha* on his vehicle tortoise, holding *varada*, snake, snake and noose and the other, ascribable to *circa* twelfth century A.D., is seated in *lalitāsana* holding in his four hands a lotus with stalk, *gadā,* noose or snake and *varada.*[20]

In one example, we find Dharaṇendra represented in bronze also. Housed in the Seattle Art Museum in America it shows the richly bejewelled *yaksha* "seated in *sattva-paryaṅkāsana* on a lotus which rests on a tiered pedestal. The right hand of the figure is broken, but the left holds a *vīja-pūraka*. A multiheaded serpent canopy[21] serves as a halo as seen in images of Pārśvanātha."[22] This Deccan bronze may be dated to the late ninth century A.D. on stylistic grounds.

We thus see that all the extant images show the *yaksha* as human-faced only and none as elephant-faced as enjoined in the Śvetāmbara texts. All these images show the *yaksha* either as two-handed or as four-handed. We have noted above that all the texts describe the *yaksha* as four-handed with the exception of *Aparājitapṛichchhā* which refers to the six attributes in his hands. In two instances only has the *yaksha* been depicted with his vehicle, the tortoise. The extant examples reveal that he could be depicted with three-, five-, or seven-hooded canopies. The attributes in his hands, too, are not always the same as prescribed in the iconographical texts.

No independent image of Pārśvanātha's *yaksha* is known from any other region. This paucity endows every new discovery with a great importance. So we publish here a new image discovered by us from the village Badli in the Jhajjar tahsil of district Rohtak, Haryana.[23]

Badli (28°36'N and 76° 45'E) is situated on the Jhajjar-Najafgarh road, about 40 km west of Delhi, only a few km from the border of the Union Territory of Delhi.[24] The whole village is studded with old *havelīs* and is partially located on a mound which yields old relics from time to time. Some sculptures were recovered from an old well some years ago and some are placed in the Śiva Temple in the village. The latter include a beautiful almost complete image of Sūrya and Gaṇeśa and fragmentary reliefs of Sūrya, Vishṇu, Mahishāsuramardinī, Śiva-liṅga, Nandī, architectural pieces etc.[25] They all belong to the early medieval period. Some carved pieces are fixed besides the outer wall of Chaudhary Randhir Singh's *havelī* and have thickly been coated with whitewash. They include fragments of the images of Vishṇu, Umā-Maheśvara, door jamb and Dharaṇendra, the last of which is being described and discussed here.

That Badli was an important village with Jaina population is indicated by its references in the *Kharataragachchha-Bṛihadgurvāvali* which gives an authentic account of the Jaina *āchāryas* of Kharataragachchha from the eleventh to the fourteenth century A.D.[26] It is said that having obtained the permission of Āchārya Jinachandra, his disciple Vardhamāna came to Delhi and Badli— *Tato guroḥ sammatyā nirgatya katichinmunisameto Ḍhillī-Vādalī-prabhṛiti-deśeshu samāyātaḥ.*[27] Āchārya Jinachandra himself also visited this place in V.S. 1222 (= 1165 A.D.) to set up golden *kalaśas* in the temple of Pārśvanātha-*Saṁ. 1222 Vādalī-nagare Śrī-Pārśvanātha-bhavane vā. Guṇabhadragaṇi-pitāmaha-Lāle-śrāvaka-kārita-sauvarṇa-daṇḍa-kalaśau pratishṭh-āpyāmbikā-śikhara-yogyaṁ sauvarṇa-kalaśaṁ cha pratishṭhāpya, Rudrapallyāṁ vihṛitāḥ.*[28] Reference to the temple of Pārśvanātha shows the popularity of this Tīrthaṅkara at Badli.

The image under reference shows Dharaṇendra as a hybrid figure, half-human, half-snake (Pl. 48.1). The *yaksha* sits on a *triratha* pedestal under the canopy of nine-hooded snake with serpentine legs entwined artistically with tapering tails falling outwards. Dharaṇendra, the Lord of the Nāga-Kumāra class of semi-divine beings,[29] is appropriately endowed with a cylindrical crown. His right hand, raised to the level of the shoulder, is broken but seems to have been originally disposed in the protection affording pose. The left hand holds a *kalaśa*, water-pot. On his proper right is a diminutive half-human, half-snake female (?) figure in *añjalimudrā* in profile. The snake-hood over her head indicates that she is Padmāvatī, the spouse of the *yaksha*. On the corresponding left side is another hybrid figure in profile with folded hands. At the level of the chest are two small figures, one on either side, holding some musical instrument in their two hands across the chest. On the top corners of the back-slab are shown *vidyādharas*, holding long garlands and hovering in the sky. The two sides of the back-slab are slightly concave but the top is convex. Since the image has been whitewashed repeatedly, the whole image bears a thick encrustation concealing the details of the *yaksha* and other subsidiary figures.

The *yaksha* is two-handed like the early images known from Osian, Gyaraspur and the Deccan. The attributes in the two hands are similar to those of Digambara figure from the Mālādevī Temple. This image, too, is obviously a Digambara one. It, however, betrays the peculiarity of having a nine-hooded canopy and being hybrid, half-human, half-serpent. Stylistically, it may be dated to *circa* tenth century A.D. to which date most of the other images from Badli may be assigned. The importance of this image of Dharaṇendra, unique in form and the first to be discovered from Haryana, cannot be overstated.

NOTES AND REFERENCES

1. B.C. Bhattacharya, *The Jaina Iconography*, 2nd revised edition, Delhi, 1974, p. 83.
2. From *Pārśvanāthacharita* as quoted by Bhattacharya, *ibid.*
3. *Vāstuśāstra* (Mss Jnana-mandir, Baroda), *ibid.*
4. Pādalipta Sūri, *Nirvāṇakalikā* (ed. Mohanlal Bhagwandas, Bombay, 1926), XVIII. 23.
5. Amarachandra Sūri, *Padmānanda Mahākāvya* (also called *Chaturviṁśati-Jina-Charitra*), Mss, L.D. Institute of Indology, Ahmedabad, Appendix-Pārśvanātha, XCII-XCIII as quoted by M.N.P. Tiwari, *Jaina Pratimāvijñāna*, Varanasi, 1981, 232.
6. Hemachandra, *Trishashṭiśalākāpurushacharitra* (GOS, Baroda), IX. 3, 362-63; *Devatāmūrtiprakaraṇa* (ed. U.M. Sāṅkhyatīrtha, Calcutta, 1936) VII. 62; Maṇḍana, *Rūpa-Maṇḍana* (ed. Balram Srivastava, Varanasi, V.S. 2011) VI. 20; Bhavadeva Sūri, *Pārśvanāthacharitra* (eds. H.G. Das and Bechar Das, Varanasi, 1911) VII. 827-28; Vardhamāna Sūri, *Āchāra-dinakara* (2 Vols., Bombay, 1923) XXXIV, p. 175 etc. All these texts have been quoted by Tiwari (*loc. cit.*) along with the *Mantrādhirājakalpa* of Sāgarachanda Sūri (Mss, L.D. Institute of Indology, Ahmedabad) III. 47.
7. Bhuvanedeva, *Aparājitapṛichchhā* (ed. P.A. Mankad, GOS, Boroda, 1950), 221.55.
8. Vasunandi, *Pratishṭhāsārasaṅgraha* (Mss, L.D. Institute of Indology, Ahmedabad) as quoted by Tiwari (*loc. cit.*).
9. Āśādhara, *Pratishṭhāsāroddhāra* (ed. Pt. Manoharlal Shastri, Bombay, V.S. 1974), III. 151.
10. Tiwari, *op. cit.*, pp. 232-33.
11. Tiwari (*ibid.*) dates the earliest images to ninth century A.D.
12. Devendra Handa, *Osian: History, Archaeology, Art & Architecture*, Delhi, 1984, p. 189, Pl. 145. We had mistaken it with Pātāla yaksha. Tiwari (*op. cit.*, p. 233) has identified it rightly.
13. Handa, *loc. cit.*, Pl. 144.
14. Tiwari (*loc. cit.*) has not identified the attribute of the right hand and is mistaken in taking the object in the left hand as snake. Bow and arrow have been prescribed in the hands of Pārśva *yaksha*, though in six-handed variety, in the *Aparājitapṛichchhā*.

15. We had earlier mistaken it as dolphin, the vehicle of Pātāla yaksha (Handa, *op. cit.*, p. 189).

16. Tiwari (*loc. cit.*) refers to citrus in this hand.

17. Handa, *op. cit.*, p. 189, Pl. 144.

18. Tiwari, *loc. cit.*

19. *Ibid.*

20. H.D. Sankalia, "Jaina Yakṣas and Yakṣiṇīs", *Bulletin of the Deccan College Research Institute*, Poona, Vol. I, Nos. 2-4; A Ghosh (ed.), *Jaina Art and Architecture*, New Delhi, 1975, Vol. III, p. 566, Pl. 348; Tiwari, *loc. cit.*

21. Five-headed.

22. Ghosh, *op. cit.*, p. 552, Pl. 331.

23. We had explored the site in December 1989 along with our friends Dr. Ashvini Agrawal and Dr. Manmohan Kumar.

24. There is another Badli near Delhi on the Delhi-Ambala railway section within the Union Territory of Delhi, quite close to Rohini. So the village Badli in the Jhajjar tahsil is generally called Jhajjar-Badli to avoid confusion.

25. Most of these pieces are still unpublished.

26. Āchārya Jina Vijaya Muni (ed.), *Kharataragachchha-Bṛihadgurvāvali*, Bharatiya Vidya Bhavan, Bombay, V.S. 2013, Introduction, p. 6.

27. *Ibid.*, p. 1.

28. *Ibid.*, p. 20.

29. Umakant P. Shah, *Jaina-Rūpa-Maṇḍana*, Vol. I, New Delhi, 1987, p. 3.

49

CONCEPTS BEHIND THE ORIGIN OF THE DHARMACHAKRA STUPA AT SANGHOL

G.S. GAUR

The Sanghol Mahāstupa of Hiuen Tsang description,[1] partly excavated by R.S. Bisht in 1968-69,[2] was fully exposed in 1984-85 by G.B. Sharma, K.K. Rishi et al., of the Department of Cultural Affairs, Archaeology & Museum, Punjab. Only lower brick courses of this stupa are now preserved; albeit its complete plan is available. Some Hūṇa coins coupled with other archaeological indicators, both from the contemporary deposits and the surface, suggest not only the presence of the Hūṇas but their authority as well. And, this suggestive evidence could well indicate that the superstructure of this stupa may have been destroyed by the invading hordes of Hūṇas in the 5-6th century A.D.

Restricting the scope only to the Sanghol stupa with Dharmachakra Plan, we propose to delineate in this paper various stages of time and space manipulation by man for architectural purpose in the Vedic and later and post-Vedic period. This will, in particular, be seen how the concept of time and its divisions have played major role in it.

Before coming to the actual theme of the paper, a few words about ancient Sanghol are perhaps necessary.

Sanghol (30°47' N and 76°23' E) is 40 km west of Chandigarh on the Chandigarh-Ludhiana road in district Ludhiana, Punjab. Located on the Uttarāpatha, Sanghol has all along been an important playground of continuous human activities and cultures right from the Late Harappan (Bara) to the recent times. But the play of human endeavours and spirit has possibly been at its best (only) during the Kushan period as revealed at Sanghol. It was in this period when the Mahāstupa at Sanghol was built.

The Kushan township at Sanghol was divisible into three distinct though well-knit and integrated parts—fortified citadel, main city and peripheral religious zone.[3] To the north of the main city stood once majestic Kushan citadel with provision of triple moat. It was in the peripheral zone, away from but contiguous to the main city that all religious edifices including stupas and monasteries were built. Not only the exposed Mahāstupa and two stupas of smaller dimensions along with extensive monasteries, but also some still buried and others totally or partly destroyed stupas have been located in this zone. There seems to be similarity between the religious edifices found at Sanghol and those described by Hiuen Tsang who says:[4]

> ....and reached the country called "She-to-tu-lu". It was about 2000 li in circuit, ...and its capital was 17 or 18 li in circuit, ... In the capital there were about ten monasteries, but they were desolate and the Brethern were very few. About three li to the south-east of the capital was an Ashokan Tope about 200 feet high....

She-to-tu-lu is identifiable with Sanghpura or Sanghol and the stupa to be the one which was originally constructed by Asoka. It has to be made absolutely clear that no remains, whatsoever, of Asokan period have been found in and around the stupa at Sanghol. The possibility is that the Asokan (mud?) stupa, if at all existed, may have become nucleus or core of the later stupa which was expanded and built during the Kushan period. Such evidences elsewhere in the country are not wanting.

It would possibly not be out of place to mention here that a hoard of 117 stone members of the railing including sculptured pillars, crossbars, etc., once possibly enclosing the stupa, were found from a nearby pit. Some of the sculptures, particularly *śālabhañjikās,* are epitome of female beauty and masterpieces of Indian art.

As regards the architectural plan of the stupa, it is like the Dharmachakra or *rathachakra* (spoked-wheel) within a 17-m square platform. It had three concentric circles of brick masonry with intervening spaces divided by radiating spokes of similar brick masonry at regular intervals. All three circles—inner, middle and outer—have 12, 24 and 32 radiating spokes with similar number of intervening spaces, respectively. Almost triangular spaces between spokes were filled with earth and brickbats to form a solid structure. The core of the stupa consists of a thick circular wall of brick masonry-filled with earth in which a steatite relic casket bearing an inscription in Kharoshthi of the first century B.C.--first century A.D. was found. The inscription reads Upasaka, Ayabhadasa. The reading suggests that the casket belonged to an *Upasaka* or lay-disciple named Āryabhadra.

The brick sizes usually are 33x22x5 cm and 30x20x6 cm Staircases were attached to the platform on all four sides. The stupa is surrounded on the three sides by an extensive monastic complex and few votive stupas. At a distance of about 100 m from the stupa was a Kushan well in the south.

We shall now discuss various concepts behind the origin of the Dharmachakra stupa.

The basic premise is that the Dharmachakra stupa is a descendant of the *rathchakrachiti* which is one of the Chitis where the ritual of Somayāya was performed in Vedic period. Chitis of various form have been unearthed in some archaeological excavations, namely Kausāmbi, Purola, Sanghol etc. The architectural form of this Chiti must have undergone several suitable changes and modifications before it was adopted by Buddhists in the stupa architecture. The stupa with the *rathachakra* plan was a Buddhist borrowal from Vedic people.

Distinguished by cyclic movement (chhando-gati), the Chakra symbolises the Sun or Time (Kāla chakra), Cosmos (Bhava chakra), life (Jivana chakra) and the transcendent creative power (Brahma chakra). The number of spokes may vary as 3, 5, 6, 12 etc. depending on the varying division of time units in the year which is conceived as Kala chakra.

In order to decide the right time for Vedic sacrifice, need was felt to work out some norms which, in turn, may have given the initial impulse for astronomical observations. In fact, these rituals (sacrifices) mark the beginning of abstract and speculative thoughts in ancient India. And these Chitis (Yajnasālas) were possibly the first laboratories of mental devices to comprehend concepts basic to the quest for knowledge, namely, what is whole? what is part of whole? what is principal? what is subsidiary? what is the original form? what is the variation? etc.

In *Vedanga Jyotisha*, it is remarked that the Vedas arose for the purpose of sacrifices and sacrifices are enjoined according to the order of the time.

As regards the construction to an altar (Chiti) in the form of a wheel, the simple *rathachakrachiti* without spokes in the first stage and an elaborate Sararathachakra Chiti with spokes in the second (stage) were constructed. The Vedic people had devised geometrical methods by which squares could be turned into circles and the vice versa. Baudhāyana and Āpastamba Sutras clearly illustrate these methods.

References quoted below would show that the concept of Time and its division as (symbolically) applied to the Sanghol stupa were also present in the seed form in the Vedic literature.

In Ṛgveda (Rv.I.35.6)[5] three spheres are mentioned. These three regions of space are called in the Ṛgveda as avama (lower), madhyama (central) and parama (upper).

Nāsatyas are said to be the three wheels of (your) triangular car in the Ṛgveda (Rv.1.34.6).[6] Ṛgveda enumerates number of sets of three, namely, *trivṛta ratha*, *tri chakrah*, etc. *Satapatha Brāhmaṇa* indicates the drawing of three concentric circles, each with a larger metre.

There is further reference in the Ṛgveda that the pradhis (segments of a circle) are twelve, the wheel is one, three are the axles (nābhī), but who knows it? Within are collected 360 spokes, which are, as it were, moveable and immovable (Rv.1.164.48).[7]

The Ṛgveda further states: The wheel of *ṛta* has twelve spokes; it revolves round the heavens; O Agni! in this (wheel) seven hundred and twenty sons in pairs abide.... One wheel and twelve rims (of the wheel) and three naves ...; in that (wheel i.e. year) are placed together three hundred and sixty were unstable nails (Rv.I.164.11.-13).[8]

Thus, metaphorically, a year is divided in three, five or six seasons, twelve months, 360 days and 720 days and nights (when calculated separately).

The twelve-spoked wheel is said to be divided into 720 equal parts and, thus, the concept of half-a-degree emerged (Rv.I.164.11).[9]

The Ṛgvedic Aryans had already evolved and conceptualized the sexagesimal system which is the basis of modern clock, and the same system, as we shall see, governs the architecture including plan of the Sanghol stupa.

Briefly, this would be summarized in the following words.

The circle is at first divided into 60 equal parts by arpitas or khīlas (at a displacement of 6° each) and then each division is further divided into six equal parts by putting five śaṅkus between the two khilas (or two-anpitas) each. Thus, each śaṅku corresponds to an angular displacement of 1°. This can be visualized in our twelve-hour clocks, which have twelve major divisions (Pradhis) I, II, III...XII; in all 60 divisions round-the-clock each representing one minute (khīlas) or arpitas. A rotation through 6° corresponds to one minute; by the use of 5 saṅkus between the two-minute marks one can have an angle equal to 1°.[10]

The view that the sexagesimal system of degrees, minutes and seconds used by Ptolemy was of Babylonian origin does not appear to be true. As stated elsewhere the Ṛgvedic Aryans had fully conceptualized this system.

If we now compare the divisions of time as enshrined in the Vedic literature and those symbolically available in the Sanghol Mahāstupa, it becomes evident that the Sanghol stupa with rathachakra-plan was conceived as the year-wheel (*Kālachakra*). There concentric circles of the stupa are represented by three spheres of space. Twelve (12) and Twenty-four (24) spokes in the inner and middle circles of the stupa stand, respectively, for Twelve (12) months and Twenty four ardhamāsas (24) of a year which, as stated, was conceived as the year-wheel. We shall now see the symbolic meaning of the Thirty-two (32) spokes of the outermost circle. Thirty-two spokes are indicative of days of a month including the additional time-difference resulting from the calculation of the intercalary month which results from the varied movement of the Sun (tropical year) and the Moon (lunar year).

Before describing how the number '32' after necessary computation was arrived at, some references to the intercalary month seem necessary.

In Ṛgveda (I.164.15),[12] it is said: 'They say that the 7th of those that are born together is born of one; there are only six twin sages born of the gods'. Here, there is reference to seasons, six of which have two months each, the 7th has only one (viz. 13th or intercalary month) and that the 13th month is not fit for religious rites.

The Vedic Saṁhitas and Brāhmaṇas speak of a 13th month which was intercalated. About Varuṇa, the Ṛgveda (Rg.I.24.8.)[13] says, 'He knows the twelve months with their progency (the days) and also the month that is added'.

The Taittiriya Saṁhita (IV.6.7.9-2)[14] refers to a year of twelve months and also of 13 months.

How and when the month was inserted in the Ṛgvedic times is not clear. What is clear is that one month was added here, therefore, we have two calendars—one a purely sacrificial of 360 days (12 months of 30 days) and another calendar where a month was added in order to bring the year in line with visible astronomical data.

The Atharvaveda (V.35.4)[15] also states that Saṁvatsara has twelve spokes and the months have 30 spokes. Kautilya speaks about the insertion of two intercalary months, one at the end of $2^1/_2$ years and the other at the end of five years.[16]

A year of 360 days was in later times in India called a Sāvana one (from Savana meaning extracting of *soma* juice in a sacrifice) and a month was added after about 30 months to bring the lunar year (of 354 days) in line with the solar (of $365^1/_4$ days).

After calculations, this would appear that, in the course of six years, there becomes a difference of 30 to 32 days, amounting to a month. This month is intercalated as the 13th in the sixth year. We have two suggestions in respect to the measure of the intercalated month, one of 30 days and the other of 35 days. It seems that these suggestions were followed alternatively giving an average intercalation of $^1/_2(30+35) = 32^1/_2$ which is a very close to the value of $31^1/_2$ on the basis of the tropical year measuring $365^1/_4$ days.

Thus, the sixth civil year (360 days) is behind tropical year $31^1/_2$ days. To show the number $31^1/_2$ in any architectural scheme, particularly as spokes in circle, must have posed the problem, for a spoke could not be shown in-a-half. Even if it is so done, its very purpose is defeated. Therefore, a practical solution was found by making $31^1/_2$ as 32 (on-an-average). And, this very number '32' as shown in the forms of spokes in the outer circle of the Sanghol Mahāstupa, represents days including additional intercalary difference in a month of a year.[17] In fact, in later Vedic period, this was clearly stated: 'One divides the area lying between felloe and nave into thirty-two parts'. [(B.S.I.396(V.22).]

Another stupa with a six-spoked circle (wheel) and smaller dimensions was also exposed at Sanghol (SGL-5). Six spokes of this architectural wheel represent six *ritus* of the year-wheel. The number six stands for the six seasons of a year.

It may also be inferred that the number of spokes as 6, 12, 24, etc., denote the solar calendar (tropical year), and may, therefore, have its association with the Theravāda.

It is now seen that the basic idea of this Buddhist stupa, both in its architecture and plan, was enshrined in the Vedic literature, as has been made amply clear through various references quoted in the foregoing. It was, possibly, in the historical period when the concept behind this model or the model itself was borrowed, modified and adopted by Buddhists in their stupa architecture.

How these divisions created by circles and spokes, etc. were useful from the standpoint of engineering and architecture is not within the scope of this paper. This may, however, be said in passing that these divisions were possibly suitable architectural devices through which the load of such a high structure could be equally distributed. To precisely understand it, a separate study is required.

To conclude, the Sanghol stupa with its given plan and architecture was conceived as the time-wheel represented by three circles as three spheres of space, and twelve, twenty-four and thirty-two spokes in the inner, middle and outer circles as twelve months, twenty-four *ardhamāsas* (fortnights) and 32 days (including additional intercarlary monthly time-difference), respectively. The nucleus of the stupa denotes the centre of Absolute power (Parama Brahma) from which emanates time through all manifestations of universe.

NOTES AND REFERENCES

1. Gupta, S.P. (ed.), *Kushan Sculptures from Sanghol,* New Delhi, 1985, pp-22.
2. *Indian Archaeology–A Review,* 1968-69, pp. 25-26.
3. Margabandhu, C. & Gaur, G.S., *Purātattva*-16, 1985-86, pp. 75-73.
4. Gupta, *op. cit.*

5 to 15 are quoted from Swami Satya Prakash Saraswati's Book *Geometry in Ancient India,* Delhi, 1987.

16. *Arthas'āstra* II, Chap. 20 (Des 'akālamāna), p. 109.
17. Swami Satya Prakash Saraswati, *The Critical and Cultural Study of the Satapatha Brāhamana,* Delhi, 1988.

50

ANGA-ŚIKHARA IN THE DECORATIVE SCHEME OF ORISSAN REKHĀ DEUL

GYANENDRA NATH SRIVASTAVA

The curvilinear spire is one of the most dominant architectural forms of medieval Indian temple and the temples having such superstructure are referred to in canonical writings as *rekhā prāsāda* or *rekhā deul,* the latter term particularly used in Orissan texts. This form is found well established in the seventh century A.D. In fact, the style was in vogue about that time in northern India excepting Kashmir.[1] The early *rekhā-śikhara* (Figs. 1 & 4) is noticed till the ninth century A.D. However, in succeeding centuries diverse regional styles were evolved. The innovative experiments on ground plan as well as in elevation of the main shrine and ancillary structures brought about revolutionary changes in the overall design of the temple. Among these innovations, introduction of *aṅga-sikhara,*[2] variously termed as *uraḥ-śriṅga kūṭa-stambha, Nāgara-Kūta,* etc. represents a landmark in the development of *rekhā śikhara* and effective placing of these resulted in a number of regional styles of *nagara* temple. Thus, in Gujarat and Rajasthan it developed in Mahā-Gurjara and Māru-Gurjara styles with aggregate units of *aṅga-śikharas.* Similarly, under the Paramaras of Malwa a new Bhūmija style (Fig. 3) was enunciated. In this style, the *śikhara* has four spines (*latās*) with the usual decoration of *chaitya* motif on the central *rathas* and the quadrants in between the spines are filled with miniature *śikharas* (*kuṭa-stambhas*) of diminishing height arranged in 5 to 7 storeys of 3 to 4 horizontal rows.[3] Another visually spectacular diversification of *rekhā* order is seen under the style floated by the Chandelas of Jejākabhukti, typified by the magnificent group of temples at Khajuraho and epitomised by the Kandariya Mahādeva temple (Fig. 2) there. This is the *uraḥ-śriṅga* type of superstructure with applique overlaps of half miniatures of the *rekhā śikhara* in a rising crescendo.

In the eastern zone, Orissa produced a distinct indigenous *śikhara* of *rekhā* order.[4] In its early phase it is squat and almost vertical in profile (Fig. 4) in contrast to the tapering *śikhara* of

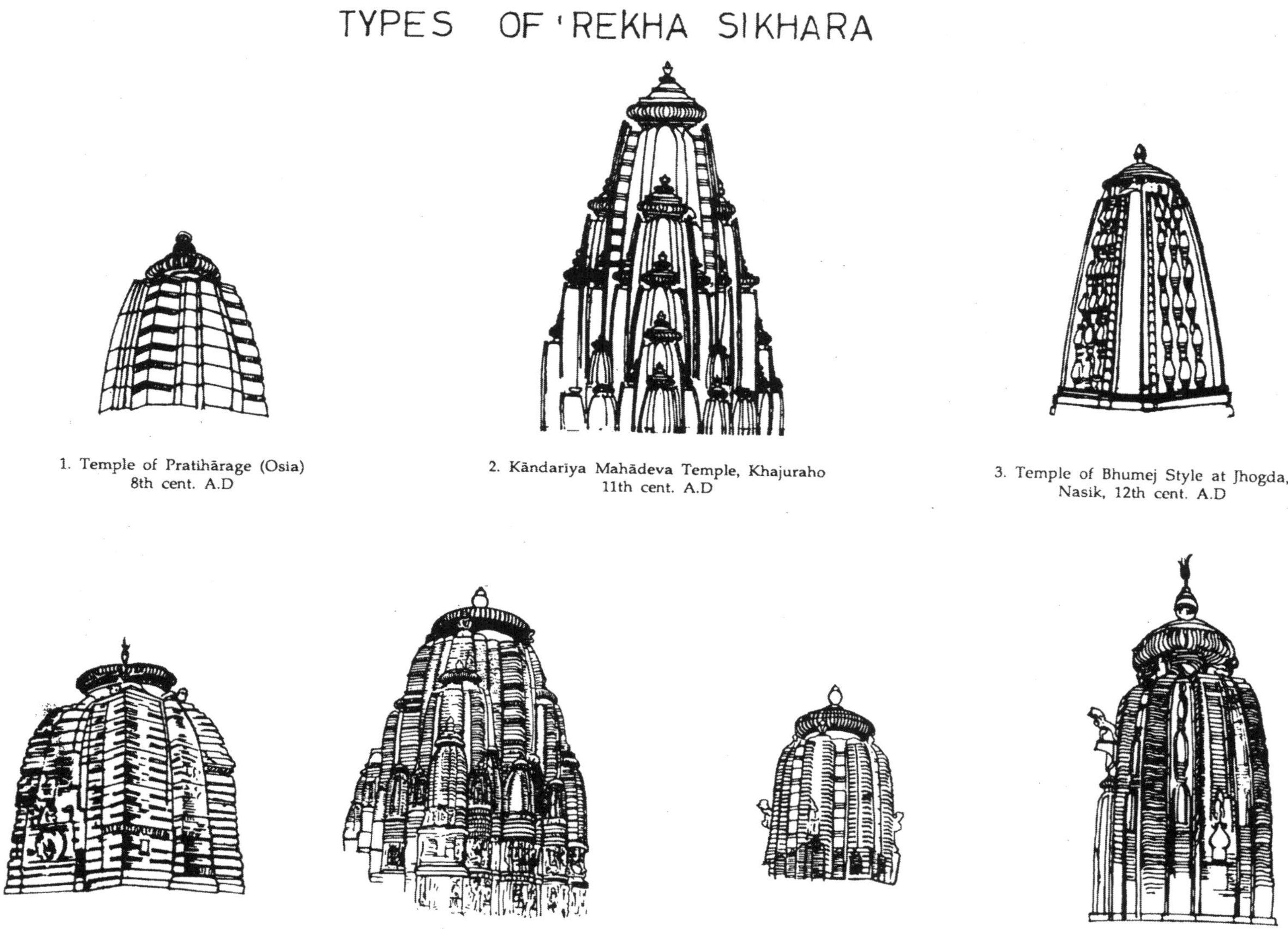

1. Temple of Pratihārage (Osia) 8th cent. A.D

2. Kāndariya Mahādeva Temple, Khajuraho 11th cent. A.D

3. Temple of Bhumej Style at Jhogda, Nasik, 12th cent. A.D

4. Parasuramesvara at Bhubaneswar 7th cent. A.D

5. Rajarani at Bhubaneswar 11th cent. A.D

6. Bramesvara at Bhubaneswar 11th cent. A.D

7. Lingraj at Bhubaneswar 11th cent. A.D

Fig. 1.: Types of *Rekha Sikhara*

Pratihāra age (Fig.1) in upper India. The course of evolution in Orissa was towards a greater elaboration of the plan and elevation and increasing sophistication of the ornamentation. The early temples with a modest sized squat *śikhara* showing naive sculptures and ornaments, mature into elaborate structures of soaring height, embellished with exuberant sculptural and decorative wealth. In this process the decorative scheme of *śikhara* (*gaṇḍi* in Orissan terminology) was much affected by new trends coming from outside Orissa as well as the product of local innovations. Among these innovations the *aṅga-śikhara* motif once greatly dominated the straight-lined profile of Orissan *rekhā śikhara* witnessing obvious extraneous influence in the indigenous style, discernible most boldly in the temples known as Rajarani Dakra-Bhimesvar and Ekamresvar, all in Bhubaneswar.

At Bhubaneswar, a cluster of magnificent temples constitutes virtually a complete record of Orissan temple architecture almost from its beginning to its culmination, and the experiments with *aṅga-śikharas* in various phases can be traced in those temples. It is already mentioned that the most pronounced execution of *aṅga-śikhara* was done in the three temples of the place. Among these the Rajarani (Fig. 5) is well-known for its exotic nature and superb workmanship being conspicuously located amidst the vast stretches of open land while the latter two are devoid of ornamental carvings and sculptural embellishments. The first one, *i.e.* Dekra-Bhimesvar is located near Liṅgarāja temple on the road leading towards ORT Garage, the other one, *i.e.* Ekamresvar is standing inside Liṅgarāja temple complex being lost in the crowd of more than one hundred subsidiary shrines.

In each of the above three temples, *aṅga-śikharas* primarily cluster the base of *śikhara* (*gaṇḍi*). These are like miniature turrets and aligned on the *kaṇika* and *anuratha pagas* and the recess in between both the *pagas,* the latter being an applique work obviously having no basal support. The central facets or *raha pagas* are fashioned with an overlap of two larger *aṅga-śikharas.* The lower one springing directly from the projected eave over the upper *jaṅghā* niche is sharply pronounced while the upper one is broad and flattened; it is leaning to the curvature of *rāha.* These two *aṅga-śikharas* cover about 2/3rd part of *rāha.* The upper part of *rāha* is bare with usual horizontal mouldings, all these temples simulating a common pattern. However it is only the Rajarani temple which attained the graceful and harmonious execution of *aṅga-śikharas* with their staggered elevation.

The above temples stand just like the intruder in the land of Orissa as the temples built in succeeding phases testify a move towards maintaining indigenous tradition. Thus, we find in the Brahmesvar temple (Fig. 6) at Bhubaneswar that the *deul* assumes more traditional *pañcharatha* plan on a square unlike that of the Rajarani tending to be circular with multiple offset projections. The *varaṇḍa* effectively separates the *gaṇḍa* from *bāda.* However, the presence of *aṅga-śikharas* at the base of *gaṇḍi* is the only survival of those outside innovations. These are placed on the *kanikā* and *anuratha pagas,* one on each rising up to the first *bhūmi* of *kanikā* and larger one at the base of *raha paga.* The former have no link with the *bada* but the latter is springing from the *piḍhā* roof of upper-*jaṅghā* niche and thus partly disrupting the division of *varaṇḍa* mouldings. The flattened body of these *aṅga-śikharas* and their location in a limited space on the *anuratha* and *kanika* without any interruption of the continuous contours of the *gaṇḍi,* suggest a tendency for their assimilation in native trend. In the Liṅgarāja temple (Fig. 7) even more emphasis is given to show the divisions of elevation. Here all the component parts of temple elevation are neatly demarcated from each other. In this move, the earlier arrangements of *aṅga-śikharas* noticed at the Brahmesvara are totally changed by removing them from the *kanikā* and the *rāhā* and placing on *anuratha pagas* only along the vertical plane of *gaṇḍi* matching the elevation of spire. In this arrangement the *anuratha* is decorated with a series of four *aṅga-śikharas* which begin a little higher up the *varaṇḍa* (the middle of second *bhūmi* of *kanika*) and diminish in size progressively to the top of *gaṇḍi*. In the later temples either of the above two modes of *aṅga-śikharas*; *viz.* (*i*) that of Brahmesvar type (Fig. 6), aligning horizontally and *(ii)* that of the Liṅgarāja temple (Fig. 7), the vertical placing on *anuratha,* is followed; however that of the Rajarani type remained unpopular though not abandoned completely as its repetition is noticed in the Chateśvara temple at Kishenpur, district Cuttack datable in late thirteenth century A.D.[5]

The above survey of some representative temples of Kaliṅga order shows that the motif of *aṅga-śikhara* entered the land of Orissa as a dominant style; however the attempts at its suitable integration in the typical Orissan *śikhara* are evident in the simultaneous constructions. The course of modification was towards the flattening of sharply projecting *aṅga-śikharas* and placing them in a limited space avoiding any abrupt disruption of usual contours of *gaṇḍi*. Such adjustments were the constructional requirements of Orissan builders who employed the astylar corbelling technique solely for all constructions. This resulted in the starkly vertical build of *gaṇḍi* of the *rekhā deul.* But this vertical rise did not provide any basal support to the projecting *aṅga-śikharas,* therefore we notice that Orissan architect had to add multiple offset projections to the plan of temples having such designs: namely Rājārāṇī, Dakra Bhimeśvara and Ekāmbreśvara. These projections continue in elevation-like buttresses to support the highly pronounced *aṅga-śikharas* those on the *anuratha* and *kaṇika pagas.* Similarly, the lower *aṅga-śikhara* on the *rāhā* was footed upon the projected eave covering the upper *jaṅghā* niche, though much placing disrupted the regular division of verandah but it was necessary for constructional stability. Thus, we see that in adopting the projecting *aṅga-śikhara* style Orissan architect had to commit a lot of changes in the original plan and elevation of a typically established Orissan temple, overruling the canonical norms of the land. Contrary to Orissa, in other parts of India, the pillar, lintel corbel framework was the major technical formula for carriage of load at any given level.[6] In this mode of construction the framework carries the whole load and leaves the wall free for containing the *uraḥ sriṅgas* (in case of Chandela temples) or *kūṭastambhas* (in case of Bhumija ones). The steady recession of *śikhara* provides basal *bhūmis* for erecting successive series; its tapering profile helps to contain those turrets and leaning replicas within the plumb line of perpendicular walls. Further, the multiple offsets and the projected balconies provide a firm footing to those clustering the *śikhara* at its base and overlapping the central facets. However, such arrangements were lacking in Orissan temple and therefore we find that Rājārāṇī temple, which was a product of a follow-up action of the Chandela temples at Khajuraho, could not produce a gradual and harmonious vertical thrust which was achieved in the temples of Chandelas as well as in *Bhumija* type and rather produce a truncated silhouette. On the other hand, the canons of the Orissan architecture developed towards personification of temple forms in *Purusha* and *Prakriti* or male and female and prescribed ritualistic mode of construction, therefore, the component parts of the temple body were executed in detail with their more distinctive placings. In those conditions the scope for the display of *aṅga-śikharas* was limited and therefore those were adjusted accordingly in suitable location.

NOTES AND REFERENCES

1. *Rekhā Prasada* is prolific generally in north India upto Lower Deccan. The Lower Deccan and coastal Andhra were the meeting point where temples of *rekhā* order, typical of north India as well as the south Indian *Vimana* type stand side by side. See K.V. Soundararajan, *Invitation to Indian Architecture*, New Delhi, 1984, pp. 18-19, also the *Indian Temple Styles* by the same author.
2. Though these various terms are identical in common usage but they are applicable in respect of that particular regional style. It is translated into English as 'clinging spire,' 'miniature-turret,' 'shrine-replica,' etc.
3. K. Deva, 'Bhumija temple,' in Pramod Chandra (ed.), *Studies in Indian Temple Architecture*, Bombay 1975, pp. 90-113; Soundararajan called it 'Sringahara', see *ibid.*, p. 20.
4. In the early phase Orissan *rekhā deul* either constructed as a single unit or combined with porch (*jagamohana*) of clerestoryed (*dvichhādya*) roof. In the developed phase the clerestory roof was replaced by a pyramidal roof and such construction was known as *pīḍhā deul*. In a typical Orissan temple both the *rekhā deul* and the *pīḍhā deul* form the component parts of a single architectural scheme. Another important development in Orissan temple architecture was the greater divisions of temple body and defining them by appropriate nomenclature.
5. T.E. Donaldson, *Hindu Temple Art of Orissa*, Vol. II, p. 762. It is also curious that the vertical series of *aṅga-śikharas* upon *anuratha paga* in Jagannātha temple at Puri are found originally absent (as noticed after deplastering) but in plastered condition there were *aṅga-śikharas* in the style of Liṅgaraja temple, therefore, it seems that the fashion of *aṅga-śikharas* in Liṅgaraja style again gained popularity in the late 13th-14th century A.D.
6. This was a highly popular mode of construction. The style is discussed by Fergusson in *History of Indian and Eastern Architecture*, Vol. I, Delhi—Reprint 1967, pp. 314-15 and astylar corbelling, p. 324. The pillar lintel corbel frame is termed by Soundararajan in early *Kaliṅga Art and Architecture*, Delhi, 1984, 24. This mode of roofing is very old and termed in Sanskrit literature as '*Karṇāta*'. See T. Bhattacharya, *The Canons of Indian Art—A Study of Vastuvidya*, Calcutta, 1986, pp. 55-56.

51
KHAR PALACE AT LEH, LADAKH

H.L. RAINA

Ladakh is the northernmost district of Jammu & Kashmir state cradling in the Himalayan ranges between 32° 15' to 36° N latitude and 75° 15' to 80° 15' E longitude. There are many attractions in Ladakh, the most visible being its monasteries, big or small. They can be seen in every village/town, in the isolated passes, on the spurs of cliffs, sometimes crowning peaks of hills. The choice for such difficult and almost inaccessible locations has been for two reasons: *(a)* the belief that higher the location of the monastery, the greater will be the proximity of the monk to the Buddha; and *(b)* to protect the wealth of the monasteries.

A good number of lamas reside in the monasteries who look after the spiritual as well as the mundane matters. In addition to the monasteries, other which attract attention as one moves through this land notably are the palaces (*e.g.* Khar Palace, Leh), *gonphas* or monasteries, *Chortens, Mane* walls, rock-cut sculptures, caves and huge stupas.

The maintenance and conservation of these buildings is a challenging task particularly because of climate and remoteness of Ladakh. The conservation of one important building is discussed here to give an idea of the magnitude of the task.

In Leh, the capital of Ladakh there is a towering structure of huge dimensions built a atop a hillock commanding attention from all parts of the town. This building is locally called "KHER", which in Ladakhi means a palace. There are other palaces in Ladakh, among which the palaces at Stok and Shey are worth mentioning. The Leh palace is a masterpiece of builders' art. It was built above 300-500 years ago with stones, mud bricks (sun-dried) and at some places even pisé walls. It consists of nine storeys of imposing height and its effect is further heightened by the hillock on which it is built. The walls slope inwards so as to keep the structures intact and to counteract the thrust of the hill face. The contours of the hills over which it has been built have meticulously been made use of. The roof is flat and a small parapet wall is constructed all around.

Sengye Namgyal is said to be the greatest builder of Namgyal dynasty. It is said that he had initiated the construction of many buildings which were finished long after his time by his son. Leh palace is considered to be the best example of its type. This building was completed in three years. The other remarkable building is the Maitreya monastery at Basgo above the ruins of the ancient fort. The form of the religion of Sengye Namgyal and his great Lama was that of Red sect. It is worth mentioning here that there are two sects of Lamas in Ladakh, the Red sect and the Yellow sect.

Rainfall in this region is scanty, the annual average being a mere 5 cm. The temperature of the region ranges from 31°C in summer to near arctic cold in winter. These aspects have been taken into consideration while constructing all buildings. The Leh palace has been constructed on the natural contours of the hill and different heights of the hill have been marvellously utilized. The width of the bottom portion of walls over rocks varies from one metre to three metres and it proportionately decreases as the height increases. The stones bearing natural faces have been placed in the structural walls in such a manner that it appears that these have not been placed but have been chiselled out from the rock. Not a single hammer drop or chisel has been used yet the placement of stones is perfect and beyond one's imagination.

Mud has tremendous adhesive power of binding especially the earth containing more of alumina and sand particles. The lower storey walls are of stone masonry laid in mud mortar. The width of the bottom walls is greater than the width of the walls in the upper storeys. Sun dried mud brick walls have been used as the height of the walls increases. Interestingly, the size of these bricks is bigger than the normal brick. The brick walls are surmounted at some places with pisé walls.

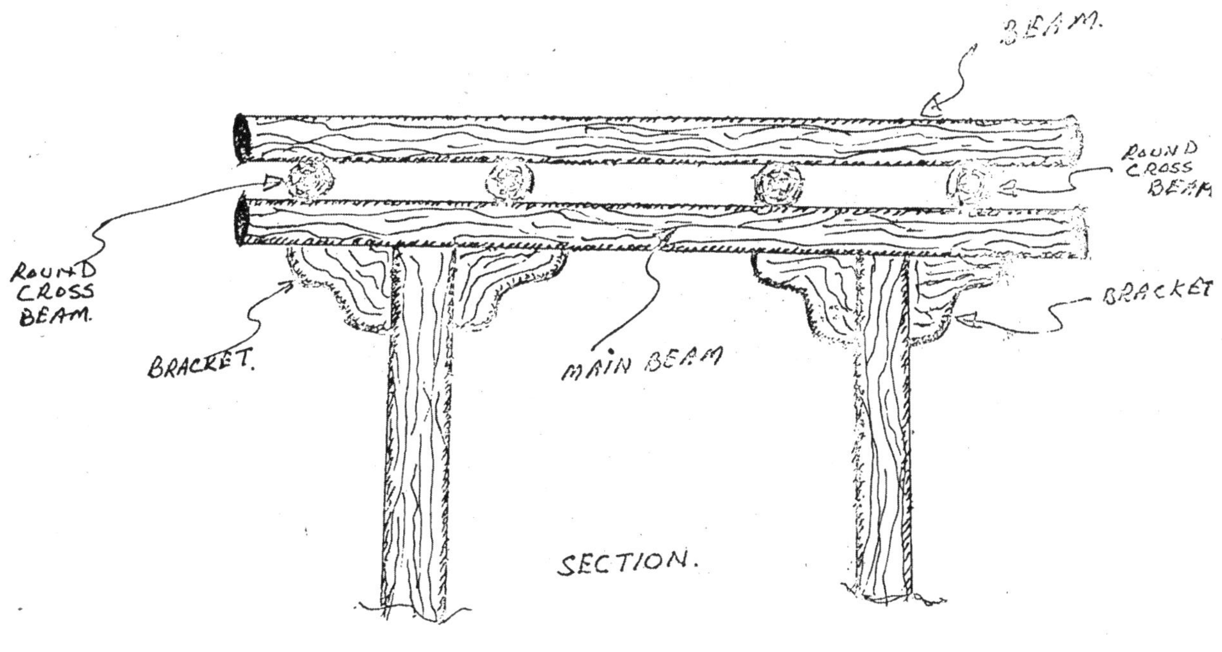

Fig. 1. Vertical pillars, brackets, crossbeams and main beams

Doors and windows are made up of local wood, which is either poplar or willow. The Ladakhi version of this wood is *youlat* and *yulap* respectively. In fact, the region is bereft of any forests and one wonders wherefrom all this wood has come. Pillars, brackets, beams; cross-beams and other items are all made of wood. There is one version that Leh was surrounded by thick forested hills and all the forests were cut down and made use of in the palace; wood was also procured from neighbouring areas. As a result the mountains surrounding the area were denuded of forests.

It may be worth mentioning here that the trees after felling down were used by them to the best of their ability. It may not be out of place to mention here that each component of these trees was suitably made use of in this building. The main logs were used for vertical pillars, brackets, crossbeams and main beams. The logs of wood were seasoned by peeling off the trunk and put in open space for sometime till the moisture evaporated away. The arid and dry atmosphere hastens in taking away the moisture in the wood. It may be interesting to know that there are no white ants in Ladakh as none of the wooden structures has been seen eaten by them. Perhaps this may be the reason as to why the necessity of using some chemicals as wood preservatives did not occur to the builders of the huge buildings.

Even the smaller branches of the trees were used efficiently as in case of ceiling. The branches are cut into equal small sized twigs. These small twigs were spread horizontally over the little gaps of crossbeams so as to bridge the gap in between them. In order to beautify the ceiling, these small twigs are peeled off their bark. This operation imparts them the natural white colour unlike the usual wooden tint. These twigs would be placed in different patterns resulting in creation of beautiful decorative fashions adding grandeur to the beauty of the ceiling. A number of designs with different patterns still exist at number of places in the ceiling although a lot of additions and alterations have been made in the past. Some of the patterns are shown. (Fig. 2)

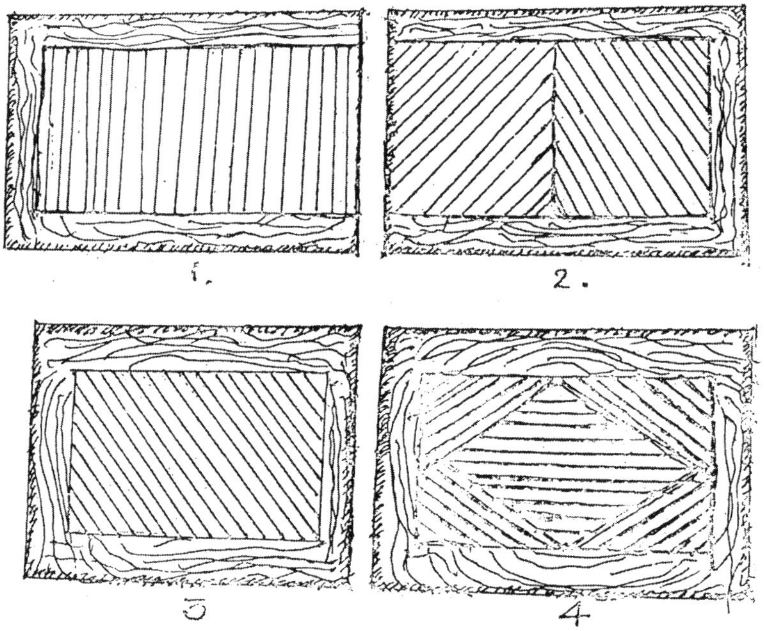

Fig. 2. Arrangement of twigs in ceilings

There may have been several other decorative patterns originally but with the passage of time are now lost.

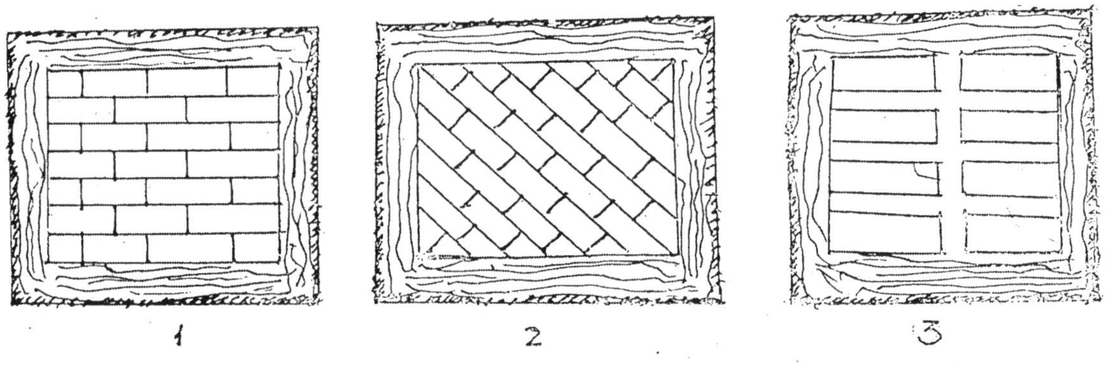

Fig. 3. Arrangement of Wooden pieces in floors

The custom of sitting on the floor has been the practice there since the temperature during winter is near-arctic and sitting on floor without any flooring of non-conducting material is next to impossible. Small pieces of wood have been used for flooring. Due to high cost and non-availability of wood its use was restricted only to such places which were considered to be important. These small pieces of wood were arranged in the following patterns. Not only sawn wood from the trees was made use of but the peeled off barks, branches, leaves and other peeled off twigs were also used. The thinnest branches were used for decorative purposes over door and window lintels. The peeled barks and the leaves were laid over the decorative twigs. On these leaves and barks, mud clay was laid and packed with dry earth which would serve as sub-base for the flooring of the next floor. All subsequent floors too would be filled up in similar pattern; the final coat of the roof would be laid with *markala* (special clay) with hay and goat hair or other material and would be packed up with *thapies*. The roof is usually flat. Laying of *markala* mud layer with water would mean filling up all the cracks and gaps that may have cropped up after compaction. The *markala* earth has a unique property of binding like cement and would render the top surface watertight. Use of wooden gutters at the fringe of the roof for draining of the melted snow water was in vogue. The snow which falls here in Leh has a very low volume of water content. As soon as snowfall takes place it is swept by brooms immediately otherwise it soon gets frozen. In case the snow is allowed to remain on the roof, it starts melting and the melted water will find its way for the drainage of which the wooden gutters are provided.

The flat roof is provided with parapet walls so as to enclose the roof and for protection of load-bearing walls from percolation of the melted snow-water.

Providing of semicircular or flat type of coping over these parapet walls was in vogue for which stones were laid in mud mortar and the top was finished with *markala* mixed plaster so as to render it watertight.

Both the inner as well as the outer walls are plastered (excepting those where natural faced stones have been provided) with mud mortar mixed with hey, husk or sometimes with animal hair which was not suitable for weaving purposes.

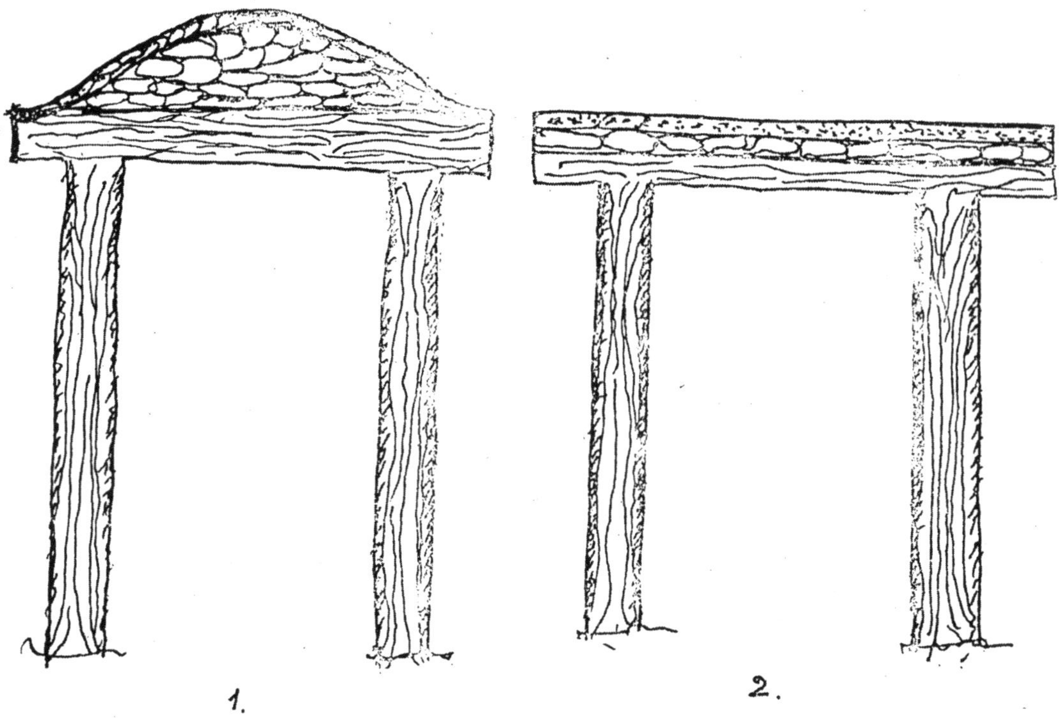

Fig. 4. Types of Coping

These places have undergone a lot of changes ever since they were built. These were either abandoned or their maintenance and repairs were beyond the capacity of the owners which ultimately resulted in their present state of deterioration. With the passage of time deterioration has set in and the cracks, leakage and falling of plasters in these huge buildings demand immediate conservation measures. Conservation of these monuments was taken up in 1978 after the Archaeological Survey of India started functioning there.

52
DHYĀNĪ BUDDHAS ON THE STELE OF BUDDHA

JITENDRA NATH

Portrayal of Dhyānī Buddhas on the stele of Buddha is not only rare but interesting also which suddenly appeared in the late Vajrayāna phase. Though the concept of Dhyānī Buddhas originated around the beginning of Christian era and the earliest representations are dated back to second century A.D. *i.e.*, Kushana period, but barring a few exceptions they were depicted on the crest or stele of Bodhisattva image only.

Around tenth-twelfth century a few images of Buddha with Dhyānī Buddhas on the stele were carved which have been reported from Kirtail, Dinajpur, Khalisady, Bareya and other places.

The one from Kirtail[1] depicts the scene of Buddha's descent from Tushita heaven. It shows Buddha in transparent drapery, standing in *tribhaṅga* on double lotus with right hand in *varada* and the left holding the score of drapery flanked by Brahmā on the right and Indra on the left holding an umbrella over the head of Buddha. Figures of five Dhyānī Buddhas are shown in their respective *mudrā* just above the umbrella. Dhyānī Buddha Akshobhya in *bhūmisparśa mudrā* is portrayed at the apex. On the right are Dhyānī Buddha Ratnasambhava and Amoghasiddhi in *varada* and *abhaya mudrā* and on the left are Amitābha and Vairochana in *dhyāna* and *dharmachakramudrā* respectively (Pl. 52.1).

The panel from Dinajpur[2] which depicts the scene of *Mahāparinirvāṇa*, shows five Buddhas seated in a row on the upper portion. Another panel, which is from Bareya[3], depicts Buddha in *bhumisparśamudrā* and five Dhyānī Buddhas on the stele in their respective *mudrā* (Pl. 52.2).

The one from Khalisady[4] represents Buddha in *abhaya mudrā* and the five Dhyānī Buddhas on the stele in their respective *mudrā*.

Such representations are also found in Nepal. A wooden panel of 16th century A.D., painted with Buddha's life scenes in the National Museum collection (Acc. No. 76.500) depicts

Śākyamuni seated in *bhumisparśa mudrā* within an architectural frame resembling a sort of *toraṇa* on which five Dhyānī Buddhas are shown seated in their respective *mudrā* (Pl. 52.3).

So far, these depictions of Dhyānī Buddhas on the stele of Buddha images have not been corroborated by literary sources but are congruous to the developments in later Buddhism which was heterogeneous in all respects.

Buddhist art from its early simple art medium metamorphosed into a variety of complexities, both in art forms and iconography. It was perhaps due to the emergence of a number of schools and sects with thoughts of varying shades, which were inextricably mingled in the course of time. Even the Buddha was not spared. The mortal teacher became god and then the embodiment of the Supreme. More and more idealization of Buddha's personality ultimately resulted in the concept of previous Buddhas and later on the five Dhyānī Buddhas, who represent the five cosmic elements which constitute the world. Relationship between mortal and Dhyānī Buddha was established.

Some Buddhist sects believed that Śākyamuni assumed the form of Vajradhara,[5] the primordial or Ādi Buddha. According to the *kula* system, the five Dhyānī Buddhas have their family with a consort, a Bodhisattva and a Mānushī Buddha, the earthly reflex of Dhyānī Buddha. Śākyamuni belongs to Amitābha family and is considered to be his earthly reflex. But Śākyamuni in one of his forms, known as Durgatipariśodhana, the principal deity of Durgatipariśodhana Maṇḍala, is supposed to be the embodiment of Mahāvirochana.[6] In Vajrāsana form, he is supposed to be the embodiment of Dhyānī Buddha Akshobhya.[7] All these suggest that different Buddhist sects and philosophers came out with different views to highlight Buddha's personality, who considered him to be omnipresent, everlasting and primordial god invested with supernatural powers and legendary attributes. So the motive behind the depiction of Dhyānī Buddhas or the symbols like *vajra*, trident, crown and ornaments, etc. in a Buddha image is understandable as all these enhance the significance of the Buddha who was believed to be the embodiment of supernatural powers.

It may also be seen as an extension of tradition of early Buddhist art where Hindu gods were frequently depicted in the case of life scene's of Buddha to mark the importance of the event and similar concept might have influenced the later Buddhists to depict Dhyānī Buddhas.

It is obvious from the finds that this type most probably originated in eastern India and was confined to that region barring a few exceptions. The fewer number of sculptures suggests that it was not a very popular type, but the possibility that this type of sculpture might have been used for some specific ritualistic purpose, cannot be ruled out.

NOTES AND REFERENCES

1. Huntington, Susan, L, *The Pala-Sena Schools of Sculptures*, Leiden, 1984, fig. 232.
2. *Ibid.*, fig. 238.
3. *Ibid.*, fig. 222.
4. *Ibid.*, fig. 223.
5. *Catalogue of Tibet House Museum* , New Delhi, 1965, p. 21.
6. B. Bhattacharya (ed.), *Niṣpannayogāvalī of Abhayakar Gupta,* GOS No. 109, Baroda, 1949, p. 66.
7. Alice Getty, *The Gods of Northern Buddhism,* Oxford, 1928, p. 36.

53
THE PEARL MOSQUE IN DELHI

JOSÉ PEREIRA

The range of Islamic architecture extends unbrokenly from the Pacific to the Atlantic, from the Philippines to Morocco. No geographical unit within this range has such a diversity of styles as has the Indian subcontinent. From the 11th century to the 17th century, this subcontinent produced a complex of provincially circumscribed stylistic modes in north, south, east and west, each with its distinctive features. But in the 17th century, under the rule of the Mughals (1526-1858), these modes fused in a Pan-Indian style. The Mughals, whose name is synonymous with opulence, were perhaps the most magnificent of all Muslim royalty, and none of their monarchs more so than Shah Jahan (1592-1666, emperor 1628-58), who commissioned the jewel-encrusted Peacock Throne of massive gold, resplendent symbol of imperial dominion, and the white marble Taj Mahal, embodiment of the Throne of God raised over paradise. The Pearl Mosque (*c.* 1658-59), elegant epitome of the palace mosque, seems to have been the last structure erected by the emperor, before he was deposed by his rebellious son, the fanatical Aurangzeb, murderer of his brother, prince Dara Shikoh, the renowned Sufi mystic.

Islamic in its function and basic features, the Mughal style is unmistakably Indian in its symbolics and aesthetics. In the Pearl Mosque one can see features created by Buddhist and Hindu architects, such as the following: *pointed and cusped arches,* that is, arches with small arcs ending in a point; *bulbous domes,* shaped like bubbles to symbolize the evanescence of things that the Buddha had emphatically proclaimed; *the lotus,* crown of all Indian monuments, a flower representative of the grace, beauty and elegance of Indian civilization; and *pot finials,* which surmount the lotus on Indian temples, and symbolize the water that gives life to all living things.

There are also the forms that Indian architects especially created for Muslim buildings. They include the *guldastas,* or pillar-like finials, usually topped by motifs like lotus buds; *chhatris,* miniature pavilions or kiosks, placed above *guldastas* in the Pearl Mosque; *curved caves,* accentuating the mosque's central bay; and the *triple-arched façade,* echoing the also typically

Indian *triple cluster of domes* above. Among these domes, the middle one is raised higher than its companions, thus creating the central emphasis and pyramidal configuration beloved of Indian architects.

Fig. 1.

In addition there are three features of symbolic meaning. The first is the *whiteness of the Pearl Mosque.* Mughal architects were fond of using two colours for their buildings, sandstone red and marble white, as though to symbolize the earthy and the celestial respectively. For their large mosques they began with using only red sandstone, but later introduced white marble as inlay into the various parts of the building, finally marbling the entire dome surface, with sandstone being occasionally added for emphasis. The exclusive use of marble they reserved for tombs, for it was the tomb (like the Taj) and not the mosque that came to be India's chief Muslim monument. India is the homeland of Buddhism, a religion whose principal structure is not the temple, but the tomb (the stupa). The Indians also preferred white on their sacred monuments; the great Sanskrit writer Bana compares the white effulgence of a temple to the "massed reflection of the constellation of stars lifted out of the seas" (*Kadambari*).

Second, the *raising of the mosque on a podium or platform.* In other parts of the Muslim world, mosques are generally on street level, as though to affirm the equality of the world outside and of the Muhammadan believers inside the mosque. But the Hindu temple is built on a platform, for it is meant to embody the deity envisaged as the Supreme Man (*parama purusa*). It has thus to be raised above the profane world.

Third, and last, the *triple cluster of domes,* which echoes the Hindu doctrine of the triformity of God (*trimurti*), or the Buddhist one of the Triform Body of the Buddha (*trikaya*).

But none of this symbolism conflicts with Muslim mystical teaching. The luminous star-like whiteness of the Pearl Mosque symbolizes Allah who, as the Quran says, "is the light of the heavens and the earth. His light may be compared to a niche that enshrines a lamp, the lamp within a crystal of star-like brilliance" (*sura* 24, verse 35). As for the raising of the mosque on a podium, while the mosque does not embody the deity, it contains the mihrab, the symbol of the invisible presence of the Prophet, the Perfect man (*insan-e-kamil*). And Sufi mysticism is willing to concede, in the words of the 18th century poet Hatef-e-Isfahani, that "the mystery of Oneness" can be conceived in triune fashion, for in manifesting Himself, the one God, "the eternal Witness, flashed rays from His shining face into three mirrors" (*Tarjiband*, chapter 2, verses 11 and 12).

54
A HARIHARA SCULPTURE FROM KHAJURAHO

K.M. SURESH

Khajuraho (lat. 24°-51' North and long. 79°-56' East), one of the capitals of the Chandellas who ruled the central India in the early medieval times from *circa* 9th to 12th centuries A.D., is situated in Chhatarpur District of Madhya Pradesh. The tract round Khajuraho was known during ancient times as Vatsa, in mediaeval times as Jejakabhukti and as Bundelkhand from 14th century onwards. This place made a significant contribution to the development of art and architecture, as is very well-known.

A composite image of Śiva and Vishṇu is called Harihara. Among the different anthropomorphic forms worshipped in India, the Harihara image is undoubtedly one of the most important. The combination of Hari and Hara in one image, forms the theme of this icon.[1] '*Devam Hariharam vakshe sarvapātakanāśanam Dakshine Śaṅkarasyārdhaṁ ardhaṁ Vishṇoścha Vāmataha*' emphasises the reconciliation between the two major cults, Śaivism and Vaishṇavism.

The earliest literary reference to Harihara is to be traced in the *Harivaṁśa*.[2] In the Epic and Puranic accounts we find that each divine personality has a tendency to merge with the other. The *Purāṇas* relate many episodes of how the two gods Hari and Hara became one and the same. The *Liṅga Purāṇa*[3] furnishes an interesting story in this connection. It stated that 'once Vishṇu had been to the Dāruvana in the guise of a woman and there Śiva and the woman-Vishṇu became one'. A similar account is also found in the *Bhāgavata Purāṇa*,[4] which states that Śiva heard that Vishṇu had assumed an enchanting female form, to satisfy his curiosity he went to him with Bhavānī, Vishṇu assumed that form again to satisfy Śiva, Śiva became passionate and ran after that female form and embraced her, the female-Vishṇu got out of the embrace and reassumed his own form, Śiva was then restored to himself etc.

Brahaddharma Purāṇa[5] states that there is no difference between Śiva and Vishṇu. These two deities live in one place and those who worship Śiva worship Vishṇu also. They are described as water in two different jars.[6] The *Vāyu Purāṇa*[7] also states that 'all things in this world are the manifestations of Rudra-Nārāyaṇa'. In the *Skanda Purāṇa*,[8] it is stated that after the marriage of Gaurī with Rudra-Śiva, a fight ensued between Hari and Hara, Brahmā intervened and said, 'Let both of you be of established reputation as Harihara'.

The worship of Hariharamūrti as a chief image in temples came into existence after the reconciliation between the two major cults of Śaivism and Vaishṇavism, that Śiva and Vishṇu are one and the same and both are essential for the creation, protection and destruction of the universe. Some Śaiva *Saṁhitas* and *Āgamas* contain elaborate rules about the construction of temples and images. The *Suprabhedāgama, Kamikāgama, Aṁsumadbhedagam, Karṇāgama* and *Śilpartna* throw a flood of light not only on Harihara but also other branches of Brahmanical Hindu iconography.[9] The growing spirit of harmony between these two Hindu sects found expression not only in the literary accounts but also in the epigraphy and sculptures of early mediaeval India. Gopinatha Rao,[10] in his '*Elements of Hindu Iconograpy*', has discussed all the above sources and presented a good number of this composite form of Harihara sculptures of different schools of thought.

One of the earliest stone reliefs representing this deity in south India, is found at Badami in Bijapur District of Karnataka, the capital of Eastern Chālukyas. The clear vertical line of demarcation between the *jaṭāmukuṭa* of Śiva and the *kirīṭamukuṭa* of Vishṇu runs throughout. The two different types of earrings, that is, *sarpakuṇḍala* in the right and *makarakuṇḍala* in the left ear are also very prominent. He is four-armed and standing in *samabhaṅga* posture on a pedestal. The back hands hold a *paraśu* with a snake round it and the *śaṅkha* while the front right hand is broken and the left hand rests on the thigh. A number of dwarfish figures of the Śaiva *gaṇas,* some playing musical instruments and others dancing, are carved on the lower portion.[11]

Images of Harihara clearly represent the efforts made for bringing about a reconciliation and rapproachment between the followers of the different cults[12] and illustrate a combination of the two divinities, Vishṇu (Hari) and Śiva (Hara), the former normally occupying the left-half, that is of female and the latter, the right-half, that is of male. According to Banerjea,[13] this may have hidden allusion to the Purāṇic story of Vishṇu's assumption of the female form of Mohinī while distributing the nectar churned from the ocean, between the gods and the demons and Śiva's love for Vishṇu in that beautiful form. Further, Gopinatha Rao[14] mentions, 'Umā, Durgā or Devī is also considered to be a female aspect of Vishṇu and Durgā, the consort of Śiva is represented in all the sculptures with *śaṅkha* and the *chakra*, the weapons characteristic of Vishṇu.'

The *Purāṇas* and other ancient texts on Hindu iconography furnish a detailed description of this composite god Harihara or Śaṅkara-Nārāyaṇa, mainly on the basis of the attributes held in the hands of Vishṇu-half and Śiva-half as given in the *Vishṇudharmottara Purāṇa*.[15] Harihara should have a *varada mudrā* and *triśūla* in his right hands and a *śaṅkha* and *chakra* in the left. Sometimes *chakra* is replaced by *gadā, śaṅkha* or by the *kaṭihasta*. He should be shown with Nandi (bull) to the right and Garuḍa to the left side. Hemādri's *Chaturvarga Chintāmaṇi* describes '*Dakshiṇe Vṛshabha pārśve Vamevihamgaraditi*'. The text of *Rūpamaṇḍana*[16] differs only in expression but has the same impression. According to *Abhilaśitaratha Chintāmaṇi*,[17] 'the right-half (Śiva) should be shown exhibiting *varada mudrā* and carrying *triśūla* in the hands whereas the left-half (Vishṇu) should be holding *śaṅkha, chakra* or *gadā*. The Śiva-half should be of white complexion, adorned with a *jaṭāmukuṭa* with a crescent moon, *nāgakuṇḍala* or *patrakuṇḍala*, wearing an elephant skin, whereas Vishṇu-half should be of darkish colour, wearing *ratnakirīṭa, makarakuṇḍala* and yellow garments'.

According to *Aṁśumadbhedāgama*,[18] Harihara should exhibit *varada mudrā* and carry a *paraśu* or *triśūla* by his right hands and *śaṅkha* and *kaṭihasta* by the left hands respectively. On the head, in the Vishṇu-half should be *kirīṭamukuṭa* set with precious stones and *makarakuṇḍala*. The arms should be adorned with *keyūra, kaṅkaṇa* and other ornaments, draped with a yellow silk garment. The colour of Śiva-half is to be snow-white and that of Vishṇu-half, either green or bluish-brown. Harihara should be shown standing in *samabhaṅga* posture. The right-half should be terrific and left half pacific. Behind the head of Harihara, there should be a halo.

One of the earliest stone reliefs representing Harihara from north India is found from Girdharpur Tilla[19] near Mathura of Kushana period, which is preserved in the Mathura Museum.[20] A Gupta seal discovered at Balanda[21] has depicted the composite figure of Harihara. A sandstone column from Jutari,[22] which is preserved in the Allahabad Museum, contains the face of Harihara which is damaged but the *kirīṭamukuṭa* and *jaṭāmukuṭa* over the head can be discerned on the left and right side respectively. The sculpture is of 5th century A.D. A stone head of Harihara from Ujjain, 8th-9th centuries A.D., is exhibited in the Gwalior Museum.[23]

A unique image of Harihara from central India belonging to the Pratihāra period of 11th century A.D., is exhibited in the National Museum, New Delhi.[24] The deity is shown in *ālīḍha* pose[25] and both the arms are damaged. He is identified by his composite crown which is *jaṭamukuṭa* on the right-half and *kirīṭamukuṭa* on the left-half. A sculpture of Harihara from Bihar, which is displayed in the Indian Museum, Calcutta,[26] depicts the composite figure of four-armed Harihara, carrying a *triśūla, śaṅkha* in the upper hands and a skull-cup and *chakra* in the lower hands. He is accompanied by Sūrya and Buddha on either side, which suggests it to be the cult deity of worship and demonstrates the combination of Hindu deities, Śiva and Vishṇu and Sūrya but also of Buddha.[27]

The famous Liṅgarāja temple at Bhubaneswar in Orissa, is a combination of both Vishṇu and Śiva, that is, Harihara and not Hara alone. A natural line that exists in that *svayambhu liṅga* (*Liṅgarāja*) is pointed out as the line demarcating Śiva and Vishṇu portions of the same deity which is invoked as Harihara and the leaves of *bilva* and *tulsi* are used in daily worship.[28] The Harihara cult developed in Orissa from the early mediaeval period and that is partially reflected in the cult of Jagannātha[29] which in turn assimilated certain ideas from Vaishṇavism and Śaivism and even from Śāktism and Buddhism.[30]

A close observation and study of the available evidences disclose the fact that the worship of Harihara became popular in north India from the times of Guptas and the spirit of conciliation and compromise seems to have pervaded the relation between the two sects of Vaishṇava and Śaiva.

The actual representation of Harihara is invariably shown as standing in *samabhaṅga* posture, either two-or four-armed, with Śiva on the right and Vishṇu on the left-half. The clear-cut features of Śiva and Vishṇu are distinguished by a clear line of demarcation starting with the headdress, that is, *jaṭāmukuṭa* and *kirīṭamukuṭa, kuṇḍalas,* ornaments, attributes, the attendant figures and the *vāhanas.* A slight deviation from this normal way of representation is when Harihara is shown as seated in *yogāsana* with combination of Śiva, Vishṇu, Sūrya and Brahmā, known as Harihara-Hiraṇyagarbha.[31]

A beautiful sandstone sculpture of Harihara from Khajuraho (Pl. 54.1) exhibited in the Archaeological Museum, is standing in *samabhaṅga* posture on a lotus pedestal. He has four arms. The lower right hand, partly broken, is held in *varada mudrā* with rosary, the upper right hand holds a *triśūla* whereas the upper left hand holds *chakra* and the lower left hand is unfortunately broken and missing. The deity is characterised by his headdress which is composed of *jatāmukuṭa* and *kirīṭamukuṭa.* The *jaṭāmukuṭa* of Śiva is adorned with crescent moon and single hooded *nāga.* He wears *patrakuṇḍala* in the right ear and *ratnakuṇḍala* in the left ear, necklaces, armlets, wristlets, *yajñopavīta,* waist-girdle with tassels hanging on the thighs and in between the two legs, long *vaijayantīmālā* coming up to the knees are common and identical for both the halves. He is provided with a *prabhāvali* and a *kīrtimukha* at the top and also double *śiraśchakra* at the back of the head.

The right half portion of *prabhāvali* depicts Śaivite figures. At the top is seen a standing four-armed Bhairava, which holds *ḍamaru* and *triśūla* in the upper hands. The lower right hand is held in *varada mudrā* and the lower left hand holds a *kamaṇḍalu.* He is accompanied by Nandi and wears a *jaṭāmukuṭa, kuṇḍalas,* necklaces, *yajñopavīta,* armlets, waist-girdle and *vaijayantīmālā.* Below Bhairava, is depicted a seated two-armed Kārttikeya. The right hand is held in *abhaya mudrā* and left hand holds *śakti.* Below Kārttikeya is depicted two-armed Gaṇeśa, his right hand held in *varada mudrā* and the left hand holds *modaka.* Below Gaṇeśa is depicted a *āyudhapurusha* of *triśūla,* standing in *tribhaṅga* posture on a pedestal. He has two hands, the right hand is held in *vyākhyāna mudrā* and the left hand holds a *triśūla.* His hair is tied up in the form of a *jaṭāmukuṭa* and wears *kuṇḍalas,* necklaces, *yajñopavīta,* and *vaijayantimāla.* Below the right hand palm of Harihara, is depicted Bhikshāṭanamūrti standing in *tribhaṅga* posture. He has two hands, the right hand holds a skull-cup and the left hand holds a *khaṭvāṅga.* He wears *kuṇḍalas,* and other ornaments. His face is worn-out. By the side of Bhikshāṭanamūrti is shown a Nandi (bull), the *vāhana* of Śiva. At the end of the right portion of *prabhāvali* are depicted other subsidiary figures along with *gaja-vyāla,* etc.

The left half portion of the *prabhāvali* depicts, right from the top, the Daśāvatāras of Vishṇu from Matsyavatāra to Kalki *avatāra.* The Matsya and Kūrma *avatāras* of Vishṇu are shown in simple animal forms of a fish and a tortoise. The next incarnation of Vishṇu is shown as Bhū-varāha, standing with left foot on a *pīṭha.* He has four hands, the lower right hand placed on the right thigh in the form of *kaṭihasta,* the upper right hand holds *gadā* while the upper folded left hand holds *chakra* and the lower left hand holds *śaṅkha,* which is resting on the folded left knee. Bhūdevī is shown seated on the folded left arm of Varaha. The snout of Varāha is raised towards Bhūdevī.

The next incarnation of Vishṇu is shown as Narasiṁha *avatāra.* He is shown with the lion face and tearing the belly of demon king Hiraṇyakaśipu, who is placed on his laps. The next incarnation is of Vāmana, shown seated in *ardhaparyaṅkāsana* on a pedestal. He has two hands, the right hand is held in *abhayamudrā* and the left hand holds an umbrella. Below Vāmana is shown Rāma *avatāra* of Vishṇu, in *vīrāsana* posture. He too has two hands, the left hand holds a bow and the right hand is in the act of taking out an arrow from the quiver. The next incarnation of Vishṇu is Paraśurāma, shown seated in *mahārājalīlāsana* posture on a pedestal. His right hand is held in *abhaya mudrā* and the left hand holds a *paraśu* (battle-axe). Below Paraśurāma is shown Balarāma, seated in *ardhaparyaṅkāsana* posture on a pedestal under the canopy of three-hooded *nāga*. His left hand rests on the left lap and the right hand holds a ploughshare.

To the right side of Balarāma is the next incarnation of Vishṇu, of Buddha, standing in *dvibhaṅga* posture on a pedestal. His right hand is held in *vyākhyāna mudrā* and the left hand rests on the left thigh. The last and tenth incarnation of Vishṇu is shown as Kalki *avatāra*. He is riding on horseback, his right hand holds a sword and the left hand is holding the reins of the horse. He wears a short *karaṇḍamukuṭa* and other ornaments on the body.

On the left hand side of Harihara is shown a *chaurī* bearer, standing in *tribhaṅga* posture on a pedestal. He has two hands, the right hand holds a *chaurī*, the fly-whisk and the left hand rests on the left thigh in the form of *lola* pose. He wears *kuṇḍalas* and other ornaments. By the side of the left-hand side *chaurī*-bearer, is shown *āyudhapurusha* of *Chakra,* standing in *dvibhaṅga* posture. His right hand rests on the pedestal and left hand holds *chakra* which is chipped off. His face is also chipped off.

Below the feet of Harihara is shown Lakshmī seated in *padmāsana* on a *kūrma* with her hands held in *añjali mudrā*. She is flanked by *nāgakanyās* on either side with hands held in *añjali mudrā*. Harihara is flanked by *vidyādharas* on either side with hands held in *añjali mudrā*.

On the top centre of the *prabhāvali* is shown a deity, probably Buddha seated in *padmāsana* with hands held in *dhyāna mudrā* flanked by *vidyādharas* and *gandharvas* on either side.

This sculpture of Harihara is one of the best specimens of the Chandella art representing the popularity of cult-deity of Harihara, and characteristic of the trend of iconographic evolution during the mediaeval period in Indian history which was set to assimilate the ideas and ideals of different schools of religion like Śaivism, Vaishṇavism, Buddhism, Śāktism and so on. It is now exhibited in the Archaeological Museum, Khajuraho.

NOTES AND REFERENCES

1. T.A. Gopinatha Rao, *Elements of Hindu Iconography,* Vol. II, Part 2, p. 170.
2. *Harivaṁśa II, Adhyāya* 129, 40 ff.
3. *Liṅga Purāna, Pūrvārdha, Adhyāya* 96.
4. *Bhāgavata Purāṇa*, VIII, 6-7.
5. *Brahddharama Purāṇa, Pūrvarkhaṇḍa, Adhyāya*, 9. 39-47.
6. *Ibid., Adhyāya* 25, 20-26.
7. *Vāyu Purāṇa, Adhyāya* 25, 20-26.

8. *Skanda Purāṇa*, VII, 2, 17, 187 ff.
9. Gopinatha Rao, *op. cit.*, pp. 268-171.
10. *Ibid.*
11. *Ibid.*, Pl. XCIV; & J.N. Banerjea, *Development of Hindu Iconography*, Pl. XIVI, No. 3.
12. Banerjea, *op. cit.*, and *EHI*, Vol. II, part 2, p. 133.
13. J.N. Banerjea, *JISOA*, Vol. XIV, p. 48.
14. Gopinatha Rao, *op. cit.*, pp. 332-33.
15. *Ibid.*, p. 171.
16. *Rūpamaṇḍana,* Chap. IV, vv 30-31.
17. *Abhilaśitāratnachintāmaṇi*, 3 1/785.
18. *Aṁsumadbhedāgama*, 73.
19. *JUPHS*, p. 44, Pl. 18, Figs. 2 & 3.
20. *Ibid.*, Acc. No: 1336.
21. *MASI*, 66, Pl. 3.
22. Chandra, P., *Some Sculptures in the Allahabad Museum*, p. 91, Pl. LXVIII, 203 a.
23. Bhagwant Sahai, *Iconography of Minor Hindu and Buddhist Deities*, p. 137.
24. B.N. Sharma, *Journal of Oriental Institute*, Vol. XVIII 1 & 2, pp. 157/159, Fig. 1.
25. Bhagwant Sahai, *op. cit.*, p. 139, Pl. 23.
26. J.N. Banerjea, *DHI*, p. 547, Pl. XLVIII-1.
27. *Ibid.*, Pl. XLVI-4 & LVIII-3.
28. K.C. Panigrahi, *Archaeological Remains at Bhubaneswar*, p. 257.
29. H.K. Mahatab, *History of Orissa*, p. 511.
30. K.C. Mishra, *The Cult of Jagannatha*, p. 157.
31. Kalpana Desai, *Iconography of Vishṇu*, p. 55. & DHI, pp. 510-11.

55

AN INTERESTING INSCRIBED MAKARA TORANA FROM HULI, DISTRICT BELGAUM

K.P. POONACHA, M.V. VISWESWARA and T.M. KESAVA

Huli, referred to as Pūvalli, Pūli, etc., in the medieval epigraphs (75°14' long.; 15°47.5' lat.; Savadatti Taluk, Distt. Belgaum) was prominent amongst the 18 *Agrahāras*[1] during the Kalyāna Chālukyan times. Recently prehistoric implements of the lower and middle Palaeolithic cultures have been collected from the seasonal rivulets and at the foot of the hills of the village. Earliest epigraphical reference[2] to the place (*Kiruvattakere*) occurs in the copperplates of the Bādāmi Chālukyan period and Rāshtrakūṭa records[3] are also noticed here. An inscription[4] of the place refers to Siddhanañjēsa, author of *Rāghavāṅka Chāritra* as hailing from this place.

Epigraphs of the Kalyāna Chālukya period are far numerous in the place and provide vital information on various aspects of the socio-religious conditions and the architectural edifices built during the period. During this period, Huli, apart from being a *mahāgrahāra,* was an important Kālāmukha centre. An inscription[5] of the times of Someśvara-II mentions Puliyadeva, Lakulīśadeva, Vakkhaṇidēva, Yogi Vidyāsēna and Somadeva as eminent saints of *Kālāmukha* sect, besides informing that Jñāśakti Paṇḍitadēva was held in high esteem by the king. The Chālukyas of Kalyāṇa also built or renovated more than a dozen temples at Huli, especially of Śaiva faith *viz.,* Madanāsura, Kāsīviśvesvara, Agastyeśvara, Kalmeśvara, Tārakeśvara, Sidheśvara, Trikūṭeśvara, Nirmala Liṅgeśvara, Māleśvara, Pañchaliṅgeśvara and Andhāsura[6] to name a few. One of these *in situ* epigraphs refers to the *makara tōraṇa*[7] in the temple which will be discussed later.

Amongst the temples, the one dedicated to Andhāsura was an important seat of Kālāmukha activities. A record of Vikramāditya-VI dated Śaka 1019 (A.D. 1097)[8] refers to this temple and another[9] of A.D. 1104 records donations made to it. Obviously the temple pre-dates the above records and it could be surmised that it was constructed around A.D. 1060-75. This *drāviḍa dvikūṭa* temple (Pl. 55.1) has east-west orientation with an ornate entrance at south. In plan it has two *garbhagṛihas* at the extremities, connected to a common *mahāmaṇḍapa* (Pl. 55.2) through an *ardhamaṇḍapa* each. In elevation, the temple has an evolved *adhishṭhāna* and the *bhitti* is treated with double pilaster *drāviḍa* turrets with a typical *drāviḍa dvitala śikhara* atop. The western sanctum houses a Śiva *liṅga* and the eastern is empty at present.

The ornate *makara tōraṇa* (Pl. 55.3) spanning the front two pilasters of the western *archamaṇḍapa* is of great interest and forms the topic of the present paper. Such *tōraṇas* are a characteristic feature in medieval Indian religious art. *Kāmikāgama*[10] refers to *makara tōraṇa* as one amongst the three types of *tōraṇas* depicted in embellishments. Normally such *tōraṇas* are to be seen at the entrance as a lintel piece of the main door frame and occasionally spanning the pilasters of the *ardha-maṇḍapas* also. In all the other known specimens the trinity depictions have Śiva *tāṇḍava* as the centre-piece flanked by Brahmā and Vishṇu—the deities being depicted singly or with consorts and the usual retinue of the *dikpālas* forming the backdrop. The *makara tōraṇas* of the Kalleśvara temple, Kuruvatti, and other places may be cited as examples.

The *makara tōraṇa* under reference forms a class of its own for three reasons: 1. It depicts Vishṇu as Vaikuṇṭha; 2. it is inscribed; and 3. it mentions the name of the sculptor. The sculptural composition of the said *makara tōraṇa* was wrongly identified as "Durgā dancing on the back of a crouching demon with Sarasvatī on her right, another goddess on her left, and the eight *dikpālas* in a row above her".[11]

This massive *tōraṇa* (7' 4" X 2' 3") has much stylised, ornate *makaras* at extreme ends (Pl. 55.4) lead by snarling, moving lions in front. Astride *makaras* are Varuṇa and Vāruṇī. From the open grunting jaws of these *makaras* issue highly ornate, twisted, five-arched, jewel-studded, *ratna toraṇa* held in position at the apex by *kīrtimukha* (Pl. 55.5 & 55.6).

Śiva *tāṇḍava: Astabhuja* Śiva (Pl. 55.7) dances in all grace beneath the *kīrtimukha* on Apasmārapurusha lying on his chest and head slightly raised, with a drawn out sword in right hand. Phālāksha-Śiva bears *khaḍga, triśūla, khatvāṅga, pānapātra* and *agni.*[12] The other hands are in the gestures of *lōla, japa* (*abhaya* — mutilated), and *khasūchi* or *svarga hasta*. To the right of dancing Śiva at knee is a drummer and to the left are a flautist and *tālavādaka* (or a *gāyaka*).

Chaturmukha Brahmā : To the right of Śiva is Brahmā (Pl. 55.8) seated over a *padmapīṭha* in *lālitāsana*. He is playing on a *viṇā* with front pair of hands placing the *viṇā* across left shoulder. The upper right bears *sruk-sruva* and the lower left is in *lōlā*. Swan is shown facing left on the pedestal.

Vaikuṇṭha-Vishṇu : Depicted to the left of dancing Śiva, Vaikuṇṭha Vishṇu (Pl. 55.9) forms the most important sculptural renderings in the present *tōraṇa*. Vaikuṇṭha is carved as *chaturbhuja* Vishṇu, seated on *padma pīṭha* in *maharājalīlāsana*. All the hands are mutilated at wrist but the position of lower right and left hands, held in front of the chest indicates the deity as engaged in playing *tāla*, to keep notes for the dance of Śiva. The upper right hands are upraised sideways almost touching the *toraṇa*. The index and curved thumb of the upper right hand are held as if to support the *prayoga chakra*. Thus it could be surmised that the attributes were *tāla* in lower hands, *chakra* and *padma* in the upper right and left. The mace is placed upside down just behind the body at the available space, which otherwise could have been the attribute in lower

Fig. 1. *Chaturmurti Vishṇu,* c. 4th Cent. A.D., Mathura Museum

left hand. It looks more like a wrestler's club with short handle and elongated, less bulbous head with a "lotus bud-like" apex.

The three faces are as per textual prescriptions,[13] the central (eastern) face is *saumya*, Narasiṁha face is to the south *i.e.,* to the proper right of the image and the face to north *i.e.,* to the left of the image is Varāha. Since the sculpture is of high relief the face of Kapila (west face) is not shown. All the three aspects of the deity are endowed with *kīrīṭamukuṭa*. The face of Narasiṁha exudes the sentiment of fierce (*raudra*), with open jaws and revolving protruding eyes with heavily arched eyebrows. The snout of Varāha juts out firmly with open jaws and unfortunately 1/4th of the snout at front is mutilated. Right in front of the lotus pedestal couchant Garuda in fully anthropomorphic form with hands in *añjali*, looking front in all readinesss to fly is depicted. Above the trinity, *ashṭadikpālas* with their respective spouses have assembled astride their respective *vāhanas* to watch the mesmerising dance of Śiva.

It is a well-known fact that the Vaikuṇṭha form of Vishṇu is the *chaturmūrti* aspect symbolising and synthesizing the principal form of Vishṇu with some of his incarnations. As per the *vyūha* theory of *Pāñcharātra* tradition it is an integration of the emanatory forms *viz.*, Saṅkarshaṇa, Pradyumna and Aniruddha, with Vāsudeva the supreme being as the central piece. Iconographically, the earliest representation of Vaikuṇṭha aspect is of Kushāṇa times (Fig.1) followed by the one of Gupta times (Fig. 2) both kept in the Mathura Museum (6th cent. A.D.). The former has three busts attached to the central figure, one on the top and two at the shoulders. In the latter, already in a standardised iconographic form of the typical Gupta period, the image has lateral disposition of heads as per iconic specifications.[14]

Fig. 2. *Vaikuṇṭha-Vishṇu*, c. 6th Cent. A.D., Mathura Museum

It may not be out of context to consider here the only sculptural representation of Vaikuṇṭha-Vishṇu (Pl. 55.10) so far known from the Karnataka area. This specimen reported by Sundara[15] hails from the Banashankari temple, Basavakalyāṇa, district Bijapur. It is a relief sculpture executed on a rectangular sandstone slab. Significantly it represents the Lakshmī-*sahita-vaikuṇṭha* form described in the *Jayākhya Saṁhita*.[16]

In the Basavakalyana specimen, *Chaturbhuja* Vishṇu is depicted as *Garuḍārūḍha* in *ardha padmāsana,* the left leg folded and accommodating Lakshmī on the lap thus formed. His three faces are clearly shown. In accordance with the canonical prescriptions, the front face adorns with a somewhat tall cylindrical *kirīṭa,* shows the *saumya* aspect, the right side has fierce Narasiṁha and Varāha on the left. The deity holds *chakra* and *gadā* in the upper right and left hands, the lower left embraces Lakshmī whereas the right holds *padma. Gadā* is shown in a minuscular fashion near the extreme left. Lakshmī holding *pushpa* in her hands is supported by a lotus. Front facing Garuḍa with fluttering wings holds an *amṛitakalaśa* in his hands. A pair of devotees are depicted in the lower extremities on either side of Garuḍa. Stylistically this sculpture could be ascribed to 12-13th centuries.

In Kashmir and north-western parts of India, Vishṇu as Vaikuṇṭha was a popular cult deity during 8th to 10th centuries. Kalhaṇa's *Rājataraṅgiṇī*[17] refers to the installation of Vaikuṇṭha images known as *Chaturātman.* However, in south India, this aspect of Vishṇu appears not to have gained the status of a cult deity but still is seen represented as a rare form occasionally depicted as at Basavakalyāṇa and Huli. The depiction at Huli especially speaks of the artists' freedom in expression on the one hand and signifies the absorption of the Vaishṇava element into the fold of the Kālāmukha sect.

The two-lined inscription in Kannada characters eulogises the *makara tōraṇa,* 'Has the lotus born (Brahman) in exceeding delight fashioned this or has Viśvakarman with joy executed this or has the Lord of the western region (Varuṇa) constructed this archway with a pair of monsters?'[18] It concludes that Mārtāṇḍa, skilled in arts and devoted to his master was indeed fortunate to have executed this *tōraṇa.* This Mārtāṇḍa obviously is the sculptor.

This epigraph further informs that Jñānaśakti got this *makara tōraṇa* made. We know from other records[19] that Jñānaśakti, revered by the royal families, was the *āchārya* of the establishment of the Andhāsura temple. As the inscription rightly claims, this *makara tōraṇa* is '*dhātriyoḷ vinūtanataram*'—it is indeed a unique one of the class for its terrific yet enchanting dance of Śiva in all anger yet serenity, full of rhythm, poise and grace accompanied by no less than the deities like Brahma and Vaikuṇṭha-Vishṇu as the musical accompaniments.

NOTES AND REFERENCES

1. S.L. Shantakumari, *History of the Agrahāras : Karnataka 400-1300 A.D.,* Madras, 1986.
2. Karnataka State Gazetteer, *Belgaum District* (Bangalore 1787), p. 89.
3. Information kindly provided by Dr. R.M. Shadaksharaiah, Director, Kannada Research Institute, Dharwad.
4. The epigraph is noticed in the recent explorations and the text is being edited.
5. *Epigraphia Indica,* Vol. XVIII, No. E, pp. 189-96.

6. *Ibid.*, Ins. No. D, pp. 182-89.
7. *Ibid.*, Ins. No. K, pp. 206-07.
8. *Ibid.*, Ins. No. E.
9. *Ibid*, both the inscriptions are engraved on the same slab.
10. C. Sivaramamurti, *Amaravati Sculptures in the Madras Government Museum* (Bulletin of Madras Govt. Museum, Vol. 4, p. 129).
11. *Epigraphia Indica, op. cit.*, pp. 206-07.
12. Though the flames cannot be clearly discerned, it could be surmised by the gesture of the hand that it was endowed with Agni.
13. *Saumyam tu vadanam pūrvam Nārasiṁham tu dakshiṇaṁ* I
    Kāpilam paśchimam Vaktram tathā Vārāhamuttaraṁ I I
    Vishṇudharmōttara Purāṇa (Baroda 1958), Vol. III, Ch. 44, 11b-12a.
14. Kalpana S. Desai, *Iconogaphy of Vishṇu*, New Delhi, 1973, p. 40.
15. We are thankful to Dr. Sundara for having kindly provided with the photograph of the said sculpture for study purposes and permitting to publish it.
16. *Jayākhya Samhitā*, Baroda 1931, XXXIII, 54-65.
17. Kalhana's *Rājataraṅgiṇī*, V. 25, cited by Kalpana S. Desai, *op. cit.*, p. 46.
18. *Epigraphia Indica, op. cit.*, Ins. No. K, p. 207.
19. *Ibid.*, Ins. No. E, pp. 189-96.

56
SOCIAL SETTING OF THE MEDIEVAL TEMPLES

KRISHNA DEVA

Feudalism crept into the Indian body politic from about the fifth century A.D. The system of payment in the form of land grants to the civil and military officers and the profuse religious grants to the temples and the Brahmins gradually brought about a change in the socio-economic pattern which tended to feudalization. There emerged now a politicc-economic system based chiefly on the distribution of land. The territory directly administered by the king or the central power shrank and the kingdom became a loose pyramid made of a hierarchy of chiefs and feudatories of different gradations owing allegiance to the overlord. As the king depended more and more on the army of the feudatories, his power grew weaker and that of the feudal chiefs, who amassed large chunks of land, property and armed might, grew stronger.

The liberal grant of land and titles to the chieftains and the military character of the feudal relationships mainly contributed to the rise of the Rajput clans which forms a distinctive trait of the medieval politico-economic structure. The Rajput was bred and brought up in an atmosphere of heroism and gallantry and armed conquest was uppermost in his thought. To die in the battlefield was the greatest ambition of the Rajput who glorified warfare and regarded armed expeditions as *vijaya-yātrās* or victory-pilgrimages.

The Rajput chiefs, who were able to carve out principalities for themselves, invariably tried to glorify their families and claimed high pedigrees irrespective of their actual origin. For the recognition of their social status they depended upon the support of the Brahmins who were won over by the performance of *pūrtadharma* which mainly took the form of liberal gifts to the Brahmins and the building of temples.

The upper classes associated with the temple construction believed in magic. The magico-religious beliefs of the high society are amply reflected in the literature, epigraphs and arts since the early medieval times. Increasingly during the medieval age, sex and war became the dominant preoccupations of the aristocracy and magic and stars were believed to assure success in these ventures. The Kāmaśāstra prescribed magical formulae and auspicious dates and time for amours. Magical and astrological considerations played an important role also for military adventures. The soothsayers and the astrologers were held in high esteem and granted land. The march of the army and the timing of the campaigns were dictated not so much by military considerations as by astrological calculations. When the king marched on an expedition, the streets were adorned with auspicious sights and evil omens were scrupulously avoided.

The feudal tendencies, which gradually intensified the decentralisation of political power and the growth of local units of economic production, promoted regional consciousness in many spheres of social life and culture including language, script, costume and visual arts. The inevitable concomitants of feudalism and regionalism were conventionalism and drying up of creative reservoirs.

Literature now produced very little of original writing and more of commentaries with scholastic elaborations and *alaṅkāras* (embellishments). In the field of visual arts strict canons were laid down and the painting and sculptural art and architecture were bound down by prescriptions of proportions and rigid formulae of poses, postures and attributes. All creativity and originality were stifled under the rigours of canonisation. Regarding the medieval sculptures Nihar Ranjan Ray has noted: "A procession of endless monotony of form, uninformed by any inner experience and without any registration of individual creative genius, meets the eye. It is only in rare instances that images were expressions of the artist's creative genius and attained high artistic standards. But such examples are few and far between."[1] In short, there was a great stress on form and embellishment both in literary and visual arts.

The medieval period was also the age of local annals and *praśastis* (recitations of praise) by the bards and the court-poets, giving exaggerated and colourful accounts of the attainments of their princely patrons, emphasizing particularly their heroism in battles and sexual virility. Blatant ostentation characterised also the land-grants and other epigraphs which credited even minor princes with high-sounding, almost imperial titles and with exaggerated and often false claims of conquests. Similar tendencies of egoistic display are reflected also in the keen competition among princes and feudatories to excel others in building ever larger and grander temples adorned with sculptural profusion. The race was joined by the queens and other members of the family and the ministers and other dignitaries.

The socio-economic conditions of the times, which were not conducive to promotion of trade and commerce, induced the princes and the feudatories to invest their surplus wealth in the patronage of arts and crafts, in luxuries, in visiting places of pilgrimage, in the *dāna* (charities) to the Brahmins of cash and kind and land and above all in building and decorating temples which would earn them both merit and fame. Temple building was regarded by the Purāṇas as more meritorious than the performance of the *aśvamedha* or any other Vedic sacrifices.

Land-grants were made to the Brahmins and the temples together with all fiscal immunities and surrender of police and administrative functions in favour of the donees. The result was that the state became poorer and weaker and temples were converted into rich and powerful organizations. The enormous riches amassed in the medieval temples may be estimated from the accounts of the temples at Somanātha and Mathura furnished by the Muslim travellers. The

Somanātha Temple was endowed with 10,000 villages, had 500 *devadāsīs* and 1,000 priests. Inside the temple hung a golden chain with bells attached, weighing 200 maunds. The *maṇḍapa* was supported by fifty-six pillars inlaid with jewels. The value of the wealth plundered by Sulṭān Maḥmūd from this temple amounted to more than twenty million golden *dīnārs*. Regarding the main temples of Mathura, Sulṭān Maḥmūd remarked that it would have required not less than one hundred thousand golden *dīnārs* and two hundred years for the most able craftsmen to build the temple. Maḥmūd found there five images of gold, each 15 feet high and at least 200 images of silver, so heavy that they could not be weighed without breaking them to pieces. Al Utbi stated that the accumulated wealth of the Indian temples was so enormous "that the backs of camels would not carry it, nor vessels contain it, nor writer's hand record it, nor the imagination of an arithmetician conceive it."[2]

Rājarāja Chola (A.D. 985-1014) built the Brihadīśvara Temple at Tanjore and presented it 500 lbs (troy) of gold, jewels of about half that value and over 600 lbs (troy) of silver and endowed it with several villages yielding an annual income of 1,16,000 *Kalams* of paddy. Four hundred *devadāsīs* were also maintained, besides 212 other employees comprising dance-masters, musicians, drummers, tailors and goldsmiths, each getting fixed shares of paddy. The rich temple wielded tremendous power in the contemporary socio-economic life, acting at once as the landlord, employer, bank, school, museum, hospital and theatre.

It has also been recorded that the Chedi king Yuvarājadeva I (c. A.D. 915-45) assigned 3 lac villages in Ḍāhala, roughly one-third of the entire kingdom, to the Mattamayūra ascetic Sadbhāvaśambhu or Prabhāvaśiva, the founder of the monastery known as Golakī Maṭha. Rāshṭrakūṭa Govinda IV (A.D. 930-33) gave 400 villages and 32 lac coins to temples on the occasion of his coronation. The Solankī king Jayasiṁha (A.D. 1094-1143) is recorded to have distributed for religious charities ten million coins every year. The Orissan kings are known to have dedicated their kingdom to Lord Jagannātha and ruled as the god's viceroy. King Dhaṅga is referred to as having dedicated an emerald *liṅga* to a Śaiva temple at Khajuraho.

Many medieval temples also owned houses, house-sites and shops from which they collected rent and some of them were also assigned a portion of the tolls and transit taxes. The temples in Kashmir had become so wealthy that king Kalaśa of Kashmir (A.D. 1063-89) confiscated villages belonging to them and his son, king Harsha, appointed a special officer to collect wealth and golden images from them.

Wealth and power, combined with the presence of the *devadāsīs* (temple-maidens) and the philosophy of sex preached and practised by some of the extremist Śaiva and Tantric sects vitiated the holy atmosphere of many medieval temples and their priests succumbed to the temptation of luxurious living and immoral sexual practices. The *Rājataraṅgiṇi* (V, 465; VII, 13) states that the temple priests were organised into corporations which wielded political power and took part in the internal politics of the kingdom. The Verawal inscription of Bhāva Brihaspati records how the Somanātha Temple was ruined by many evil-disposed Gaṇḍas (Pāśupata priests) and greedy servants of the king. Merutuṅga has noted in the *Prabandhachintāmaṇi* that a Śaiva teacher agreed to act as a priest of the Tripurushaprāsāda built by Solankī Mūlarāja on the condition that he was supplied daily a specified quantity of saffron, musk and camphor for massaging his body, and was given in addition 32 *vārāṅgaṇās* (courtezans) as attendants, a white umbrella and a land grant. Dāmodaragupta and Kshemendra in their satires refer to the love adventures of the Pāśupata teachers and temple officials with prostitutes. We come across actual sculptures of religious teachers attended by women on medieval monuments such as the Lakshmaṇa and Chitragupta temples at Khajuraho.

The *devadāsī* institution, which in origin had fertility associations and was recommended by the Purāṇas for subserving the important temple rituals of dance and music, became so popular in medieval times that no prestigious temple could do without it. Developed medieval temples of all regions had provision for dance and drama and the special hall constructed for the purpose was significantly known as *nāṭa-mandira* in Orissa, *sabhāmaṇḍapa* or *raṅga-maṇḍapa* in Gujarat and Rajasthan and *nritya-maṇḍapa* or *Utsava-maṇḍpa* in south India. As regards Khajuraho temples, dance and music performances were probably held in the *mahāmaṇḍapa*. While we have copious historical, literary and epigraphic references to the temple *devadāsīs* from other regions of India, we get only two epigraphic allusions to the system from the Chandella records. A fragmentary pillar inscription dated A.D. 1130 in the Nīlakaṇṭha Mahādeva Temple at Kalanjar mentions Mahānachani Padmāvati, while there is a short inscription in the *mahāmaṇḍapa* of the Kandariya Mahādeva Temple at Khajuraho referring to probably a donation from the *varastrīs* (courtezans).

In the luxurious atmosphere of the medieval temple, the performances of dance, drama and music could not retain their pristine purity and got increasingly alloyed with secular *śriṅgāra* and sensuous appeal. As a consequence the *devadāsī* institution became notorious for breeding corruption and moral laxity. Further, the temple was often used for staging sensuous plays like Harsha's *Ratnāvali* (as stated in Dāmodaragupta's *Kuṭṭanīmatam* of the 8th century) and was even abused as a rendezvous of the lovers, the prostitutes and their paramours and the travellers seeking the company of women. As the temples grew larger, there was a corresponding expansion of the space for sculptural ornamentation and the artists had a free go at the representation of the erotic theme which had become an absorbing passion of the medieval art. It will thus be seen that the ascetic idealism became out of tune with the aristocratic feudal society which revelled in embellishment and aggrandization. The outburst of sexual depiction therefore accorded well with the luxurious atmosphere of the medieval temple, which was hardly different from that of the court.

NOTES

1. *History and Culture of Indian People*, ed. R.C. Majumdar, Vol. V, p. 643.
2. H. Elliot and J. Dowson, *History of India as told by its own Historians*, Vol. II, p. 34.

REFERENCES

Devangana Desai, *Erotic Sculpture of India* (Delhi, 1985).

Krishna Deva, *Khajuraho* (Brijbasi Printers, Delhi, 1987).

57

BRAHMANICAL DEITIES IN JAINA PANTHEON AND RELIGIOUS ART : THEIR MUTUALITY

MARUTI NANDAN PRASAD TIWARI

Jainism claims hoary antiquity as one of the three principal religions of India. While much work has been done on Jaina philosophy and religion, Jaina art and iconography, especially in respect of the assimilation of Brahmanical legendary characters and deities in Jaina pantheon and consequently their expression in visual and iconic forms, have remained largely ignored. The core of the Jaina pantheon and so also the visual manifestations representing the concretization of thoughts and myths into figurative and pictorial art, was the 24 Jinas or the Tīrthaṅkaras who were adored as the Devādhideva, the invincible supreme deities. The Jainas further developed their pantheon by assimilating and transforming different Brahmanical legendary characters and deities in Jaina creed which could distinctly be gleaned through their vast literature as well as repository of surviving visual imagery.

While embracing Brahmanical deities, the Jainas have never compromised with their basic tenets of meditation and bodily abandonment represented by the Jinas who were *vītarāgīs* (free from passions and desires) and hence could neither favour nor frown at anybody. It is for this apparent reason that the Jinas were never shown as safety-bestowing or boon-conferring deities as was the case with Buddha, Śiva, Vishṇu, Gaṇeśa and others. But the religion obviously can thrive only with the active support of the masses and this fact was very much in the minds of the Jaina *āchāryas*. The majority of the worshippers aspire for worldly and material possessions from the deities which, however, could not be obtained from the worship of the *vītarāgī* Jinas and hence several deities were conceived and incorporated in Jaina pantheon to cater to the need of the common worshippers. It was done through the inception of the *śāsanadevatās* or the *Yakshas* and *Yakshis*, joining the Jinas on two flanks as guardian deities, who bestow upon the worshippers the desired boons. This socio-religious requirement paved the way for assimilation and mutual understanding between the Brahmanical and Jaina sects.

If we look at the ancient map of India we come across several such sites which have yielded temples and gamut of sculptures related to both the Brahmanical and Jaina sects, the most important of them being Mathurā (U.P.), Osiāñ (Rajasthan), Ellorā (Maharashtra), Khajurāho (M.P.) and Aihoḷe, Halebi and Bādāmī (Karnataka). Besides, Deogarh (U.P.), the Vimalvasahī and Lūṇavasahī (Rajasthan), Tāraṅgā and Kumbhāriā (Gujarat) and Śravaṇabeḷgol (Karnataka) were the Jaina sites of great consequence which had produced profuse amount of Jaina icons. The iconic data at these sites bear testimony to the multidimensional mutual influences. The Pārśvanātha Jaina temple at Khajurāho (*c*. A.D. 950-70), containing all around its facade the figures of Brahmanical deities like Śiva, Vishṇu, Brahmā, Rāma, Balarāma, Kāma, Agni and Kubera along with their respective Śaktis in *āliṅgana* pose, is a remarkable example of coherence and understanding between the two sects. Such figures in *āliṅgana* pose are indeed the violation of accepted norms of the Jaina tradition and were actually carved under the influence of Brahmanical sculptures at Khajurāho. On the other hand, the Jinas also find representation on some of the Brahmanical temples at Khajurāho (Kandariyā Mahādeva and Viśvanātha temples—11th century A.D.), Osiāñ (Sūrya and Harihara temples—8th-9th centuries A.D.) and Bhubaneśvara (Mukteśvara temple—10th century A.D.).

The Jainas in their list of 63 *śalākāpurushas* (great men),[1] finalised during the Kushāṇa-Gupta period, include a number of Brahmanical deities and legendary characters, the most important of which are Bharata Chakravartin, Rāma and Balarāma as Baladevas (or Balabhadras), Lakshmaṇa or Nārāyaṇa and Kṛshṇa as Vāsudevas (or Nārāyaṇas), and Aśvagrīva, Tāraka, Niśumbha, Madhu, Kaiṭabha, Bali, Prahalāda, Rāvaṇa and Jarāsandha as Prativāsudevas (or Pratinārāyaṇas). It may be noted that independent texts were also composed on Rāma and Kṛshṇa; they are the *Paümachariya* of Vimalasūri (A.D. 473), *Padmapurāṇa* of Ravisheṇa (A.D. 678), *Uttarapurāṇa* of Guṇabhadra (9th-10th century A.D.), *Harivaṁśapurāṇa* of Jinasena (A.D. 783) and *Trishashṭiśalākāpurushacharitra* of Hemachandra (mid-12th century A.D.). Of all the deities borrowed from Brahmanical tradition, Rāma and Kṛshṇa, the two great epic characters, undoubtedly occupy the most exalted position in Jaina worship and religious art. They were incorporated in about first-second century A.D. The rendering of Kṛshṇa along with Balrāma begins as early as in the Kushāṇa period. Balarāma and Kṛshṇa were associated with the 22nd Jina Arishṭanemi or Neminātha as his cousins and as a consequence they find representation in the image of Neminātha from Mathura, belonging to the Kushāṇa period. In one instance (State Museum, Lucknow, J 47), the seated figure of Neminātha is flanked by the figures of four-armed Balarāma and Kṛshṇa-Vāsudeva. Balarāma holds *mūsala, hala* while Kṛshṇa bears mace. Another image of late Kushāṇa period shows Kṛshṇa with mace and *chakra*. This association distinctly explains the process of adoption and transformation of Brahmanical deities in Jaina worship. The subsequent examples of such images are known from Baṭeśvara (Agra, U.P.) and Deogarh (Temple No. 2, Lalitpur, U.P.). Owing to the explained kinship of the two, Balarāma and Kṛshṇa were also carved in different narrative panels at Kumbhāriā and Vimalavarahī (11th-12th century A.D.), showing the life of Neminātha. These scenes include the water sport and trial of strength between Neminātha and Kṛshṇa. According to the Jaina tradition and also in visual expression Neminātha is portrayed as victor in a trial of strength with Kṛshṇa which was intended to establish the superiority of Jainism.

Vimalavasahī and Lūṇavasahī (c. 1150-1250 A.D.) exhibit some very interesting renderings of *Kṛshṇalīlā* and other Vaishṇava themes which include *Kāliyadamana* (Pl. 57.3), Kṛshṇa playing *holī* with *kanakaśṛṅgakosa* (as found in *Harshacharita*) with *gopas* and *gopikās*, the episode of Bali and Vāmana, *samudramanthana* and vivid carvings pertaining to Kṛshṇa *janma* and his *bālalīlās*.[2] As compared to Kṛshṇa, the rendering of Rāma was not so popular in Jaina art and the sculptural examples are found only on the Pārśvanātha temple at Khajurāho whereat the figures of Rāma-Sītā-Hanumāna (Pl. 57.4) and Sītā sitting in *aśoka-vātikā* and receiving the message and the ring of Rāma from Hanumāna are carved.[3]

Apart from the above epic characters, several other deities were assimilated directly in Jaina worship with identical iconographic features. The concept and names of such deities are found in the early Jaina works datable between c. third and seventh century A.D. but their detailed iconographic features are enunciated mainly in the works assignable between c. eight and fourteenth century A.D. The list of such deities comprises Gaṇeśa (Jaina *devakulikās* at Osiāñ and Neminātha temple at Kumbhāriā—11th-12th century A.D.), Kshetrapāla (Deogarh and Khajurāho, Pl. 57.7), Lakshmī, Sarasvatī (Mathura, Deogarh, Khajurāho, Pallū, Vimalavasahī, Lūṇavasahī, Kumbhāriā, Humchā—Kushāṇa to 12th century A.D.), Ashṭadikpālas (sometimes their number being ten including Nāgarāja Dharaṇendra and Brahmā), Navagrahas (Pl. 57.1), Ashṭavasus (carved on the Jaina temples of Khajurāho), 64 yoginīs, Indra Brahmaśānti *Yaksha* (Pls. 57.2 & 57.6) and several other deities. In concurrence with the Brahmanical tradition, the *ashṭadikpālas* and the *navagrahas* were carved respectively on the cardinal points and door-lintels of almost all the Jaina temples.

Gaṇeśa, as the remover of obstacles and bestower of success, was incorporated into Jaina pantheon during the early medieval times. According to the *Āchāradinakara* of Vardhamānasūri (A.D. 1412), Gaṇeśa is propitiated even by the gods in order to obtain desirable things. On the basis of the available instances showing Gaṇeśa with rat mount and as carrying lotus, goad, tusk, axe, spear and *modaka* or *modakapātra*, the bearing of Brahmanical iconography is clear (Pl. 57.5). Jaina Sarasvatī also has distinct bearing of Brahmanic Sarasvatī. Their proximity could be ascertained on account of their identical *vāhana* (swan or peacock) and attributes namely, manuscript, vīṇā, rosary, water-vessel, goad and noose.[4] In one of the images carved in the ceiling of Vimalavasahī (A.D. 1150), Sarasvatī is joined by the figures of *sūtradhāra* Loyaṇa and Kelā, the chief architect and sculptor of the temple. She is thus visualized here as the goddess of fine arts.

There are few such Jaina deities who were borrowed but with some changes either in respect of their names or the iconographic features or even both to suit the requirement of Jaina creed. The Brahmaśānti and Kaparddi *yakshas* are the foremost among such deities who occupied important position in visual representations at Śvetāmbara Jaina temples in western India. They distinctly reveal the bearing respectively of Brahmā and Śiva. Likewise, several *yakshas* and *yakshis* associated with the Jinas show such features which suggest that they are the transformations of Vishṇu, Śiva, Brahmā, Kārttikeya, Kāli, Gaurī and Vaishṇavī. In some cases only the names like *Garuḍa* and Kumāra *yakshas* and Kālī, Mahākālī *yakshīs* have been adopted. The *śāsanadevatās* of Ṛshabhanātha, the first Jina, are Gomukha and Chakreśvarī who apparently represent Śiva and Vaishṇavī (Pls. 57.1 & 57.2)

The figures of Saptamātṛkās finding no mention in Jaina works were also carved in some of the examples known from Mathura, Gyaraspur, Vimalavasahī and Khaṇḍagiri. These figures are carved usually in the *parikara* of Ambikā and Gaurī images while at Khaṇḍagiri (Navamuni *Gumphā*—11th century A.D.) they are carved with the Jinas as *yakshīs*, albeit with the features of Indrānī, Kaumārī and other Mātṛkās. We also encounter the figures of several such deities, mainly the female ones, at the prolific Jaina sites like Vimalavasahī, Lūṇavasahī and Kumbhāriā which could not be identified on the testimony of available textual prescriptions. Most of the deities in such cases show the influence of Brahmanical goddesses. Vimalavasahī alone has 16 such goddesses, some of which with bull as mount and holding either *triśūla* or *sarpa* or *triśūla* in both the hands have distinct Śaivite stamp.

Apart from the deities borrowed either directly or indirectly we come across several such icon types at Jaina sites which virtually do not find any textual support and instead their concept and forms appear to have been inspired by Bhrahmanical images. The Jaina *chaumukhī* (*pratimāsarvtobhadrikā*), representing the figures of either the same or different Jinas on four sides, is one such icon types. The earliest examples of Jaina *chaumukhī* are procured from Mathura and are assignable to first century A.D. These images were popular in subsequent centuries, the examples of which are found from all prolific Jaina sites. Scholars generally believe that the conception of Jaina *chaumukhī* was based on the early conception of Jina *samavasaraṇa* showing some advancement upon it.[6] But this view is not acceptable since it does not stand to reason. While it is difficult to find any traditional basis of the conception of Jaina *chaumukhī* in the Jaina works, we come across a number of such sculptures in the Kushāṇa or even earlier art whcih might have inspired the Jinas to carve Jaina *chaumukhī*. It is not impossible that some such representations as the Sārnāth and Sāñchī lion capitals and multifaced *yaksha* figure may have been the source of inspiration.

The conception of *dvitirthī* and *tritīrthī* Jina images, depicting two or three Jinas together, are also perhaps inspired by the syncretic icons of Brahmanical tradition. The Hariharapitāmaha images from Ellorā, Abaneri Khajurāho and elsewhere show the figures of Brahmā, Vishṇu and Śiva either standing or sitting on single pedestals. The Pāla Jina images from Rājgir (Bihar) in some examples show the five- or seven-hooded snake canopy (representing Supārśvanātha and Pārśvanātha) but the cognizances on the pedestal are either conch (of Neminātha) or bull (of Ṛshabhanātha) or elephant (of Ajitanātha) which suggest that inspired by the Brahmanical syncretic icons the Jinas also attempted at such innovatory forms which have never been referred to in any of the Jaina works. The above examples thus represent the syncretic images respectively of Supārśvanātha-Neminātha, Pāśvanātha-Ajitanātha and Pārśvanātha-Mahāvīra.

Besides the rich repository of Jaina images from various sites we have numerous literary references as well which connote Brahmanical influence. The two Jaina epical works namely *Mahāpurāṇa* and *Trishashṭiśalāka-puruṣcharitra*, are of enduring importance from this standpoint. These works have several references to the worship of Śiva and other Brahmanical deities, besides the episodes of Nala-Damayantī, Ahilyā, Bhagīratha and descent of Gaṅgā. Ṛshabhanātha, bearing close semblance with Śiva, has been eulogized in the *Ādipurāṇa* of Jinasena (c. 9th century A.D.) with 1008 appellations which distinctly illustrate how liberally different Brahmanical deities have been imbibed. These names include Svayambhū, Śambhu,

Śaṅkara, Sadyojāta, Trinetra, Jitamanmatha, Tripurāri, Trilochana, Śiva, Īśāna, Bhūtanātha, Mṛtuñjaya, Maheśvara, Mahādeva, Kāmārī, Jagannātha, Lakshmīpati, Dhātā, Brahmā, Hiraṇyagarbha, Viśvamūrti, Vidhātā, Pitāmaha, Chaturānana, Indra, Mahendra, Sūrya, Āditya, Kubera, Vāmanadeva, Rāma and Kṛshṇa.[7]

NOTES AND REFERENCES

1. The earliest list of 63 *śalākāpuruṣas* is found in the *Paümachariya* and some *Āgamic* texts while the detailed anecdotes of these great men are enunciated in the *Mahāpurāṇa* and *Trishashṭiśalākāpurushacharitra*.
2. Consult, Maruti Nandan Prasad Tiwari and Kamal Giri, 'Vaiṣṇava Themes in Dilwara Jaina Temples', *Vājpeya—Prof. K.D. Bajpai Felicitation Volume* (Eds. A.M. Shastri et al.), New Delhi, 1987, pp. 195-202.
3. Maruti Nandan Prasad Tiwari, *Elements of Jaina Iconography*, Varanasi, 1983, pp. 115-16.
4. Maruti Nandan Tiwari and Kamal Giri, 'Images of Gaṇeśa in Jainism', *Ganesh—Studies of an Asian God*, (Ed. Robert L. Brown), New York, 1991, pp. 101-14; 'Sarasvatī in Jaina Tantric Worship,' *Archaeology & Art—Krishnadeva Felicitation Volume* (Ed. C.R.P. Sinha), Pt. II, Delhi, 1990, pp. 311-25.
5. U.P. Shah, *Jaina Rūpamaṇḍana*, Delhi, 1987; Maruti Nandan Prasad Tiwari, *Jaina Pratimāvijñāna*, Varanasi, 1981.
6. U.P. Shah, *Studies in Jaina Art*, Varanasi, 1965, pp. 94-95; *Jain Journal* (Calcutta), Vol. IV, No. 1, July 1971, p. 27.
7. *Ādipurāṇa*, 25, 100-217.

58
ŚIVA TEMPLE, PANAHEDA, RAJASTHAN

P.K. TRIVEDI

I. Introduction

The Paramāras with fluctuating career ruled over a large part of Indian territory for about 500 years. They began their career by the end of the eighth century from Malwa and in due course established their subordinate branches in Rajasthan *viz.* Chandrāvatī, Bhinmal, Kirāḍū and Vāgaḍa. The Vāgaḍa branch was founded by Ḍambarsiṁha, the younger brother of Vairisiṁha and the son of Upendra Raj. The territory of Vāgaḍa country is represented by present districts of Banswara and Dungarpur in south-eastern Rajasthan, adjoining Malwa and Gujarat. A large number of temples in this region at Arthuna, Baroda, Chitari, Galiakot, Talawara and Panaheda were built under their patronage. An excellent temple at the last named place, attributed to one of these illustrious rulers, in the district Banswara, is the scope of the present paper.

II. Site

Panaheda (23°34.5'N; 74°14'E) is mounted on the Topo Sheet No. 46$^1/_2$ of the Survey of India. It is situated about 8 km. due east-north-east of Garhi, the headquarters of a tehsil in Banswara district. Its ancient name was Pāṁśulkheṭaka.[1] The nearest locality is Gopīnatha-kā-Ghoda which in turn is connected by a metalled road by a regular bus service. The surrounding topography is undulated and low hills represent the scattered ranges of the Aravallis.

III. Description of the Temple

The imposing temple complex under reference is built on a low hillock (3.50 m high) serving as a *jagatī*, near *kachchā* road between Panaheda and Gopinātha-Kā-Ghoda. The *jagatī* is partly built with bricks and measures 45x30 m. To the east of the temple complex is a water reservoir, locally called as Nagelā *tālāva* (ancient *nagna taḍāga).*[2] The *pañchāyatana-prāsāda* facing the east, on plan, includes a *pañcharatha garbhagṛiha, antarāla, sabhā-maṇḍapa* with lateral transepts (*pārśvālindas*) and an *ardha-maṇḍapa* approached through a flight of steps (*sopānas*). In the same axis exists a Nandī-*maṇḍapa* (Fig. 1). The temple proper measures 16.50 m in length and 10.50 m in width. The four corner shrines (*karṇa-prāsādas*) identical in plan and composition face the east and west directions (Pl. 58.I).

Elevation

The temple proper is raised on *kharaśilā* over which rests *pīṭha* constituted by a pair of plain courses of *bhiṭṭa, jāḍymba, kaṇi* and a deep *antarāpatra* followed by *kapotāli* punctuated with *chaitya* dormer. Above this lies an incipient band of *(i)* three-pronged (*gagāraka*) motif, *(ii) grāsapaṭṭī* in case of *garbhagṛiha, antarāla* and a part of *sabhāmaṇḍapa* whereas remaining portion of assembly hall and *mukhamaṇḍapa* exhibits courses of *rājasenaka, vedikā* and *āsanapaṭṭa* profusely embellished with alternate arrangement of bell motif, boldly incised *kīrttimukhas* and *chaitya* arches. This is followed by *kakshāsana* stones tastefully designed with circles (*vṛittas*) encompassing the boldly worked figurines of swan (*haṁsa*), parrot (*śuka*), Śiva, Gaṇeśa, couples playing on musical instruments, monkeys shaking a tree and amorous (*līlāsana*) scenes. This is overlain by a band of *vasanta-paṭṭikā*. On the northern side, the *pīṭha* is pierced by a *makara-praṇāla* with its mouth bedecked with a dwarf figurine.[3] *Vedibandha* consists of plain *khura,* neatly chiselled *kumbha* embellished with a median *maṇibandha* and vertically arranged diamonds like a floral design and *chaitya* decor. The plain *kalaśa* is followed by plain *antarāpatra kapotāli* carved with semicircular *chaitya* design, again *kapotāli* punctuated with conical *chaitya*-arches and suspended square *lumās*. The *jaṅghā* show *salilāntaras* and is adorned with vertical repertoire of *nāgara-śikhara* as met in Bhūmija temples of central India and some shrines at Arthuna. A broad *chaitya* band coupled with diamond motif seen here is also noticed in other contemporary and later temples of Vagada area. The *jaṅghā* is relieved with deep niches on cardinal directions, harbouring beautiful images of Chāmuṇḍā on the north, Naṭeśa on the west and Andhakāntaka-Śiva on the southern *bhadra-khaṭṭakas*. Each *khaṭṭaka* covered with a projected roof consists of small pillars (*stambhikās*) crowned by *udgama* dormer which in turn is carved with *induśālikās*. The upper portion of *jaṅghā* reveals *mahā-kevalya*, a projected ribbed awning (*kūṭachhādya*) followed by a pair of *varaṇḍikā* above which begins *śikhara* (Pl. 58.2).

The curvilinear brick built *śikhara* of Bhūmija variety shows *latās* with decoration of *chaitya* arches on the central *rathas* and grouping of three rows of horizontal and five vertical rows of *kūṭastambhas* (miniature *śikharas* resting on pilasters). On the basis of prominent *sūrsenaka* at the base on three principal sides it could be safely attributed to Bhūmija style of temple architecture popular during the time of imperial Paramāras.[4] The *āmalaka* is missing. Further, owing to the damaged superstructure above vestibule and assembly hall, the nature of *śukanāsikā* could not be determined. Like other Bhūmija shrines, the edifice is *niraṅdhāra*.[5] The vestibule exhibits two rows of *stambhakūṭas*. The roofs of *sabhāmaṇḍapa* and *ardhamaṇḍapa* appear to have undergone renovations and show empty shallow niches meant for small icons.

Interior

The square sanctum (2.30m x 2.30m) of *vairāja* class enshrines a big *yonipaṭṭa* with its *vinirāgama* towards north. On it is placed a small Śiva-*liṅga*.[6] The walls of *garbhagṛiha* are plain.

It contains a loose twenty-armed image of Vaikuṇṭha. The ceiling is of *samatala-vitāna* type carved with three whorls of petals of a full blown lotus (*utphulla-kamala*) and boldly worked *grāsa-mukhas* on each *vikarṇa* inside the bejewelled border. The entrance of the *garbhagṛiha* is provided with a moonstone (*chandraśilā*). The moulded door-sill (*udumbara*) exhibits a semicircular projected *mandāraka* adorned with stalked lotus scrolls and is flanked by a bold *kīrttivaktra* on either side. The lintel (*uttaraṅga*) was originally bedecked with a panel of nine planets of which only figurines of Rāhu and Ketu survive on the extreme right besides a seated male devotee in *namaskāra-mudrā*. Presumably *lalāṭa-biṁba* was represented by a figurine of Gaṇeśa which has been defaced now.

The opening of door-frame measures 1.75m x 0.9m. The *dvāra-śākhā* is of *pañchaśākhā* variety attributable to Nandinī class. Its vertical branches are distinguishable to *patra-śākhā, padmapatra, śākhā, rūpastambha* topped by *uchchālaka, patra-śākhā* and the outermost plain *khalva-śākhā* (Pl. 58.3). The lower portion of *pedyās* shows four-armed Śaiva-*pratihārīs* accompanied by male and female attendants, inside a *virālikā-yukta-parikara* surmounted by *makara-mukha* oozing out lotus scrolls and topped by a *grāsa-mukha*. The plain buffer walls (*kapili*) connect the sanctum with *sabhāmaṇḍaspa*. An *antarāla* measuring 2.30m x 1.40m is introduced by means of a pair of *bhitti-stambhaps*. The latter at the base exhibit *kumbha* decorated with indented half diamonds, the shaft (*yashṭi*) relieved with a niche portraying a lady in *tribhaṅga* pose, carrying a pot and akimbo. The niche is crowned by pediment (*udgama*). The upper portion reveals *uchchālaka, hīragrāhṇaka* and plain *bharaṇī*. The *samatala-vitāna* of vestibule is carved with three medallions.

The *sabhāmaṇḍapa* measures 8.65m x 6.40m and consists of a central hall and lateral transepts (*pārśvālindas*). A stone inscription dated A.D. 1059 of king Maṇḍalīka of the Vāgaḍa branch of the Paramāras incised in Devanāgarī characters in Sanskrit language is fixed in a niche of the hall. The central ceiling (*karoṭaka*) composed of concentric rings rests on eight pillars and pilasters of *miśraka* order, a feature of Marū-Gurjara style.[7] The pillars are octagonal (*ashṭāśra*) at the base and show: *(i) kumbha* carved with indented half diamonds, *(ii) varaṇḍikā*, *(iii) yashṭi* relieved with deep niches containing figures of four-armed Śiva and Māheśvarī. Śiva is shown carrying *abhaya, sarpa, khaṭvāṅga*, bowl or *abhaya, sarpa, triśūla* and *bījapūraka* whereas Māheśvarī holds *abhaya, sarpa, khaṭvāṅga* and *bījapūraka* as attributes, *(iv) parṇabandha*, *(v)* plain circular band, *(vi)* circular lion frieze, *(vii)* circular band of *varaṇḍikā* punctuated with *chaitya* motif, *(viii)* plain circular band, and *(ix)* plain *bharaṇī* above which rests bracket figures represented by a warrior with bow and arrow, seated Māheśvarī displaying *varada, triśūla, sarpa, bījapūraka*, Gaṇeśa holding radish, *paraśū*, indistinct and sweet balls, an arrow shooter in action, Śiva seated in *ardha-paryankāsana* holding *varada, ḍamarū, triśūla* and *bījapūraka* and a monkey in action.

The central ceiling (*karoṭaka*) is attributable to *sabhāmārga* order.[8] It is formed by: *(i)* the lowermost *karṇadardarikā*, *(ii)* a band of plain *gagāraka*, *(iii) grāsapaṭṭī*, *(iv)* knife-edged *kaṇi*, *(v)* plain *kolā*, *(vi) gagāraka*, *(vii) grāsapaṭṭī*, and *(viii) rūpadhārā*, bedecked with various scenes *viz.* worship of Gaṇeśa, Śiva-liṅga, music and dancing scenes. This tier is further beautifully enriched by sixteen tastefully modelled *devāṅganās* resting on *vidyādhara*-brackets (Pl. 58.4). Of them, only five survive *viz.* Kanudkā, Alasā, Chāpāvatī, Viṇā-Vādinī and Subhagāminī. This tier is followed by two courses of *gajatālu* and four rings of *kolā* which ultimately encompasses a central hanging *padmakeśara* now missing.[9] The *kolā* course on its edge shows small male figurines in *namaskāra-mudrā*.

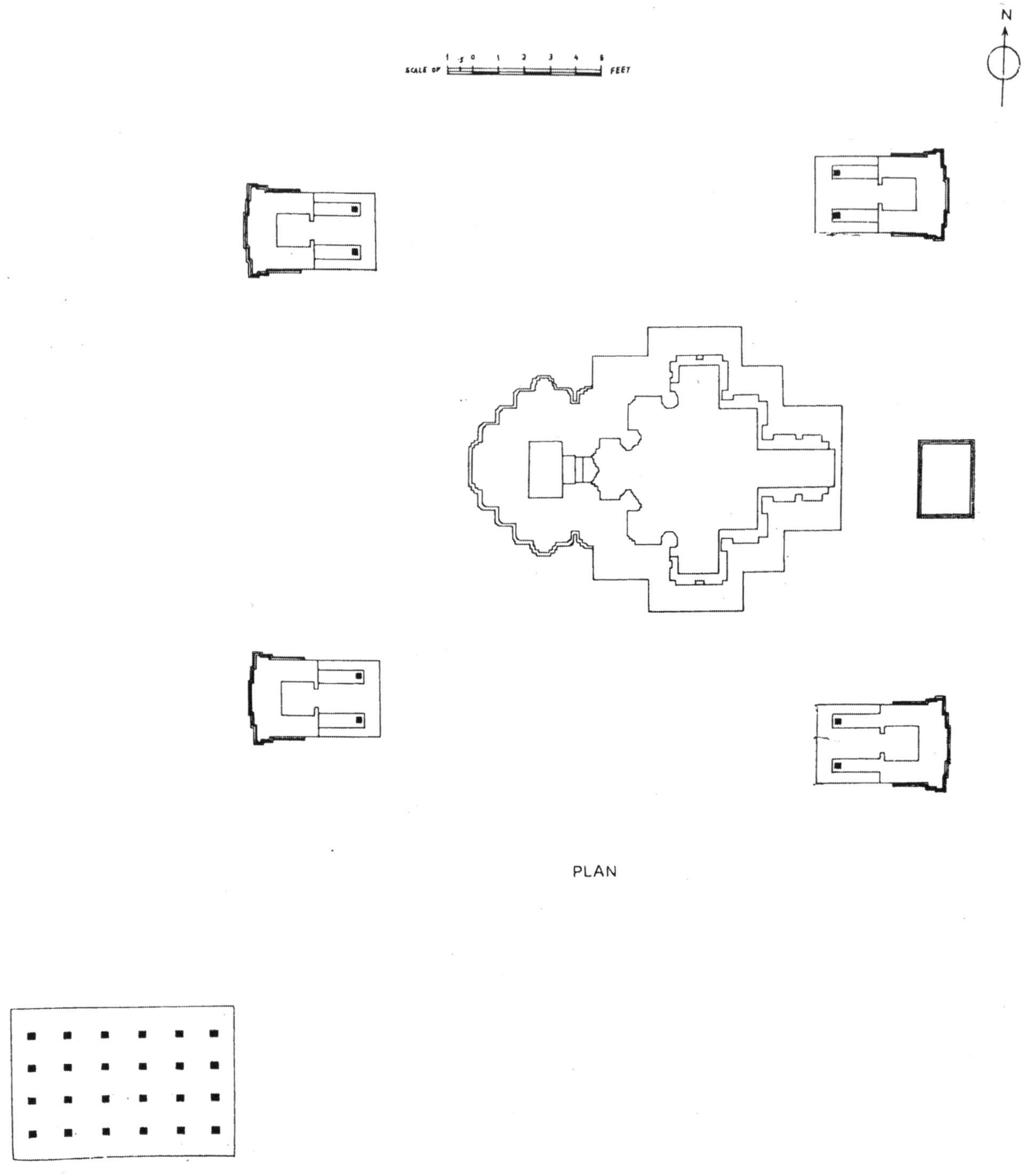

Fig. 1. Śiva Temple & Monastery, Panheda, Rajasthan.

The *pārśvālindas* resting on dwarf pillars (*kuḍyastambhas*) exhibit *samatala-vatāna* variety of ceiling bedecked with full blown medallions. The *mukhamaṇḍapa* (2.90 x 3.35 m) is also provided with a similar ceiling. The architraves supporting the ceiling are carved with war scenes, horse riders, soldiers with swords and musicians, etc.

Nandī-Maṇḍapa

This small construction almost square (2.22 x 2.13 m) on plan is raised on a 0.90 m high platform. It is roofed by a domical superstructure of bricks. Its interior reveals a flat ceiling (*samatala-vitāna*) carved with a full blown medallion. It retains two statues of couchant Nandī, assignable to *circa* eleventh century.

Monastery

Towards the southwest corner of the temple complex exist the remains of an edifice. Its components show affinity with temple complex. Presumably this single-storeyed construction served as a monastery for Śaiva teachers.

IV. Sculpture

(a) The *kakshāsana* and *vedikā* are embellished with attractive *līlāsana* panels, beautifully designed beaded circles encompassing a separate couple *viz.* a lady with boar, *purushṭiya, viparītarata*, cunnilingus (*kākila*), another scene of bestiality, amorous group (*goūthika*), etc. The cause of their depiction appears to be certain magico-religious beliefs and practices associated with sex under the influence of Tantrism and conventionalism.[10]

(b) The parrot (*śuka*) is shown in an enchanting manner inside the *vṛittas* on *kakshāsana*. Here a pair is depicted with beaks joined together. Two monkeys shaking a tree and *haṁsa* eating pearls are also portrayed.

(c) Two stone images of *śaivāchāryas* are lying in *sabhāmaṇḍapa*. In the first image the bearded teacher, seated in *padmāsana* on a plain two-tiered, high cushion, is shown with flying *gandharvas* and *vidyādharas* on either side of his head. On the top of *toraṇa*-arch formed by lotus scrolls emerging out from *makara-mukha* inside a niche is depicted a seated Lakulīśa figurine. This suggests that Śaiva teacher was the superintendent of Śaiva monastery and the temple (Pl. 58.5).

The other specimen illustrated in the same photograph reveals more prominent treatment. The central monk is modelled seated on a comparatively low two-tiered *pīṭha* adorned with lotus stalk scrolls. The stalked object held in hands is damaged. The carefully arranged bun of matted locks (*jaṭā-jūṭa*) is conspicuous, *i.e.* the uppermost tier is shown more tapering as compared to previous image. The flanking standing monks with folded hands are carved more minutely. Above on either side of the head is depicted a flying *vidyādhara* holding a *mālā*. The upper portion reveals a niche crowned by a plain triangular pediment dormer on either side on the top of a pilaster carved in low relief. Inside niches are displayed a male musician and a male dancer. On the top of *toraṇa* oozing out from crocodile mouth was presumably shown a Lakulīśa figure inside a niche (now damaged) as found in the other specimens.

Stylistically both of these images could be assigned to third quarter of eleventh century. These images confirm that Panaheda was an important centre of Lakulīśa-Pāśupata cult during Paramāras in Vāgaḍa country. It was visited by Śaiva ascetics and followers to imbibe knowledge under their masters. These images represent distinguished teachers, *maṭhādhipatīs* or heads of temple institutions. They were not only preceptors but also looked after the worship and maintenance of temples and monasteries. They also propagated tenets of Śaivism.

V. Iconography

(a) Vaikuṇṭha

Assignable to *circa* eleventh century, this three-faced composite deity is carved on a faceted pedestal. The central figure of Vishṇu wearing *kirīṭa-mukuṭa* is modelled seated in *ardha-paryaṅkāsana* on a cushion, carved with Garuḍa in human form. The face of Vishṇu is roundish with an incipient chin. The side faces are shown putting on headgear of *jaṭā-jūṭa*. The hands preserved exhibit different attributes, some of which in clockwise fashion are identified as *varadāksha, aṅkuśa, vajra* in proper right hands and *kheṭaka, abhaya, vismaya-mudrā, pāśa, tarjani-mudrā* and *śaṅkha* in the left hands.[11] On his proper right side of back is seen an arrow-case (Pl. 58.6). Above on either side are depicted tiny figurines of Brahmā carrying *varada, sruka, pothī* and *kamaṇḍalu* and Śiva holding *varada, triśūla, sarpa* and *bījapūraka*. Similar images are known from Arthuna also in which side faces are shown more distinctly. One such image is stored in National Museum, New Delhi.

(b) Chāmuṇḍā

Ten-armed goddess portrayed as northern *bhadra-deva* with ferocious look and sunken eyes is modelled, showing a scorpion on her sunken abdomen. She puts on *jaṭā-mukuṭa, sarpa-kuṇḍalas, sarpa-hāra, sarpa-udarabandha, vyāghracharma,* a long *muṇḍamālā, valayas,* etc. Her right hand displays *varada, triśūla,* horn (*śriṅga*), *śakti* and kettle drum while left hands carry *khaṭvāṅga, vismaya-mudrā,* mutilated and a bowl carved with a fish.[12] Below right is depicted a corpse resting his head on left hand. To the left are shown *pretas.*

(c) Naṭeśa

Dancing Śiva is modelled gracefully on a pedestal with his face towards right and thrusting the weight on left leg. He wears *jaṭa-mukuṭa,* ear and neck ornaments, a long *vanamālā,* etc. He displays *varada-mudrā, tarjani, triśūla, sarpa,* kettle-drum, *khaṭvāṅga, sarpa,* bow, *khappara* and *siṁha-karṇa mudrā* in clockwise fashion. Below is seen a male drummer playing on *ūrdhva-mridaṅga* and Vṛishabha, the mount. This god depicted on rear niches of Śiva temples in Banswara district is a characteristic feature of this area.[13]

(d) Andhakāntaka-Śiva

Ten-armed standing Śiva in *aliḍha-mudrā* is carved keeping his left leg on *padma-pīṭha.* He is adorned with *jaṭā-mukuṭa, ratna-keyūras, kaṭaka-valayas,* neck ornaments, *pāda-valayas* and *pāda-jālakas.* His face is turned towards right. He pierces the demon through a *triśūla* held in two hands. The other attributes in clockwise fashion are identified as *khaḍga, bāṇa, ḍamarū, dhanusha, pāśa, tarjani* and *kapāla.* To the left below is carved Vṛishabha with its head turned left while on the right side is depicted an emaciated Yogīśvarī seated on her knees, below the *padma-pīṭha* (Pl. 58.7). She holds a dagger in her right hand whereas the left one carries a cup for catching blood drops as they trickle down.[14]

VI. Date

A stone inscription affixed on the walls of *sabhāmaṇḍapa* informs that this temple was built by king Maṇḍandeva in honour of Śiva in V.S. 1116 (A.D. 1059).[15] This excellent and well-preserved temple complex is perhaps the least known but solitary example of the Bhūmija mode in the Vāgaḍa country. Regarding chronology it could be placed at par with famous Udayeśvara temple near Vidisha.[16]

Acknowledgements

I am grateful to Sarvashri Surendra Kumar Acharya and R.P. Mathur for preparing the line drawings and photographs. The copyright of the photographs rests with the Archaeological Survey of India.

NOTES AND REFERENCES

1. *C.I.I.*, Vol. VII, Part II, p. 282.
2. *Ibid.* The water of this *tālāva* is still used for cultivation and other purposes by the villagers. The devotees could take bath in *nagna-taḍāga* and directly ascend the temple to offer prayers.
3. This sort of *praṇālas*, a feature of Marū-Gurjara temple, have been reported from Mahāvīra temple, Kumbhaṛia and Chandrāvatī assignable to eleventh century. See M.A. Dhaky, 'The "Praṇāla" in Indian, South-Asian and South-East Asian Sacred Architecture', *Rūpa Pratirūpa*, Alice Bonner Commemoration Volume, (ed.) Bettina Baümer, Biblia Impex Private Ltd., New Delhi, 1982, pp. 121-22, pls. 1-2.
4. Krishna Deva, 'Bhūmija Temples', *Studies in Indian Temple Architecture*, (ed.) Pramod Chandra, American Institute of Indian Studies, New Delhi, 1975, pp. 90-91.
5. *Ibid.*
6. This Śiva-*liṅga* is not original.
7. M.A. Dhaky, 'The genesis and development of Marū-Gurjara Temple Architecture', *Studies in Indian Temple Architecture*, p. 137.
8. J.M. Nanavati and M.A. Dhaky, 'The Ceilings in the Temples of Gujarat', *Bulletin of Baroda Museum and Picture Gallery*, Baroda, Vols. XVI-XVII, Baroda, 1963, p. 77, pl. 59. Similar ceilings are invariably found in *sabhāmaṇḍapa* of contemporary large temples at Arthuna, the capital seat of the Paramāras of Vagada.
9. In 1981 it was seen by the author.
10. Devangan Desai, *Erotic Sculptures of India—A Socio-Cultural Study*, Munshiram Manoharlal, New Delhi, 1975, p. 86.
11. These attributes, however, require re-verification.
12. Agrawala, R.C., 'Some Paramāra Brahmanical sculptures from Banswara, Rajasthan', *Art of the Paramāras of Malwa*, (ed.) R.K. Sharma, Agam Kala Prakashan, Delhi, August 1979, p. 23.
13. *Ibid.*, p. 22.
14. *E.H.I.*, Vol. II, Part I, p. 193.
15. *C.I.I.*, *op. cit.*, p. 92. Record bespeaks that Udayeśvāra temple was commenced in A.D. 1059 and completed in A.D. 1080.

59

RELIGIOUS SYNCRETISM IN THE PALA-SENA ART

PRANABANANDA JASH

Dissemination of religious syncretism is the major contribution of the Pāla-Sena art in the realm of Indian religious studies. Considering the extensive time and space covered by the Pāla-Sena art and also its prolific output of variegated nature, it is difficult to throw light on each and every aspect of the religious bearings and significance of the objects. It is needless to point out that these art objects occupy an extremely significant position not only in the annals of Indian art, but they also exhibit conspicuous contemporary religious systems as well as religious environment.

An attempt has been made in this paper to show the religious toleration and mutual concordance among the different sects of the Pāla-Sena period. Though it cannot be said that there was no religious rivalry or persecution whatsoever at any time during the long stretch of time of their rule, the fact remains that the evidence for persecution is very limited indeed, and the nature of it is such that it pales into insignificance when compared to examples in the history of some other parts of the world, or when compared with examples in the later history of India itself.

In the entire history of ancient India, there are so few alleged or authenticated cases of persecution by kings that one hardly gives importance to them. There are some who almost take for granted that great religious tolerance and viable adjustment in religious performances prevailed in ancient India in all times. In their understanding the phenomenon of tolerance is an integral part of 'Hindu thought'. S. Radhakrishnan thus believed :

> The Hindu view is not motivated by any consideration of political expediency. It is bound up with its religion and not its policy.[1]

In fact, from the earliest times various schools of thought propounded the doctrines of agnosticism, atheism and materialism. Jainism, Buddhism, and later on, Christianity, Islam and other religious sects were professed and practised their respective religions alongwith Brahmanism or Hinduism side by side. They built their places of worship and established their respective ways of life. From the earliest days this kind of environment in the realm of religion seems never to have been denied. As Max Weber opines :

> It is an undoubted fact that in India, religious and philosophical thinkers were able to enjoy perfect, nearly absolute, freedom for a long period. The freedom of thought in ancient India was so considerable as to find no parallel in West before the most recent age.[2]

There is, in fact, no denying the fact that rivalry did exist but it is only one of the features of the religious life of the times. It is to be noted that "side by side there developed a syncretistic attitude in religion— a spirit of tolerance and mutual give and take. A modified monolatry, which maintained the supremacy of the particular supreme deity of the community while at the same time admitting the existence and right to worship of other gods, made its appearance. Śaṅkarāchārya has been credited with the initiation of the *Pañchāyatana-Pūjā*— the worship of the five gods, Vishṇu, Śiva, Śakti or Devī, Sūrya and Gaṇeśa, the principal deity of the worshipper being placed in the middle and the other four in the four corners of a square. But whether it is Śaṅkara or Kumārila or somebody else that introduced it, the fact remains that the idea caught the imagination of the public as the best solution of the rather perplexing problem of harmonising monotheism with polytheism and allaying communal bitterness and religious quarrel."[3]

It is thus interesting to note the custom and character of the *Pañcāyatana-Pūjā* of the Smārtas who are eclectic in their religious concepts. The principal object of worship in it was usually in the form of an aniconic emblem which symbolised five major cult deities of Hinduism. Monier Williams has described the worship of *Pañcāyatana-Pūjā* as he noticed it being practised by the devotees of central and southern India:

> Five stones or symbols believed to be permeated by the essences of the five chief deities are-
>
> (1) the black stone, representing Vishṇu;
>
> (2) the white stone representing Śiva's essence;
>
> (3) the red stone representing Gaṇeśa;
>
> (4) the small piece of metallic ore, representing the wife of Śiva; and
>
> (5) the piece of crystal representing the sun.
>
> All five symbols are placed on a round open metal dish, called *Pañcāyatana*, and are arranged in five different methods, according to the preference given to any one of the five deities at the time of worship."[4]

The cult affiliation of the worshipper is to be known from the particular mode of placing in the centre the symbol of any one of the five cult deities. The *Pañcāyatana-Pūjā* of the Smārtas is also known from the architectural peculiarities of the early and mediaeval temples of India. In this type of temple construction the central shrine housing the chief deity is surrounded by four smaller shrines on the four corners of the quadrangle containing four other deities.[5]

Any way, we are here primarily concerned with the phenomena of religious liberty and tolerance which are projecting on the syncretistic sculptural representations of the Pāla-Sena period. Against a general background of the theory pertaining to the emergence of the concept of syncretistic icons, we propose to deal specifically with the Pāla-Sena iconographical representation and its religious bearings on the subject under review.

Without entering into subtle sculptural peculiarities of the Pāla-Sena art or the medium of its expression which have been analysed by competent scholars,[6] it is rather befitting to reproduce a group of icons that explicitly exhibits adequate religious feelings of the contemporary age. The basic stylistic character of the Pāla-Sena sculpture appears to have been predetermined by its purpose, which is distinctly religious. It usually depicted the human forms representing various deities, male as well as female. As produced to occupy a pedestal in a shrine each of them is almost invariably frontally conceived and wrought in a stela background. The larger part in the centre of the stela is covered by the image itself, while the left out spaces around are found to be covered by decorative designs, motifs and attendant figures. Though frontally conceived, the central figure, *i.e.* the image proper, is always in high relief and through the passage of time it shows a trend to become a sculpture in the round and almost detached from the stela. This progressive tendency towards rounded plasticity may also be noted in the decorative designs, which are mostly floral and sometimes architectural, as well as motifs representing leogryphs (*śārdūla*), singly or an elephant (*gajasiṁha*), swan (*haṁsa*) and aquatic monsters (*makaras*), arranged in an ascending order on the two sides of the principal image converging sometimes to a *kīrtimukha* motif on the top of the stela. The outer edge of the stela is generally bordered with beads, scrolls, flames and some other motifs. The architectural forms usually noticed on the stela include pilasters with lintel, three-lobed niches and in later examples the facade of a temple.[7]

The deities are found standing or seated on lotus-seats placed on a pedestal which in its turn shows *ratha* projections counting three to seven. A close scrutiny of these minor aspects of a sculpture is not only helpful to study the spirit or motive behind the origin of the theme, but it is also helpful in determining its date on stylistic ground. Of course, it is to be noted cautiously because during the long period of the Pāla-Sena sculptures, motifs are found to be introduced, withdrawn and reintroduced from time to time. So it is needless to say that exclusive reliance on the representation of a single motif is liable to an error in judgement. Moreover, some of the pre-Pāla sculptures from Paharpur bear close affinities with that of the Pāla art. Thus some scholars would think that at Paharpur we have "a vigorous school of sculpture, already differentiated from Gupta art and foreshadowing the characteristics of Pāla art."[8]

With this brief observation about the characteristic features of the Pāla-Sena art we may now proceed to explain a few syncretistic icons of the Pāla-Sena period exhibiting the spirit of catholicity and tolerance among the various sects of Hinduism, or even of Buddhism too. Of course, as we have already pointed out, it does not mean that animosity and rivalry did not exist among the votaries of different sects. The unmitigated sectarian rivalry and bitterness are manifested in the representations of Śiva in the form of Śarabhesa[9] punishing Narasiṁha and in the Ekapāda Trimurti of Śiva or its Vaishṇava counterpart, Śiva or Vishṇu occupying the central position, Brahmā being invariably projected as a lateral accretion in the attitude of bowing to the central deity.[10]

But evidences, both literary and archaeological, are not wanting to believe that positive efforts were being made for bringing about rapprochment and reconciliation between the members of the rival sects "even from a very early period when some of them had not come into being and others that had originated were being systematised."[11] Available evidences at our disposal disclose the fact that the worship of syncretistic cults, *viz.* Harihara, Ardhanārīśvara, Mārtaṇḍa-Bhairava, etc., became popular in northern India from the time of the Guptas; the spirit of conciliation and compromise seems to have pervaded the relations between these sects since the time of the Kushāṇas.[12]

Of the syncretistic images, the names Harihara and Ardhanārīśvara, seem to have appeared earlier in Indian visual representation. A Harihara image of the Pāla period housed in a temple in the village Anti of the Gayā district (Bihar) portrays the fusion of two great gods of Hinduism.[13] The four-armed deity is characterised by his head-dress which is composed of the *jaṭāmukuṭa* and *kirīṭamukuṭa*. The deity is holding a trident and a rosary in the right hands and a discus (*chakra*) and a conch-shell (*śaṅkha*) in the left hands. There are also the figures of Nandin and Garuḍa carved on appropriate sides on the pedestal. The distinction is emphasised in the treatment of the *yajñopavīta* and the garland worn by the deity. There are also the figures of a pot-bellied Śiva-*gaṇa* and an attendant of Vishṇu on the right and the left sides respectively.

Similar interesting image of Harihara exquisitely carved on stone is now preserved in a private collection of the temple priest (Mahanta) of Bodh Gayā, Bihar.[14] This ninth century A.D. sculptural representation of four-armed Harihara is holding a trident and a rosary in his right hands and a discus and a conch-shell in the left hands. The right side has a snake with its tail coiled into a circle adorning the side of the head, a human skull tucked into the middle of the bracelet and a loin-cloth of tiger-skin. The left portion is also marked by a *kirīṭamukuṭa*, a *vanamālā* hanging down the shoulder and a *pītāmbara* serving as the lower garment. The god is flanked by two male attendants, one on each side. Nandin and Garuḍa have been placed on the right and the left sides respectively facing their masters.

Another image of the Pāla-Sena period hailing from Bihar, now housed in the Indian Museum, Calcutta,[15] may be described in this connection. This composite icon of Harihara is four-armed holding a trident and a conch-shell in the back hands, while in the front hands there are a skull-cup and a discus. The two halves of the main image are also nicely emphasised by the treatment of the headgear, the ornaments, the long garland and the respective *vāhanas* (vehicles) of Śiva and Vishṇu. But the significance and unique feature of the panel lie in the fact that Sūrya standing on his seven-horsed chariot driven by Aruṇa, and the Buddha on a double-petalled lotus, are shown accompanying the god on his either side. In fact, we have no textual evidence referring to Sūrya and Buddha as attendant deities of Harihara, nor have they been shown as mere attendants, for the manner in which separate sections of the pedestal have been allotted to them really suggests them to be cult objects for worship.[16] This outstanding representation thus betrays in a striking manner not only the combination of the Brahmanical deities, like Śiva, Vishṇu and Sūrya, but also that of the Buddha with them. This perhaps belonged to the Pāla period when Buddhism had imbibed Tantrika elements in it.[17] Images of Vishṇu-Lokeśvara are also found in parts of eastern India. Again, the images of Śiva-Lokeśvara and Sūrya-Lokeśvara also discovered from eastern India and housed in the Ashutosh Museum, Calcutta University, deserve special attention. These kinds of icons clearly illustrate a close association of Bodhisattva Lokeśvara with the prominent Hindu cult deities.[18]

The iconographic peculiarities of Vasudhārā (also known by the name of Vasundharā, Bhumī or Pṛthivī, the mother Earth) may also be noted in this connection. It represents distinct syncretistic attitude of the Buddhist and the Brahmanical ideas. Worship of this goddess was greatly prevalent among the Buddhists because of her guardianship over the riches. It is generally believed that the emanation of Vasudhārā, like Jambhala, takes place either from Akshobhya or from Ratnasambhavā. To the Buddhists Vasudhārā is the counterpart of Jambhala.[19] In the *Sādhanamālā*[20] she is described as two-armed deity carrying the ears of corns in a vessel in the left and displays the *varada* pose by the right—

> *Vasudhārāṁ pītavarṇāṁ dhānya*
> *mañjarinānāratna-varshamaṇaghaṭa vāmahastāṁ*
> *dakshiṇena varadāṁ sarvālaṁkārabhūshitāṁ...*

A four-armed image of Vasudhārā has been found from Nālandā.[21] The deity holds a lotus stalk and a pot with ears of corn in the left while the lower right hand exhibits the *varada* pose.

As time rolled on this fusion assumed more important shape and this is illustrated by the Pradyūmneśvara motif during the time of Vijaya Sena's rule in Bengal.[22] Here Śiva, Umā, Lakshmī and Nārāyaṇa are carved on both the sides of statue to harmonise—the Harihara, Lakshmī-Nārāyaṇa, Umā-Maheśvara forms.[23]

In this connection we may note an interesting icon of Ardhanārīśvara showing the amalgamation of the Īśvara (Śiva) and Nārī (Śakti). This form of image is of the late Pāla period hailing from the village of Purapara near Rampal in Bangladesh and is now preserved in the Rajshahi Museum.[24] While studying the image N.K. Bhattashali observes:

> The image appears to have had only two arms, one arm is broken away at the shoulder and the other at the elbow, and the lower part of the image beneath the knee is altogether missing. The face has also been slightly scratched in places... the contrast of the male and the female halves of the image has been ably shown and the careful observer can readily mark the differences between the right and the left halves, in physiognomy, ornaments and dress.[25]

A large number of such composite images have been found in various places of Bihar, Bengal, Benaras and Mathura. Hara-Gaurī, Umā-Maheśvara, Umā-Āliṅgana-mūrti, Umā-sahita-Chandraśekhara, etc. type of combined images of the Pāla-Sena period were very popular. It is stated in the *Rāma-charita*[26] that Bhīma, the Kaivarta ruler, worshipped this form of the deity. It is no wonder that in this region, where the Tāntrika cult developed to a great extent, these poses of the deity would be heartily welcome.[27]

It should be remembered that with the introduction of Tantrism the earlier method of worship was modified and it encouraged the inclusion of combined images of Śiva and his female energy on a large scale. The abundance of composite images of Śiva and Pārvatī indicates that the devotees worshipped Śiva and his Śakti in the Tāntrika form,[28] which popularized this type of a combined cult. It is to be noted in this connection that the Tāntrika worshippers of

Tripurasundarī, another name of Umā or Pārvatī, are required to meditate on the Devī as seated on the lap of Śiva in the *Mahāpadmāsana*,[29] and these composite images were used by them as aids for the correct performance of the *dhyāna-yoga.*

The eclectic attitude and liberal approach of the Hindu religious sects during the Pāla-Sena period are further reflected in the representation of the concept of *Tri-mūrti* image. Thus, when Brahmā was added to the image of Harihara it came to be known as the Harihara Pitāmaha and this type of images have been discovered all over India.[30]

Without citing more examples in this regard it is presumed that the syncretistic representation primarily expressed the spirit of reconciliation and cordial relations that prevailed among the followers of different sects of the Brahmanical and non-Brahmanical religious systems. And this also tends us to the irrefutable conclusion that notwithstanding the prevailing cult-rivalry, the movement of religious syncreticism and mutual amelioration and toleration was also gaining momentum during the Pāla-Sena period.

NOTES AND REFERENCES

1. S. Radhakrishnan, *Eastern and Western Thought*, Second Edition, London, Oxford University Press, 1940, p. 316.
2. Donald Eugene Smith, *India as a Secular State*, Princeton University Press, 1963, pp. 61-62.
3. *The Age of Imperial Kanauj*, Bharatiya Vidya Bhavan, Bombay, an article contributed by H.D. Bhattacharyya, pp. 327-28.
4. Monier Williams, *Religious Thought and Life in India*, pp. 411-12.
5. J.N. Banerjee, *Development of Hindu Iconography*, Calcutta, p. 542.
6. R.D. Banerji, *Eastern Indian School of Mediaeval Sculpture*, Delhi, 1933; N.K. Bhattashali, *Catalogue of the Buddhist and Brahmanical Sculptures in the Dacca Museum*, Dacca, 1929.
7. S.K. Saraswati, *Early Sculpture of Bengal*, Calcutta, 1937; *A Survey of Indian Sculpture*, Calcutta, 1957.
8. B.K. Chatterji, 'Pāla Art of Gauḍa and Magadha', *Modern Review*, Vol. XLV, p. 85.
9. J.N. Banerjee, *op. cit.*, p. 486; B.P. Sinha, *Archaeology and Art of India*, Delhi, 1979, pp. 156-70.
10. J.N. Banerjee, *op. cit.*, p. 519.
11. *Ibid.*, p. 540; for details, see Pranabananda Jash, *History of Śaivism*, Calcutta, 1974, Chapters IX-X, pp. 134 ff.
12. In an interesting gold coin of the Kushāṇa king Huvishka it is depicted— "Śiva facing, three-headed, nimbate; clad only in waist band, ithyphallic; has four arms and hands, in which are goad, wheel, trident and thunderbolt." The representation of wheel or *cakra* (the emblem of Vishṇu) in the hand of Śiva leads to suggest "the beginning of the interesting composite icon of Harihara of subsequent days." J.N. Banerjee, *op. cit.*, p. 124.
13. *Ibid.*, p. 547, Pl. XLVIII. 1.
14. Kalpana Desai, *Iconography of Vishṇu*, p. 53, Fig. 46.
15. J.N. Banerjee, *op. cit.*, p. 547.
16. *Ibid.*, p. 547, Pl. XLVI, Fig. 4.
17. Pranabananda Jash, *op. cit.*, p. 138.
18. J.N. Banerjea, *op. cit.*, pp. 554-55.

19. *Ibid.*, p. 560.
20. *Ibid.*, Pl. XLVIII, Fig. 2; two Vasudharā images from Kurkihar during the time of Rājyapāla are described in the *Journal of Indian Society of Oriental Art*, Vol. II, p. 72.
21. J.N. Banerjea, *op. cit.*, p. 560, fn. 1; A. Ghosh, *A Guide to Nalanda*, pp. 26-27.
22. N.G. Majumdar, *Inscriptions of Bengal*, III, pp. 42-56; Pranabananda Jash, *History and Evolution of Vaiṣṇavism in Eastern India*, Calcutta, 1982.
23. Pranabananda Jash, *op. cit.*, p. 143.
24. R.D. Banerji, *op. cit.*, Pl. LVI.
25. N.K. Bhattashali, *op. cit.*, pp. 130-31.
26. *Rāmacarita* of Sandhyākaranandī, 2.27.
27. Pranabananda Jash, *op. cit.*, pp. 165-66.
28. *History of Bengal*, ed., R.C. Majumdar, Vol. I, pp. 444-45.
29. *Saundaryalaharī*, verses—40 ff.
30. Pranabananda Jash, *op. cit.*, pp. 143 ff.

60

SOME OBSERVATIONS ON THE IMAGES OF KUBERA

PRITHVI KUMAR AGRAWALA

While commenting on the iconography of the Yakshas and their overlord Kubera, J.N. Banerjea illustrated a remarkable sculpture from the Lucknow Museum with the following remarks, "Reference may be made here to one such icon of the god belonging to the late Gupta period, now in the collection of the Mathura Museum. Two-armed bejewelled Kubera, slightly pot-bellied, is shown seated in the *ardhaparyaṅka* pose on a cushioned seat beneath which are two jars (of treasure, perhaps symbolising the *śaṅkha-* and *padma-nidhis*) on one of which his right leg is placed; he holds a cup in his right hand and a pouch in his left and is shown attended on either side by a bearded male" and a female (Pl. 60.2). The iconography has no doubt developed to a great extent by this period, but its former traits are not altogether obliterated.[1]

Anyway, this excellently preserved image of the fine artistic style of the seventh century A.D. deserves our closer attention here (Pl. 60.1). There may be pointed out several discrepancies in the above description of the learned authority. In fact, the sculpture under mention is not from Mathura as one may get the impression from its caption given under the illustration and on p. xxi or Banerjea's magnum opus. It actually comes from Pabhosa, Allahabad district and is preserved in the State Museum of Lucknow (not in the Mathura Museum as stated by Banerjea). Although Banerjea has given no indication of its earlier publication, the same was treated in significant details by Bhagawat Sharan Upadhyay in his excellent paper that appeared in 1942 issue of the *Journal of the Indian Society of Oriental Art*, Calcutta, with even two photographs of the image.[2] He dates the sculpture to the early medieval period and calls it as representing Jambhala though in his description of it he also mentions it as that of Kubera. Lately, N.P. Joshi while making a study of early images of Kubera in his work on ancient Indian iconography has taken into consideration the remarkable features of this Kubera image, which will no doubt be found to represent typical iconic concept of the post-Gupta stage of iconographic evolution. N.P. Joshi has rightly made the use of the name Jambhala for the Buddhist form of this deity and with this restricted application of the two names observes as follows: "In this context the Kubera image of the seventh century coming from Pabhosa and in the Lucknow Museum (Lko Mus. No. G 56), is noteworthy, in which there are, together with the attributes of *nakulaka* and *madyapātra*, two *ghaṭas* placed near his feet which had by this time become characteristic features of the Kubera icon. In this reference it would be reasonable to pay some attention to Jambhala or Buddhist Kubera. In the general depictions there is no difference between the images of Jambhala and Kubera. ... In the Kubera images the *ghaṭas* are placed normally but in case of Jambhala the *ghaṭas* are put turned upside-down yielding jewels. In these[3] images there is no indication to be seen to Kubera's *naravāhan* aspect."[4]

The two jars (*ghaṭas*) below the lower projected base of the raised seat of the god in the Pabhosa sculpture are to be no doubt identified as any two of the Nine Nidhis (treasures) of Kubera, the God of Riches. However, their identity as the *Śaṅkha* and *Padma Nidhis* cannot be ascertained for want of any specific features of the two Nidhi shapes except the fact that both are simple pitchers containing riches shown to the brim. Upadhyay was indeed quite wrong in taking these details of the *ghaṭas* to form *pāda-pīṭha* of a general type, which he described thus : "... the right one (*i.e.* leg) is supported by a double faced '*pīthī*' (footstool), carved along the ridge of the '*bhadrapītha*'.[5] "But he did not miss their identity as the pots full of riches when he observed, "Below the cushion on which the deity sits, the rectangular pedestal shows the double '*pādapīthīs*' (footstools) shaped like vessels closed with lids. It is but natural that the lord of wealth should place his feet on pots full of jewels (*ratnapātra*)."[6] In fact, the two pots-of-riches are taken here, as in certain other images of this god,[7] by the artist to serve as the rest for the god's foot suspended from the seat. This detail can hardly be described as "a double faced '*pīthī*' (foot-stool)".

Apart from the two garland-bearing males appearing on either side of the prominent lotus-halo of the god, Kubera is flanked by two miniature figures of his attendants, one male and the other female. According to Upadhyay, "On the left side, Kubera is attended by a male who carries a peculiar fly-whisk in his right hand and a long stalk in his left. Probably he is the '*Padma-nidhi*'. On the right side is a female attendant bearing a '*ratnabhāṇḍa*'."[8]

Upadhyay has identified the male attendant perhaps quite rightly but his description of the attributes with respect to this figure is, in our humble opinion, somewhat incorrect. On closer scrutiny, it will be found that there is only one attribute of a lotus-flower with a long stalk which is held in the two hands of the figure; the left one is displaying the flower to the front while the long stem of it is uplifted by the other hand over the head at the back being passed over the left shoulder of the person. In all likelihood, this purposeful delineation of the floral detail in such a conspicuous manner was intended to indicate the identity of the attendant as personified *Padma-nidhi*.

The female on the god's right is holding out a jar or *ghaṭa* in both her hands as if in a gesture of offering its contents to the deity. It was most probably not to represent a pot or container of jewels (*ratna-bhāṇḍa*) as suggested by Upadhyay. Similar presence of a female attendant on the side of Kubera's right hand bearing a *chashaka* (wine-cup) will be noticed in several Mathura reliefs of this god.

In case of relief C4 of the Mathura Museum, V.S. Agrawala observes in his *Catalogue,*[9] "Two female attendants, partly defaced, are standing to his right and left behind the shoulders. The one to right seems to hold a pitcher (cf. no. C5)." The other specimen, C5 (Pl. 60.3) of the same Museum is thus commented upon, "Statuette (ht. 12") of a corpulent male figure squatting and holding in his left hand a bag and in his right hand a cup into which a female attendant, standing on his right side, pours some liquid from a pitcher which she holds with both hands." Both these Mathura images are assigned to the Gupta period. However, this seems to be just a general dating. Closer analysis of their style and a comparison with the Pabhosa sculpture would indeed reveal that all the three specimens belong to the post-Gupta artistic phase falling roughly in the late sixth and seventh centuries A.D.

To the best of my knowledge, the above images seem to be at present the earliest specimens of this detail known. As a characteristic feature of Kubera's attendant on his right near his usual *chashaka*-bearing hand, this gesture of serving the master with a wine-container came to be accepted as a regular feature in his one significant type, fixed around the sixth-seventh century, and continuing through subsequent periods. Ramashraya Awasthi[10] has noticed the presence of a male or female attendant in wine-offering attitude in several Kubera images at Khajuraho and rightly drawn our attention to such a feature in the Mathura figures. Perhaps, this trait as an iconographic specification was derived in origin from the Kushāṇa period depiction of Kubera-as-Bacchus where in a scene of drink the intoxicated god is attended by one of his associates bearing a wine-goblet.[11]

However, we find such a female depicted below the right hand of the god in an excellent two-armed sculpture of Kubera from Baijanath, Almora, of c. 8-9th cent.[12] Another image of Kubera with his consort Ṛiddhi, found at Badoh and housed in the Gwalior Museum, showing this detail belongs to the style of c. ninth century in central India (Pl. 60.4). Further interesting is the depiction of a pair of *Nidhi-ghaṭas* below the suspended right leg of the god, in a manner which can be described as if copied after the Pabhosa figure. It may be remarked that the *ghaṭas* are usually seen placed under the seat of the god, but the depiction of a *ghaṭa* or *ghaṭas* as supporting his foot is an unusual type. There are perhaps no similar examples at Khajuraho.[13]

Attention may be just drawn to several significant iconic details of the Pabhosa image namely, the sole of his left foot exposed to view in the god's *lalitāsana* displays its marks of lines and lotus-symbol; his *ekakuṇḍalī* feature is exquisitely illustrated as he wears a round *kuṇḍala* in the left-ear-lobs only, the ear-ornament on the right ear is of floral or pearly features;[14] the god's purse in his left hand is an actual *nakulaka*, with details of its mouth, eyes and body finely shown, indicating that it was made of the skin of a mongoose. It is remarkable that the convention of showing Kubera's *nakulaka* as exuding jewels was not yet fixed by the sixth-seventh cent and was seemingly a later innovation at the hand of inventive artist of the medieval times.

NOTES AND REFERENCES

1. J.N. Banerjea, *Development of Hindu Iconography*, 2nd end., Calcutta, 1956, p. 344, pl. XIV, fig. 2.
2. B.S Upadhyay, "Sculptures in the Provincial Museum, Lucknow," *JISOA*, Vol X, 1942, pp. 182-83, pl. XI, figs. 1-2.

3. N.P. Joshi, *Prāchīna Bhāratīya Mūrttivijñāna*, Patna, 1977, p. 179.
4. This refers to the Kushāṇa and Gupta figures of Kubera.
5. Upadhyay, *op. cit.*, p. 182.
6. *Ibid.*
7. See below.
8. Upadhyay, *op. cit.*, p. 183.
9. V.S. Agrawala, *A Catalogue of the Brahmanical Images in Mathura Art*, Lucknow, 1951, p. 78.
10. Ramashraya Awasthi, *Khajurāho kī Deva-pratimāyen*, Agra, 1967, pp. 234-35.
11. See Mathura Museum, No. C2; V.S. Agrawala, *op. cit.*, pp. 93-94.
12. Illustrated by Aschwrin de Lippe, *Indian Medieval Śculpture*, Oxford, 1978, pl. 47.
13. See P. Pal, "Dhanda-Kubera...," *Lalit Kalā*, No. 18, 1977, pp. 13-26, showing no figure with this feature. However, his fig. 4 on pl. VII is remarkable as showing the god sitting in *lalitāsana* with his left bent and rested directly on a large *Nidhighaṭa* exuding coins.
14. See *Medini : ekakuṇḍala akhyāto balarāma dhanādhipe*, 29. 169. Also the reading in some manuscripts of *Amarakośa:- Kubera Chaikakuṇḍalaḥ* at 3. 205 (p. 320, edn. by Sharma and Sardesai).

61
NOTES ON TWO ORNAMENTAL MOTIFS

R. MORTON SMITH

1. I would ask Prof. Lal to excuse the smallness of this offering, (though it has called for more research than may seem), as owing to the Canadian postal situation I have had rather short notice, but I appreciate the honour of being approached. For some years I have been interested in tracing the development and use of subsidiary motifs in Indian art (especially sculpture, which has had the longest survival), in the hope of assisting the chronology of Indian art and history and also throwing light on the movement of sculptors of whom we will never know the names or the personalities.

2. First we take the merlon, or better 'ziggurat', conspicuous in Assyria, more restricted at Persepolis, found widely in the early period of Indian sculpture from the western Indian caves to Rani Gumpha in Orissa. On walls it forms a frieze — at Bharhut on the coping — but on pillars it becomes capping a scene. We also find it on the top of the *harmikā*, like a fence, which can be paralleled by its position on crowns at Persepolis. This occurs also in Gandhara, but otherwise I can find only two instances evidently capping a Medhi? stupa railing. The early form is plain and in the west it is always so, as it is on the rim of the *harmikā*. (Nasik III, Gandhara, Mathura); the plain is normal at Bodh Gaya, Sanchi (in the (western Sātavāhana realm), and can be found at Bharhut, Mathura, Kauśāmbī. But innovation seems to spring from Bharhut, where the normal is intervening opening lotus buds between ziggurats. This appears at Ananta Gumpha in Orissa, on the last (West) gate at Sanchi (which reverts in Sanchi III to plain), and belated, at Amaravati (Burgess, Notes 14.2) where it surmounts a pot which forms the base of a pillar. At Mathura we find a semicircular frond, and at Amin near Thanesar an ordinary frond between the ziggurats; and from Bharhut in the Allahabad Museum a succession of jasmine garlands. The *kuḍu* seems to supersede the ziggurat in Mathura; the instance from Amaravati seems unique at the site, and is a good instance of the normal disappearance of a motif; it is reduced in size and significance as it approaches extinction. In the western Indian caves it does not seem to survive A.D. 250. The ziggurat is not to be found on the *harmikā* at Amaravati. It had

no resemblance to the Indian temple, and could not therefore call on symbolism to its rescue. For gradual disappearance, the concave scallop on the halo, prominent on early images, it is barely noticeable on the Sarnath Buddha, and on one of Marshall's Sanchi images, must be looked for.

3. The other motif we may consider here is the lozenge in rectangle. It may form a band under a ceiling, an external string course, or a band on a pillar that before extinction may descend to ground level. *A priori* I would expect the plain smooth lozenge to be the original, but my researches have given no evidence of this. The lozenge as floret has the flower symbolism, but there does not seem to be a Moslem preference for plain. In fact the first instance of the motif I can find is a floret in rectangle, single and not in a band on the top step/sill of the entry of the Chaunsath Yogini temple at Khajuraho (*c.* 800 if in original position). The rectangle becomes a square, but curiously though the square rosette filling a square goes back to Bharhut and before, the square flower standing on the tip of a petal in a square seems to have to wait on the lozenge floret in rectangle, and even then till about 1430. The late date for our motif may be supported by Stern's observation that the export of motifs to Greater India ceased around A.D. 600, and our motif is not found outside India (though the square rosette in square can be found in Cambodia), and in India is not found east of Deogarh, where I can find it once on a probably 11th (+) century column, base ornament.

4. There is a diamond in a diamond in a square at Mirpur Khas (Cousens, ASI *Antiquities of Sindh*) which I would put in the 5th century, but I have found no other possible ancestor for our motif. The first clear instance (continuous) is at the Qutb Mosque on a reused pillar of the 8/9th century. It is plain, but on the neighbouring pillar (also reused) the lozenge is already a floret. The next plain is at Abu, 1031, Vimala, but the floret is there too. Plain can be found down to the 19th century (step-well at Isanpur), and seems especially favoured in west India, and there *ca.* 1450-1510 (Champaner/Ahmedabad). We mention the step-well at Ghumli and the gate at Dabhoi in Hindu context, or Gwalior, little Sas Bahu (early) 12th century.

5. The floret would seem to spread further south than the plain, and we find it in the late Chālukyan Kundgol and Annavatti of the 13th century, Annavatti, Degamva, while at Belgaum it is wholly vegetated, all these being lozenge. At Kundgol and Belgaum the upright of the rectangle is portrayed as a pillar, but this is not normal. The floret seems to have remained the more popular, and we find it widely in the western area from the 11th to the 16th centuries. It is not taken over in the northern Islamic area (Indus/Ganges basins), but I find it once at Tatta (ASI *Antiquities of Sindh*, Pl. XXXIII), late, where it is the square form.

6. This square form seems to appear in the 2nd quarter of the 15th century, the rectangle being reduced to a square, and the lozenge/rhombus accordingly so also, but still standing on an angle. The earliest I find is at Ranakpur temple addition of 1439; it occurs at Dholka Jami Masjid (1450) and in step-wells from late 15th-17th centuries, at Ahmedabad and Champaner. We can find an 8-point floret in a square at Mahmudabad step-well soon after 1500, but it does not seem derived from the square one, and the same for the one at Ahmedabad (Sidi Saiyad) about the same time, but its uprights seem to be reduced pillars, and the derivation seems uncertain. But our motif does seem to have invaded textiles, as we

find it on a Pahari representation of a saddle-cloth of the 16th century. There is no clear evidence of it from the exports of textiles recovered at Fostat in Egypt. The motif is not found in eastern India at all, but in the square form we find it in a window at Somnathpur Keshava temple and with elaboration of the dividing vertical, at Madurai (*Living Architecture; Indian of A Wohlwashen,* pl. 82, 85 (square) and also 82 (lozenge) of the 17th century.

7. The lozenge in rectangle does not seem to be used twice on the same wall or lintel or column; the only cases I can find are on a Mohammedan sarcophagus at Cambay, and on a thin subordinate pilaster on the mihrab of Hilāl K͟hān G͟hāzī's mosque at Dholka. On the column the position seems to vary from the bracket to the base.

62
FRESH LIGHT ON TANJORE TEMPLE

R. NAGASWAMY

Four Records

Four inscriptions of historic interest were recently discovered in Tanjore, throwing fresh light on the temple. One was a fragmentary inscription, built upside-down, in the front *maṇḍapa* of the main shrine, of the Bṛhadīśvara temple noticed by the present writer. The second inscription was found on a pillar by a villager in Tanjore town. The other two were noticed by the Archaeological Survey of India during the course of their cleaning and conservation of the temple. The four inscriptions throw valuable light on different aspects of the temple, which form the subject matter of this paper.

Tanjore under the Pallavas

The first inscription of which only two lines are visible, is a fragmentary record, written in Pallava grantha characters and reads —

...*Koṭi visrana prakhya*
...(*Ba*)*ttam yaṁ Śri Danti*

The inscription is obviously in *anushṭub śloka* but not much can be made of it except the name Śrī Danti, which is the name of the Pallava ruler, Danti Varman, who ruled from 795 to 850 A.D. with his capital at Kanchi. The inscription can thus be ascribed to the first half of the 9th cent. A.D.

It is known that a family of chieftains, known as Muttaraiyar was ruling the region around Tanjore. A certain Perumbidugu Muttarayan, who also had the name Cuvaran Māran was the Lord of Tanjore. He is known as *Tanjaiyarkon* and *Tanjai Narpuhaḻālan*. He built a temple to Kālā piḍāri at Neman. The records referring to this construction are now found in Sendalai near Tanjore.

Another member of the same family is seen excavating a cave temple at Malaiyadipatti in the reign of Dantivarman Pallava. This place is not too far away from Tanjore. From Ponvilaindanpatti village, near Tanjore, an inscription of Pallava Nandivarman II, the father of Danti has been noticed. This village has also yielded a lovely bronze image Tripurāntaka of the same age now in the Tanjore Art Gallery. From other inscriptions of the Pallavas it is seen that the Tanjore region came under the sway of the Pallavas from the time of Siṁhavishṇu, the father of Mahendravarman, in the 6th cent. A.D.

Thus it is known that Tanjore region was under the Pallavas but it is for the first time a record of the Pallava is found in Tanjore proper confirming that Tanjore continued to be under the Pallavas till the reign of Dantivarman, whose fragmentary record has been found now in the Bṛhadīśvara temple.

Though this fragmentary inscription has been found in the Bṛhadīśvara, it obviously belonged to another monument in Tanjore and was brought and reused in building the big *maṇḍapa* in and around 16th cent. A.D. It shows that there was a Pallava monument at Tanjore in the time of the Pallava Dantivarman. The second point of interest is that the Pallava art tradition was very much alive in Tanjore. It is towards the end of Dantivarman's reign, or perhaps the beginning of his successor's rule, Tanjore seems to have been captured by Vijayālaya Chola, that laid the foundation for the Chola empire. Vijayālaya consecrated an image of Nisumbha-sūdani at Tanjore, when he captured the city. It is at the same time, Cuvaran Māran, the Perumpidugu Muttaraiyan consecrated the image of Kālāpiḍāri at Nemam, near Tanjore. The inscription of Danti found in the big temple of Tanjore is immediately before the capture of Tanjore by Vijayālaya.

Sanskrit Poetry

The second inscription is that of Rājarāja Chola, in Sanskrit, written in grantha characters. The inscription was on a plain granite pillar, like the pillar found in the great temple. The pillar was found lying buried about four feet below the ground while digging a foundation for house. The finder broke the pillar into pieces, out of fear and to hide the information about the find, lest the Archaeological Department might take over his house site. The matter soon came to light and the present writer was able to secure an estampage. It turned out to be a good Sanskrit composition with an eye on poetry, eulogising Rājarāja. It also shows that Sanskrit poetry received great patronage in the hands of Rājarāja. It is known that Tamil classical poetic tradition was also greatly favoured, for some of Rājarāja's inscriptions as at Thirukkoyilur are couched in the poetic tradition of Sangam Tamil. Rājarāja also appointed 50 *Tevāram* singers (including two instrumentalists) to recite the Tamil hymns in the big temple. He also appointed *Āryam Pāḍuvār* and *Tamil Pāḍuvār* — singers of Sanskrit songs and singers of Tamil songs. Thus both Tamil and Sanskrit received equal attention in the royal court. So far as Sanskrit inscriptions are concerned, they are found mostly in *praśastis*. But the present Sanskrit record is purely a poetic composition in *kāvya* style, eulogising the emperor.

The Shrine of the Goddess

The third and the fourth inscriptions are in a way related. They are found on the walls, flanking a shrine in the northern part of the *prākāra*, immediately behind the present shrine of the goddess Bṛhadnāyaki. An image of Gaṇeśa is found inside the shrine which was probably consecrated, when renovations were undertaken by the Maratha ruler Serfoji II in A.D. 1802-3 when a number of *liṅgas* were also consecrated in the *prākāra*. The Maratha renovation is recorded in the temple and also in the Modi records. In all probability the shrine was empty before that time. However from the inscriptions under discussion it is clear that this shrine of the enclosure, housed an image of goddess Umāparameśvarī, in the time of Rājarāja as seen from both the inscriptions referring to the gifts made by one administrative officer of the temple (*śrīkāryam*) to the goddess Umāparameśvarī in the shrine of the *prākāra* of the temple. The specific mention in the inscription that the gift was made to the "Umāparameśvarī in the *ālaya* of *Thiruccuṟṟumāligai* (enclosure) of the temple" shows unmistakably, the shrine referred to is the one where the inscriptions are found flanking the shrine. A similar example is an inscription of referring to the Gaṇeśa of the *parivārālaya* in the same temple (No. 36 of S.I.I. Vol. II). The inscription is found on the wall of the shrine (*parivārālaya*) in the north-west of the enclosure. It refers to a gift of a vessel to the Gaṇapati of the *Parivārālaya* in the time of Rājarāja. An image of Gaṇeśa is enshrined in this shrine, and that was the one consecrated by Rājarāja is evident from the style of that figure. The presence of this Gaṇeśa is of great value.

The Āgamas prescribe the location of the *parivāra devatās*, and stipulate that the *parivārālaya* of Gaṇeśa should be in the *Nṛriti* region (south-west corner), for example, the text *Īśānagurudeva Paddhati* prescribes that Gaṇeśa shrine should be located in the north-west— "*Gajavaktrasya Nairṛte*" (Ch. 35, verse-56), the same place where the Gaṇeśa shrine is located in the time of Rājarāja and that the inscription is also found in the same place.

Similarly, the shrine of Umāparameśvarī according to the Āgamic texts should be in the northern part of the *prākāra*. The same *Īśānagurudeva paddhati* says—

"*Vāyavyām atha va Aiśānyām*
Umā Durgālayaḥ Smṛtaḥ" (—*Īsānaguru* — 35, 57—)

The shrine could be in the north or as an alternative, it could also be in north-east. In the big temple, the shrine is located in the north of the *prākāra*.

The texts of the two inscriptions and their translations are given at the end.

Since the inscriptions are dated in the 29th year of Rājarāja Chola, and also mention the shrine of Umāparameśvarī, it is evident that it formed part of the original layout of the temple. The location of the shrine of the goddess raises a point of historic interest.

Scholars have drawn our attention to the fact that in early Saivite temples no separate Devī shrine is noticed, and whereever they are found, they are clearly later foundations and not contemporary with the original temples. The earliest temple dedicated to the goddess Parvatī is a Śiva temple said to be the Sivakāmi Amman Temple in the Naṭarāja temple at Chidambaram. However it may be of interest to note the following view of Dr. T.V. Mahalingam in this regard.

Differing Views

"The need for building a separate shrine for the Devī arose only in the late Chola period, which witnessed a movement in the elaboration of temple complexes and rituals. During this time the development of the Devī cult reached a degree hitherto unknown and the worship of Jyēshṭā and Saptamātas on the decline to give perhaps a smooth going to the worship of Ambā, the universal mother. This coupled with the fact that later Chola builders had a flair for building adjuncts in their elaborate temple circuits has resulted in the construction of Devī shrines from the eleventh cent. onwards. Even in the Bṛhadīśvara temple, Tanjore, the shrine for the goddess is not coeval with the main shrine as regards its date, as it appears to have been built under Konerinmaikondan. Its architectural style is also recognisably posterior to that of the central shrine and its axial adjuncts. But in the temple of Bṛhadīśvara at Gangaikonda Cholapuram built during the next generation we find an original Devī shrine. This has been presumed to be the earliest extant Devī shrine which is chronologically coeval with the sanctum in the same temple complex. That Rājendra's reign was thus epoch-making in the regard is indicated by two other pieces of evidence, in an inscription of the same ruler from Ennayiram, in the South Arcot district, mention is made of Pārvatī; a record of the same ruler is incised on the wall of the Mangalambika shrine in the Śiva temple at Kandiyur that the Devī shrine might have existed during the time of the engraving of the inscription."[1]

By way of comment it may be mentioned that the present Devī shrine in the Gangaikonda Cholapuram temple is not the original Devī shrine. It was a Śiva temple converted to a Devī shrine, very much later.[2] "There was no independent Amman shrine in any of the S. Indian temples till the days of Kulottunga I. It seems that the Sivakama Sundari Amman shrine built by the later Cholas was the first among independent Amman Shrines."[3]

The inscriptions now found in the big temple, Tanjore, prove that the Śiva temples in Tamil Nadu, in the time of Rājarāja I (much earlier to the time so far suggested by scholars) did have an independent shrine for the goddess Umā, as a part of the full temple complex. This has an important bearing on the religious and philosophical history of south India. From the time of Kulottuṅga Chola I, c. 1100 A.D. separate Devī shrine within the Śiva temple complex, assumed more dominant role and came to be called *Thiru Kamakkottam Udaiya Nachiyar* temple.

Superintendent of Inscriptions

The second inscription in the same wall adds a further interesting information. It refers to a gift made by a dignitary to the same goddess Umā Parameśvari. He was an officer under Rājendra Chola in his 3rd year — (the last year of Rājarāja)—and was also a cavalier. His name is given as Ravipalur Uḍaiyān. The point of great significance is that he is mentioned as the officer supervising the engraving of inscriptions on the stone walls. It is clear that Rājarāja, known for his meticulous organisation of administration had appointed one of his able commanders to supervise engraving inscriptions on the temple wall. It is not out of place to mention that Tanjore temple inscriptions are the best drafts and very neatly engraved in the history of the south and it is to this officer Ravi we owe such an admirable series of inscriptions.

Texts and Translations of the two Inscriptions found on the wall of the shrine in the enclosure on the northern side:

(1) *Svasti Srī: Uḍaiyār Srī Rāja Rājēśvāram Uḍaiyārkku Srīkāryam Ceykinra Āṛṛūr uḍaiyān Nakkan Toṇṛi. Ālaiyattu Umāparamēśvariyārkku, Uḍaiyār Srī Rājendra Chola devarkku Yāṇḍu mūnrāvadu varai, kuḍutta Venkālamum Tarāvum, Āḍavallān ennum Tulākkōlāl niṛai eḍuttu kallil Veṭṭinapaḍi, Veṇkalamaṇḍai onṛu, niṛai nārpattu muppalam Tarā Kalasappānai onṛu, niṛai aimpattu on Kalam.*

Translation: Svasti Sri

This is a gift made by Nakkan Toṇṛi alias Ārrūr Uḍaiyān (of Āṛṛūr) serving as an Administrative Officer of the temple of Rājarājeśvaram. The gift was made till the third regnal year of Udaiyar Sri Rājendra Chola deva. It consisted of bronze and zinc measured by the weight standard Āḍavallān and was inscribed on the wall of the temple. One bronze receptacle weighing 43 *palas*. One *Kalasa* pot made of zinc weighing 59 *palas*.

(2) *Svasti Srī: Uḍaiyār Srī Rāja Rājēśvaram Uḍaiyārkku*
Srīkāryam Ceykinṛa Nakkan Tonṛi,
Uḍaiyār Kōyilil Thiruccuṟṟu māligaiyil Ālaiyattu
Umāparameśvariyārkku,
Uḍaiyār Srī, Rāja Rāja Dēvarkku yāṇḍu irupatton-padāvadu varai Kuḍuttana, Kallil Veṭṭiyatu.
Umā Parameśvariyārkku cātti aruḷa kkuḍutta Tāli onṛu,
Pon Āḍavallānāl pon iru kalanjarai
Ivarkke Srī Rājendra Chola devar cirudanattu,
Iraṭṭa kulakālatterinda uḍanilai kuḍurai c cevakaril
Uḍaiyār Kōyilil Kallil eḻuttu veṭṭuvikkinṛa
Arumoḻideva Vaḻanāṭṭu Vaṇḍālai Vēlūr Kūṛṛattu
Sāttankuḍi Veḷḷālan Iravi Pālūr Uḍaiyār.
Srī Rājendra Choḷa devarkku yāṇḍu mūnrāvadu varai
Kuḍutta Paṭṭaikkārai onṛu
Pon Āḍavallān ennum Kallāl niṛai Mukkāle mūnṛu Mañjāḍi.

Translation: Svasta Sri

This is a gift by Nakkan Tonṛi, an Administrative Officer of the temple made to

the goddess Umāparamēśvari in the shrine of the enclosure of the temple of Rājarājeśvara,

till the end of the 29th regnal year of Sri Vḍaiyār Rājarāja Chola deva,

One golden *Tali* weighing $2^1/_2$ *Kaḻañju* of gold, for adorning the goddess Umāparamēśvari.

To the same goddess was gifted one golden *Pattai Karai*, weighing 18 *mañjāḍi* by the weighing stone *Ādavallān*.

The gift was made by one Ravi, Pālūr Uḍaiyār, a veḷḷāla of Sāttan Kuḍi, in the subdivision of *Vandālai Vēlūr Kūrram*, in the territorial subdivision *Arumoḻi deva valañḍu*.

He was a cavalier, in the selected Cavalry, "*Iraṭṭa Kulakāla terinda udanilai kudurai-c-cevakar.*" In addition he was a *Sirudana* —an Officer of Sri Rājendra chola devar.

He was getting the inscriptions engraved on the stone walls of the temple of Sri Rāja Rājēśvara.

NOTES AND REFERENCES

1. T.V. Mahalingam, *The South Indian Temple Complex,* Dharwar, 1970, pp. 58-59.
2. R. Nagaswamy, *Gangaikonda Cholapuram,* Madras, 1970; also see, *Encyclopaedia of Indian Temple Architecture—South India—Lower Dravida Deśa,* American Institute of Indian Studies, New Delhi, p. 2w1.
3. B. Natarajan, *The City of the Cosmic Dance* , New Delhi, 1974, p. 69.

63

TWIN VARĀHĪ PANEL IN INDIAN ART MUSEUM AT BERLIN

R.C. AGRAWALA

Scholars of Indian art are fully aware of the depiction of boar-headed Vārāhī as one of the Seven Mothers independently or on Mother Panels in Indian sculpture. Vārāhī is usually shown as *Mahisha-Vāhanā* though in fifth-sixth century sculptures from Shāmalājī and Āmjhara she is riding on a boar as well as cited in *Vārāhī Tantra* and the mediaeval text *Goraksha Saṁhitā*. In the Buddhist text *Nishpañña Yogāvalī*, she is associated with an owl (*pechaka*) which is yet to be substantiated by the actual sculptures.

The depiction of boar-faced Vārāhī, as attendant on subsidiary figure, in some sculptures is equally interesting. In the dancing Kālī or Chāmuṇḍā sculpture (tenth century), now in the Fogg Art Museum at Harvard in U.S.A. we notice a four-armed goddess with a boar face seated to the left of the main goddess;[1] the *Vārāha mukhī* goddess (attendant) carries a bell in left upper hand, a sword in the right lower while the left lower is placed on her left thigh. The face of the female on the opposite side is damaged but she too was probably a boar-headed female figure.

The tenth century inscribed Vārāhī Yoginī image from Antarā (near Shahdol, Madhya Pradesh) is equally interesting whereto we notice two-armed boar-headed female attendant on both sides of the goddess seated on a buffalo,[2] the one attendant to left holds a cup in the right hand while the other on right carries a *nara muṇḍa*; the pedestal of the main image bears the inscription *Śri Vārāhī* in bold letters of the tenth century.

Still more interesting is the exterior of Jarai Mātā Temple at Baruā Śāgar (near Jhansi), datable to the eight-ninth century. Just above the entrance of the main sanctum of this Pratihara edifice,[3] the third panel presents the 8 Guardians of Quarters (*Dikpālas*) in a single row. In the centre of this particular panel are also carried two miniature figures of boar-headed females seated on a common lotus seat and facing each other. Both are shown as *mātrikās* carrying a child in left lap and both of them hold a lotus flower in the right hand; both are seated in *lalitāsana*. Their exact identification is really a mystery; who are these twin Boar-Headed Mothers (?) (Pl. 63.1)[4], this grouping of two females of the same type is quite interesting.

During my visit to Berlin West (now unified Berlin)in May 1986 at the invitation of the Director, Indian Art Museum, Berlin, Dr. H. Hartel—the then Director of the Museum very kindly showed me in his Museum's Reserve collection, a mediaeval independent rectangular stone panel (No. I. 5922; ht 23 cm, width 36 cm). Here too can be seen[5] (Pl. 63.2) two boar-headed *devis* seated on a cushion; both have placed one of their hands on the seat while the other carries a cup placed in front of the mouth-suggesting some *Tāntric* association. The lotus halo behind their heads suggests their divine association beyond any doubt. Still more, both are accompanied by female attendants and garland bearing *Vīdyādharas* flying above. This particular panel, curved as an independent piece probably served the purpose of worship during the contemporary period but the exact identification of these twin *Vārāha mukhi Devīs* is still a problem. The *Agni-Purāṇa*[6] (chapter 146, verses 23-24) refers to 8 types by boar-headed goddesses amongst the Vārāhī family; the two were to be worshipped likewise, their names are enumerated as *Tālu Jihwā, Raktākshī, Vidyujjihvā, Karaṅkiṇī, Meghanādā, Prachaṇḍogrā, Kālakarṇī* and *Kali Priyā*. Dr. M.T. de Mallmann also refers to another boar-headed goddess *Viśālākshī* who carries a bell and a dagger in her hand, (*ibid.*, p. 296).

The Berlin Museum Twin Vārāhī Panel is of reddish sandstone and probably hailed from Madhya Pradesh. It is earnestly hoped that experts of Indian iconography and scholars of Sanskrit literature will be able to suggest some tangible identification of the above motif in Indian art. The Indian Art Museum at Berlin is to be congratulated for having acquired such an unusual specimen of mediaeval Indian iconography. Compared with the Baruā Sagar relief, it becomes quite chear that this particular motif was carved under some specific literary injunction. Identification of the boar-headed female attendants in the Kālī-Chāmuṇḍā and Vārāhī sculptures cited above is equally essential. Their motherly aspect is quite evident on the Baruā Sāgar panel under scrutiny.

NOTES AND REFERENCES

1. A. Lippe, *The Art of India*, 1962, New York, Plate 40; sculpture from Khajuraho area, ht. 27 inches.
2. R.C. Agrawala, 'Some interesting sculptures of Vārāhī from N. India,' *Bhāratī*, B.H.U. Varanasi, nos. 12-14, (1968-71), pp. 134-36, Plate II; Vidya Dehjeia, Yoginī Cult and Temples, Delhi, 1986, plate on p. 168.
3. S.D. Trivedi, *The Jārāi Temple at Baruā Sāgar*, Jhansi, 1985, p. 29, photo on cover page and plate 4.
4. Photograph kindly supplied by the Director, American Institute of Indian Studies, Varanasi, Neg. No. A 4-64.
5. Unpublished Relief; photograph kindly supplied by Dr. Mrs. M. Yaldiz—the Present Director of Indian Art Museum, Berlin. I stand obliged both to Dr. Hartel and Dr. Yaldiz in the study of this unique panel.
6. M.T. de Mallman, *Les Enseignements Iconographiques de L' Agni Purāṇa*, Paris, 1963, p. 293. The *Vārāhī Tantra*, also refers to 5 types of boar-headed *Devīs*.

64
ICONOGRAPHIC GLEANINGS OF GOVINDADEVA TEMPLE

R.C. SHARMA

The temple of Govindadeva at Vrindaban is an outstanding specimen of Mughal period temple architecture in the northern India. It imbibes innumerable architectural peculiarities of which some have been discussed and highlighted by the art historians but a number of them have yet to be analysed. This paper aims at discerning mainly the iconographic merits of this great edifice.

The artistic and architectural grandeur of ancient Vraja first became the target of fierce attack of the barbarous Huns towards the close of the 6th century A.D. All Buddhist establishments, Jaina *stūpas, chaityas* and Brāhmanical temples and other places of worship were destroyed and razed to earth. The devastation to some extent was compensated by some enthusiastic Rājpūt chiefs but after about half a millennium history repeated itself and the region again fell prey to the evil intentions of the bigoted iconoclastic invaders.[1] The centuries of catastrophes resulted in demolition of buildings, particularly the religious ones and migration of citizens to safer places.[2] The exodus of artisans, masons, sculptors and painters was also a natural phenomenon under such precarious conditions.

Once the hub of social, religious, political, cultural and artistic activities the twin towns were reduced to the graveyards of our luxurious opulence of different forms of arts. It lost the political status as well and even in the Mughal period the administrative headquarter of the region was Sahār and not Mathurā. The heaps of neglected and dismantled monuments gathered coats of dirt and dust which finally assumed the shape of mounds. We come across such situation in hoary past also when the utter neglect caused great harm to the glorious city of Ayodhyā and Kālidāsa has furnished elaborate description.[3] It appears that the poet was an eyewitness to the wonderful monuments of Mathurā with beautifully chiselled railing pillars.

Vrindaban had also become a neglected and isolated region imparting a forest look, full of trees, wild creepers and shrubs. With the writing of *Bhāgavata* in south[4], *Gītagovinda* in east[5] and emergence and development of devotional (Bhakti) movement, the followers of Vaishnavism or Bhāgavatism longed to rediscover, relocate or recreate the holy spots associated with their deities, particularly Krishṇa whose deeds and philosophy appealed them most. The saints, seers and their followers thronged from different directions. The pioneer among them was the illustrious saint and scholar known through different names as Chaitanya, Krishṇa Chaitanya, Viśvambhara, Gaurāṅga and Nimāi. The credit of identification or discovery of several holy spots including Vrindaban goes to him.[6] Subsequently, his disciples Rūpa, Sanātana and Jīva followed his mission.

Several factors combined to shape Vrindaban as a temple town from the last decade of the 16th century to the present day. The seed was sown by the visits of Chaitanya, his followers and other Vaishṇava saints. Akbar's policy of religious harmony gave a further impetus. At the same time he felt greatly indebted to his outstanding Hindu military commander, Man Singh of Jaipur whose martial valour and warfare planning resulted not only in crushing the rebellions but also in further expanding and strengthening the Mughal empire.[7] It was just natural that he allowed the temples to come up to please his faithful Hindu ministers, princes and subjects. Govindadeva temple thus stood on the foundation of this socio-political and religious urges in the last quarter of the 16th century A.D.

This was, however, not a one-way traffic. If the emperor Akbar felt it necessary to be tolerant and considerate towards the Hindu sentiments, the Hindus also cared and adjusted with the Muslim feelings. This mutual concession under the changed scenario is amply reflected in the contemporary Hindu edifices and the temple of Govindadeva is no exception to this fact. The exterior is conspicuous by almost total absence of anthropomorphic representation.[8] This is in contrast with the earlier practice of temple architecture at Khajurāho and other places where the divine, semi-divine or fabulous figures occupy the major part of composition. In Govindadeva these have been replaced by plain mouldings, occasionally filled in with geometrical, floral or symbolical representations like full vase, lotus and creeper.

To what extent the court policy and the contemporaneous circumstances influenced the construction of Govindadeva is a matter of deeper probe by the art historians but the fact remains that the builder (Mān Singh) thought it fruitful to take adequate precautionary steps to safeguard this marvellous abode of God from some further vandalism. Being very close to the Emperor and a dominating personality of the court he was also aware and conscious of the inner politics and could also guess the future impediments. The liberal views of his master were not acceptable to all his henchmen and the life style and thoughts of the envious and frustrated would-be successor to the throne were rather unpredictable. As such the measures adopted by the Rājā do reflect his farsightedness and this worked well at least for a century. The subdued iconographic aspect and projection of nature or symbol appear to be the revival of older convention of Kushāṇa and Śuṅga age formulae of art and architecture when the nature played a dominating role and the human figure had yet to make its presence felt.

A very significant issue which deserves our attention is the treatment of entrance gate to the cella or *garbhagriha*. Following the traditions of the Gupta temple door pattern the Govindadeva inner shrine looks a real frame to the cella of idol. It consists of the jambs with one central and two side friezes divided into several compartments one running over the other and to be viewed from three sides. Each of the niches contains human figures and the subject matter is Krishṇalīlā. This door frame is important from several angles. It adequately compensates the absence of human figures on the exterior. Secondly, being first monument after the rediscovery of Vraja-Vrindāban it introduces the basic mythology of Vraja. It also serves as mirror to study the life style of Vraja recaptured from the traditions followed in Rājasthān. It represents both royal and folk conventions. While Krishṇa wears a princely attire, the female figures are adorned with Rājasthānī garments *orhnī* and *chunni* which are in vogue in the Vraja region also.

The appraisal of iconographic aspects of the Govindadeva complex reveal that it has retained some of the earlier forms, motifs and features or these have somehow reappeared. There seems a good deal of resemblance between the ladies (*gopīs*) depicted on the cella entrance and some railing pillars of Mathurā of the Kushāṇa period. The lady with pot on head from Kankālī mound now in the State Museum, Lucknow is a notable example.[9] The lady under tree (*śalabhañjikā*) or playing on flute[10] or busy in dance[11] etc. are some of the common citations. It appears that the carving or sculpting traditions of Vraja were not altogether dead and some of these withstood the most chaotic conditions during the centuries of repeated attacks.

Alternatively, the migrating artisans or sculptors who established themselves in safer place continued to practise the same style of carving through ages and this was inherited from father to son. Ultimately, it became their family tradition. As has been observed elsewhere by the present author,[12] a few Buddha images unearthed at Kauśāmbī and recording the installation under the Mughal rulers were carved in the earlier Kushāṇa traditions of Mathurā as the family must have migrated from Mathurā to Allahabad but the older connections of Mathurā art were continued to be practised. The statement is further supported by the fact that several Śaka-Kushāṇa features are noticed in the Mug͟hal miniatures. After all, the stitched drapery, trimmed beard, pointed or padded shoes, embroidery work, high caps, the cognizable features of the Śaka-Kushāṇa sculptures of Mathurā and Gandhāra regions, do appear again and again in one form or the other. The Taj manufacturing traditions have continued for about four hundred years in the miniature form at Tajpura Agra, a locality near the Taj and the trade is flourishing.

One more reason of the continuity or reappearance of earlier tradition is that some early Śilpa texts could survive the ravage of the natural calamities and human agency. In this context mention may be made of a Jaina text *Rāyapaseniya*[13] which must be dated to the pre-Gupta age. It gives a detailed description of the architectural complexities of the monuments which stood at Mathurā in the 1st-2nd century A.D. There has been a prolific tradition of manuscript writing in India and Sarasvatī Bhandaras of Jains are stocked with such handwritten documents. The region of Vraja also possesses innumerable number of old manuscripts. It may, therefore, be conjectured that some of these treatises were available to the planners of the Govindadeva temple and it seems appropriate to conclude that the older features reappear in the natural process.

The gate to the sanctum of the deity (Govindadeva) is really the gateway to Vraja culture, revival of earlier traditions and also a gate to the resettlement of Bhāgavatism or Vaishṇavism in the Vraja region and its further transmission in other parts of the country, particularly the north India.

The nomenclature of the temple also deserves our attention. The inspiration for the commencement of the great temple was given by the Goswamis, Rūpa and Sanātana who hailed from Bengal which is known for Durgā or Devī worship. They themselves were staunch Vaishṇavas but the cult of goddess was not altogether forgotten. It remained prevalent in one way or the other. Rādhā had already emerged as a potential force in Vaishṇavism. This strong wind of sublime form of feminine worship originating in the Bay of Bengal was blowing towards west. Rājā Mānsingh who himself was the devotee of Durgā[14] (Śilādevī) had no reservation in welcoming the new concept of Devī worship. The story of discovery of the idols of Govindajī and of goddess Yogamāyā or Vrindā and their consecration in the temple supports the theory of assimilation of Vaishṇava and Śakti cults.

There are other stories associated with the despatch of idols of male and female deities from Orissa to Vrindāban for installation in the sanctum of temple.[15] Govinda alone was not happy and he did need a companion for his divine play (*līlā*). Necessity was, therefore, felt to install and worship the *Jugala Chhabi*. The process of assimilation was accomplished in two ways. A separate shrine of Yogamāyā was put up on one side of the main temple and the statue of Rādhā or Vrindā was also provided for worship to the left of Krishṇa (Govinda). The sentiments behind the unity of male and female aspects were so strong that the temple was called as 'Govinda Devī' temple and this term remained in vogue even up to the recent past as Percy Brown writing in the first quarter of the 20th century referred the name of temple as Govinda Devī and not Govindadeva.

The projection of Gaṇeśa in the centre of the lintel of door to cella (*lalāṭabimba*) and at some other places also supports this view. This should, however, be clarified that by this time Gaṇeśa had established himself as Vighnāntaka and the depiction and worship of his figure had developed as an essential part of almost all social, religious and domestic ceremonies and rituals. His name 'Śrī Gaṇeśa' had become synonym for an auspicious beginning leading to the fruitful end 'Siddhi'. He was, therefore, praised as 'Siddhidāyaka or Siddhivināyaka'.

This may, however, be pointed out that the principle of unity or eclecticism has been an important characteristic of Vraja area from ancient time. The very name 'Vraja' negates stagnation. It denotes constant movement and change which could be achieved by assimilation. All the three major sects of early India *viz.* Hinduism, Buddhism and Jainism flourished simultaneously in Vraja. The statement is amply corroborated by discovery of a large number of statues from 1st century B.C. to the Gupta period. Even from one site icons belonging to different sects have been recovered. There are a few sculptures in which several deities have been shown in one.[16] Similarly, cosmic form of one deity begins in the Kushāṇa period and it became more popular with the representation of Krishṇa as Viśvarūpa. Combined figure of Śiva and Pārvati as Ardhanāriśvara or Śiva and Vishṇu as Harihara appear for the first time at Mathurā. Depiction of Balarāma and Krishṇa with the 22nd Jina, Nemināthа is an exercise in the same direction. The union of Govinda and Devī in the Govindadeva temple reminds us the earlier tradition of religious harmony of Vraja region.

The sculptures in or on the temples may be classified under the following categories:

(a) Images in or for worship

(b) Divinities *in situ* as Gaṇeśa in different forms

(c) Krishṇa and his male companions — *Sakhās*

(d) Rādhā and her companions — *Sakhīs*

(e) Semi-divine figure as nymphs (*apsarās*), *Vrikshākas*, etc.

(f) Devotees and attendants holding fly whisk, stick, garland, wreath, flower and musical instrument

(g) Persons busy in household activities, applying cosmetics, carrying water or milk pot, churning milk, performing *Rāsa* as part of Krishṇalīlā

(h) Krishṇa lifting Govardhana being central theme above the lintel of the sanctum

(i) Animals—cows, elephants, lion (on door sill) etc.

(j) Birds

(k) Attributes and postures

(l) Garments and ornaments

(m) Hair styles

(n) Symbols and decorative motifs

All these aspects deserve detailed treatment for proper understanding of sculptural delineation of Govindadeva. Here only a few basic elements and principles behind the iconographic rendering of the temple have been discussed.

NOTES AND REFERENCES

1. K.D. Bajpai, *Vraja kā Itihāsa*, p. 114.
2. *The Struggle for Empire*, Bombay, 1957, p. 499 and *The Delhi Sultanate*, Bombay, 1960, pp. 146-47 and 626.
3. *Raghuvaṁśam*, XVI, 9.21.
4. M.S. Randhawa, *Kangra Paintings of Bhāgavata Purāṇa*, New Delhi, 1960, p. 22.
5. *Gītagovinda*, Kapila Vatsyayana (ed.), 1983, pp. 9, 25-26.
6. Kennedy, *The Chaitanya Movement*, p. 47.
7. Brown, P., *Indian Architecture*, 1956, p. 158.
8. *Ibid.*
9. *Kushāṇa Sculptures from Sanghol* (Ed. S.P. Gupta), 1985, fig. 22.
10. R.C. Sharma, *The Splendour of Mathura Art and Museum*, 1994, p. 124.
11. *Ibid.*, p. 129, fig. 45.
12. R.C. Sharma, *Buddhist Art of Mathura*, 1984, pp. 210-12.
13. R.C. Sharma, 'Art Data in Rayapaseniyam,' *Bulletin of Museums and Archaeology in U.P.*, No. 9, June 1972, pp. 38-44.
14. R.K. Das, *Temples of Vrindāban*, 1990, p. 67.
15. *Ibid.*, p. 73.
16. R.C. Sharma, *op. cit.* (1994), pp. 118-19, 148, 154, 156, 158, etc.

65
ZANSKAR: THE HIDDEN TREASURE

R.S. FONIA

Zanskar at the extreme west is one of the driest and least known Buddhist land of the entire western Himalayan range. It comprises an area of 3,000 square miles and most of its villages and monasteries are distributed along the two great branches of the Zanskar river *i.e.* Doda and Lingti and their tributaries in a general direction from south-east to north-east. It is bounded in the north by Ladakh, by Rukchu in the east, in the south by Lahul and in the west by Purig. Access to Zanskar from all sides is difficult. However, the easiest approach to Zanskar leads from Kargil through Suru valley during summer *i.e.* July-August by motor road and from Nemu (Leh) to Padam during winter via Chadar road all along Zanskar river.

Zanskar is among the rare places in the Himalayan region, where Buddhist religion and traditional way of life and culture continue to exist from the ancient time. The landscape of the entire region is adorned by rows of *mane* walls carved with invocation "*Om mane-padme-ohum*", blue poppies, primitive carvings and countless stupas. It is the land adored by great yogis and monks. A land with cave monasteries, it is indeed watershed of the two great cultural traditions *i.e.* Indian in the west and Tibetan in the east. It has also produced several saints, temple builders and took part in sponsoring the Buddhist religion through the media of art. It is for this reason that for centuries together whether it may be a primitive rock carving or rock-relief, bronze image or mural, ritual object or *thanka*, stupa or gonpa, religion which played a vital note almost in every sphere of art. Its simplicity, therefore, recalls its antiquity.

Historical Survey

The religion of Zanskar, Ladakh and Tibet is a modified form of Indian Buddhism. This faith was introduced into the region during the reign of emperor Aśoka in the third century B.C.[1] The association of primitive rock-carvings of ibex and *chorten* which dot the valley symbolises the interrelation between the nomads and Buddhist monks who followed each other into Central

Asia via Zanskar, Ladakh and Tibet during the reign of emperor Aśoka and subsequently during the reign of Kushāṇ emperors too and this was the main reason for the spread of Buddhism in the region. Thus it was the nomads and monks who brought these into a region and played significant role in the cultural history of the region. The chronicles of Zanskar state that before the arrival of Tibetans *i.e.* ninth-tenth century A.D., the country was subject to Kashmir. Whether Kashmir in fact exercised any political and military control over Zanskar during this period cannot be stated with certainty, but its cultural and religious influence was certainly felt on the paintings and bronze images at Sumda, Sani and other monasteries.[2] Buddhism entered the region through two channels, the ancient monks brought it from India and the Dards from Gilgit.[3] Buddhism was further strengthened by the emigration of many Buddhist monks from Kashmir. The emigration did not take place in consequence of severe persecution; it had its origin in the general decline of Buddhism in Kashmir, which deprived the monks of their sources of revenue. The time of this emigration from Kashmir can be roughly fixed at about eighth-tenth century A.D.[4] but when Ḳashmir finally fell to Muslim rule in A.D. 1337 its Buddhist influence in Zanskar, as on Ladakh decreased rapidly. Zanskar being hidden behind the inaccessible mountain ranges remains a Buddhist land up to present day. It has retained close cultural and religious contacts with Ladakh, Guge, Central Tibet and after seventeenth century A.D. also with Bhutan. Its political status also depended upon the strength and weaknesses of Ladakh in the latter part of the eighteenth century and thereafter. Finally, in 1842, after the Dogra conquest under the leadership of General Zorawar Singh, Zanskar together with Ladakh became a part of Jammu and Kashmir.

Survey of Monastic Development

Before the spread of Buddhist religion in the region, the primitive rock carving representing ibex formed an important clue to the sociological and cultural history of the region. The rock carvings of ibex are widely distributed in the whole of Zanskar and Ladakh region and are believed to have been the representation of the fertility god of the prehistoric people who once lived here long before Buddhism entered the Himalaya. During the time of emperor Aśoka, Buddhism became widespread in Himalayan region and this was probably the time when ibex was worshipped as God by primitive man in Zanskar, because tradition says that ibex is also associated and worshipped in the region as Lord Buddha in deer incarnation.[5] Even today the local people visit the boulders carved with ibex figures inscribed upon them in particular to pray to be blessed with the birth.[6] The association of the symbols of ibex and *chorten* indicates the existence of Buddhism in the land at a very early period. Even the rock cut sculptures found in the region are a witness to the existence of Buddhist religion long before the arrival of Tibetans in Zanskar particular and Islam in Purig, Kargil, Sod, Surm and Batalic regions later. It is thus clear that Zanskar took an active part in sponsoring and establishing the Buddhist religion from third century B.C. to present day. It produced several learned historical personalities who laid the foundation of the monasteries at Sumda, Sani, Phe and Karsha. All these early sites are attributed to the great Tibetan translator-scholar and temple-builder Ṛinchen-byabgo-po (A.D. 958-1055) who was sponsored primarily by a religious king of Gu-ge, namely y-Shes-od. The inscription at Sumda monastery, written probably at the end of the seventeenth century claims that it was built by Rinchen-Zangpo.[7] There are other places in Zanskar where artistic and iconographic remains indicate early foundation, attributed to the Zanskar translators Phag-s-pa-Shes-rab (more or less contemporary with Milaraspa, A.D. 1040-1133), Zhad-pa-Dorje and Kunga Cheyolok. There are other early foundations in Zanskar which are not associated with the translators of Zanskar. These are Sani, Dzonkhul and Tonde. The first is associated with Guru Padmasambhava and second with Naropa and third with his Tibetan successor Marpa. After all both Gura Padmasambhava and Naropa were historical persons who selected this holy land for meditation in the eighth and the eleventh centuries respectively and spread Buddhism in the Himalayan region.

With the arrival of the Gelugspa order from Tibet in Zanskar and Ladakh in fifteenth century, a number of the old monastic foundations were taken over by them and redecorated. This order was founded by Tsong-kha-pa (A.D. 1375-1419) in Tibet. There were several learned men belonging to Gelugspa order who were active in Ladakh and Zanskar in the fifteenth century of whom Zhad pa-Dorje and Kanga Cheylok became the most renowned. By the second half of the fifteenth century A.D. this order was firmly established in this region and received full support by the royal families under the inspiration of Tsong-Khapa. In seventeenth century A.D. another religious order known as Brug-pa gained considerable strength in Zanskar.

In view of above, the main eras of cultural development — their beginning and cultural cumulations particularly in respect of monastic establishment in the region — can be divided into five different periods:

(i) The oldest remains which are pre-Buddhist and testify ancient occupation of Zanskar since the earliest times as represented by boulders with carvings of ibex *i.e.* pre-Buddhist period.

(ii) The rock-cut sculptures of Buddhist deities which indicate existence of early Buddhist religion before the arrival of Tibetan Buddhism in the region and can be dated between the third century B.C. and seventh-eighth century A.D.

(iii) The early monasteries attributed to Guru Rinchen-Zangpos, tenth century A.D. to thirteenth century A.D.

(iv) The later monasteries which came into existence or which have been revived after fifteenth century A.D. closely related with Gelugspa order of Tibet and Brugpa order from Bhutan.

(v) Monasteries renovated or built after Sino-Indian war, 1962.

Primitive Rock Carvings

During the course of exploration in the region, attempts were made to identify rock carvings which have so far remained unnoticed. The most outstanding is the group of primitive rock engravings widely distributed in the entire Zanskar region. These older engravings are deeper, primitive and some of them have blackened and even patinated due to climatic action in comparison to later carvings with new facial expression and subject matter. The common theme of the primitive carvings is hunting and the animals shown therein are ibex and markher. The ibex is a species of wild goat that wandered in the mountains and is recognizable by its double carved horns. It was quite popular in local tradition. In the higher region of Zanskar it is believed to have been a representation of primitive god and respected as token. The Dards, until recently, placed its horns on the grave as a symbol of protection.[8] It was also considered as symbol of fertility god before the spread of Buddhism in the region. There is a local custom to make a flour ibex on the occasion of the birth of child as a thanks offering.[9] Apart from these two animals we also get sheep, fox and dog in the carvings. The only weapon represented in the carvings is bow. It is shown by a vertical line with an arrow crossing it in the middle. A large number of boulders with primitive carvings depicting hunting scene etc. have been found at Phey Tonde, Zangla and Mane in Zanskar and Bhayame Kharbu in the Suru valley. These boulders containing carvings of ibex, hunting scene, human figure are distributed either on ancient route or nearby in the cultivated fields. The later association of religious figures of the sun, *chorten* and *swastika* symbolises the interrelation among the nomads, the Dards and the Buddhist monks. The *swastika* is considered as an important symbol of Bon religion. These carvings certainly testify ancient occupation of the Zanskar valley thereby suggesting that the highest regions of the Himalayas were inhabited since the very early times. The most important factor to be ascertained and identified is the origin and chronology of these primitive rock carvings. The presence of prehistoric culture seems more plausible. This is further substantiated by the recent discovery of a fireplace or *chullah* made by the prehistoric man using three boulders on the terrace of the Indus river near Gayak about 100 km east of Leh. The fire was used by the pre-historic man to roast meat since few pieces of thick bone, possibly of ibex, were collected from the ash and charcoal and have been dated to 6710±130 years. The present discovery and presence of primitive rock carvings provide an important clue for the further studies to trace back the human activities in the region before the onset of permanent settlement in lower Indus and Kashmir valley.

The second group of best reflected and expressed rock art in the region are the Buddhist rock cut sculptures. Carved on huge rocks and isolated stones, the most impressive ones are at Kartse Khar, Padam, Sani, Sanku, Mani, Tonde, Karsha and Zanyla. It is fairly certain that before the Tibetan military expansion in the seventh century cultural inspiration came almost entirely from the west, namely from Kashmir and Gilgit area under the patronage of the Kushāṇ emperors. The existence of even more ancient pre-Buddhist rock carvings suggests that this form of artistic representation may be peculiar and throw light on the early life and culture of Zanskar. The Buddhist divinities which are represented are of Indian origin and for iconographic as well as historical reasons and these are not likely to be much earlier than the eighth-ninth century before the arrival of Tibetan Buddhist order in the region. The most impressive and prominent rock-cut sculpture is that of Maitreya, deeply carved on huge rocks at Kartse-Khar, (Pl. 65.5) in the Suru valley which is identical to Maitreya at Mulbeg and Apati in the Sod valley. The image is in standing form approximately 10 metres in height facing south-east. It is adorned with rich ornaments and holds in his left hand a vase and the right hand is in *abhaya-mudrā*. Flying *gandharvas* are beautifully carved on both sides. It could be dated to about the seventh century A.D. Moorcraft had noticed already Brahmanical card among the characteristic emblems of Maitreya sculptures of Ladakh.[10] Among the wood carvings of Śakti temple at Chhatrari in Chamba, there is four-armed Brahmā, carrying a rosary and a water-pot and accompanied by a pair of geese which are dated to about the seventh century.

Another rock carving representing Padmapāṇi Avalokiteśvara flanked by a goddess has been noticed at Bhyama Khanbu about 33 km from Kargil on way to Zanskar. On the right and left of the main image are represented lay devotees. The costume of the lay devotees is quite similar to the carving of Hanupata and Kalatse which shows Dards in their original costumes. Just below these figures there is a two-line inscription which is badly mutilated.

The other group of rock cut sculptures are the engravings of five Dhyānī Buddhas on huge rocks with their corresponding vehicles near the bank of Zanskar river at Padam. The five seated Dhyānī Buddhas (Pl. 65.6) with their vehicles, a long row of pyramidal *chaityas* and a row of men wearing three-pointed hats are also beautifully carved. Here the workmanship is found better than that of other ancient sculpture in the region. On the upper portion of the rock there are two square recesses bonded into the rock, which probably served as the reception of beams. It appears that there used to be a hall erected in front of the boulders.

Just about 75 yards from this rock, there is another similar boulder, which is carved in the north-south direction by five standing Dhyānī Buddhas and below three of them is seen the outline of the figures of lion, peacock and *garuḍa* probably carved later. The delicate aura around the head and slightly faded outline show that it is older than that of the seated Buddhas. The most interesting feature of this site is the cave underneath the boulder, which has several cells separated from each other by walls and is now filled with debris. These caves will provide valuable information about cave dwellers after a small scale excavation is carried out. Apart from these Dhyānī Buddhas, sculptures of Buddha and Maitreya are also found near the Police Control Room at Padam. According to local people, this place has been associated with a holy site where they place the ashes of dead. Some human bones are also seen there. Just close to the site near the Police Control Room, an ancient Dard grave site was noticed. The labourers found some jewellery and beads of precious and semi-precious stones, handmade pots and bronze objects. Due to howling winds and freezing cold we could not make further enquiry about the finds as most of the labourers had left for other places.

Traditionally the inhabitants of Zanskar have several ways of disposing of their dead. Due to difficult climatic conditions and limited natural resources, either they burn them or throw in the river, or they cut up the corpse and expose it to predators, the wolves and vultures. In certain cases they also bury their dead. These various forms of disposing of the dead represent the transformation of body to fire, water, earth and wind, the four elements considered to be the component of man. This traditional way of disposing of the dead body has something to do with the construction of famous Kanika *chorten* at Sani which is the earliest in Zanskar and played an important role in the dissemination of stupa cult in the region. The rectangular base of this weird-shaped stupa is supposed to represent the earth, the rounded central section or dome representing water, spire representing fire, and the crowning parasol representing wind. These are the four elements which the locals believe to be the component of universe and the elements of which man is made. A red painted wooden piece shaped like erected penis is installed on the front wall of facade. Traditionally during annual festival at Sani, the females visit this place and pray to be blessed with a child. The third group of rock cut sculptures are the representation of Buddhist divinities such as Maitreya, Tārā, Avalokiteśvara etc. and are noticed at several places in Zanskar *i.e.* at Padam, Zangla, Sani, Tonde and Karsha.

Early Monasteries

The finest monumental buildings in Zanskar are the monasteries which are located above the villages in their present form, dating back originally to the tenth-eleventh century to which have been added more structures and decorations. When the Tibetans arrived in the region they built Buddhist monasteries in the valleys below the forts constructed by the Dards and monks. These early monasteries are located at Sani, Sumda, Phey, Karsha and Padam. All these religious sites are attributed to the great Tibetan scholar, translator and temple builder, Guru Rinchen-Zangpo (A.D. 958-1055). The monastery which is fortunately intact and can be attributed to Guru Rinchen-Zangpo is at Sumda. The other monasteries whose artistic and iconographic remains indicate early foundation are located at Karsha, Phe, Sani and Phugtal. Although it is not possible to assign the work of art here to a period or after eleventh century A.D. because the monastic studies entirely depended on models and sometimes procured from distant centres of Buddhist learning and copied for hundreds of years but still the monasteries of early period can easily be distinguished. Their special features are thick door beams and lintels and ornamented wood carvings, galleries and at some places trefoiled arches, halls decorated with paintings. The centre of cult in all these early monasteries are the five Dhyānī Buddhas, attendant Bodhisattvas and other divinities. This cult is represented textually by the tantras and their commentary in which Rinchen-Zangpo and his collaborators took special interest.

The most fascinating site in Zanskar is Sani about 12 km before Padam; the Sani monastery is built on plain land just by the side of the main road leading from Kargil to Padam. It is also famous for its annual festival. On the other side across the road flows the river Thundri. The monastic complex has an enclosure wall within which are two small ancient temples and famous Kanika *chorten* at the back (Pl. 65.3). The murals on the walls have been repainted. It houses several bronze and stucco images of the later period. Another small temple there whose door is locked and sealed, contains an image of Naropa. It is believed that it was built at the spot where Naropa sat in meditation in front of Kanika *chorten*. The other temple which is neglected contains unique collection of images set in the niches. The stuccos on the wall are decorated with landscape, lakes, floral design, *chorten* and manifestation of Padmasambhava and show the influence of Kashmiri art. On the north side is a group of ten rock-cut sculptures among which that of Maitreya is the largest and is still worshipped. Sani is considered to be oldest monastery/site in Zanskar; it is still believed that Guru Padamasambhava and yogi Naropa, the famous Indian saint resided here. Its simplicity and great traditional values recall its antiquity. How old is Sani monastery, is a matter of further archaeological investigation.

It is further believed that Guru Naropa rested at Sani while fleeing from this place to a cave known as Naropa cave at D Zonkhul which is located about 20 km from Sani at a very isolated place. A five-storey monastery is also built here on the contour of the rock and rock forms back-wall of the monastery with Naropa's cave at fifth level. The lower first and second storeys are an assembly hall and contains *thankas* of Akshobhya, Padmasambhava, Mila-raspa and 84 Siddhas and kings of four quarters. A door on the left wall leads to a side room which houses wooden print blocks and other materials for printing of Tibetan books and prayer flags. The second floor of the temple contains *thankas* and stucco images of Zhad-pa-Dorje, Kunga Cheyolok and Lama

Norbu. The fourth floor leads to Naropa's cave through ladder. On the floor of the cave a stone is placed with footprints believed to be those of Guru Naropa who resided here for meditation. Stucco images of Śākyamuni, Akshobhya, Guru-Rinchen Zangpo, Naropa and Phyang-spa are displayed here (Pl. 65.4). The most important features of the monastery are the *thankas* and stucco images of all the temple builders and artists of Zanskar and Tibet who built most of the important monastery and later it became important seat of Brugpa religious order.

The other monastery which can be attributed to Guru Rinchen Zangpo on the basis of iconographic details and inscriptions is the eleven-headed Avalokiteśvara temple at Karsha. It stands on the hillside below the ancient ruined castle just opposite Karsha monastery and is remarkable for its centuries' old murals, inscriptions, wooden images of Buddha and rich collection of *thankas*. Just above the temple (*gonpa*) on the hilltop, are a number of ruined *chortens* and other structures which contain beautiful murals of five Dhyānī Buddhas on the ceiling and walls.

Later Monasteries

With the establishment of Gelugspa, Tibetan religious order in Ladakh and Zanskar, a large number of monasteries were built like 4-5 storied fortress as a place of defence on the summits of hillock. The Gelugspa order was founded by Tsong-kha-pa (A.D. 1357-1419). Several learned men and temple builders belonging to Gelugspa orders, among whom Phad-pa-Dorje and Kunga Chelok were most prominent were very active in Zanskar. They built several monasteries at Karsha, Tonde, Muni and also redecorated several earlier monasteries at Phugtal, Sani Sumda and Phe. An inscription in Phe monastery, Kunga Cheylok, a monk from Zanskar salutes his Guru after completion of decoration of monastery.

The Karsha monastery is the largest and richest monastery in Zanskar (Pls. 65.1 & 65.2). It houses about 100 monks and contains *Dukhang, Gonkhang, Kanjur, Lhakhang, Labruag, Lotsawa-Lhakhang* and Maitreya temple, all having murals and other ritual objects.

At the end of the seventeenth century A.D. another religious order *i.e.* Bragpa branch of Kagu-pa of Bhutan gained considerable strength and built several monasteries at Bardan, Dzonkhud, Tagrimo and took possession of Sani, Zangla and Sumda. Apart from these monastic complexes, several village monasteries at Dorje Dzong at Rizing, Zangla, Tagrimo, Dipting, Acting and Phe were thoroughly studied. Fortunately some of these villages and its monasteries which may date back to thirteenth-fifteenth centuries A.D. have come down today unchanged except for a certain amount of dilapidation due to negligence.

Modern Period

The closure of Tibet to outsiders on account of its occupation by China had immediate repercussion on the day-to-day maintenance of the monasteries. After Dogra conquest of Zanskar and Ladakh the monasteries no longer remained the centre of local administration under royal patronage. Open access, tourism and recent ecological changes have further endangered the centuries old monasteries in Zanskar. As such, the traditional artistic creativity of Zanskar has been sandwiched between Kashmiri militancy and Chinese communism. It has literally pushed

Zanskar into isolation. In this context monastery management has taken up the task of renovation and repainting of these monasteries. Under this process, demolition, renovation and new construction are quite frequent which has changed the original character, authenticity and sanctity of these centuries-old monasteries.

The dislocation of Buddhist learning centre of Tibet, influx of foreign tourists and antique dealers in the region have worsened the situation. Here it may be observed that in the past, religion and art were much more intimately connected than what they are today and much of this was a happy combination by which work of great intensity flourished. But the situation today has completely changed. Artists and religious persons are no longer having cordial association reflecting the urge of the society. Instead, they have exposed themselves to the outside influence to such an extent that priçeless art treasures from monasteries are being smuggled out. Here it may be observed that there are a number of places of regular worship where thankas are being produced and countless bronze images are being casted by refugee artists and are then sold as antiquities to unsuspecting buyers. If such practice will continue, very soon Zanskar together with Ladakh will be deprived of its real art and cultural heritage unless some other sources of inspiration are discovered. Today the task of maintenance and preservation of monasteries and other works of art is the duty of the entire civilized world.

After all, there is need to go again and again in this land of Buddhist art treasure which cannot be described and read but is to be seen and felt. As to how ancient and rich in antiquity is Zanskar one has yet to learn and discover.

NOTES AND REFERENCES

1. Alexander Cunningham, *Ladakh, Physical, Statistical and Historical: With notices of the surrounding countries*, London, 1854 (reprinted New Delhi, 1970).
2. A.H. Francke, *Antiquities of Indian Tibet*, Calcutta, 1914; *History of Western Tibet*, London, 1907, Reprinted with a critical introduction by S.S. Gergan and F.M. Hussnain, as a *History of Ladakh*, New Delhi, 1977.
3. Heinrich-Harrer, *Seven Years in Tibet*, London, 1953.
4. Michel Peissel, *Mustang, A Lost Tibetan Kingdom*, London, 1968.

   ——— *Zanskar, The Hidden Kingdom*, London, 1979.
5. Madanjeet Singh, *Himalayan Art*, UNESCO, Paris and London, 1971.
6. P. Pal, *The Art of Tibet*, New York, 1969.
7. P. Pal, *A Buddhist Paradise, the Murals of Alchi, Western Himalayas*, Basel, Hongkong, 1982.
8. L. Petech, *The Kingdom of Ladakh c. 950-1842 A.D.* , Rome, 1977.
9. D.L. Snellgrove, *Buddhist Himalaya*, Oxford, 1957.
10. D.L. Snellgrove and T. Skorupski, *The Cultural Heritage of Ladakh*, Westminster, 1979-80.
11. Thomas J. Abercrombie, *The Lost Shangri-la*, National Geographic Magazine, Washington DC, March 1978
12. Shering, C-A. *Western Tibet and the British Borderland*, London, 1976.

66

DEVELOPMENT OF EARLY TERRACOTTA ART IN THE MID-GANGA PLAIN—A CASE STUDY

S.C. SARAN

Mid-Ganga plain, located in the core of north India (Singh, 1971: 183), has been the melting pot of cultures through the ages. The region witnessed spontaneous development of art, technology and culture. Beginning of artistic creations by the Prehistoric man may be seen on stone and bone in the middle Ganga plain. The best examples of such expressions are the rock-paintings of Singanpur (Ghosh, 1932:32). The mother-goddess figurine of stone Baghor-I in the Son valley (Pal, 1980-81: 26-29) and bone mother-goddess (Pl. 66.1A) from Daiya on the Lohanda in the Belan valley (Gravel III) (Sankalia, 1978:7-8), both revealed from the upper palaeolithic levels. From the post-palaeolithic period onwards, the other craft which attracted the masses was the modelling of terracotta figurines and pottery making. Being made of easily available material *i.e.* clay, the terracotta art became a prolific medium of expression of the creative genius of the rich and poor alike. The material reflects the glimpse of contemporary socio-cultural, economic and artistic traditions of both urban as well as rural societies. The occurrence of terracottas has therefore been in plenty as compared to other class of antiquities.

The clay used for manufacturing of terracotta is the same as required for making pottery except that it is better lavigated. In most cases, the clay used for terracotta modelling is devoid of common tempering materials. Evidence of the profuse mixture of tempering materials like husk, sand, lime has been noticed in the Kushan, Gupta and even in the later periods as well.

Though early terracotta art of India is a widely discussed subject, its in-depth systematic study covering the evolution, gradual development based on characteristic features and technique still remains to be done in its regional perspective. In this paper, an attempt has been made to study the gradual evolution of plastic art in the mid-Ganga plains from the earliest times down to the 2nd century B.C.

Besides representation of animal and other objects, the earliest examples of terracotta human figurines in the region comprise mainly the depiction of mother-goddess figurines which could have been necessitated due to the prominence of the mother-goddess cult. These figurines are generally crudely modelled specimens which may be categorised as "archaic" having occasional pinhole decoration. The terracotta mother-goddess figurines from the neolithic levels of Chirand are the best examples of the archaic types.

Recent archaeological excavations at Chirand, Sonpur, Buxer, Oriup, Kumrhar (Patna) and Champa in the middle Ganga plain and its neighbouring area at Tamluk in lower Ganga plains and sites like Hastinapur, Atranjikhera, Lal Qila, Sringverapura, Jakhera, Ayodhya, Sonkh and Mathura in the upper Ganga plains have yielded a rich evidence of terracotta art beginning from neolithic age down to the pre-Mauryan period. Chirand is located on the north bank of the Ganga about 10 km east of the district headquarter of Chapra in north Bihar. The earliest level at Chirand *i.e.* neolithic has revealed one of the finest specimens of the artistic activity of the neolithic folk. The best example of the earliest plastic art of this region are the handmade underfired terracotta figurines of bull, snake, and a bird-like figure resembling that of a dove, male and archaic female and miniature linga type object (Sant, 1991:116). The specimen of a longitudinal crudely modelled terracotta female figurine (probably representing mother-goddess) has also been reported from the same level with part below the waist being broken (Pl. 66.1B). The head is crudely modelled and a few pinching marks on the upper portion indicate eyes, nose, mouth and ears. The figure shows well defined, fully developed breasts (left partly broken), slender waist and broad hips. The navel part is indicated by a depression and the right lower part perhaps indicates the right leg while left being completely broken. These specimens possibly represent the earliest attempts to make icons representing objects of sacred worship. But these may be reckoned to be the example of one of the earliest attempts by man to exploit the plasticity of well levigated clay found in abundance in the Ganga valley. Besides plastic art, fine examples of paintings may also be noticed executed on the ceramics. A few potsherds contain post-firing ochre paintings (Verma, 1970-71:21).

In the regions away from mid-Ganga plain, the Harappan culture was flourishing simultaneously. Though there is no direct evidence of contact of these two cultures, yet the close affinity in respect of painted motifs in pottery, beads, bone implements and archaic type of terracotta figurines show the presence of certain common elements in art traditions. Besides, some cult objects like *linga* (phallus) type object, archaic bull figurines, snake, amulet, painted *pipal* leaf pattern on pottery which are present in Chirand neolithic assemblage, show a close resemblance with those of the Harappans (Saran, 1990:63-70).

Examples of archaic figurines have been encountered from Oriup in chalcolithic context. The terracotta figurines from chalcolithic levels generally depict a plump physiognomy, stumpy legs and a plain body devoid of decorative treatment. Most of the figurines reported are headless. It is significant to mention here that the mother-goddess figurines of bone and terracotta from Stone Age culture of the mid-Ganga plain are generally longitudinal in shapes while in chalcolithic context the shape invariably becomes geometrical particularly triangular and in a good frequency.

Oriup is a small hamlet situated on the right bank of river Ganga between Antichak and Patharghata hills in the district of Bhagalpur (Bihar). The handmade terracotta female figurine in triangular shape represents mother goddess (Pl. 66.1C). The head and arms are indicated by simple projections. The other characteristic features are the fully developed breast and pinching decorations. This is a unique specimen as only a few human figurines of this type have so far come to light from the chalcolithic levels.

The artistic heritage of mid-Ganga plain and its neighbouring regions is so vast and rich that it is not possible to assess it in its entirety in the present context but a few examples of early art traditions of the neighbouring regions also cannot be ignored. The discovery of two terracotta female figurines from the O.C.P. levels at Lal Qila (Bulandshahr district of Uttar Pradesh) bear witness to this fact (Sankalia, 1978:78-79). This well preserved terracotta female figurine (measuring 8 x 5 cm) may be reckoned to be unique example of this period (Pl. 66.ID). Unlike female figurines from Indus and other sites, the nose, eyes and lips are well modelled and physical appearance is well maintained. The bust is prominently shown. There is a hole on the right shoulder while left is broken. The author presumes that the hole was intended for hanging the deity on the wall for worship purpose.

The continuance of this tradition has also been marked in the PGW levels particularly in the upper Ganga plain. Three terracotta human figurines of blackish grey colour recovered from Jakhera II-B are interesting (Sahi, 1978:101-03). A unique female figure decorated with deeply incised designs has been shown wearing a *sari* in the modern fashion. In fact these discoveries have provided a new chronological setting to the 'archaic' or 'ageless' human figurines discovered in different parts of the country. The excavations at Ayodhya have also revealed a fine specimen of the early historical terracotta figurine of a Jaina. B.B. Lal identifies bust of a grey colour bald male figurine, having long ear-lobes and arms streched downwards to be the earliest representation of Jaina Tirthankara in *Kayotsarga* pose dating back to c. 4th century B.C. (*IAR*,1976-77:53, Pl. 66.1C).

Completely hand-modelled figurines from Buxer may be reckoned to be one of the earliest examples from pre-NBP levels of the mid-Ganga plain. It is significant to note that the pre-NBP terracottas from Buxer are handmade and what is most important is that the animal figurines are painted with horizontal parallel lines in yellow colour. Terracottas that have been reported from Hastinapura from pre-NBP level are much more crudely made and have no paintings on them (Sinha, 1979: 139-40, Pl. 38). Two terracotta female figurines from Buxer are beautiful. The eyes are incised, nose pinched, breasts full and rounded, and one of these is wearing punched ear-lobes. The technique though primitive, is quite successful, and the modelling shows good craftsmanship. The hand and the fingers of the broken female torso have been very naturally made resting on knee (Pl. 66.2, A & B). Another figurine from Buxer (Pl. 66.3) has rounded face with prominent cheek and very expressive lips. Almond shape eyes with arc shaped eyebrows are indicated with incised eyeballs. Abstract shape ears are elongated with punched ear-studs, hair has been depicted by a series of incised lines, and the nipples in the prominently shown breasts are indicated by pinholes. Though there is a contradiction in proportions yet it exhibits attractive modelling. Except two ear-studs it is devoid of any ornamentation or decoration (Desai, 1986). The other complete one shows diamond-shaped incised eyes, hands folded on breasts and the lower part the body represented in three-legged manner (Pl. 66.4). The conception of portraiture is very clear in this early specimen.

From the early northern black polished ware (hereafter NBP) level at Champa, dated to 6th-5th century B.C., were discovered a large number of antiquities which include a broken ivory figure, stone mould and terracotta *Nagi* figure. The terracotta *Nagi* figure whose head portion is represented by snake god, and the remaining portion including legs, represents abstraction of a human figure. This is the early representation of the concept of the semi-*Nagas*, having human form as described in early literature [Sinha, 1972-73 : 71-73; Pl. IV(A)]. Perhaps this is one of the earliest examples of the composite figurine in plastic art. Another significant evidence from Chirand (*c.* 4th-3rd century B.C.) is a terracotta mask (measuring 35 cm. in length) which reflects an insight into the social amusements of the period [Sinha, 1972-73 : 73; Pl. 89.3 (B) & (C)].

The characteristic feature of terracotta from this level generally shows the crude modelling and application of pinching technique for decoration and indication of facial features. Besides complete hand-modelling we start getting the specimens having moulded face and hand-modelled body from the third century B.C. onwards. The limitation in decoration of moulded face was supplemented by applique decoration. So far as modelling is concerned the figurines of this type can be divided into two groups: (I) completely hand-modelled, and (II) luting of the moulded head while remaining part of the body being hand-modelled. In later period the entire figurine is found to be made out of a single mould. Red and grey shades were achieved by introduction of different methods of firing.

Further elaboration is noticed during 300-200 B.C. in the figurines from sites like Buxer (Pl. 66.5), Vaisali (Krishna Deva and Mishra, 1961, Pl. XII, A, B), Rajghat (Narain and Agrawala, 1978, Pl. I & II), Mathura, Ahichchhatra and Kausambi. Various methods of decoration in the form of applique bands punched, incised and finger-tipped decorations are found which may be reckoned to be the main characteristic features of the Mauryan terracotta art. Specimens from Mathura (Joshi and Margabandhu, 1976-77; Fig. 5, 1-3), Ahichchhatra (Ancient India 4, Pl. XXXI A, No. 1-9), Rajghat (Narain and Agrawal, 1978; Pl. I No. 1, 2) of this hand-modelled group show elliptical section. This element could have inspired the emergence of plano-convex plaques of the Sunga period. The best examples of the earliest terracotta Sakti-goddess with weapons round the top of the plaque have been found from the late phase of the NBP strata at Champa (Pl. 66.6), assignable to the Sunga period (Sinha, 1972-73 : 73). Besides, a good number of terracotta plaques of this period have been reported from almost all the early historic sites of northern India.

Specimens of terracotta female figurines of group II found from Buxer (Desai, 1986, Fig. 6), Rajghat, Kausambi (Sharma, 1960, Pl. 44, 4-5) and Mathura (Joshi and Margabandhu, 1976-77, Pl. II, Fig. 6) are very interesting, Notable feature of this group is the introduction of moulded head along with applique decorations and ornamentation. The bust from Buxer (Desai, 1986, Fig. 6) is a fine specimen of this group. Moulded face does not show sharp features which is the characteristic of a cast from a much used mould. Yet it is beyond any doubt, that it is an example of beautiful portraiture of a smiling lady with sharp nose, dimpled cheek and prominent chin.

Profuse decoration in applique style is finished with incised and punched motifs. Female figurines from Sonpur, Bulandibagh are the other fine specimens to be mentioned here. Mathura figurine (Joshi and Margabandhu, 1976, Pl. II, Fig. 6) is a beautiful specimen of this group. It has moulded charming face with less pronounced vegetal characteristic showing coronet of lotus flowers behind the head having ample ornamentation covering almost the entire body. Facial expression and modelling achieved the treatment of fine portrait making excells in its intricate treatment similar to that of Buxer lady. Moulded head bears the conception of portraiture aesthetic development. It is also linked up with the mass production of figurines as per the demand of the society.

We do not get evidence of the use of mould from the pre NBP levels in the Ganga Valley. It might have been introduced sometimes in early 4th-3rd century B.C., and that too in very restricted manner at sites like Buxer and Mathura. The tradition of group II type terracotta *i.e.* fully hand modelled, dominates the production at several sites in mid-Ganga plain. The reference to the use of moulded face in pre-Mauryan and post-Harappan times (Verma, 1986, Pl. 117) can hardly be accepted as the author has failed to quote any such examples.

Specimens unearthed from neolithic, chalcolithic and pre-NBP levels very well represent continuity in the terracotta art tradition in this region. The view held by different scholars that the technique of moulding has been due to foreign influence in India, cannot thus be accepted. Creative mind always looked for some inventions and potter cannot be an exception to this mostly their inventions evolved out of their regular work. If in the pre-Mauryan period, the artists could evolve the technique of punching design on their own moulding techniques is not at all far-off. The evidence of moulding and casting of ornaments had already been in practice in Champa during the 6th-5th century B.C. (Sinha, 1979: 1445; Pl. 12).

Besides these, a good number of unpublished terracotta of the neolithic and pre-NBP strata from Chirand, Buxer and Champa are preserved in Patna Museum and in the Department of Ancient Indian History and Archaeology, Patna University, Patna (Bihar) which require further study and may throw more light in the development of terracotta art.

NOTES AND REFERENCES

1. Agrawala, V.S., 1947-48. "The Terracottas of Ahichchhatra", *Ancient India, No. 4,* New Delhi.
2. Desai, D., 1986. "The Social Milieu of Ancient Indian Terracottas 600 B.C.-600 A.D.", Amy. G. Poster (ed.), *From Indian Earth 4,000 years of Terracotta Art,* New York.
3. Deva, K. and Vijaykant Mishra, 1961. *Vaisali Excavations 1950,* Allahabad.
4. Ghosh, M., 1932. "Rock-Paintings and other Antiquities of Prehistoric and Later Times", *Memoirs of the Archaeological Survey of India,* No. 24, (Reprint 1991, Chapt. III, pp. 9-10).
5. *Indian Archaeology : A Review,* 1976-77.
6. Joshi, M.C. and Dr. C. Margabandhu, 1976-77. "Some Terracottas from Excavations at Mathura—A Study", *Journal of the Indian Society of Oriental Art,* New series ,Vol. VIII.
7. Narayan, A.K. and P.K. Agrawala, 1978. *Excavations at Rajghat (1957-59, 1960-65),* Part IV, terracotta human figurines.
8. Pal, J.N., 1980-81. "Upper Palaeolithic Cultures of the mid-Son Valley", *Puratattva, No. 12,* New Delhi.

9. Sahi, M.D.N., 1978. "New Light on the Life of the Painted Grey Ware People as Revealed from Excavations at Jakhera (Dist. Etah)", *Man and Environment*, Vol. II, Ahmedabad.

10. Sankalia, H.D., 1978. *Pre-historic Art in India*, Delhi.

11. Sant, Urmila, 1991. *Neolithic Settlement Pattern of North Eastern and Northern India*, New Delhi.

12. Saran, S.C., 1990. "Harappan Elements in Chirand", *Archaeology and Art*, Krishna Deva Felicitation Vol., Part-I, (Chief Ed. C.R.P. Sinha).

13. Sharma, G.R., 1969. *The Excavations at Kausambi* (1957-59), Allahabad.

14. Singh, R.L., 1971. *India—A Regional Geography*, Varanasi.

15. Sinha, B.P., 1972-73. "Some Rare Antiquities from Recent Excavations in Bihar", *Puratattva, No. 6*, Delhi.

16. Sinha, B.P., 1987. "Origins of Art in the Central Gangetic Valley", in B.M. Pandey and B.D. Chattopadhyay (eds.), *Archaeology and History*, Essays in memory of Sh. A. Ghosh, Vol. II, New Delhi.

17. Sinha, B.P., 1979. *Archaeology and Art of India*, New Delhi.

18. Verma, B.S., 1970-71. "Excavations at Chirand, New light on the Indian Neolithic Culture-complex", *Puratattva, No. 4*, New Delhi.

19. Verma, N., 1986. *Terracottas of Bihar*.

67

A GANDHARAN RELIEF IN THE NATIONAL MUSEUM COLLECTION

SHASHI ASTHANA

Gandharan art with some elements of West Asian--Graeco-Roman idioms is known for its predominantly Buddhistic content. The Gandharan artists indeed surpassed all others in depicting the largest number of events from the life of Buddha, major and minor both. They adopted narrative style to illustrate the episodes vividly which was absolutely essential for the neo-converts in the Gandhara region who certainly knew very little of the Buddha whose following till the Ist century B.C. was mainly confined to eastern, western and southern India. A large number of such plaques have been reported from various Gandhara sites and are presently available in various museums of India and abroad for study.

1. It has been found that the Gandharan artists were fond of depicting the life scenes of Buddha in sculptural reliefs in narrative style with events placed in proper sequence; for example, the panels of the Birth, Enlightenment, First Sermon and Mahāparinirvāṇa are placed one following the other. But sometimes they depicted the events which occurred at different points of time together in one single frieze, irrespective of time and space as well as sequence in which they had occurred.

2. Gandharan artists were experts in presenting detailed as well as the concise versions of the same event, generally depending upon the availability of space.

3. Each episode has been carved according to the proper contents of the story but sometimes two episodes, completely different in their content, are presented in such a manner that it becomes difficult to identify exactly the episodes in question. Still some minor clues do help us in identifying them. To our mind such examples are late in chronology when the faithfuls became fully conversant with the life stories of the Master.

To illustrate these characteristics a Gandharan stele is presented here (Pl. 67.1). This sculpture is presently housed in the National Museum, New Delhi,[1] where it was received from Chandigarh Museum in exchange. Originally it belonged to the Lahore Museum and it was given to Chandigarh Museum as Indian share at the time of Partition. Its exact provenance is unknown. It is carved out of greyish schist and can be dated to 1st-2nd century A.D. It is conceived as a gable commonly used in decoration of Buddhist stupas and placed at the base of the dome, either on one or all four faces of the monument. The vertical relief is divided in four panels in the centre, set one over the other. The sides of the stele are decorated with musicians in six small compartments on left side, arranged vertically one above the other. The Buddha and Boddhisattva images depicted in various *mudrās* and set in six compartments on the right side are also placed vertically one above the other. The relief is bordered on the right side with a thick stem with diamond -shaped leaves and left side has a band of acanthus leaves.

Four square panels, presented in the centre, are important for this study. They depict four important episodes from the life of Buddha. While the first panel from top presents the scene related to the conversion of Jaṭilas, the second incorporates the Māra-attack or the Enlightenment. The subject of the third panel has as yet not been properly identified. The fourth compartment is carved with the subject known as conversion of Aṅgulimāla. Each of them occurred at different points of time in Buddha's life and are also not at all interrelated. For example, conversion of Jaṭilas occurred later than the Enlightenment. Therefore each of these four panels is complete in itself in time and space.

From the point of view of iconography, the second panel is very important as it depicts the scene related to Māra-attack and Enlightenment though neither Buddha is shown seated under the Bodhi tree in earth-touching posture nor is Māra presented in the scene along with his three daughters, three sons and army. In this panel, Buddha along with Vajrapāṇi (?) is shown standing near the Bodhi tree under which a human figure, probably the tree-spirit, is visible. Both the tree and the human figure, are worn out. The identification is, therefore, based on similar representations, one housed in the Prince of Wales Museum, Bombay[2] and one in Peshawar.[3] In the first representation Buddha is shown seated near the tree in *abhaya mudrā* with a female figure standing under the tree. On the other side of the tree Māra, the god of love, is standing alongwith his daughters. The tree is shown emerging out of the base made of stone decorated with geometric designs. This base is exactly like the one which is represented in the present panel.

In the second relief Buddha is shown standing near the Bodhi tree, a human figure is emerging out of the base on top and the earth-goddess is shown in front of the base emerging out of the foliage. Another figure accompanying the Buddha is damaged. Māra and his daughters are shown on the other side of the tree. If we compare this with our relief we will see that Buddha is standing exactly in the same posture. In this relief the attendant figure is shown on his left side while in our relief it is placed on the right side. The tree with human figure emerging from it is portrayed in the same way. The earth goddess is missing in our relief. The most important feature of this theme is the depiction of Māra and his daughters, but it is missing in this relief probably due to the shortage of space.

The identification clearly attests that the scene relates to the Māra-attack and Enlightenment. Thus the artists did depict the concise version of this theme besides a number of plaques presenting the theme on a large scale.

The lowermost panel is carved with the scene of the conversion of Aṅgulimāla. But the scene completely tallies with another subject also, *i.e.* Dīpaṅkara Jātaka. Even the most casual look at this relief makes its identification as Dīpaṅkara Jātaka. The whole setting appears to be in accordance with the episode where Dīpaṅkara Buddha stands facing Sumati who scatters flowers with his raised hand. In the next stage he has prostrated himself before Buddha and finally Sumati is raised in the air. But the depiction of sword on the pedestal changes the whole of arrangements and it identifies itself with a completely different subject *i.e.*, the conversion of Aṅgulimāla, which the artist has presented here.

According to a legend, a Brahman, called Ahiṅgsaka was studying at Taxila. As he excelled in the school, the other students became jealous of him. They made a false allegation against him by telling to the *guru* that he took liberties with the wife of the teacher. His *guru* became furious and he chalked out a wicked plan in order to take revenge. He refused to educate him any more unless he killed a thousand persons and brought their fingers as a proof of their death. Ahiṅgsaka tried to prove himself innocent, but he could not. Due to his great desire for learning he made himself ready to carry out the orders. He murdered many persons in the forest who passed by and wore the garland of the fingers. Thus he assumed a new name 'Aṅgulimāla'. When he completed the murder of 999 and only one remained, his mother heard about her son. She reached the forest with the food to bring her son into senses. But the moment he was about to kill his mother, Buddha appeared on the scene. As Buddha knew about his merit and virtues he thought of converting him. As Buddha prevented him, he tried to attack Buddha also. But the Buddha's words proved like a miracle and he threw his sword and jewels on the ground and prostrated himself at the feet of the Buddha. He repented, and was immediately converted.

In sculptural art this subject is presented in the following manner. Aṅgulimāla is ready to kill his mother on one side; Buddha appears and prevents him from doing this; he tries to attack him too, but finally submits himself in prostrate posture after throwing the sword and jewels.

In this panel Buddha is shown standing facing Aṅgulimāla who is ready to kill his mother as shown above and at the intervention of Buddha he turns towards Buddha to attack him too with his raised hand. Finally, he lies prostrate at the Buddha's feet. His sword, thrown by him, is shown nearby.

In other examples, like the one from Sahri Bahlol,[4] the representation is much more dramatic and detailed. The sword along with diadem is shown lying on the ground. This part of the representation is very much similar to the National Museum relief.

Though the contents of Dīpaṅkara Jātaka and conversion of Aṅgulimāla are poles apart, the depictions of both the episodes bear a striking similarity. In both the representations, Buddha is shown facing a person who has a raised hand, a human figure is shown on higher ground and a person is shown in prostrate posture before the Buddha. The sword lying on the floor is however only distinctive identification mark in these two scenes.

Thus this vertical frieze is an important Gandharan sculpture reflecting some unique characteristic features of the Gandharan art.

NOTES AND REFERENCES

1. National Museum, New Delhi, Acc. No. 68. 173.
2. Moti Chandra, *Stone Sculpture in the Prince of Wales Museum*, Bombay, 1974, cat. No. 26.
3. Ingholt, H., *Gandharan Art in Pakistan*, New York, 1957, Fig. 62.
4. *Ibid.*, Fig. 119.

68

VAISHṆAVA IMAGES IN KHAIRAGARH MUSEUM—A CRITICAL STUDY

SHIVA KANT DWIVEDI

Vaishṇavism, or the worship of the god Vishṇu, was an important cult which claimed a large number of adherents among the people in ancient India. It occupied a unique position in the Hindu religious pantheon whose popularity in the form of Vāsudeva Kṛshṇa, Rāma, Buddha and many other manifestations may be imbibed in the temples and independent images. Although the whole of the State of Madhya Pradesh is girdled with a large number of Vaishṇava temples, but Chhattisgarh region (ancient Dakshiṇa Kośala) is not far behind in the temple structural activity of the Vaishṇava cult. The south-eastern region of Dakshiṇa Kośala is quite rich with regard to the development of Vaishṇavism. As a result many temples from *circa* tenth century A.D. to fourteenth century A.D. were erected, such as Tumman, Janjagir, Shivari-Narayana and the ruined Vishṇu temple at Dhamadha.

The Indira Kala Sangit Vishwavidyalaya, Khairagarh, is situated in Rajnandgaon district which lies in Chhattisgarh region of M.P.; the collection of the art and archaeology museum of this University is from this region only. The collection is confined to only a few manifestations of Vishṇu such as Lakshmī Nārāyaṇa, Vāmana and a few Dhruvaberas, etc.

These sculptures range between tenth and thirteenth century A.D. and were executed during the reign of the Kalachuris of Ratanpur branch.

This paper aims to throw light on the critical study along with the description of the images of Vaishṇava cult preserved in this museum.

The images in chronological order are described below:

Lakshmī Nārāyaṇa (*Acc. No. KM. 156*): Made of blackish-brown sandstone, this beautiful image is from Kawardha. It measures 88 x 60 x 19 cm.

This image of Lakshmī Nārāyaṇa is a prototype of Umā Maheśvara form prevalent in contemporaneous period. Lakshmī Nārāyaṇa is seated on Garuḍa, who is shown in flying posture. The *vāhana* Garuḍa is in human form. His pointed and elongated nose and hair are done in *piṅgalordhva* fashion. As he is shown lifting the couple, he is supporting the right foot of Vishṇu on his raised right palm. The goddess Lakshmī is seated on the left thigh of Vishṇu. Vishṇu and Lakshmī, both are seated in *lalitāsana* in *āliṅgana* attitude. Both are four-armed. Vishṇu is holding *gadā* in his upper left and *padma* in his upper right hand whereas his lower left is touching the breast of Lakshmī in *āliṅgana* and the lower right holds the *śaṅkha*. The lower left hand of Vishṇu in embracing attitude also holds *chakra* which is a peculiarity. The right lower hand of Lakshmī is placed around the neck of her lord. She holds *sanāla padma* in her upper left whereas upper right is shown holding *añjana-śalākā* in *vitarka* attitude and the lower left holds the *śṛingāra-mañjūshā* in the same fashion as is commonly found in the hands of Umā in Umā-Maheśvara images.

Vishṇu is encrowned with *kirīṭa-mukuṭa* and wears necklace, *mekhalā, yajñopavīta, udarabandha, keyūra* and *kaṅkaṇa* along with the *chakra-kuṇḍalas. Vaijayantīmālā* is also partly visible. Lakshmī is embellished with necklace, *mekhalā, muktā-māla* which is hanging below in U'-shape across the breasts. She also wears *chakra-kuṇḍalas, keyūra* and *kaṅkaṇa*, finger rings and is attired in *uttarīya* in a typical fashion.

The *parikara* of the image is adorned with *prabhāmaṇḍala* along with *kuḍū* pattern on either side and *makaramukha* as a part of upper decoration of the *siṁhāsana* on both the ends. The exterior of the image is covered with the depiction of the *daśāvatāras* and *āyudha purushas*. On the left is *śaṅkha-purusha* and on the right is the *chakra-purusha* as attendants holding *chaurī*. On the top above the *prabhāmaṇḍala* is *matsya* and the *kūrma* on the right and left respectively. On either side of the halo is *varāha* and *Nṛsiṁha* in pillared niches at the right and left respectively. On the right exterior, are Balarāma, Rāma and Buddha and on the left are Vāmana, Paraśurāma and the Kalki. The exterior is also adorned with the *śārdūla* motifs. On stylistic ground, the image may be assigned to *circa* twelfth century A.D. (Pl. 68.1).

Lakshmī Nārāyaṇa (Acc. No. KM. 158) : This image made of blackish-brown sandstone has been procured from Kawardha and measures 1.00x48x25 cm.

This image of Lakshmī Nārāyaṇa is in *āliṅgana* attitude showing the goddess Lakshmī seated on the left thigh of Vishṇu. The couple is seated in *lalitāsana* on Garuḍa, the *vāhana* of Vishṇu, who is shown in flying posture in conventional form. His hair are in *piṅgalordhva* fashion. The face is bearded and there is shown a *nāga* around his neck in the fashion of *kaṇṭhahāra* along with the necklace. He is shown lifting the couple. Both the hands are broken. Both Vishṇu and Lakshmī are four-armed. Vishṇu is holding *gadā* in his upper left and his lower left is holding *chakra* while embracing and almost touching the breast of Lakshmī. His both right hands are broken. Lakshmī is holding *añjana-śalākā* in her upper right and the *śṛiṅgāra mañjūshā* in her lower left hand. The right lower hand is placed around the neck of her lord. Her upper left hand is broken. Vishṇu is crowned with *kirīṭa mukuṭa* which is partly broken. He wears *chakra kuṇḍalas, hāra, mekhalā* and the *keyūra* whereas Lakshmī is embellished with *chakra kuṇḍalas, keyūra, kaṇṭhahāra, kankana* and the *muktā māla* along with the *mekhalā*.

The style of seated attitude of the couple is in *sammukha-mudrā* gazing each other. Behind the couple is the *prabhāmaṇḍala* in low relief and depicted only in linear pattern. On either side of the *prabhāmaṇḍala* is the figure of a *vidyādhara* holding garland in floating pattern.

As far as the exterior decoration of the image is concerned, *makaramukha* as a decorative part of the *siṁhāsana* and *śārdūla* are shown on either side. Below the *śārdūla* on the right exterior is standing a male *chaurī* bearer. Amongst the *daśāvatāras,* the figure of Nṛisiṁha, on the top of the left exterior and Rāma, Vāmana and Kalki in the lower part of this portion are shown, which indicates an irregular form of the depiction of the *daśāvatāras.* Apart from the *daśāvatāras* a very rare and exceptional image of four-armed *Hayagrīva* seated in *ardhaparyaṅkāsana* is carved on the top of the right exterior. In the lower portion of right exterior Balarāma incarnation and the *śaṅkha-purusha* are shown side by side in *dvibhaṅga* posture.

The *pādapīṭha* of the statue is decorated with the figure of Bhūdevī in the centre, worshipped by a *nāga* in *añjali mudrā* on either side. On either side of the *pādapīṭha* is shown a seated male devotee on the right and the female devotee on the left as worshippers.

In view of the anatomical details, ornamentations and expression along with the later adoption of unsystematic placing of *daśāvatāras* and the *āyudhas* of Lakshmī, this image may safely be placed in latter half of *circa* twelfth century A.D. (Pl. 68.2).

Lakshmī Nārāyaṇa (Acc. No. 149) : Made of blackish brown sandstone, this image has also been procured from Kawardha. It measures 73x38x14 cm.

This statue of Laskhmī Nārāyaṇa is almost similar in the form to the above statues excepting in exterior decoration and expression. The couple is seated on Garuḍa, the *vāhana* of Vishṇu, who is in human form and shown in flying posture, supporting the right foot of Vishṇu on his right palm and left foot of Lakshmī on his left palm. His pointed nose and hair done in *piṅgalordhva* fashion are in conventional style.

Lakshmī Nārāyaṇa is seated in *āliṅgana* attitude showing Lakshmī seated on the left thigh of Vishṇu and placing her right lower arm on the shoulder of Vishṇu around his neck. Vishṇu's lower left hand to be conventionally shown touching the breast of Lakshmī is invisible due to broken left breast and arm of Lakshmī.

Both Nārāyaṇa and Lakshmī are four-armed. Vishṇu is holding *gadā* in his upper left and *padma* in his upper right hand. In his lower right is *śaṅkha* and the lower left is broken. The right lower hand of Lakshmī is placed around the neck of her lord and the right upper hand holds the *añjana śalākā.* Her lower and upper left hands are broken. Vishṇu is bedecked with *kirīṭa-mukuṭa* and is embellished with *chakra kuṇḍalas, kaṇṭhābharaṇa, muktāhāra, keyūra, kaṅkaṇa* and *mekhalā.* He also wears *udarabandha* and is endowed with *śrīvatsa* symbol on the chest. Lakshmī wears *karṇa-kuṇḍalas, kaṇṭhahāra, muktā māla* and the *mekhalā.*

The *parikara* of the statue covers four *avatāras* of Vishṇu, *i.e.* Matsya, Kūrma, Varāha and Nṛsiṁha.

This image in view of the form and slightly balanced anatomy along with better expression is assignable to *circa* latter half of the eleventh century A.D. (Pl. 68.3).

Lakshmī Nārāyaṇa (Acc. No. 148) : This beautiful image, made of blackish brown sandstone, hails from Kawardha and measures 55x39x18 cm.

This image of Lakshmī Nārāyaṇa is also in *āliṅgana* attitude, portraying the goddess Laskhmī seated on the left thigh of Vishṇu. The divine couple is seated in *lalitāsana* on Garuḍa, the *vāhana* of Vishṇu, who is shown in conventional form. His face is bearded and the hair arranged in *sīmanta* fashion is the peculiarity of this particular representation. He wears the *kuṇḍalas, graiveyaka, ekāvali-hāra, udarabandha, kaṅkaṇa, kaṭimekhalā* and the *pādavalayas*. He is shown in flying posture, supporting the right foot of Vishṇu on his right palm and the left foot of Lakshmī on his left palm.

Lakshmī and Nārāyaṇa, both are four-armed. Vishṇu is holding *chakra* in his upper left and his lower left is shown touching the breast of Lakshmī. His upper and lower right hands are broken which might have held *gadā* and the *śaṅkha*. Lakshmī is holding *añjana-śalākā* in her upper right and the lower right is placed around the neck of her lord. Her upper left hand holds the *mṛṇāla-padma* and lower left is holding the *sṛiṅgāra mañjūṣā*.

Vishṇu's head is now chopped off. He wears *graiveyaka*, two-stringed *hāra, yajñopavīta, udarabandha, mekhalā, kaṅkaṇa* along with the *chakrakuṇḍala*. *Vanamālā* is also partly visible. Lakshmī is embellished with the *mukuṭa, kaṇṭhahāra, ekāvali-hāra* falling in U-shape across the breasts, *mekhalā, pāda-kaṭaka* and the *nūpura*. She also wears the *chakrakuṇḍalas, kaṅkaṇas*, finger rings and moreover she is attired in *uttarīya* in a typical manner.

The exterior of the image is covered with the depiction of the *daśāvatāras* and the female worshippers. On either side of the stele, the Varāha and Nṛisiṁha incarnations are depicted in conventional manner. The left exterior is covered with Vāmana, Rāma and the Kalki while Balarāma, Paraśurāma and Buddha incarnations are depicted at the right exterior. The figure of Balarāma is shown in conventional manner with serpent hoods on the head. He holds *ghaṭa* and the *hala* (plough) in his two hands.

In view of the anatomical details, ornamentation, expression and irregular symmetry along with the unsystematic placing of the *daśāvatāras*, this image may be placed in the latter half of the twelfth century A.D. (Pl. 68.4).

Vāmana (Acc. No. 105) : This image represents the Vāmana incarnation of Vishṇu depicting the earlier part of the whole mythology. It has been procured from Khatutola, a ward of Dongargarh town in district Rajnandgaon (M.P.). It is made of white sandstone and is in very mutilated condition. It measures 87x62x23 cm.

The appearance of this statue reminds the Vāmana-Vishṇu conception furnished in the *Ṛgveda* (R.V; I, 155, 6), where Vāmana is conceived as a Yuvā-Kumāra, *i.e.* the mendicant (*Brahmachārī*). Unfortunately the maximum portion of his head and the face is now chopped off. It is a dwarfish figure having plump body and straight limbs. His all the four hands are broken from elbow, hence the attributes held in his hands are not visible. His chest is marked with the *śrīvatsa* symbol.

The image is shown standing in *samabhaṅga* posture on a plain pedestal. He wears the *chakrakuṇḍalas, graiveyaka,* two-stringed *hāra, keyūra* studded with the *maṇis, yajñopavīta, kaṭimekhalā, uru-jālaka, pādakaṭaka, nūpura* and the *vanamālā* falling up to his knee. In the lower exterior, he is flanked with the goddesses Śrī and Bhūdevī standing in *dvibhaṅga* posture holding *kalaśa* and an indistinct object in their hands, possibly *padma*. A female *chauri* bearer holding *chauri* and a lotus bud is shown attending the God at the lower left exterior. To the left side of the pedestal, a long bearded worshipper is depicted in *añjalihasta mudrā*. In the centre of the pedestal, a small figure of his vāhana, Garuḍa, is shown in anthropomorphic form in flying posture with folded hands. In the right *parikara*, a figure of *mālādhara* floating amidst the clouds is shown in a small niche.

The God might have held his usual emblems, *viz. śaṅkha, chakra, gadā* and the *padma* in his lost four hands.

On stylistic ground, this image may safely be placed in the first half of the twelfth century A.D. (Pl. 68.5).

Vishṇu worship was also prevalent in the form of *vyūhas* in Chhattisgarh region throughout the centuries. All the 24 varieties of Vishṇu have been worshipped by the people of this region. Such images are either installed in the temples or worshipped independently. Generally, the complete forms of *Vishṇu-Vyūhas* are not found together in the temples of central India. But Chhattisgarh region is an exception in this respect. The door jamb of the temple at Tumman (Bilaspur, M.P.) and the *jaṅghā* portion of Vishṇu temple at Janjgir (District Raipur, M.P.) is embellished with the complete 24 forms (*Dhruvaberas*) of Vishṇu. The Vishṇu temple at Shivarinarayan (District Bilaspur, M.P.) is also noteworthy in this regard, where the streams of *avatāravāda* and the *vyūhavāda* are shown enjoined with each other in the form of sculptures caused by the Kalachuri rulers of Ratanpur branch. During survey of the temple architecture and other monuments, even specially in the Vishṇu temples of this region, I found that in whole of Chhattisgarh region, some selected forms of Vishṇu were more prevalent and worshipped by the people. These form are Govinda, Mādhava, Vāsudeva, Trivikrama, Saṁkarshaṇa, Vishṇu and Hṛishikeśa.

In the collection of Khairagarh Museum, two *sthānaka* images of Vishṇu procured from the village namely Birkha-Bilahari, district Rajnandgaon (M.P.) are preserved.

The first image (Acc. No. KM. 108) is made of brownish sandstone and represents Mādhava variety of Vishṇu according to the *Rūpamaṇḍana*. It measures 76x50x17 cm. The deity is standing in *samabhaṅga* posture on a plain pedestal. As per the broadly accepted order of emblems, which starts from the lower right hand in the clockwise direction, he holds the *gadā, chakra, śaṅkha* and the *padma*. At the lower right portion of the image, his *vāhana*, the Garuḍa is shown in anthropomorphic form in *añjalihasta* posture, while at the left, a manifestation of Vishṇu's emblem, the *Padma-purusha* is shown standing in *tribhaṅga*. He wears the *kirīṭa-mukuṭa, chakra kuṇḍalas*, plain and heavy *graiveyaka, hāra, Yajñopavīta, keyūra, kaṅkaṇa, kaṭisūtra, pāda-kaṭaka, pāda-valaya* and the *vanamālā*.

Varāha and *Nṛisiṁha* incarnations are shown on the *parikara*. Behind the head of Vishṇu, a halo carved in the sunrays pattern (*sphurat-prabhā maṇḍala*) or radiating halo indicates the cosmic power of the deity and enhances its divine beauty.

On stylistic ground the image may be ascribed to *circa* latter half of the thirteenth century A.D. (Pl. 68.6).

The second image (Acc. No. 107) is also made of brownish sandstone and measures 75x45x15 cm.

It is shown standing in *samabhaṅga* posture on a lotus pedestal. The upper right and left hands and also the upper left part (shoulder) of the body of the image have been lost. The lower left arm is broken above the elbow while the paw of lower right hand is partly damaged.

As is already mentioned above that the two hands are lost, the placing of emblems cannot be ascertained. In this specimen, the order of emblems starts with *gadā* and ends with the *chakra*. In the list of *chaturviṁśatimūrttis* furnished in the *Rūpamaṇḍana*, Vishṇu and Saṁkarshaṇa hold the same order of emblems. Thus, this image either represents the Vishṇu variety or Saṁkarashaṇa variety of Vishṇu.

This image holds *gadā* and the *chakra* in its lower right and the left hands. He wears *kirīṭa-mukuṭa, chakra-kuṇḍala, hāra, kaṭimekhalā, bhujabandha, kaṅkaṇa, yajñopavīta* and the *vanamālā.*

An interesting feature of this image is the representation of different *vibhavas* and *vyūhas* together in a very peculiar way. The Nṛisiṁha and the Kūrma *avatāras* are shown at the right exterior along with the representation of Mādhava and Hṛishikeśa. Achyuta, Vāsudeva and Mādhava forms of Vishṇu are depicted at the left exterior. The *parikara* of the right side is endowed with the *Kṛishṇāvatāra* narrating the episode of Kāliya-mardana very prominently. On stylistic ground, this statue may be assigned to *circa* thirteenth century A.D. (Pl. 68.7).

Critical Study

Vaishṇava images in the museum as described above, although meagre, are typical in character from the point of view of eleventh-twelfth century sculptural art of the Kalachuris of Ratanpur and Tumman. The images assignable to *circa* eleventh-twelfth century A.D. are the *āliṅgana mūrtis* of *Garuḍāsīna* Lakshmī-Nārāyaṇa in majority. This style is prevalent and is found in many of the art centres particularly at Janjagir, Shivarinarayana, Ratanpur and Bhoramdeo. The same stylistic pattern with a slight variation can be noticed in the collection of two Lakshmī Nārāyaṇa images preserved in the open air at Bhoramdeo and a few in Bilaspur and Raipur Museums. In the Śiva temple at Pali, this slight variation is also visible in these images.

If the style of these Lakshmī-Nārāyaṇa forms is compared with the images of Ḍāhala school, the difference is only noticed in Itālamāna, facial features, composition, ornamentation, particularly in exterior decoration and to some extent in the *āyudhas.* The similarity is only in depiction of Garuḍa in anthropomorphic form having beard and moustaches, hair in *piṅgalordhava* fashion and embellished with the *sarpa hāra*, lifting his lord and the goddess with support of his both the palms, in flying posture. The pointed and elongated nose of Garuḍa is nothing but the convention of local artists. Besides these, the similarity can be observed in the U'-shaped *muktāhāra* passing from the centre of the breasts of Lakshmī shown four-armed.

As far as the difference in both the schools is concerned, apart from *tālamāna* and facial features, the difference of the *āyudhas* is more prominent, since the artist of Ratanpur school has particularly introduced the *añjana śalākā* and the *śṛiṅgāra-mañjūshā* and commonly adopted in almost all the images of Lakshmī Nārāyaṇa, held by Lakshmī in her hands, which is rarely found in Ḍāhala school. It is not only in the case of Lakshmī Nārāyaṇa, but the *añjana śalākā* and *śṛiṅgāra mañjūshā* are found in the hands of Umā-Maheśvara images also wherever these images are found in both the schools.

The faces in Ratanpur school are wider and flat with side profile whereas the facial features of Ḍāhala school are elongated with pointed chin. The eyes are much more expressive in Ḍāhala school showing the depth of lids whereas this expression of eyes is absent in Ratanpur school. In anatomy, the curvature of the body is more elastic with sharp curvature in profile of the waist.

The exterior decoration of the images in Ḍāhala school is commonly similar almost in majority of images, in the delineation of *prabhāmaṇḍala, vidyādharas,* Hindu triad on the *parikara, gaja-śārdūla* and the *āyudha purushas.* But the sculptures of twelfth century or onward are not found following any common pattern due to which there is slight variation in different images. *Vidyādharas* and *Trideva* on *parikara* are not found in majority of images. Likewise *āyudha-purushas* have not been taken into consideration as an essential element of the sculpture. Placing of Bhūdevī and Nāga-Nāgī figures in conventional form is also not unanimous in these images. Brahmā and Śiva are almost absent in majority of sculptures who have been depicted within small niches on the stele. It is actually a very prominent aspect in other contemporary schools of art of M.P., *viz.* the Paramāras, the Chandellas, the Kachchhapaghātas and the Nāgas of Bastar.

In the images of Ḍāhala school, Vishṇu's *vāhana* Garuḍa and Lakshmī's *vāhana siṁha* have no doubt been adopted in the conventional pattern. The *siṁha*, as the vehicle of Lakshmī, has not been depicted in majority of sculptures.

Amongst the *āyudhas*, *chakra* in the lower left hand of Nārāyaṇa is very prominently shown and this hand is mostly seen embracing Lakshmī and touching her left breast. Lakshmī mostly holds the full blossomed lotus with stalk in her upper left hand. The *śṛiṅgāra mañjūshā* and lotus are bigger in size in comparison to the whole composition of the figures. The *śrīvatsa* symbol on the chest of Vishṇu is prominently shown in flower pattern while the *kaustubha* is absent in almost all the figures, but the similar Lakshmī-Nārāyaṇa images noticed from a part of Chhattisgarh region, located in the north of Mahānadī are embellished with *kaustubha*. Even this *ratna* is decked in the centre of the *graiveyaka* also, worn by Vishṇu. Such depictions are frequently found in the sculptures of Vishṇu temple at Janjagir, district Bilaspur, M.P.

Apart from the images of Lakshmī Nārāyaṇa, there are two images of four-armed Vishṇu, standing in *samabhaṅga* in Khairagarh Museum. But these images lack vigour, charm, composition and rhythm. Though they represent the *vyūha* forms of Vaishṇavism, but the expression of facial features is not attractive. Even the eyes are devoid of lids and seem to be projecting out of their sockets.

The entire stele of these Lakshmī-Nārāyaṇa images is almost covered with the ten incarnations of Vishṇu. They are placed in sequence, but sometimes the sequence has been ruled out by the artist. Either sides of upper stele represent Matsya and Kūrma followed by the Varāha and Nṛisiṁha respectively. In place of Kṛishṇa, the depiction of Balarāma seems to be more popular.

It is thus evident that the later art of Chhattisgarh region has to some extent lost its charm and the aesthetic beauty which resulted in the crudeness in form and even lost the expression, but this art style has its own identity and peculiarity. It may be pointed out here that the four-armed Lakshmī is the originality of the Kalachuri school of Ratanpur and Tripurī which is almost absent in the contemporary art schools of the Paramāras, Chandellas and in the Kachchhapa-ghāṭas.

69

SOME REFLECTIONS ON ART HISTORY AND ART CRITICISM

SUSMITA PANDEY

It is a common assumption of modern historiography that it is value neutral. The historian is indeed called upon to write the history of values themselves as reflected in cultural and creative embodiment of values. The general principle should hold that the history of art should thus confine itself to the description and analysis of facts namely the objective features of the work of art, the conditions of its origins and dissemination, its actual social reception and role. An account of its actual evaluation by critics and its audience through the generations would also be a part of the factual account. If the analysis of the work of art itself could throw light on its origins or received evaluations that too could also be a part of value-neutral factual analysis.

However since the 18th century the histories of art have also tried to elucidate the trends and patterns of growth and decay in art traditions.[1] In the hands of Hegel and his followers art history has been sought to be connected with the changes in general aesthetic ideas and values.[2] More detailed works in art history have sought to connect the underlying values of creativity in art with the general environment of socio-cultural values, needs and patronage as also with the conditions of technical fabrication. All these types of analysis and attempted correlations may be deemed more or less factual provided the aesthetic values of the historian do not obtrude.

One respect in which such obtrusion occurs now more or less universally is through the notion of evolution. The evolution of the art form or the attempt to realize some particular model of aesthetic evalution may be considered as factual trends but the application of the concept of evolution to different art forms, values or repertoire of techniques clearly imports the subjective values of the historian, even though they are widely shared today.

Thus since the days of Fergusson, western critics and historians have considered the history of art in the West as the model from which to judge the history of art in India.[3] It is true that historians like Havell and Coomaraswamy tried to correct this by highlighting the autonomy of Indian aesthetic values.[4] Nevertheless there is a renewed danger now on the emergence of a facile universalism among some Indian historians of art. Archaism, classicism, impressionism, etc., are taken as universal constants and changes in techniques such as the use of geometrical or aerial perspective or of the use of material such as stone or clay or of colours are taken to constitute the inner history of artistic creativity as if art and craft were the same and imaginative creativity parallel to scientific technology.[5] It is, therefore, necessary to bestow some thought on the nature of art itself to see what is essential to it and what is only accidental. Every historian has to avoid making the accidental features of artistic creativity into its essential ones. Croce has defined art as imagination and art objects may be defined as the objective content of an intuitive imaginative experience with the twin dimensions of felt immediacy and the sense of clarity or significance.[6] Alternatively it could be described as an integral image conveying an immediate sense of value.[7] This art object may be embodied in an external or material medium to become the familiar art object of common parlance. This secondary or material art object being detached from the psychic environment of the original image is no longer capable of functioning as an art object by itself. It needs to be psychically reappropriated so that it may reflect the original image. Thus the material object has to evoke the psychic image which in turn expresses value. It is true that the relationship of the material object to the image or of the image to value varies in different art forms. In architecture thus a building may not be simply an object of art but also a useful object. In the latter aspect it would be necessarily material. The same is true of artistic crafts. In music the externally audible sound and the imagined or remembered sound have complete correspondence and the situation is largely similar in the visual arts. In the literary arts on the other hand the distance is the greatest between what is externally embodied and what is immediately intuited in imagination; thus the external art object continues in various proportions elements of presentation, representation, and symbolism, of material production plastic form and what may be called language. Clearly skill in engineering, drawing, modelling, chiselling, voice articulation, rhetoric and the like belongs to the production of the secondary or external object. These are skills which are teachable, their products analysable and easily duplicated by craftsmen who need not be artists in any significant sense. On the other hand creative imagination is unique, unanalysable and unteachable. That is why there has always been a theoretical difference between the poet and the versifier, the artist and the craftsman, the composer and the player. In the future ages of advanced technology, the task of duplicating material art objects or producing similar ones is not likely to present much difficulty. Synthetic electronic music, computerised versification, three dimensional projections, electronic and photographic recordings etc. are examples of what would undoubtedly exceed present imagination. Just as the works can no longer be confused with the use of muscles or calculation with reasoning, creative imagination cannot be confused with the skills and techniques of material manipulations or representations. The growth of such techniques as of geometrical or photographic representation thus is primarily part of the history of technology, not art. Art is not a mode of human power over nature but of self-expression.

The essence of art thus is the creation of an 'image' expressive of value, an image being understood not as a presentation but as a sign and symbol, a significant structure or form. The suggestion and expressing power of the image necessarily depends on its cultural and experimental associations. The image thus functions within world of taste and cultural education. Its recreation in the minds of the audience requires that the latter should be initiated into this world. The understanding of the image depends far more on the understanding of its cultural world than on the understanding of the techniques employed in its material embodiment.

It is necessary to distinguish between two kinds of values which are expressed in art.[8] There is on the one hand a kind of value which is peculiar and characteristic of art. This art-value may be said to live in the mode of expressiveness of the image, its capacity to evoke a sense of admiration by its flawlessness or perfection, its evocativeness which produces a sense of significance even without any definite content.

These art-values are the easiest to recognize and even create the aestheticist illusion that they alone give value to art. As a matter of fact they only characterize the mode in which art expresses value. The peculiar value of being expressive receives its substance from the values which it expresses. These values which art expresses may be called life-values, ultimately the intimations of the self or humanity.

Art thus is the expression of twofold values through imaginative creation further embodied in a material medium for public communication. The historian of art should be expected to give an account of the cultural and aesthetic value perceptions of the artists and their milieu, the imaginative forms and structures created, the materials and techniques used and the conditions of the public consumption of art. Concentration on the material object and its public consumption to the neglect of its inner values and original image would plainly be one-sided.

NOTES AND REFERENCES

1. Periodization of classical art was the first to be standardized.
2. On Hegelian art history and the new trend of formal aesthetics, Vide Inwood (ed.), *Hegel*, pp. 203ff.
3. J. Fergusson, *History of Indian and Eastern Architecture;* V.A. Smith, *History of Fine Art in India & Ceylon;* Marshall in *CHI*, Vol. I.
4. *E.g.*, Coomaraswamy, *History of Indian & Indonesian Art.*
5. The historical unity of art and craft stemmed from the originally artistic impulse of craft.
6. Vide Croce (tr. Ainslee), *Aesthetics*, p. 8.
7. So Abhinavagupta describes *Natya* as *Sākṣātkāra kalpa-Natyasastra* (Parimal), Vol. I, p. 177.
8. Cf. G.C. Pande, *Mulya Mimansa*, p. 214; cf. Ingardin's distinction between artistic value and aesthetic value— Osborne (ed.), *Aesthetics*, pp. 46ff.

70
MANASĀ IN LITERATURE AND ART

UMESH CHANDRA DWIVEDI

Manasā, the snake-goddess of the Hindus is one of the most popular folk-goddesses. Her worship is still very popular in eastern India, particularly in Bengal, which takes place on the fifth lunar day of Śrāvaṇa (Nāgapañcamī). Manasā is identified with Jaratkāru, the sister of the Nāga king Vāsuki.

According to *Mahābhārata,*[1] provoked by an act of disobedience of her sons, Kadru, the mother of snakes, cursed them with destruction by fire at the snake killing sacrifice of king Janamejaya. The snakes then met to search the device through which they could escape from the consequences of the awful curse. Elāpatra, a Nāga chief told them that he had come to know through a vision that saint Āstīka, born of their sister Jaratkāru, married to a Brāhmana husband of the same name, would save them from the threatened destruction. Vāsuki, the Nāga chief, was requested for arranging the marriage of her sister Jaratkāru with the Brāhmaṇa Jaratkāru.

Sage Jaratkāru, who belonged to a clan of nomad (*yāyāvara*) Brāhmaṇa, was not interested in marriage and settled life. However, a vision of his forefathers losing their places in heaven due to his childlessness, finally induced him to think of marriage. But he decided to marry only under certain conditions. The conditions were that the girl must be of the same name, she must be offered to him unsolicited, that he shall not be required to maintain her and finally, he would be at liberty to foresake her on her first offence.

The agents of Vāsuki, who were watching for the appearance of Jaratkāru and change in his views, now informed Vāsuki,who approached Jaratkāru and offered him his sister. When the saint was satisfied that the girl was of the same name and the bride's party was ready to accept his terms and conditions, the marriage took place and all went well for some time. During this time, the sister of Vāsuki became pregnant. However, one day an accident occurred. The saint's wife offended him by preventing him from an untimely sleep. The sage became angry and decided to leave his wife. However, he assured her that a great sage would be born to her, and went away.

But, by this time, the purpose of the Nāgas had been served. Sage Āstika was born to Jaratkāru and he subsequently saved the Nāgas from the snake-sacrifice of Janamejaya by begging the king the cessation of the sacrifice.

Manasā is now generally identified with Jaratkāru, but surprisingly, in the *Mahābhārata* there is no indication of the deification of Jaratkāru, mother of sage Āstika, as a snake goddess, *i.e.* mother of the snakes (*nāgamātā*) and their mistress. She is also not credited with the possession of the supreme knowledge (*Mahājñāna*) nor with the power of counteracting poison, the two most prominent characteristics of the snake goddess Manasā. The term "mother of the snakes" in the *Mahābhārata* always denotes Kadru.

In the Brāhmaṇas,[2] we meet with the term Sarparājñī which literally means queen of snakes. She was the seer of a hymn of the Ṛg-veda (X-189). But the connection of this Sarparājñī with snakes is not unquestioned. Sāyaṇa explains that Sarparājñī was the earth, incarnated as a goddess, who attained the knowledge of Brahmā, the Supreme Soul in that guise. One commentator Mahīdhara, however, states that the term denotes Kadru in the guise of Earth.[3] It may also be noted that Kadru is given as a synonym for Manasā in the dictionaries.[4] Thus it seems that the first identification of Manasā, the snake-goddess, was not with Jaratkāru, but with Kadru. Subsequently, however, as in the *Brahma-Vaivartta Purāṇa*, attempts were made to identify Manasā with Jaratkāru and they give the latter a deified character.

There is no doubt that the position of Snake-goddess Manasā is obscure in the Brahmanical pantheon. The name does not occur in the *Mahābhārata*, or in the work of Pāṇinī or in *Amarakośa*. The medieval grammarians and lexicographers mention the name, the former citing it as an illustration of an irregular *Samāsa*[5] (*Aluk-Samāsa*:- Manasā Sṛshṭā devī = Manasā devī) which explains her name as "the mind-born of Kāśyapa" for which there appears no authority other than the *Brahmavaivartta-Purāṇa*, obtained a footing by the time. The absence of her name in early literature, and the evidence of attempt for explaining her name in medieval literature, point to the possibility of being Manasā not a goddess of Vedic or Puranic age, but an assimilation from outside. A careful study of her legends and Dhyānas shows that there was a great difference of opinion among the learned persons who tried to enlist the goddess in the Brahmanical tradition. Evidences that she probably was first identified with Kadru and not with Jaratkāru are already known. Even when the identification with Jaratkāru was established, considerable difference prevailed in working out the details.

The Dhyāna, which is commonly recited now-a-days in the ceremony of the worship of Manasā, but whose source is unknown, makes swan her vehicle.[6] According to the Dhyāna, "I adore the goddess, the mother of the snakes, who is graceful and generous and whose face is like the moon, who rides on a moon (?), wears a red garment and lavish of gifts, always giving everything (asked for); who has a smiling face, whose body is decked with gold, gems and many jewels obtained from serpents; who has prominent breasts, is anchorite, who can take any shape at will and who is accompanied by eight snakes." On the basis of this Dhyāna, Bhattasali observes that she was contemplated as identical to Brahmāṇī or Sarasvatī. However, this Dhyāna does not ascribe any distinctive attribute in the hands of the goddess.

The identification of Manasā with Sarasvatī is also confirmed by the following Dhyāna which Dhanvantarī addressed to Manasā,[7] "I adore the goddess, the supreme mistress of snakes, whose vehicle is a huge snake. The complexion of her body is like the Champaka flower. She is beautiful in every limb. She has a pleasing expression of face marked by a faint smile. She is decked with fine garments and jewelled ornaments. She looks beautiful with a sumptuous chignon. She feels with her devotees and protects them from all evils. She is peaceful, versed in all kinds of knowledge and also imparts them (her devotees)."

In the *stotra* following, Manasā is once called daughter of Kāśyapa, and again, distinctly, daughter of Śiva, and the latter parentage is upheld in the Bengali ballads which are sung in her honour throughout the country. In these ballads, which cannot claim a Puranic origin, the explanation of her name attempted in the *Brahma-Vaivartta-Purāṇa* that she is called Manasā because she had her origin from the *manas* (mind) of Kāśyapa, is not repeated; instead, it appears an account how she was fashioned out in the northern region by an artisan employed by Vāsuki, the king of serpents, from the seed of Śiva, which was placed on a lotus leaf, had impetuously travelled down through the stem to the place of Vāsuki. At another place,[8] there is compromise between the two versions of the origin of the goddess. She is there the mind born of Kāśyapa, but spiritual daughter of Śiva, who gave her the Supreme Knowledge. But even this spiritual fatherhood of Śiva is undermined by the statement that she was instructed by Śiva himself to go to the holy place Pushkara and to meditate there on the Divine Śrīkṛshṇa. Thus she became a Vaishṇavi, received favours of Kṛshṇa-Vishṇu and was first recognised by him.

At another place,[9] in an inscription the vehicle of the goddess Manasā is denoted by the term Nāgendra which normally means 'a huge snake'. But Nāga also means an elephant.

These attempts to connect her variously with Brahmā, Vishṇu and Śiva; the attempts to explain her name; the difficulties mentioned in the Bengali ballads, this goddess had to surmount before she could establish her worship in this country, are all very remarkable, and these point to the probability of her coming from outside and she had to fight her way into the Brahmanical pantheon and obtain an identification with Jaratkāru.

Undoubtedly, the worship of Nāga was popular from quite early period but the origin and development of Manasā cult are shrouded in obscurity. The only fact which we can claim with certainty is its popularity in Bengal area. However, it had a Bengal origin or it was transplanted into Bengal by some migrating clan, is difficult to clarify with certainty in the present state of our knowledge.

Kshiti Mohan Sen advocates its southern origin. According to him, a snake goddess called Manchāmmā or Mother Manchā is still worshipped among the Telugus and the Canarese-speaking people of southern India. The stories of the struggles of Manasā to get recognition as a goddess, are also current in southern India with name Ambāvaru, a goddess who appears to have control over snakes. Sen suggests that the goddess Manchā of the Dravidians has obtained in Bengal the semi-Sanskritised name of Manasā and appropriated to herself the legends of Ambāvaru in Bengali forms. According to Bhattasali,[11] "When we remember that the name does not occur in the earlier grammars and lexicographies that the medieval grammarians and lexicographers had difficulty in explaining this ungrammatical name, we gladly recognise that Prof. Sen has probably found the right origin of the name."

Manasā appears to have been imported into Bengal from the southern India at the crest of a Brahmanical revival. She quickly outdid Jānguli, as her name stands, meaning the goddess of the wild. She is daughter of the Śabaras (Śabara-Kumārī) or the wild tribes of India. She is a charmer of snakes and is invoked against snakebite. She has four arms. She plays on the lyre by her two normal hands, bestows boon by the extra right hand and holds a white snake in the left. She appears to have been a divinity of the aboriginal tribes of India and was admitted into the Buddhist pantheon in a fairly early period. According to a Saṅgīti in the *Sādhanamālā*, she is as old as the Buddha himself, and the secret of Jāṅgulī and the mantra for her worship are said to have been imparted to Ānanda by Lord Buddha himself. In this context, the *Atharvaveda* may be remembered. A little girl of the Kirātas (a wild aboriginal tribe), in the *Atharvaveda*, digs a remedy against snakebite with a golden shovel upon the ridges of the mountain. Later on, possibly, the same girl is called Tāudī and Ghṛtāchī and devotees take shelter under her 'poison-spoiling track'. When we remember that Ghṛtāchī is only another name of Sarasvatī and that Sarasvatī herself is spoken of, in one passage, in the *Atharvaveda* as a destroyer of poison and also take into consideration the fact that Jāṅgulī has the attributes of Sarasvatī, some conclusions begin to take shape. The Vedic goddess Sarasvatī, in one of her aspects, was a destroyer of snake-poison and was often invoked in that capacity. Sarasvatī, in this aspect, was a girl of the Śabaras. This aspect did not develop in the Brahmanical pantheon, but the Mahāyāna Buddhists accepted this snake-goddess and called her Jāṅgulī and did not forget her connection with the Śabaras. Later on, while tracing the origin of Manasā, some scholars identified her with Vedic Sarasvatī, the curer of snakebites. Thus goddess Manasā finally succeeded in absorbing Jāṅgulī within herself. However, at certain places they called Manasā even Jāṅgulī. The most popular Dhyāna of Manasā popular in Bengal specially mentions,[12] "I adore, the lotus-born goddess of the wilds (Jāṅgulī), the healer of the effects of poison, and daughter of Śaṅkara. She is resplendent as gold, has a pleasant face, is beautiful like a lotus and has a hood of king of serpents over her head. Her body, covered with snakes, is smeared with celestial unguents and all her limbs are graceful. She constantly holds Protection and Boon in her two hands." A clear invocation of Jāṅgulī is used here in the worship of Manasā.

The Senas came from south India and settled in Bengal-Bihar region in the middle of eleventh century A.D. They were probably worshippers of the snake goddess Mañchā, and their rise probably gave an impetus to her popularity. The decline of Buddhism by this time gradually transferred the honours paid to Jāṅgulī to Mañchā, who became Manasā at the hands of the Brāhmin theologists.[13] The Karnats of Mithilā may have also helped in this cause.[14]

The cult of Manasā is still a very popular cult in Bengal and the number of poets, who composed songs in her honour, is very large. The biographer of the Chaitanya states that the worship of Manasā used to be performed during Chaitanya's time (fifteenth century A.D.) with great splendour. Vijaya Gupta of Phullasri (Bakerganj district), the most famous poet of Manasā songs in south-east Bengal, states that the first poet of the Manasā song was the one-eyed Hari Datta, who, according to Bhattasali, may have been living in the eleventh-twelfth century A.D.[15]

These poems composed in the honour of Manasā refer to the opposition offered by the merchant-prince Chandra to the introduction of the worship of Manasā. According to the legend, the ladies of Chandra's household had already accepted the popular worship of Manasā, but Chandra, only after a long resistance agreed for its worship. The Chandra kings of East Bengal rose to power towards the middle of the tenth century A.D. The date of Sri Chandra Deva, the most powerful prince of the family, may be approximately fixed as A.D. 975-1000 and one feels tempted to suggest that Chandra, the above-mentioned merchant-prince, may have been member of the family of the Chandra kings of East Bengal, may be Sri Chandra Deva himself.[16]

A large number of stone sculptures of Manasā of the tenth-twelfth century A.D. which have been noticed throughout Bengal, testify to the established character of her cult during the period. From the Raghurampur excavations, pots and utensils with figures of snake on them, evidently used in the worship of Manasā were found in good number. The excavations conducted by the Varendra Research Society of Rajśāhī in a part of the large tank of Deopāḍā, from the bank of which was discovered the famous stone inscription of Vijaya Sena Deva, also yielded similar objects, as well as a large number of images of Manasā belonging to the tenth-twelfth century A.D.[17]

However, it is interesting to note that the popular worship of the goddess does not take place in her anthromorphic forms, rather on the occasion of Nāga-Pañcamī a milky hedge plant (*Euphorbia jingularum*) is planted on a raised mound of earth in the courtyard of the house and in form of this plant the goddess Manasā is worshipped.[18] In the popular legend she is said to have been told that she lives in the cactus tree (*Euphorbium Pentandra*).[19] This form of worship shows on the other hand an ancient origin. It is, therefore, more convincing to hold that snake worship in the above-mentioned form was prevalent in Bengal as in the other parts of India for a very long time and it was only in the later period that such worship was associated with goddess Manasā. We must remember that Snuhi tree, known in Bengal as *Sij*, is associated in the Sanskrit texts with the worship of Manasā and is still an indispensable article in her worship.[20]

A remarkable Dhyāna of the goddess found quoted in the commentary of Kāśīrāma Vācaspati on *Tithyādi Tattvam* by Raghunandan (Section 79) gives us an idea about her iconographic features. According to this Dhyāna, "I take shelter unto the goddess, the mother of Āstịka. She has a young child (on her lap). She shines like the golden lotus. Huge snakes always attend on her from all sides. She has full and prominent bosoms. She holds two snakes in her two hands. She has a smiling countenance and is decorated with the ornaments of shining snakes."[21]

This Dhyāna represents the goddess as a four-armed deity. She is to hold a child on her lap and should be holding two snakes with the remaining two hands. It should be noted that this description strongly reminds one of the Buddhist goddess Hāritī. According to Bhattasali, a comparison of some of the images of Manasā that conform to the above Dhyāna and those of Hāritī, will be an interesting study and may point to another probable source of her origin.

The majority of the images of Manasā found in the country represent her as sitting on a lotus with the right leg pendent. Seven snakes spread their hoods like a canopy over her head and the goddess holds the eighth snake in her left hand. In her right hand, she holds a fruit in *varada mudrā.* To her right is represented an emaciated bearded man, while a crowned male figure sits to her left.[22] The marked emaciation of the figure to the right points him out as Jaratkāru or his son Āstika. The figure on the right, on the basis of his crown, may be identified as that of the Nāga king Vāsuki, brother of the goddess. In many images, a fine pitcher appears underneath the lotus seat of the goddess. The 20-inch high image of Manasā made of black stone in the Dacca Museum, corresponds to the above description.[23] However, on this image, which was obtained from the Dinajpur district by Sarat Sasi Datta, the pitcher looks very much like *linga* attached with its *arghya.* However, two snake-like things are shown coming out of it. A very fine specimen of this type of image was discovered from village Bhadisvar in District Birbhum as well.[24] Here a nicely carved large size pitcher or *kalaśa* is noticed under the double-petalled lotus. This image is very nicely carved and is completely intact.

A nicely carved image of Manasā is in the library of Rangpur Sahitya Parishad.[25] This is a four-armed seated figure of Manasā, who is shown on a double-petalled lotus issuing from a very big lotus stalk carved on a very high pedestal. A portion of the pedestal is carved in a manner that it looks like a row of pitchers. Here the upper right hand of the deity holds a rosary or *akṣa-mālā* while the lower right hand placed on her knee is in *varada mudrā.* Her upper left hand holds an indistinct object while her lower left hand supports the child placed on her left lap. One bearded man and one clean-shaved man are noticed respectively on her right and left sides. They may be identified with Jaratkāru and Vāsuki respectively.

We have a very interesting image of Manasā from Bihar preserved in the Indian Museum, Calcutta. The image shows a goddess in the meditation pose, sitting with legs crossed. A hood of seven serpents is over her head. Her two left hands hold a book and a pitcher of nectar. Her two right hands are shown carrying rosary and in *abhaya mudrā* respectively. To the right is carved a *liṅga* and to the left is a miniature figure of Gaṇeśa. A prominent pitcher is placed below the seat of the goddess from which two serpents are coming out and crawling off in opposite directions. According to Bhattasali, the attributes of the goddess are entirely those of Sarasvatī, had the serpent-hood over the head of the goddess and the pitcher below her seat with serpents crawling out, been absent. R.D. Banerji, however, doubts that the upper hand of the goddess probably holds a shield.[26]

The excavations at Antichak have brought to light another image of Manasā,[27] which is, however, in a very mutilated condition. The lower portion and the left hand of the goddess are broken. The right hand of the goddess is placed over her knee in *varada mudrā* and the broken left hand shows remains of a snake in it. A canopy of seven serpent-hoods was over the head of the goddess Manasā; however, one of the hoods is now broken and missing. The goddess Manasā is well-ornamented. Besides other ornaments, she is wearing a *mukuṭa* also. A Śiva-*liṅga* on *Gauripaṭṭa* is carved on the top portion of the pointed stela. A flying *Vidyādhara* is also on the left side of the stela. This black stone sculpture can be placed in the eleventh century A.D. The fully intact figure may have certain other things worth mentioning.

Another interesting sculpture of Manasā is from Śilghāta in Assam.[28] Here the goddess is shown standing on a double-petalled lotus, though she is represented in sitting posture generally. Her right hand is in *varada mudrā* and the left hand holds an indistinct object. It may be a stalk of flower or lower portion of a snake(?). A canopy of five serpenthoods is over her head. A Nāga-Kanyā is represented in the upper right corner of the stela. Another point of interest here is that the goddess is being attended by two female figures and one perhaps carries a *vīṇā*(?). Both these figures are shown standing on a small double-petalled lotus seat. Under the main lotus seat, on which Goddess Manasā is standing there is an elephant. On the left side is a crawling figure of a female probably Nāga-kanyā in *añjalī-mudrā*. This very sculpture carries the inscription in which the vehicle of the goddess is denoted by the term Nāgendra. Ordinarily it would mean 'a huge snake'. But Nāga also means an elephant and in this image of Manasā, the vehicle of the goddess is an elephant itself.

Besides this, a stone sculpture has been discovered in the ruins of Koi-Sārigaḍa in Orissa.[29] She wears a head-dress of serpent-hoods consisting of seven serpents and clasping a bowl with both her hands and presents with her closed eyes the attitude of meditation. The people of this place know her by the name of Kotāsanī, probably due to its worship in the fort of the Vairata ruler. This figure can easily be identified with Manasā, the chief deity of serpent-worship.

At the village of Tundārā, district Balasore of Orissa, another ancient image of Nāga goddess has been discovered.[30] This goddess is two-armed and seated on a lotus. She is adorned with various ornaments and has a canopy of seven serpent-hoods. On her left thigh is seated an infant whom she encircles with her left arm, while in her right hand, she holds a cobra. N.N. Vasu has identified it as a figure of Skanda Ṣaṣthī on the basis of a *tantra* quoted by him.[31] However, his identification is very much doubtful because the *tantra* which he quotes nowhere refers to that she should have a snake in her hand and there should be a serpent-hood over her head. On the other hand, Bhattasali[32] has identified it as that of Manasā on the basis of the *dhyāna* quoted in the commentary of Kasirama Vachaspati on *Tithyādi Tattvam* and he seems to be correct.

Bhattasali has tried to identify an image of Gautami and Sākya-Siṁha described and illustrated in the book *Archaeological Survey of Mayurbhanj* by N.N. Vasu as that of Manasā on the basis of the Nāgas here and there and the Snuhi tree on the back.[33] However, this identification of Bhattasali is doubtful because representation of lion just under the seat on which they are sitting creates grave doubt about the identification. Moreover, whether represented things are snakes or not is also not clear.

At least four images of Manasā were discovered from Māldā district of West Bengal, which are now preserved in the Malda Museum, Malda.[34] In one of the sculptures, the four-armed goddess is shown seated on a full-blown lotus with the pendent proper right leg resting on a lotus. Her right hand touches the knee and is in the *varada mudrā* holding a fruit while the proper front left hand holds the child who is placed on the lap of the goddess. There is a serpent-hood over the head of the goddess. This sculpture from Bāmangolā (Māldā) can be placed in twelfth century A.D.

From very Bāmangolā (Māldā) itself, another figure of this goddess was also discovered which is dated to eleventh century A.D. This mutilated figure of Manasā also carries a child placed on her lap. Here the goddess is only two-armed.

We have yet another figure of this goddess in this museum, whose head is missing. This black stone image from Māldā can be dated eleventh century A.D. Here the proper right hand touches the knee and is in the *varada mudrā,* while the proper left hand holds a snake.

We have another piece of art from Māldā preserved in this museum depicting serpent hood. According to Malayasankar Bhattacharyya, this formed a part of a Manasā image. This piece of sculpture can also be dated in the eleventh century A.D.

Besides the above-mentioned stone sculptures, we have some metal sculptures of Manasā also from eastern India. One of the best bronze images of Manasā is from Narakāsura ruins of Kāhilipārā, district Kāmrup of Assam.[35] This bronze image is 8 cm in height and 7 cm in width and is solid cast. Here the goddess is sitting in *lalitāsana* upon a lotus pedestal, in front of which there is a jar from which a snake is shown coming out. That snake is held by the left hand of the goddess. The right hand of the goddess, resting on her right knee, is in *varda mudrā*. In addition, she has a canopy of hoods of five snakes. She is flanked by two seated figures having serpent-hoods over them. These figures may be identified as that of Vāsuki, her brother, and Āstika, her son. This image is placed in the twelfth-thirteenth century A.D.

There is another bronze from Kāhilipārā, preserved in the State Museum, Gauhati[36] (Assam) depicting the goddess seated gracefully on a lotus seat placed on a pedestal. Her oval *prabhā* is decorated with a border of flames. She is being attended by two female figures on the projected corners of the pedestal, who are standing in a beautiful bent posture, one of whom is carrying a snake in her hand. This figure can be placed in the Pāla period on the basis of its refined finish and style.

We have a brass image of Manasā from North Bengal, presently preserved in the Indian Museum, Calcutta.[37] She is seated in *lalitāsana* with right leg resting on a double-petalled lotus placed on a *pañcaratha* pedestal. In her right arm, she is holding a leafy branch by the stalk and in the left arm snake. Over her head, there is a canopy of seven-headed serpent-hood. A child holding snakes in either hand with a serpent-hood on the head is noticed on her left lap. The figure on her lap can be easily identified with her son Āstika. This image is dated in the twelfth century A.D.

We have another miniature metal image of goddess Manasā, preserved in Varendra Research Society, Rajsahi (Bangladesh).[38] Here the goddess has a canopy of seven hoods of snakes and is shown with a standing figure, with folded hands, on her left leg. This figure may be that of a devotee. The image is placed in the eleventh century A.D.

Thus we see that the cult of Manasā was quite popular in eastern India and was worshipped in human form at least since the Pāla period.

NOTES AND REFERENCES

1. The Ādiparva of *Mahābhārata* gives us the detailed account.
2. *Aitareya Brāhmaṇa*, 5/24/4; *Satapatha Brāhmaṇa*, 1/4/29.
3. *Śatapatha Brāhmaṇa*, translated by Pandit B.S. Shastri and published by Bangiya Sahitya Parishad, Vol. II, pp. 28-29.

4. N.K. Bhattasali, *Iconography of Buddhist and Brahmanical Sculptures in the Dacca Museum*, p. 217.
5. Evidently with the aid of the *Sutra* of Pāṇinī, 6/3/4.
6. N.N. Vasu, *Archaeological Survey Report of Mayurbhanja,* part I, p. xxxviii.
7. *Brahma-Vaivartta-Purāṇa, Śrī-Kṛṣṇa-Janma-Khaṇḍam*, Ch. 51.
8. *Op. cit.*, Prakṛti-Khaṇḍam, Ch. 42.
9. Inscribed on a stone sculpture discovered from a tea-estate near Silghāt in Assam.
10. Pravasi, 1929, B.S., pp. 380-95.
11. N.K. Bhattasali, *op. cit.*, p. 221.
12. This Dhyāna is found on page 97 of the ritual book for the worship of Dharma, edited by Pandit N.G. Bandyopadhyaya and published by the Vangiya Sahitya Parisad and is quoted by N.K. Bhattasali.
13. N.K. Bhattasali, *op. cit.*, p. 224.
14. M.C.P. Shrivastava, *Mother Goddess in Indian Art, Archaeology & Literature*, p. 170.
15. N.K. Bhattasali, *op. cit.*, p. 224.
16. *Ibid.*, p. 225.
17. *Ibid.*, p. 225.
18. Vogel, *Indian Serpent Lore,* p. 278.
19. B.A. Gupta, *Hindu Holidays and Ceremonials*, p. 148.
20. N.K. Bhattasali, *op. cit.*, p. 226.
21. This Dhyāna was hunted out by Shri Dinesh Chandra Bhattacharyya for Shri N.K. Bhattasali. However, Pandit Vacaspati omits to note the source from which this Dhyāna is quoted.
22. N.K. Bhattasali, *op. cit.*, p. 226.
23. *Ibid.*, p. 226.
24. R.D. Banerji, *Eastern Indian School of Medieval Sculpture* , p. 122, pl. LXIV B.
25. *Ibid.*, p. 122, pl. LXIV A.
26. R.D. Banerji, *op. cit.*, p. 122, pl. LXIV C.
27. The *Journal of the Bihar Puravid Parishad*, Vol. II, p. 171, pl. XXI, fig. 6.
28. N.K. Bhattasali, *op. cit.*, p. 220, pl. LXXIII.
29. N.N. Vasu, *Archaeological Survey of Mayurbhanja*, pl. XXXVII, fig. 14 A.
30. *Ibid.*, p. xxxviii, fig. 15.
31. *Ibid.*, p. xxxviii.
32. N.K. Bhattasali, *op. cit.*, p. 227.
33. *Ibid.*, p. 227.
34. Malaysankar Bhattacharyya, *Art in Stone: A Catalogue of Sculptures in Malda Museum*, pp. 21-22.
35. Arun Bhattacharyya, *Icons and Sculptures of Early and Medieval Assam*, p. 30, fig. 83.
36. Bimal Bandhopadhyaya, *Metal Sculptures of Eastern India*, p. 64.
37. Bimal Bandhopadhyaya, *op. cit.*, p. 45.
38. *Ibid.*, p. 136.

71
A RARE LAJJĀ GAURĪ PLAQUE FROM TARSANG (GUJARAT)

V.H. SONAWANE

Lajjā Gaurī, a legendary goddess, is one of the mysterious cult divinities of Hindu mythology, whose identity and antiquity are yet to be completely understood in their proper perspective. The images depicting conventionalised form of Lajjā Gaurī began to appear from *c.* 2nd century B.C. and continued to occur until about 12th/13th centuries A.D. Though the Lajjā Gaurī sculptures are reported from different parts of our country, it seems, its concept originated and flourished more widely in parts of the Deccan covering areas of Maharashtra and Karnataka.

Over a period of three decades several scholars have attempted to study the nature and significance of the images of Lajjā Gaurī.[1] However, because of the non-availability of any textual description, the nomenclature and iconography of the goddess still remain more or less enigmatic. Let it be clear at the outset that this author has no new solution to offer at this juncture on this critical issue. My intention in writing this article is to place a unique plaque of Lajjā Gaurī before the scholars for their comment which might help some one in unravelling the problem of her historicity.

The aforesaid image was discovered by the author while exploring an area around Tarsang in search of rock shelters and rock paintings. Tarsang (22° 56' N, 73° 28' E) is a small village situated about 30 kilometres north-west of Godhra in the Panchamahals district of Gujarat State. The plaque under consideration representing the goddess Lajjā Gaurī (Pl. 71.1) is carved out in fine-grained dark grey talc serpentine chlorite schist measuring 8.5 x 8.5 x 1.5 cm. The lower right corner of the plaque is broken. Though the figure has been carved in a low relief, the structural details of execution are quite bold and clear. The goddess is shown seated as usual in her characteristic manner, keeping legs stretched apart and hands resting on the knees, raised upwards in a typical *trikoṇabaddhāsana* posture. Most likely, she holds a flower, probably lotus, in each of her hands. Unlike the other common representations, she is not shown nude here. There is a suggestion of folds of her lower garment on the left leg of the figure. The image is decked with simple traditional ornaments such as *ekāvalī*, multiple armlets, bracelets, long circular *patra kuṇḍalas* and bejewelled *kaṭimekhalā*. The simple halo-like *prabhāvalī* behind her head adds charm to the entire composition and signifies her divinity.

Owing to the inclusion of a stylised *triśūla* and just immediately below it, the feet (*Śrī pāda*) on the upper left corner, this plaque represents an unusual character of its composition.[2] The damaged figure on the lower left may be that of a devotee, if the sculpture follows the usual arrangement of attributes that have been observed in many other representations of the goddess wherein this corner is occupied by a female devotee often in an *añjalimudrā*. Likewise, just above the broken lower right corner there is a Śiva-*liṅga* adorned with a *brahmasūtrarekhā*. The modelling of the figure under review shows some resemblance in its anatomical features with the other sculptures reported from the same site. Particularly, the prongs of stylised *triśūla* and breasts as well as abdominal portion of the goddess described here are reminiscent of the female-half representing Pārvatī in the composite image of Ardhanārīśvara found from Tarsang dated to c. 6th century A.D.[3] It is worthwhile to note that the sculpture of Lajjā Gaurī of the same period is reported by Gorakshkar from Gharapuri (Elephanta) caves near Bombay.[4]

Though the depiction of Lajjā Gaurī in association with Nandī, Śiva-*liṅga*, Gaṇeśa and a female devotee occurs sporadically in the sculptures of early centuries of the Christian era, apparently it becomes an almost regular feature of the sculptures during the sixth and succeeding centuries of this class. In this context, the Lajjā Gaurī plaque obtained from Tarsang is still quite unique owing to the addition of *triśūla*, *Śrī Pāda* and *prabhāvalī*, which have so far not been noted in other reported depictions of this goddess. Originally, there may have been Nañdī and Gaṇeśa also on the now missing lower right portion of this image, just below the Śiva-*liṅga*. The association of Nañdī, Gaṇeśa, Śiva-*liṅga* and *triśūla* with Lajjā Gaurī leaves no doubt regarding her Śaiva affiliation. Thus in the light of above evidence, she can very well be considered as a manifestation of the Śaktī aspect of Śiva. Secondly, the presence of an attendant or a devotee in her composition clearly suggests that she was worshipped or was given due recognition as a regular goddess. The depiction of *prabhāvalī* also signifies the attainment of divine position by this deity.

In the present state of our knowledge, we have at least fifteen sites in Gujarat from where images of Lajjā Gaurī have been reported. This number is quite substantial in proving the popularity of this cult image in this province, mainly covering parts of south and central Gujarat, Kutch and Saurashtra peninsula. In Gujarat, this tradition appears a bit late around the beginning of the Christian era but seems to have continued until about 12th/13th centuries, following the main currents prevailing in the Deccan. Though the Gujarat specimens show in general a predilection for human-headed representations, there are at least two examples of the lotus-headed Lajjā Gaurī sculptures also. These mixed trends provide evidence of the continuity in tradition as well as subtle change in the regional style. Likewise, though there are more number of figures carved in the form of handy stone plaques, we do get the terracotta plaques as well as images meant for structural decorations.[5]

Coming back to the Tarsang Lajjā Gaurī image, as has been said earlier, it is different from those reported from other sites. Leaving aside other features of its composition, the most striking observation is that the Tarsang human-headed Lajjā Gaurī is not shown nude. Similar image is carved in front of cave no. 21 at Ellora.[6] In a recent article Dhavalikar expresses his reservations in including the Ellora image in the category of Lajjā Gaurī for the simple reason that it is shown with a human head. Further, he says that the goddess does not appear to be nude as is thought by some scholars.[7] I, however, believe that in the composition of Lajjā Gaurī the main focus of attention or the mark of identification is her typical pose in which she is shown seated rather than her head or nudity aspect. It is true that in her earlier depictions she is shown nude without head. But in course of time, particularly during the post-Gupta period, besides her usual depictions we do get some slightly altered iconographic forms showing the deity with a human head often associated with Nañdī, Gaṇeśa, Śiva-*liṅga*, female devotee and rarely wearing sārī. Such depictions are common in Gujarat and sporadically they occur in Maharashtra[8] and Rajasthan.[9] In the Lajjā Gaurī sculptures reported from Pauni and Kesaragutta the genital organ of the goddess is covered by a loin-cloth.[10] These varied representations clearly show how a sensitive artist can avoid monotony by enjoying restricted freedom keeping proximity to the tradition or the myth. Such depictions certainly show that the "predilection of the artist sometimes predominates more than the tradition" as rightly observed by C. Sivaramamurti.[11]

In this context, it is interesting to note how Dhavalikar's own observation contradicts his own comment whether to term human-headed Ellora image as Lajjā Gaurī or not. Dhavalikar admits, he was convinced by the artist of "Warli Paintings" in which traditional headless goddess "Palghāt" is shown with a head because of its commercialisation. On his enquiry, the artist explained to him that the people do not like to purchase paintings of a headless goddess and hence they have started showing the goddess Palghāt with a head.[12] The same explanation can be offered for not showing goddess Lajjā Gaurī nude in some of her later sculptures. Thus from the foregoing discussion it would be more obvious to believe that in a process of transformation, considering the choice and liking of the people, some artists might have shown Lajjā Gaurī in a slightly innovated form maintaining its traditional iconographic features as those found at Tarsang, Ellora, Pauni and Kesaragutta.

To sum up, in the absence of a well-defined textual description and the lack of standardized iconography, the scholars unanimously believe that the goddess under review is one of the Śaktī aspect of Śiva and was not only worshipped for procuring an offspring but also for warding off droughts, signifying thereby child as well as vegetative fertility.

NOTES AND REFERENCES

1. a. Stella Kramrisch, "An Image of Aditī-Uttānapād," *Artibus Asiae*, Vol. XIX, 1956, pp. 259-70.

   b. H.D. Sankalia, "The Nude Goddess or 'Shameless Woman' in Western Asia, India and South-Eastern Asia," *Artibus Asiae*, Vol. XXIII, 1960, pp. 111-23.

   c. J.N. Tiwari, *Goddess Cults in Ancient India (with special reference to the first seven centuries A.D.)*, New Delhi, 1985.

   d. R.C. Dhere, *Lajjā Gaurī* (in Marathi), Pune, 1978.

   e. C. Margabandhu, "Some Mother Goddess Plaques from Western India and their cultural significance", *Homage to Historian*, Prof. N. Subrahmanyam Felicitation Volume, Madurai, 1976, pp. 205-16.

f. S. Setter, "Roots, Relations and Relevance : The Chalukyan Backdrop," *In Praise of Aihole, Badami, Mahakuta, Pattada-kal*, Marg Publications, pp. 19-21.

g. T.V.G. Sastri, "Lajjā Gaurī from Alampur and its symbolism", Paper presented in *National Seminar on Karnataka Archaeology*, Mysore, December, 1985.

h. C.R. Bolon, Prof. of Indian Art History at the University of Chicago is writing a monograph on Goddess Lajjā Gaurī (by personal communication).

2. Sometimes symbols of faith like lotus, *triśūla, chakra*, feet (Śri-Pāda), etc. were chosen with the figures of the worshippers (as shown in the Lajjā Gaurī plaque from Tarsang) for inspiring the devotees.

3. V.H. Sonawane, "Mātrīkā sculptures from Mataria and Ardhanārīśvara from Tarsang (Panchmahals)", *Journal of the Indian Society of Oriental Art*, New Series, Vol. IX, 1977-78, pp. 46-49, Pl. XX.

4. Sadashiv Gorakshkar, "The Parel Mahādeva reassessed and two newly discovered images from Parel," *Lalit Kala*, No. 20, 1982, p. 23.

5. V.H. Sonawane, "Some remarkable sculptures of Lajjā Gaurī from Gujarat," *Lalit Kala*, No. 23, 1988, pp. 27-35.

6. Sankalia, *op. cit.*, Fig. 7, p. 114.

7. M.K. Dhavalikar, "The Goddess of Mahakut," Paper presented in National Seminar on "Karnataka Archaeology", Mysore, December 1985. (Page 14 of the cyclostyled copy of his paper distributed at the Mysore Seminar).

8. Sankalia, *op. cit.*

9. U.P. Shah, "Some early sculptures from Abu and Bhinmal," *Bulletin of the Baroda Museum and Picture Gallery*, Vol. XII, 1955-56, pp. 55-56, Pl. XXI, Fig. 10.

10. Amarendra Nath, "Lajjā Gaurī and her possible genesis," *Lalit Kala*, No. 25, 1990, p. 47, Figs. 1 and 3.

11. C. Sivaramamurti, "Gajendramokṣa," *Madhu : Recent Advances in Indian Archaeology and Art History*, Ed. M.S. Nagaraja Rao, Delhi, 1981, p. 219.

12. Dhavalikar, *op. cit.*, p. 17.

72
MOTHER–GODDESS OF CURDI-GOA AND SOME PARALLELS

V.R. MITRAGOTRI

During the first seminar on History of Goa, a paper on the mother-goddess of Curdi was presented.[1] Some archaeologists and the author of the present paper were doubtful and expressed apprehensions about the identification of this laterite sculpture as mother-goddess. This was mainly because no other specimen of mother-goddess from other regions of India could be furnished. However, we did not hesitate to accept it as a specimen of folk-art which is timeless. Prior to the presentation and publication of the above paper, an official from the Archaeological Survey of India expressed his doubts about the identification of the sculpture as the mother-goddess and went to the extent of saying that this sculpture may have been chiselled by one of the masons who was building the Mahādeva temple of Curdi during his leisure.[2]

Numerous mother-goddess sculptures reported from south India are labelled as *Lajjā-Gaurī*[3] These figures have lotus in place of head (*mastake padmam*), the waist is excessively broad and the vagina is shown in many sculptures. Hence, the depiction of the lotus, broad waist and the reproductive organs has been associated with fertility aspect.

1. Parallels

The mother-goddess of Curdi (Pl. 72.1) has no *mastake padmam* (lotus in place of head); instead of *padma*, normal head has been chiselled out. This factor was also responsible for doubts about the identification of the sculpture as mother-goddess. We were eagerly tracing the parallels which could facilitate in dating the mother-goddess of Curdi and provide justification for our claim as unique mother-goddess. Our search brought us to *Mohenjo-daro and Indus civilisation*, Official account of the Excavation conducted during the years 1922-1927, Vol. III, plates CL IX, figures 0-10.[4] The mother-goddess from Mohenjo-daro belongs to the period of *c*. 3000 B.C. and is from western India. However, on the basis of the mother-goddess plaque from Lauriya, north-eastern Bihar, it may be stated that before *c.* 800 B.C. worship of the mother-goddess had spread right up to eastern India.[5] Numerous stone-discs depicting mother-goddess belonging to Maurya and Śuṅga periods have been found in north-western as well as eastern India. These stone-discs were used for some rituals or were meant for votive purpose.[6] But no *purusha* is depicted adjacent to the mother-goddess of Curdi. The tiny figure is of the child and is depicted in between the hands and the waist. If it was of *purusha* it would not have been small but would have been shown prominently. The ears and the position of hand are similar to Mohenjo-daro mother-goddess or mother-goddess in gold plaque from Lauriya or the mother-goddess depicted on stone discs of the Mauryan period. Embellishments or minute carvings could easily be done on gold or fine grained stone but laterite is not suitable for intricate carvings. Hence, only the form of the mother-goddess was carved on the laterite. However, in addition to minute carvings even Mauryan polish can be seen on stone discs belonging to Mauryan period on which mother-goddess has been chiselled.

2. The Association of Megaliths with Mother-Goddess

The aforesaid gold plaque of mother-goddess from Lauriya (Pl. 72.3) was discovered near Nandangarh in northern Bihar in the excavation of funerary mounds of pre-Buddhist period.[7] The association of mother-goddess with burials is found not only in north-eastern India but it has been reported from Udainattam in South Arcot district of Tamil Nadu. In Mottur village of North Arcot which is about 25 km away from Udainattam, second Lajjā-Gaurī figurine was discovered. The megalithic Cists of Wynad in Kerala and different places from Karnataka and Kerala have yielded similar Lajjā-Gaurī figurines.[8]

The mother-goddess of Curdi was very close to cairn circles.[9] Therefore the mother-goddess of Curdi might be also of the people who have been architects of the cairn circles of Curdi.

3. Diffusion and Date

In pre-Mauryan period the cult of the mother-goddess was yet in formative stage and was not yet fully developed. Moreover, the female figurines are not numerous in pre-Mauryan period. However, in Mauryan period there is a remarkable development in the cult of the mother-goddess and diffusion of the cult in many regions of India can be noticed. In May 1951, in a suburb of Patna, twenty-one stone discs showing mother-goddess belonging to Śuṅga period were discovered.[10] In the numerous terracotta figurines as well as stone-discs were found representations of the goddess sometimes with her partner (*purusha*).[11]

The mother-goddess representations either in stone or burnt clay (terracotta) or on stone-discs found from the period of Mohenjo-daro up to Śuṅga period in north-western India and eastern India have been dated and the dating of mother-goddess from these sites was much easier. The mother-goddess found in Mohenjo-daro excavation could be dated to *c.* 3000 B.C. Lauriya gold plaque is dated to *c.* 700 B.C. or stone discs showing the mother-goddess representation have been dated either to Maurya or Śuṅga period.

The mother-goddess from Curdi is only associated with cairn circles from Curdi and does not provide any other clues on the basis of which the said mother-goddess could be dated. The material on which the mother-goddess has been chiselled out is laterite and it is not suitable for carving minute details. Hence, the mother-goddess of Curdi is a simple cult figure, with no decoration and does not provide any scope for comparative study of mother-goddess from various sites.

The date ascribed to the gold plaque of mother-goddess from Lauriya is *c.* 700 B.C. as gold is one of the early metals discovered by man and the gold ornaments have been reported from many Chalcolithic and Harappan sites of the subcontinent. Therefore, *c.* 700 B.C. for gold plaque from Lauriya is most reasonable date. But for chiselling out stone-disc or Aśokan lion capital or the pillars iron tools were indispensable. Hence, sculptures carved in stone have to be dated to the period when the regular use of iron became common.[12] The use of iron tools led to increase in agricultural production. Even thickly forested belts could be cut and the land could be brought under cultivation. Taking the above facts into consideration the mother-goddess of Curdi has to be dated to the period when regular use of iron spread to this coastal region. Therefore, the question would arise, who were the people with whom the mother-goddess of Curdi could be associated. It seems that from Bihar Gavdas migrated to the coastal region of Goa during *c.* 400 B.C. or slightly later.[13] The Prākrit-speaking Gavdas may have brought the concept of mother-goddess and chiselled out the figure on the laterite. The Gavdas were the worshippers of the mother-goddess Sāteri and Bhauka.

The mother-goddess in many places of northern India and south India was adorned as Kottavi. The mother-goddess of Curdi was also called Kottavi.[14] According to recent researches north-eastern Indian tribe which had horns as totem migrated to Kasargod which is part of Kerala. They were worshippers of the mother-goddess and their mother-goddess was standing on horns.[15] In many sculptures of Mahishāsuramardini of Pallava period, the goddess (Devī) is depicted standing on the head of buffalo and no buffalo was chiselled out fully and no lion and no army of the demon is depicted. When tribes could reach the parts of west coast beyond Goa, the above theory seems to be plausible. There are examples to show north-east Indian contact with Goa during the lifetime of Buddha himself. A merchant named Punna Buddhist reached Goa to preach the principles of Buddhism. He lived at Jambauli in Sanguem taluka.[16] If the mother-goddess is of slightly later period that is pre-Mauryan or Mauryan by then there were regular contacts between north-eastern India and south India. The trade and commerce had increased during this period. Rajgir to Pratisthān (Paithan) in Maharashtra was the ancient trade route.[17] Chandragupta Maurya is supposed to have gone to Shravanbelagola along with Bhadrabahu, the Jaina monk and ended his life there only. The route of Chandragupta was through Konkan.[18] During the reign of Aśoka contacts with eastern India and southern India increased considerably. This is indicated by the edicts of Aśoka found in Sopara on the west coast itself. The edicts of Aśoka are found in Sannati, Maski, Jatinga Rameshwar, Palkigundu, Gavimath near Hampi and Brahmagiri; all these find spots are in Karnataka. The Northern Block Polished ware (NBP) which is closely associated with Mauryan and post-Mauryan period was found in Nevasa and Nagarjunakonda. This also indicates north Indians' contact with south India.

The aforesaid facts clearly reveal that contacts with north-eastern India increased during Mauryan period. Therefore it would not be incorrect to assign the date of *c.* 300 B.C. to the mother-goddess of Curdi.

The megalithism continued right up to the period of Sātavahanas. Therefore, it would not be incorrect to assign the date of *c.* 300 B.C. to the mother-goddess of Curdi.

The mother-goddess of Curdi is unique and one of the early laterite sculptures belonging to pre-Christian era on the west coast of India.

NOTES AND REFERENCES

1. P.P. Shirodkar, 'A rare find of Mother-goddess at Curdi', in *Goan Society Through the Ages,* B.S. Shastry (ed.), Asian Publication Services, New Delhi, 1987, p. 15. The mother-goddess of Curdi has been transplanted in Veranyapura (Verna) in Salcete taluka of Goa in May 1988 as it was to be submerged under Salauli Dam waters. The present location of the mother-goddess is in the vicinity of ancient Mahālsā temple. Mahālsā is a well known goddess in Goa. Also see M.S. Deshpande, 'Mother-goddess a great leap from Curdi to Verna', *Purabhilekha-Puratattva,* Vol. VII, Number one, pp. 78-79. This paper with illustrations furnishes the transplantation of mother-goddess to Verna.

2. S. Rajendrappa, 'Goveya Curdi devalad Vandu adhyana' in *Manavika Karnataka* (Kannada), Vol. XV, No. 4, Mysore University, 1985, p. 28.

3. R.C. Dhere, *Lajjagouri,* Srividya Prakashan, Pune, 1978. Refer to also Chandrashekhar Gupta, 'Some interesting plaque of Lajja from Paunar' in *Giridharari Prof. G.S. Dikshit Felicitation Volume,* A.V. Narasimha Murthi and K.V. Ramesh (eds.), Agam Kala Prakashan, Delhi, 1987, pp. 45-50. See also I.K. Sharma, Beginnings of temples architecture, Raw material religious impact, *Essays in Memory of Shri A. Ghosh,* Vol. II, B.M. Pande and B.D. Chattopadhyaya (eds.), Agam Kala Prakashan, Delhi, 1985, p. 549.

4. John Marshall, *Mohenjo-Daro and the Indus Civilisation,* Vol. III, plates, Aurthur Probsthain, London, 1931, plates CL IX, figures 9-10. See also Sham. Ba. Joshi, *Rigvedadasar Nagapratima Vichar* (Kannada), Prasaranga, Mysore University, 1971, figure 7 B for mother-goddess from Mohejo-daro, for mother-goddess on stone-disc from Taxila, figure 12 B.

5. Ananda K. Coomaraswamy, *Introduction to Indian Art,* Munshiram Manoharlal, Delhi, 1969, fig. 7. See also by the same author, *History of Indian and Indonesian Art,* Munshiram Manoharlal, New Delhi, 1972, p. 10. Refer to also Benjamin Rowland, *The Art and Architecture of India,* Penguin Books, Maryland, U.S.A., 1970, fig. 13, p. 46.

6. *Annual Report of the Archaeological Survey of India,* H. Hargreaves (ed.), Government of India, Central Publications Branch, Calcutta, 1931, pp. 66-67. See also Balaram Srivastava, *Iconography of Śakti,* Chaukambha Orientalia, Varanasi, 1978. Ring stone from Patna, fig. 3 and Lauriya gold plaque depicting mother-goddess, fig. 4. Refer to P.K. Agrawala, *Goddess in Ancient India,* Abhinav Publications, New Delhi, 1984, plate No. 72. See also Devendra Handa, 'Some ancient cities and towns in Punjab', in *Indological Studies in Memory of S.P. Singhal,* ed. by author himself, Caxton Publications, Delhi, 1987, plate 8, p. 329. See also Devangana Desai, Social background of ancient terracottas c. 600 B.C. to A.D. 600, in *History and Society, Niharanjan Ray Felicitation Volume.,* Debiprasad Chattopadhyaya (ed.), K.P. Bagachi and Co., Calcutta, 1978, p. 150. Also see J.N. Banerjee, *Development of Hindu Iconography,* Munshiram Manoharlal Publications Pvt. Ltd., Delhi, 1974, pp. 170-73, plate No. 12.

7. Romila Thapar, *Aśoka and the Decline of the Maurya,* Oxford University Press, Delhi, 1985, p. 232. Also see Benjamin Rowland, *op. cit.,* Fig. 13, p. 46.

8. R. Nagaswamy, 'Kundalini from pre-historic visirikhal to historical chakra', in *Dimensions of Indian Art Pupul Jaykar Seventy* (Felicitation Volume), Lokesh Chandra and Jyotindra Jain (eds.), Agam Kala Prakashan, Delhi, 1984, vol. 1, pp. 323-26.

9. Romila Thapar, *op. cit.,* p. 323. Refer to also *Indian Archaeology 1984-85—A Review,* p. 146; B.R. Mani and K.P.S. Bhadoria of the South-Western Circle of the Archaeological Survey of India discovered seven cairn circles (measuring 4.50 to 10.30 m). In the vicinity of the Mahadeva temple of Curdi, a human figure carved in high relief on the rocky surface was also noticed.

10. Devendra Handa, *op. cit.*, p. 329.
11. J.N. Banerjea, *op. cit.*, p. 170.
12. M.S. Nagarja Rao, 'Graves of the early iron using people at Komaranahalli, recent evidence', in *Archaeology of Karnataka,* A. Sundra and Bhattasuri (eds.), Directorate of Archaeology and Museums, Mysore, 1990, p. 319. Thermoluminescene dates of the aforesaid site are 1440 B.C. (the earliest) and the latest is 1130 B.C.
13. Author's paper on cultural contacts of Goa with north India and south India presented in local History seminars of Goa held in February 1990, under print.
14. P.P. Shirodkar, *op. cit.*, pp. 13-14. See also V.S. Agrawal, *Ancient Indian Folk-cults*, Prithvi Prakashan, Varanasi, 1970, p. 159.
15. T. Satyamurthi, Director of Archaeology, Government of Kerala, furnished this information.
16. R. Sheno Hardy, *A Manual of Buddhism,* Edinburgh, 1860, p. 259.
17. Devangana Desai, *op. cit.*, p. 144.
18. Radhakumud Mookerji, 'Chandragupta and the Mauryan empire', in *The Age of Imperial Unity*, Vol. II, General Editor R.C. Majumdar, Bharatiya Vidya Bhavan, Bombay, 1960, p. 61.

73

KHĀṢṢ-MAḤALL: A BUILDING OR BUILDER

Z.A. DESAI

In the early years of the present century, (Khān Bahādur Maulavī) Ẓafar Ḥasan who later on rose to become Deputy Director General, Archaeological Survey of India and after partition of the country, Director of Archaeology, Government of Pakistan, Karachi, had published an inscription in Persian verse, inscribed in beautiful *Nastalīq* script on a large red sandstone slab, measuring about 3 by .45 metres, which is now preserved in the Dehli Museum of Archaeology, Red Fort, Delhi. The inscribed tablet is reported to have been originally fixed over the western archway of the main gate of a then standing dilapidated building, situated at a distance of about 200 metres to the west of the Purānā Qilā, Delhi. The building was in an advanced stage of decay and only the said gateway along with a series of arched cells stood, when Maulavi Zafar Hasan wrote. The tablet was dislodged and removed to the above-mentioned museum some time during the first decade of the present century.[1]

That the building was in ruins even towards the end of the first half of the last century is clear from the statement of the author of the *Miftāhut'-Tawārīkh*, Thomas William Beale, who gave a reading of this inscription occurring on "the gateway of the Khāṣṣ-Maḥall which is in ruins". It was also so described by Sayyid (later Sir Sayyid) Aḥmad Khān in his celebrated work on the buildings of Delhi and its eminent men, the *Āthāru's-Ṣanādīd*, as pointed out by Maulavī Ẓafar Ḥasan. The former inexplicably omitted to quote "the text of the inscription which he normally does in his work, but he did describe the building as a palace of the time of Shāh Jahān, near Purānā Qilā, Delhi, which was built in the year 1042, corresponding to the year 1632 A.D., by Zain Khān Koka's daughter Khāṣṣ-Maḥall."[2]

It was perhaps these two contradictory views of Beale and Sayyid Aḥmad Khān about the building—Khāṣṣ-Maḥall as the name of the building taken by Beale and Khāṣṣ-Maḥall being the name of the builder—which gave rise to the speculation and difference of opinion about the exact nature of the building and its builder, among the scholars including officers of the Archaeological

Survey of India. This misunderstanding was not less due to the fact that the correct purport of the epigraph, which was not that ambiguous as was made out to be, was not properly understood.

As a result, Maulavī Ẕafar Ḥasan was not very sure about the nature of the building and the identity of its builder and his not very successful attempt at solving the problem *categorically*. In this article, it is intended to prove conclusively, by contemporary evidence as well as the internal evidence of the inscription itself that the building, a caravansarai, was constructed by Khāṣṣ-Maḥall, wife of Jahāngīr and daughter of Zain Khān Koka.

Sayyid Aḥmad Khān correctly stated that Khāṣṣ Maḥall was the title of the daughter of Zain Khān Koka, the founder of the building, but his statement was accepted by some and rejected by others, probably because he had not quoted any authority in support thereof,[3] nor did he refer to the fact that Khāṣṣ-Maḥall was the title of the wife of the Mughal emperor Jahāngīr (1605-28). Those who subscribed to Sayyid Aḥmad Khān's views included the famous historian of the later Mughals William Irvine, while J. Ph. Vögel, the learned scholar and compiler of the catalogue of the exhibits of the Delhi Museum of Archaeology, was inclined to differ from him and was of the view that Khāṣṣ-Maḥall refers to the building in question only, that is to say, is its name and not that of the builder.

Maulavī Ẕafar Ḥasan's position on none of these points in the matter is categorical. He appears to accept Vögel's view, when he suggests that "as the building was erected outside the newly founded city of Shāhjahānābād and as the remains of it now consist of only a row of small and pretentious compartments, it would appear to have been a caravansarai than a palace". He further argued that the building "has been termed in the inscription as a '*sarai*' which means a 'house' or 'an inn' and it is believed that the word was used in the latter sense". Then again, he states that the "erection of the building has been recorded as an act of generosity", which he felt, "would hardly be appropriate if it was really intended as a palace".[5]

Maulvī Ẓafar Ḥasan also stated that though it is known that a daughter of Zain Khān Koka was married to Prince Salīm (later on emperor Jahāngīr)—he does not quote any authority for this but has in all probability relied on Sayyid Aḥmad Khān's view—there was no evidence that she was styled Khāṣṣ-Maḥall. Therefore he concluded that "the inscription was ambiguous on this point and it lends itself to either of the view". Feeling disposed to follow the opinion of Sayyid Aḥmad Khān, he was inclined to think that Khāṣṣ-Maḥall was the title of Zain Khān's daughter, after whom the building constructed by her received the name, and so he concluded that the word Khāṣṣ-Maḥall in the second line of the inscription "signifies the name of the building and in the last line, the title of the builder".[6]

Thus, according to Maulavī Ẓafar Ḥasan, Khāṣṣ-Maḥall was the name of the building constructed as also that of its lady-builder; that though there is no evidence of Khāṣṣ-Maḥall being the name of Jahāngīr's wife who was no doubt Zain Khān Koka's daughter, he was inclined to think Khāṣṣ-Maḥall was her title; and that as the building termed *sarai* in the text meaning 'a house' 'an inn' was constructed as an act of generosity, it did not appear appropriate that it was intended to be a palace and may have been used in the sense of a caravansarai.

Before examining the above views, it must be said in fairness to him and other previous writers on the subject that some contemporary material since published, as will be mentioned presently, containing information throwing new light on a couple of points for and against these statements, was not available to them, though, at the same time, it has to be noted that at least he did not properly make out the purport of the inscription itself which would have helped him arrive at a correct conclusion.

The group of writers who do not accept the view of Jahāngīr's marriage to Zain Khān Koka's daughter includes the translator of the emperor's memoirs, the primary source of information, namely the *Tūzuk-i-Jahāngīrī*, Alexander Rogers, who while translating the word in the printed Indian edition of that work صبیہ *ṣabiyya*, as 'cousin' instead of the correct 'daughter', drew attention to two 'excellent manuscripts' which have خویش *khwīsh* (relative) in the phrase صبیہ صاحب جمال زین خان کوکہ *ṣabiyya-i-Jamāl-i-Zain Khān Koka* (the daughter, endowed with beauty, of Zain Khān Koka) — which itself was not correctly understood by him as will be seen presently. Rogers asserted that the printed Indian text of Sayyid Aḥmad Khān is not correct, though the Royal Asiatic London manuscript agrees with it and that the two excellent India Office manuscripts and the British Museum manuscript used by Erskine, have *khwīsh* (relative), which Rogers took to connote a cousin; this connotation, not necessarily exact, seems to have been suggested itself to Rogers by the much later Muḥammad Hādī, who writing the continuation of the *Tūzuk* about a century later, in emperor Muḥammad Shāh's reign, stated that Parvez's mother was the daughter of Khwāja Ḥasan, the paternal uncle of Zain Khān Koka. The author of the still later famous biographical dictionary of Mughal noblemen the *Maāthiru'l-Umarā* also makes Parvez's mother a daughter of Khwāja Ḥasan. This is also borne out by the statement not taken note of by any one so far, of a near contemporary Khwāja Kāmgār Ḥusaini who is the first to furnish this information which evidently was the source of the later writers.[8] This very Khwāja Kāmgār complicates the matter further by saying a little earlier that one Sultān Bakht was earlier born to Jahāngīr (who does not mention this fact) from Ṣāḥib Jamāl, a *khwīsh* of Zain Khān Koka, which could be though not necessarily, his cousin mentioned by the Khwāja.[9]

All these statements instead of helping one arrive at a correct conclusion complicate the matter. And so we have to turn back to Jahāngīr's own statement and decide whether it originally had صبیہ *ṣabiyya* (daughter) or خویش *khwish* (relative, cousin). Jahāngīr's words are:

پرویز از صبیۂ صاحب جمال زین خان کوکہ کہ در نسب ہمسنگ مرزا عزیز کوکہ بود...

"Parviz, by the daughter, possessed of beauty, of Zain Khān Koka, who in pedigree (or lineage) was equal to Mirza 'Azīz Koka."[10]

That Jahāngīr had written and meant *ṣabiyya* (daughter) only and not *khwīsh* (relative) in the above sentence is indirectly indicated, if not conclusively proved, by the above statement itself in which the emperor goes out of his way to stress the nobility of his wife, the daughter of Zain Khān Koka, through her father's noble lineage. This he would not have bothered to mention if the facts were otherwise. Again, were it not a fact that his own daughter and not a cousin was married to Prince Salīm, Zain Khān would not have taken the risk of incurring further displeasure of Akbar—who was already unhappy with him for the Bangash catastrophe in which

Rāja Birbal and others were killed — by sending a large contingent of horsemen to Prince Salīm, then living in utter defiance of his father at Allahabad.[11]

But the most conclusive evidence of the fact that not only Jahāngīr's wife was a daughter of Zain Khān Koka, but that her title after marriage was Khāṣṣ-Maḥall, is furnished by the explicit statement to that effect by the contemporary author and official of some standing, Shaikh Farīd Bhakkarī, the author of the earliest dictionary of biography of Mughal noblemen, the *Dhakhīratu'l-Khawānīn*. In his account of Zain Khān Koka, Shaikh Farīd writes that since his daughter, named Khāṣṣ-Maḥall, was married to His Majesty Jahāngīr, his nearness to and position with the person of the king were far more than as could be imagined.[12]

Again, more than anything else, the epigraph itself provides the unimpeachable evidence on the subject. While the text of the inscription as deciphered by Maulvī Ẓafar Ḥasan is correct except at one place where the word مهین *mahīn* (the greatest, most important) is misread as بهین *bahīn* (best), which makes no material difference as such, his translation thereof, being faulty, has created this avoidable controversy about the nature or name of the building or that of its builder. The text and translation of the main historical part of the inscription given by him are as follows:-

بنا نهاد مهین زمانه خاص محل درین زمین بکرم بنت زین خان دریاب

اگر ز سال بنایش بود سوال ترا حساب کن بسرای محل خاص جواب

(a) Know that the daughter of Zain Khan built the *Khāṣṣ-Maḥall*, the best structure of the period, on this piece of ground, through her generosity.

(b) If you would know the date of its erection, then add (the numerical value of) '*jawab*' (to that) of *Sara-i-Maḥal-i-Khāṣṣ* (the caravansarai of Khāṣṣ-Maḥall) 1052.[13]

In the first verse above (a), the phrase مهین زمانه خاص محل *mahin-i-zamāna Khāṣṣ-Maḥall* can be taken both as the subject as well as the object of the verb بنا نهاد *bina nihad* (constructed). Maulavī Ẓafar Ḥasan preferred to take it as an object and translate it as "Khāṣṣ-Maḥall, the best structure of the period". But in the second verse, the phrase *sarā-i-Khāṣṣ-Maḥall* is correctly translated by him as "the caravansarai of Khāṣṣ-Maḥall" and not as the caravansarai intended to be called Khāṣṣ-Maḥall, which would have been the case, if the term Khāṣṣ-Maḥall was intended to apply to the structure, as Maulavī Zafar Hasan himself took it to be in the first verse. From this context of Khāṣṣ Maḥall of the last verse, it is clear that the composer of this metrical text has meant by the phrase *mahīn-i-zamāna Khāṣṣ-Maḥall* not "the Khāṣṣ-Maḥall, the best structure of the period", as understood by Maulavī Ẓafar Ḥasan but its exact reverse, namely that Khāṣṣ-Maḥall, the best person of the time, constructed on this piece of land (a building) which the composer in the last verse identified or named as the *sarāi* of (*i.e.* built by) Khāṣṣ-Maḥall. Secondly, from the linguistic point of view also, the qualifying phrase 'the best of the period' — a better translation would be 'the best of the time *i.e.* of the world' — seems to be more apt for a person than an object; we generally say for a person the best of the time or period but not the best of the time or period for a structure.

Moreover, even if it is taken for granted that Khāṣṣ-Maḥall was the name of the structure, it is inconceivable that the author of the record would have omitted to give the name of the builder and rest content with merely mentioning her parentage in this commemorative record, the very purpose of which is to perpetuate the name of the builder. In the absence of the specific name, some other daughter of Zain Khan Koka could be mistaken for the real builder, which that worthy lady would not have liked. Therefore, it is reasonable to hold that the composer did disclose her identity in the text by calling her Khāṣṣ-Maḥall.

In view of the above, it is clear that according to the inscription itself, the best of the world, Khāṣṣ-Maḥall, daughter of Zain Khān Koka, constructed the caravansarai. Thus, both the inscription and Shaikh Farīd's explicit mention corroborate the reading *ṣabiyya* (daughter) of Sayyid Aḥmad Khān's edition of the *Tūzuk*. Incidentally, the manuscript used for the Indian edition of Sayyid Aḥmad Khān was one, if not the best, of those of the *Tūzuk* (including Muḥammad Hādī's continuation) as vouchsafed by the colophon of its manuscript in the Bodlein Library at Oxford, transcribed by Sayyid Aḥmad Khān himself, which he completed, making use of ten good manuscripts in the royal library of the last Mughal emperor Sirāj'd-Dīn Muḥammad Bahādur Shāh.[14]

Another point which indirectly corroborates Shaikh Farīd's designation of this wife of Jahāngīr as Khāṣṣ-Maḥall is that the Mughals were sticklers to privilege and protocol and they strictly enforced the *tora* (code of etiquette) under which it was considered disrespectful to call by name the members of the royal house, particularly their spouses. Consequently, the Mughal historians mention the latter, not by their names — it may be news to many of us that practically the names of all but two or three wives of the Mughal emperors are not known — but by the titles in apposition to their native place, or some other distinguishing quality or characteristic. For example, we are told about Shāh Jahān's favourite wife, Mumtāz Maḥall that "after the nuptials and marriage, in accordance with the custom and practice of the rulers of this house of caliphate, who, when they wish to distinguish with greater honour one from among those who grace the royal bedchamber of fortune, bestow an appropriate title. His Majesty, finding that incompatible lady whose auspicious name was Arjamand Bānū Begam to be of weighty dignity ... gave her the title Mumtāz Maḥall".[15] As per this practice, Mehru'n-Nisā, daughter of I'timadu'd-Daula was designated Nūr Maḥall immediately after her marriage with Jagāngīr. The Mughal queen-consorts whose names are not known are Bhakkarī Maḥall, Udaipurī Maḥall, Akbarābādī Maḥall, Fatehpūrī Maḥall, etc. Thus, it is but natural that the daughter of Zain Khān Koka was designated Khāṣṣ-Maḥall after her marriage.

Lastly, attention may be drawn to another corroborative factor. The celebrated Nur Maḥal (later on redesignated Nur Jahān by Jahāngīr) had constructed a sarai at a place now called Sarai Nur-Mahall itself near Phillaur in Jalandhar district of Punjab.[16] It would not be surprising if Khāṣṣ-Maḥall also got an idea of constructing a sarai from this structure.

In short, the dilapidated building opposite the Purānā Qilā, Delhi, consisting only of a row of small and unpretentious compartments, was a caravansarai and not "appear to have been a caravansarai rather than a palace" as hesitatingly stated by Maulavī Ẓafar Ḥasan; it was not called

Kẖāṣṣ-Maḥall; and that the builder of the caravansarai was Kẖāṣṣ-Maḥall, daughter of Zain Kẖān Koka and wife of Jahāngīr.

NOTES AND REFERENCES

1. *Epigraphia Indo-Moslemica* (*EIM*), 1913-14, pp. 11-12.
2. *Ibid.*, p. 11.
3. This he had learnt from Jahāngīr's memoirs which he had edited and published from Ghazeepore in 1863, under the title *Toozuk-i-Jahangeeree.*
4. *EIM*, p. 11.
5. *Ibid.*
6. *Ibid.*
7. Alexander Rogers and Henry Beveridge, *Tūzuk-i-Jahāngīrī* or *Memoirs of Jahāngīr* (Delhi, Reprint, 1989), p. 19; *Tūzuk-i-Jahāngīrī*, Urdu tr. I'jāzu'l-Ḥaq Quddūsī (Lahore 1968), p. 69, follows Rogers. S̲h̲ah Nawāz Kẖān, *Ma'ā̲t̲h̲iru'l-Umarā*, Eng. tr., II (Reprint, 1979), p. 1022.
8. Kẖwāja Kāmgār Ḥusainī, *Ma'āsir-i-Jahāngīrī*, ed. 'Azrā 'Alavī (Bombay, 1978), p. 16.
9. *Ibid.*, p. 15.
10. Rogers, *op. cit.*, p. 17. Incidentally Rogers has misunderstood the statement. Sahib-Jamal is not the proper name of the lady but an adjective of the daughter (or according to Rogers, cousin) of Zain Khan.
11. Shah Nawaz Kẖān, *op. cit.*, p. 1027.
12. S̲h̲aik̲h̲ Farīd Bhakkarī, *D̲h̲ak̲h̲iratu'l-Kẖawānīn*, I (Karachi, 1964), p. 124; Eng. tr. Ziyaud-Din Desai (Delhi, 1992), p. 89. Shaikh Farīd's statement has also been referred to by I'jāzu'l-Ḥaq Quddūsī in his Urdū translation of the *Tūzuk* (*op. cit.*, p. 106). But he relies on the views of Rogers and others than pronounce his own considered view.
13. *EIM, loc. cit.*, p. 12.
14. Edward Sachau and Hermann Ethe, *Catalogue of the Persian, Turkish, Hindustani and Pushtu Manuscripts in the Bodlein Library, Oxford* (Oxford, 1889), p. 117, No. 221.
15. Muḥammad Amīn Qazwinī, *Pāds̲h̲āh Nāma* (British Museum copy), f. 49b.
16. Wayne Begley, *Monumental Islamic Calligraphy from India* (Illinois, 1985) pp. 92-93.

Section E
Beyond Indian Frontiers

74
SEA VOYAGES OF BUDDHIST MONKS

ANIRUDDH SINGH GAUR

Introduction

Buddhism arose in India about the sixth century B.C. and soon began to play a vital role in the religious history of India and the neighbouring countries. India played a major role in disseminating the message of the Buddha in Southeast Asia through Buddhist missionaries who travelled with merchants during their overseas voyages. The east coast of the country served as a gateway to the Buddhist monks in spreading out their religion (*dhamma*) abroad including Ceylon in the south, to Burma, Siam and Indo-China in the east and the present day Indonesia, including Java, Sumatra and other islands there in the south-east, to Khotan, Eastern Turkistan, China, Manchuria and Mongolia and even to parts of far-off-Siberia in the north and also to the Japanese islands. Buddhist literature, *Jātaka* stories, travellers' accounts and the inscriptions throw sufficient light on this aspect.

An attempt has been made in this paper to rebuild the events with the help of above source in order to trace out the spread of civilization by Buddhist monks through sea voyages in other countries.

The first noted historical evidence, according to *Mahāvaṁsa* Raja Vallia comes in to interact with India and Ceylon in the sea voyage of the Prince Vijaya Simha, who was banished by the Bengal king Sinhaba (Siṁhabanu) and left Sinhapura in Gujarat (Simhapur in Gahilwad of Saurastra) and landed in Ceylon in 543 B.C. on the day the Buddha attained Nirvana which is beautifully painted in Ajanta cave no. 2 (Griffiths: 1896, 17). Prince Vijaya established himself as king in the island, which he called Simhala.

According to *Dīpavaṁsa*, Buddhism was introduced to Ceylon by the Thera Mahinda in the third century B.C. in the reign of Devanampiyatissa (*Dīpavaṁsa*: ch. VIII, V. 13). Aśoka sent his son Mahinda and daughter Saṅghamitrā to carry the words of the Tathāgata to the fortunate island of Lanka. Mahinda joyfully obeyed his father's commands, and started with four other monks, whose names are Itthiya, Uttiya, Sambala and Bhaddhasala. Perhaps he started his voyage from Nagapattinam because it was a port of embarkation midway to Ceylon and other countries of South-east Asia. A monastery is reported to have been built by Mahinda named as 'Dharmasoka Maharaja Vihara' (T. Watters: 1905, pp. 226-28). Mahinda presented himself at once to the king Devanampiyatissa as the son and messenger of Dharmasoka. The king's step-sister, the princess Anula was converted with five hundred women into Buddhism. The population of the capital thronged to the king's palace, where Mahinda was residing to hear his preaching and each day thousands were converted.

The *Divyavadana* relates a beautiful story of the monk Purna who began his life as a merchant and later on accepted Buddhism and became a monk (Sylvain Levi, p. 137). The acceptance of Buddhism by Purna has been simply related and is untouched by any miraculous event. It is apparent from the dialogue between Purna and the Buddha that in spite of many difficulties Purna was determined to carry on his mission. When Buddha inquired about the field of his mission, Purna pointed out to Sronaparanta which may be identified with Burma. Buddha informed him about the cruelty of the people there, but this did not deter Purna from carrying out his mission.

It seems that impressed by the miraculous power of Purna the merchant began to regard him as the presiding saint of the sea. This is evident from the voyage of Purna's brother. Acting against the advice of Purna, he undertook a voyage in search of sandalwood. After reaching an island he cut down many sandalwood trees. Infuriated at that, the presiding Yaksha of the island raised a storm in which Purna's brother almost lost his life. But as soon as he remembered Purna for succour the storm abated and he and his comrades returned safely to their country.

During Gupta period the Chinese pilgrim Fa-hien came to India. He also visited Ceylon. After staying two years in the kingdom of Tamralipti, south-west of the Ganga, he embarked on board a merchant ship going to Simhala. The voyage lasted fourteen days before the islands on the coast of Simhala were reached; these, Fa-hien tells us, numbered a hundred. He found the Buddhist religion in full prosperity, and practised with more fervour than in any country he had visited in India.

Fa-hien caught a big merchant ship from Sri Lanka which carried two hundred travellers and which was also accompanied by a smaller ship which could rescue the passengers if the larger ship met with some accident. The ship sailed in favourable wind for two days but after that it had to face a heavy cyclone and it began leaking. The merchants and the others were anxious to board the smaller ship, but those on the smaller ship feared that large number of travellers from the bigger ship might overpower them. They at once cut the rope joining the two ships. The merchants were frightened to death and fearing that their ship might be filled with water they began throwing their goods into the sea (Moti Chandra: 1977, p. 179). Fa-hien as well threw his utensils and other articles into the sea. He prayed and took a vow to devote his life to Buddhist communities in China. He said: 'I have taken such a long journey for the sake of religion, I hope that by your supernatural power you will allow me to return safely'.

After ninety days, they arrived at Java where various forms of beliefs and Brahmanism were flourishing, while the state of Buddhism there was not worth speaking of. In Java Fa-hien stayed about five months and he embarked towards China.

Among the Indian monks, who visited China is Bodhidharma (A.D. 520), the well known founder of Chan dhyana, or Zen sect who lived at the Shaolin temple (Mount Sonsshan, Henan), hailed from Kanchi. He was regarded as the third son of a royal family (Pallava) and was held in high esteem, received by no less than the Emperor Liang-Wei-ti of South China on his arrival at Nanjing (Sharma: 1982, pp. 82).

The other south Indian monks who reached China were Diṅnāga, Bodhidharma (5th century A.D.), the founder of medieval Nyāya school (one of the Buddhist sects). He hailed from Kanchi, a centre of Pali Buddhism wherefrom Vinitaruchi (A.D. 520), the founder of Dhyana school of Tonkin also hailed. From the accounts of Hiuen-Tsang we come to know that even during seventh century A.D., nearly 100 Buddhist monasteries and over 10,000 monks (*sthaviras*) were flourishing around Kanchipuram area. The account is confirmed also in the contemporary Sanskrit play *Mattavilāsa Prahasana* by the great Pallava king Mahendra-varman I. It appears then that southeast India with its long coastal lines and convenient anchorages had been in regular contact with China and other southeast Asian countries.

A Brahmin of Kasapagotra, said to have lived for 156 years (A.D. 571-727), he reached China in A.D. 693 and settled there permanently devoting rest of his life in translating Buddhist texts (Sharma: 1985, p, 82). Vajrabodhi, son of king Īśānavarman and a teacher of Pallava king Narasiṁhavarman II (A.D. 695-722) sailed to Ceylon from the Pallava country and from there to China in A.D. 720 to preach Tantrayāna. Similarly, Chinese monks also came to India in larger number during this period.

Guṇavarman, who belonged to the royal family of Kashmir was converted a Buddhist at the age of twenty. At the age of thirty he left the state and wandered for long time and finally reached Sri Lanka and preached Buddhism there. From there he went to Java and started preaching Buddhism. In A.D. 425 he received the invitation of Emperor of China, but Guṇavarman did not like to go there. Accompanied by the Indian caravan leader Nandi on a ship, he decided to visit smaller countries but the ship losing its direction reached Canton and in this way he met the Emperor of China in A.D. 431. He stayed there and translated many Buddhist works into the Chinese (Bagchi: 1927, pp. 265-66).

From the Chinese records and several Sanskrit inscriptions belonging to this period we learn that there was frequent religious intercourse between Ceylon and India and many Ceylonese monks visited the Buddhist shrines at Bodh Gaya. The Chinese text, *Hing-tchoan* of Wang Hiuen-Tsang refers to the erection of a monastery at Bodh Gaya by a ruler of Ceylon for the accommodation of monks from Ceylon (*JCBRAS*, XXIV, p. 75).

Two Sanskrit inscriptions belonging to the sixth century A.D. found at Bodh Gaya, mention the erection of a Buddhist monastery and the presentation of a statue of the Buddha to the Bodh Gaya monastery by Mahānāma, a Ceylonese monk of the sixth century A.D. (*IA*: XV, pp. 356-59).

In the fifth and sixth centuries A.D., Kanchipuram, Nagapattinam and Kaveripattinam in south India were important centres of Buddhism. The importance of Kanchipuraṁ is testified by Buddhaghosa (*ARASI*: 1928, p. 108). According to the Ceylon chronicles (CV-I, ch-XXXVII, p. 22) Buddhaghosa was born in a Brahmin village named Ghosagama near the Bodhi tree in India. According to the *Visuddhimagga* (CHJ-II, p. 239) Morandakhetaka was the home of Buddhaghosa.

As for Hiuen-Tsang, he had not the privilege of visiting Ceylon as he intended. When he reached the kingdom of Dravida in southern India, and arrived at its capital Kanchipura, which was a seaport, he proposed crossing over to the island of Siṁhala, which was only three days' distance by sea. But he was dissuaded from his voyage by two monks, who were forced to leave the country and urged him not to go there because the king had just died, and the whole island had fallen a prey to civil war as well as famine.

In seventh century the king of Kaliṅga visited Ceylon and became a monk under Jotipalathera. He was followed by his wife and minister who entered the Sangha (*Culavamsa:* Ch-XLII, p. 46).

The Ceylon chronicles refer to the introduction of Buddhism to Suvannabhumi by Thera Sona and the Thera Uttara under the patronage of the Buddhist king Aśoka of India (Dvp: VIII, p. 12). Several scholars like Vincent Smith and Kern have doubted the authenticity of Aśoka's mission to Suvannabhumi (Smith: pp. 43-55).

But old Sanskrit works like the *Kathākośa* and the *Brhatkathā* and several other books mentioned many sea-voyages between Indian ports and Suvannabhumi. These sources give us an idea about the established trade between India and Suvannabhumi. The *Mahājanaka Jātaka* refers to the visit of prince Mahājanaka with a group of merchants to Suvannabhumi (*Jātaka*-VI, p. 22). The *Suparka Jātaka* gives the story of a sea voyage of several merchants between Bharukachchha and Suvannabhumi (*Jātaka:* III-IV, p. 124). The *Bṛhatakathā-śloka-saṁgraha* records the story of Sanudasa, who went to Suvannabhumi with a group of adventurers.

The traditional belief in Siam is that Buddhism was introduced to that country during the reign of Aśoka. According to the Ceylon chronicles (DPV: Ch-VIII, pp. 8-9), Mahādhammarakkhita and Mahārakkhita introduced Buddhism to Maharattha and the Yoṇa region during the reign of Aśoka. But there is no archaeological evidence which suggests the prevalence of Buddhism in Siam as early as the third century B.C.

There are a number of *Jātaka* stories, which refer to the sea voyages.

As *Bāveru Jātaka* informs us, some merchants of Varanasi taking a direction-finding bird with themselves set out on a sea voyage to Babylonia. This voyage was performed through the Arabian Sea and the Persian Gulf.

The *Śaṅkha Jātaka* mentions a voyage to Suvarṇadvīpa. A brahmin named Śaṅkha seeing his property diminishing on account of his munificent habits, took a voyage to Suvarṇadvīpa. The ship was built by himself and loaded with cargo.

The *Mahājanaka Jātaka* gives an account of a sinking ship. The ship of Mahājanaka sailing towards Sri Lanka developed crack and began sinking. The voyagers began cursing their fate and praying but Mahājanaka did nothing of the kind; when the ship began submerging in the water then he caught hold of the floating mast. Others floating in the sea were attacked by dangerous fishes and turtles and the sea became red with their blood. After floating some distance Mahājanaka left the mast and began swimming freely. In the end he was rescued by Maṇimekhalā, the goddess of the sailors.

Samudda-vaija Jātaka says that some carpenters took advance money from some people for making furniture, but they were unable to finish their work in time. At this delay their purchasers gave them much trouble, and becoming very much dejected they decided to migrate to a foreign country. They built a big ship, boarded it and sailing with favourable wind the ship reached an island covered with trees where also grew plantains, mangoes, *jamun*, jack fruits, coconuts, etc.

From the above we can conclude that Buddhist missionaries were responsible for the spread of Indian civilization in southeast Asia from the Christian era to the eighth century A.D. through sea routes.

Acknowledgements

The author is thankful to Dr. B.N. Desai, Director, for publishing this paper. He is extremely grateful to Dr. S.R. Rao for his valuable suggestions and encouragement during the present study. He is also thankful to Sri K.H. Vora for reviewing the manuscript.

NOTES AND REFERENCES

1. Bagchi, P.C., 1927. *Le Canon Boddhique en Chine* ,Vol. I, Paris.
2. Bagchi, P.C., 1950. *India and China*, Bombay.
3. Beal, S., 1980. *SI-YU-KI Buddhist Records of the Western World*, London.
4. Chandra, M., 1977. *Trade and Trade Routes in Ancient India*, New Delhi.
5. Chaudhary, M., 1986. 'Ship-building in ancient and medieval India', in *The Cultural Heritage of India*, Vol. VI, Calcutta.
6. Ferrand, G., 1922. *Le voyage du merchand Arabe Sulayman en Inde at en Chane* , Paris.
7. Griffiths, J., 1896. *The Paintings in the Buddhist Cave Temples in India*, Khandesh, India.
8. Hazra, K.L., 1982. *History of Theravada Buddhism in South-east Asia*, New Delhi.
9. Higgins, M.K., 1914. *Jataka Mala*.
10. Jain, J.C., 1947. *Life in Ancient India as depicted by Jain Canon*, Bombay.
11. Kosambi, D.D., 1956. *An Introduction to the Study of Indian History*, Bombay.
12. Legge, J., 1886. *Fa-hien's Record of Buddhistic Kingdoms*, Oxford.
13. Ling, T., 1973. *Buddhism, Imperialism and War*, London.
14. Mookerji, R.K., 1912. *Indian Shipping*, Bombay.
15. Malalasekera, G.P., 1938. *Dictionary of Pali Proper Names*, Vol. 2, London.

16. Majumdar, R.C., 1960. *The Classical Accounts of India*, Calcutta.

17. Pillai, V.K., 1904. *The Tamils Eighteen Hundred Years Ago*, Madras.

18. Rao, S.R., 1987. *Progress and Prospects of Marine Archaeology in India*, NIO, Goa.

19. Rao, S.R., 1970. 'Shipping in Ancient India' in *India's Contribution to World Thought and Culture*, Madras.

20. Sarkar, S.C., 1928. *Some Aspects of the Earlier Social Life in India*, London.

21. Schlingloff, D., 1988. *Studies in the Ajanta Paintings*, New Delhi.

22. Watters, T., 1904. *On Yuan Chwang's Travel in India*, Vol. I, London.

75

CLOSE RELIGIO-CULTURAL BOND BETWEEN BODH-GAYA AND SRI LANKA

DEBALA MITRA

Sri Lanka (the ancient Laṅkā, Tāmraparṇī and Siṁhala) had an intimate relation with Bodh-Gaya (variously known as Sambodhi, Mahābodhi and Vajrāsana in ancient times) since the planting of a branch of the Bodhi tree (pipal tree, Ficus Religiosa), under which Śākyamuni attained enlightenment (*bodhi*) at Anurādhapura (in Sri Lanka) during the reigns of the Maurya Emperor Aśoka (*c.* 273-236 B.C.) and his Siṁhalese contemporary king Devānaṁpiya-tissa. While it received the *dharma* of Śākyamuni-Buddha from India, its contributions to the development of the establishment of Bodh-Gaya, the holiest of the Buddhist pilgrim-centres, are immense.

The communication between Sri Lanka and Bodh-Gaya was no doubt frequent since Mahendra, the son of Aśoka (according to the Siṁhalese chronicle *Mahāvaṁsa*), went to Tāmraparṇī to preach Buddhism there. However, we have little information about the routes followed by the people of the two countries. Even we are in the dark about the exact route Vijaya had to take from Sihapura or Siṁhapura in Lāḷa (usually identified with Rāḍha in West Bengal) to Laṅkā. Because of the evil conduct of Vijaya and his seven hundred followers, King Siṁhavāhu of Lāḷa banished them from his kingdom and put them on a sea-going ship. Vijaya along with his followers first landed at the haven called Suppāraka[1] (possibly Sūrpāraka, modern Sopara on the west coast of Maharashtra) and therefrom embarked and ultimately landed in Laṅka in the region called Tambapaṇṇi on the very day of Buddha's *mahāparinirvāṇa* according to the *Mahāvaṁsa*. Vijaya and his followers colonized the island after slaying the original inhabitants, called *yakshas* in the *Mahāvaṁsa*. The island was named as Tambapaṇṇi (Tamraparṇī) because of the red soil of the land and also as Siṁhala after the name of Siṁhavāhu (also called Siṁhala). Vijaya founded the city of Tambapaṇṇi. Following the foundation of settlements and villages like Anurādhagāma, Upatissagāma, Ujjenī, Uruvelā and Vijitapura by ministers, Vijaya was consecrated as the king. Before his consecration, messengers were sent by a ship to the city of Madhurā (Madura), the capital of the Paṇṇu (Pāṇḍu) king in the southern India, for his daughter to be married to Vijaya. The Paṇḍu king not only sent his daughter but many maidens (to be married to the ministers and retainers of Vijaya) who disembarked at Mahātittha (identified with Mantoṭa opposite the isle of Mannar) in Tāmraparṇī. After the death of Vijaya, Paṇḍuvāsudeva, the son of Vijaya's brother, came with thirty-two sons of ministers from Siṁhapura and disembarked at the mouth of the Mahākandara river in Laṅkā and reached the capital at Upatissagāma. Before his consecration, he married Bhadda-kachchanā, the daughter of Sakka (Śākya) Paṇḍu, who along with thirty-two girl friends boarded a ship upon the Gaṅgā and landed at Goṇagāmaka at the mouth of the Mahākandara.

After his consecration, Devānaṁpiya-tissa sent to Emperor Aśoka various precious things through his nephew Mahāriṭṭha (also known as Ariṭṭha) and three other officials who embarked at Jambukola (a harbour in northern Siṁhala), landed at the haven, possibly Tāmralipti (modern Tamluk in West Bengal), and therefrom went to Pāṭaliputra (Patna in Bihar). Aśoka also sent presents, requisites for consecration and his message towards Buddhism through his envoys who together with those who had come to Aśoka embarked at Tamalittī (Tāmralipti)[2], disembarked at Jambukola and performed the second consecration of Devānaṁpiya-tissa. After the Third Buddhist Council during the reign of Aśoka, according to the *Mahāvaṁsa*, Moggaliputta Tissa sent forth *theras* to different parts and adjacent foreign countries to preach the religion of Śākyamuni. Mahendra and four other *theras* were selected for the conversion of Laṅkā. In his thirteenth rock-edict, Aśoka included Tāmraparṇī among countries where he achieved dharmavijaya.[3] From the second rock-edict[4] it is gathered that medical services including medical treatment of men and animals, planting of medicinal herbs, roots and fruit-bearing trees and digging of wells and planting of trees along the roads were provided by Aśoka in different regions including Tāmraparṇī. Mahendra along with four *theras* and the *samaṇera* Sumana first went to Dakkhiṇāgiri (a vihāra in Ujjayinī) and next to Vedisagiri (modern Vidisa in Madhya Pradesh) to visit his mother Devī who took them to the lovely *vihāra* of Vidisagiri. From Vedisagiri-vihāra they are said to have miraculously risen up in the air and alighted on the Missaka mountain (Mihintale mountain),[5] not very far from Anurādhapura, the capital of Devānaṁpiya-tissa. The great *thera* Mahendra succeeded in his mission, and the king and his people embraced the religion of Buddha and a good number of *chaityas, ārāmas* and *vihāras* including Mahāvihāra were established. Equally miraculous is the journey of Sumana who at the bidding of Mahendra went to Aśoka and Śakra, the king of gods, to collect the relics of Buddha and brought back the relics and the *stūpa* in the Thūpārāma was constructed. Thereafter the minister Mahāriṭṭha, the nephew of Devānaṁpiya-tissa, at the bidding of his royal uncle, embarked at the haven Jambukola, came to Pupphapura (Pushpapura, Pāṭaliputra) and requested Aśoka to send his daughter, the *therī* Saṁghamitrā, to bestow *pabbajjā* on Anulā, the spouse of the brother of Devānaṁpiya-tissa, and other women and also to send along with her the south branch of the Bodhi tree of Bodh-Gaya. Aśoka having agreed and having secured the branch, Mahāriṭṭa got the branch of the Bodhi tree, Saṁghamitrā, eleven *bhikshuṇis* and others boarded a ship on the Gaṅgā and passing over the Viñjhā-mountains arrived, in one week, at Tāmralipti; after sailing from this haven the party reached Jambukola and was escorted to Anurādhapura where the branch of the Bodhi tree was planted[6] (said to be in the eighteenth year of Aśoka's reign), and Anulā with her following received from Saṁghamitrā the *pabbajjā* by giving up the household life. Since its planting in Anurādhapura, the highly-venerated Bodhi tree plays an important role in the beliefs, rituals and ceremonies of Sri Lanka. The people from all parts of the island flock to it for worship.

At the ceremony of the foundation of Mahāstupa (now called Ruwanweli or Ruvanväli Dagaba) by Gāmaṇi-Abhaya, better known as Duṭṭhagāmani (*c.* 101-77 B.C. according to W. Geiger), there was a great assemblage of monks, not only from Siṁhala but from foreign countries. The *Mahāvaṁsa* furnishes a long list of *theras* who with a large number of *bhikshus* along with them came from India to attend the ceremony.[7] Thus, the *thera* Indagutta came from the region of Rājagṛiha (Rajgir), Dhammasena from Ṛishipatana (Sarnath), Piyadassi from the Jetārāma-vihāra (in Śrāvastī), Urubuddharakkhita from the Mahāvana (monastery) in Vesālī (Vaiśālī), Urudhammarakkhita from the Ghositārāma in Kauśāmbī, Urusaṁgharakkhita from the Dakkhiṇāgiri in Ujjayinī, Mittiṇṇa from the Aśokārāma in Pupphapura (Pāṭaliputra, Patna), Uttiṇṇa from Kashmir, Uttara from his dwelling by the road through the Viñjhā forest mountains (Vindhya range), Chandagutta from the Vanavāsa (Vanavasi in Karnataka), Suriyagutta from the great Kelāsa-vihāra and Chittagutta from the Bodhi-maṇḍa-vihāra (at Both-Gaya). The routes followed by these *theras*, their numerous companion-monks and also by the *theras* and monks from Pallavabhogga (Pahlava country according to W. Geiger) and Alasanda (Alexandria, the city of the Yonas, i.e. Greeks) are not detailed in the *Mahāvaṁsa*.

The abiding overwhelming influence of Buddhism on the people of Siṁhala is reflected not merely in that country but in India as well. The cultural interflow between Sri Lanka and India was brisk and lively. The proselytizing zeal of the Siṁhalese monks and nuns who played an active role in propagating the faith and erecting Buddhist structures in different regions including India is known from the Nagarjunakonda inscriptions. Bodh-Gaya where Śākyamuni obtained his enligtenment under the Bodhi tree was particularly sacred to the Buddhists of Siṁhala. The aspiration of every Buddhist was to perform rituals of worship at the Bodhi tree and to contribute according to his ability for the constructional purpose and installation of images. So profound was their devotion to the Bodhi tree that the Siṁhalese monks lived in a large monastery built near the Mahābodhi temple. The available data are no doubt sketchy due to lack of Indian literary records and the disappearance of many structures and images, some of which presumably bore dedicatory inscriptions. Very little is known about the routes followed in olden days not only by the pilgrims but by the monks who resided permanently at Bodh-Gaya. However, from the available inscriptions and foreign accounts, it is possible to some extent to have an idea about the participation of the people of Siṁhala in the pious activities at Bodh-Gaya.

As early as the first century B.C. the pilgrims from Tāmraparṇī participated in the gift of the components of the stone railing around the Bodhi tree. As is well known, many components of this railing and also of the pavilion (built in the first century B.C.) over the promenade of Buddha are missing. But at least one crossbar (now in the Indian Museum, Calcutta, no. F) bearing the donative inscription of Budharakhita, an inhabitant of Tāmraparṇī (*Budharakhitasa Tabapanakasa danaṁ*) has survived.[8]

About the foundation of a Siṁhalese monastery in the Gupta period, is the following passage from the narrative of the Chinese pilgrim Wang Hiuen-ts'e (who arrived in Magadha in A.D. 643), made known by Sylvain Lévi. [9] 'Once upon a time', according to the narrative, 'the king of Cheu-tzeu (Ceylon), named Chi-mi-kia-po-mo which means in Chinese "cloud-merit" (merite-nuage) [Koung-te-iun] (Śrī-Meghavarman),[10] asked two bhikshus to go and visit this monastery [the monastery founded by Aśoka to the east of the Bodhi tree and later made bigger]. The elder one was called Mo-ho nan, which signifies "great-name" (Mahānāman); the other one was named Iou-po, which means "give prophecy" or "gift of prophesy" [Cheou-ki] (Upa-). These two *bhikshus* paid homage to the diamond-throne (Vajrāsana) of the Bodhi tree. The monastery did not offer them shelter; the two *bhikshus* came back to their native land. The king asked the *bhikshus*: "You went to pay your homage to the sacred places. What happy portents (omens) can be told, Oh *bhikshus*?" They replied: "In the great country of Jambudvīpa, there is no place to stay in peace." The king having heard these words sent people with precious stones for offering these as presents to the king San-meou-to-lo-kiu-to (Samudragupta). And that is why, till today, the *bhikshus* from the kingdom of Ceylon reside in this monastery.'[11] Obviously, the Ceylonese king, after obtaining the permission of Samudragupta of the Gupta dynasty, built a monastery at Bodh-Gaya.

W. Geiger is of the opinion that the 'form of this name (of the king of Ceylon), as given by the Chinese narrator, results from a confusion between *varṇa* and *varman*.' According to his chronology Siri-Meghavaṇṇa, the successor of the Siṁhalese king Mahāsena, ruled during A.D. 352-79.[12]

In the late fifth or early sixth century A.D. the virtuous *śramaṇa* Prakhyātakīrtti, a descendant of the rulers of the island of Laṅkā (*Laṅkā-dvīpa-narendrāṇāṁ śramaṇaḥ kulajo=bhavat*) and aspirant of attaining Buddhahood, performed acts of worship at the *Ratna-traya* for the peace of mankind. This is known from his record, in Sanskrit, inscribed on a sandstone coping (Patna Museum, Accession no. 113) of the railing, originally erected around the Bodhi tree in the first century B.C.[13]

In Samvat 269 (A.D. 588-89, the year 269 having been referred to the Gupta era on evidence of palaeography), the monk Mahānāman, born in the island of Laṅkā and an inhabitant of Āmradvīpa, caused to be made a white mansion (*prāsāda*) of Buddha, with an open pavilion (*maṇdapa*) on all sides, at the Bodhimaṇṇda. This is gathered from an inscription[14] on a stone slab, discovered in the course of excavations made by A. Cunningham and J.D.M. Beglar at Bodh-Gaya, now in the Indian Museum (Acc. no. 2593). The slab was originally set in a chase made on a side of a building. Mahānāman (II), according to this inscription, was a disciple of Upasena (II) and the disciple's disciple of Mahānāman (I); the last one was a disciple of Upasena (I) and disciple's disciple of Rāhula who was a disciple of the *śramaṇa* Bhava. Fleet suggested the probability of Mahānāman II being the composer of the Pāli *Mahāvaṁsa* during the reign of Dhātusena, nephew (sister's son) of Mahānāman.

Another inscription[15] of possibly this very Mahānāman[16] is found on the pedestal of a Buddhist image, discovered in the excavation made by A. Cunningham and J.D.M. Beglar at Bodh-Gaya. This short donative inscription, in Sanskrit, records the gift of an image by Śākya-

bhikshu sthavira Mahānāman who was a resident of Āmradvīpa (most probably Laṅkā is so named due to its resemblance to the shape of a mango).

Fleet had edited another Sanskrit inscription[17] on the pedestal (now in the Indian Museum, no. B.G. 119) of an image , found by Cunningham and Beglar in their excavations at Bodh-Gaya, and assigned it to the sixth century A.D. on palaeographical grounds. This short inscription records the gift (evidently of the image) by two Śākya-*bhikshus*, Dharmagupta and Daṁshṭrasena, residents of Tishyāmratīrtha. Whether this place is located in Siṁhala or not cannot be determined from this inscription. The proper name Tissa (Sanskrit Tishya) for kings and others is very common in the Ceylonese chronicles *Mahāvaṁsa* and *Chūḷavaṁsa*. The *Mahāvaṁsa* also mentions Tissārāma and Tissa-vāpi (a tank) at Anurādhapura and Tissamahāvihāra. Ambatittha is mentioned by the *Mahāvaṁsa* (XXV. 7).

Hiuen Tsang, who visited Both-Gaya in the second quarter of the seventh century A.D., left an eloquent description of the Mahābodhi-*saṁghārāma* built by a king of Siṁhala outside the north gate of the enclosure of the Mahābodhi temple. The description of this Chinese pilgrim is reproduced here, as the remains of this monastery, partly exposed by Cunningham and Beglar, are now buried inside the raised ground immediately by the north side of the enclosure of the Mahābodhi complex. 'Outside the northern gate of the wall of the *Bodhi* tree is the Mahābodhi *saṅghārāma*. It was built by a former king of Siṁhala (*Ceylon*). This edifice has six halls, with towers of observation (temple towers) of three storeys; it is surrounded by a wall of defence, thirty or forty feet high.[18] The utmost skill of the artist has been employed; the ornamentation is in the richest colours (*red and blue*). The statue of Buddha is cast of gold and silver, decorated with gems and precious stones. The *stūpas* are high and large in proportion, and beautifully ornamented; they contain relics of Buddha. The bone relics are as great as the fingers of the hand, shining and smooth, of a pure white colour and translucent. The flesh relics are like the great true pearl, of a bluish-red tint. Every year on the day of the full moon of (*the month when*) Tathāgata displayed great spiritual changes, they take these relics out for public exhibition. On these occasions sometimes a bright light is diffused, sometimes it rains flowers. The priests of this convent are more than 1,000 men; they study the Great Vehicle and belong to the Sthavira (Shang-tso-pu) school.[19] They carefully observe the *Dharma Vinaya*, and their conduct is pure and correct.

'In old days there was a king of Ceylon, which is a country of the southern sea, who was truthful and a believer in the law of Buddha. It happened that his brother, who had become a disciple of Buddha (*a houseless one*), thinking on the holy traces of Buddha, went forth to wander through India. At all the convents he visited, he was treated with disdain as a foreigner (*a frontier countryman*). On this he returned to his own country. The king in person went out to a distance to meet him, but the Śramaṇa was so affected that he could not speak. The king said, "What has so afflicted you as to cause this excessive grief?" The Śramaṇa replied, "I, relying on the dignity of your Majesty's kingdom, went forth to visit the world, and to find my way through distant regions and strange cities. For many years all my travels, during heat and cold, have been attended with outrage, and my words have been met with insults and sarcasm. Having endured these afflictions, how can I be light-hearted?"

'The king said, "If these things are so, what is to be done?"

'He replied, "In truth, I wish your Majesty in the field of merit would undertake to build convents throughout all India. You would thus signalise the holy traces, and gain for yourself a great name; you would show your gratitude for the advantage derived from your predecessors, and hand down the merit thereof to your successors."

'He replied, "This is an excellent plan; how have I but just heard of it?"

'Then he gave in tribute to the king of India all the jewels of his country. The king having received them as tribute, from a principle of duty and affection to his distant ally, he sent messengers to say, "What can I now do in return for the decree?"

'The minister said, "The king of Siṁhala salutes the king of India (Mahā Śrī rāja). The reputation of the Mahārāja has spread far and wide, and your benefits have reached to distant regions. The Śramaṇas of this inferior country desire to obey your instructions and to accept your transforming influence. Having wandered through your superior country in visiting the sacred traces, I called at various convents and found great difficulty in getting entertainment, and so, fatigued and very much worn by affronts, I returned home. I have therefore formed a plan for the benefit of future travellers; I desire to build in all the Indies a convent for the entertainment of such strangers, who may have a place of rest between their journey there and back. Thus the two countries will be bound together and travellers be refreshed."

'The king said, "I permit your royal master to take (*for this purpose*) one of the places in which Tathāgata has left the traces of his holy teaching."

'On this the messenger returned home, having taken leave of the king, and gave an account of his interview. The ministers received him with distinction and assembled the Śramaṇas and deliberated as to the foundation of a convent. The Śramaṇas said, "The (*Bodhi*) tree is the place where all the past Buddhas have obtained the holy fruit and where the future ones will obtain it. There is no better place than this for carrying out the project."

'Then, sending all the jewels of the country, they built this convent to entertain priests of this country (*Ceylon*), and he caused to be engraved this proclamation on copper, "To help all without distinction is the highest teaching of all the Buddhas; to exercise mercy as occasion offers is the illustrious doctrine of former saints. And now I, unworthy descendant in the royal line, have undertaken to found this *saṅghārāma*, to enclose the sacred traces, and to hand down their renown to future ages, and to spread their benefits among the people. The priests of my country will thus obtain independence, and be treated as members of the fraternity of this country. Let this privilege be handed down from generation to generation without interruption."

'For this cause this convent entertains many priests of Ceylon.'[20]

The construction of this monastery, which afterwards rose to great eminence and played a distinctive role in the religious services of the Mahābodhi complex, served as a momentous landmark in the history of Siṁhala's association with Bodh-Gaya.

An image of about the ninth-tenth century A.D., donated by a *bhikshu* who hailed possibly from Siṁhala, is now fixed within a niche in the central part of the east wall of a box-like structure within a pillared pavilion in the central courtyard of the quadrangular Śaiva monastery (*maṭha*) of the Mahanths of Bodh-Gaya. Worshipped as Annapūrṇā, it is covered by a cloth which leaves barely the crowned head exposed. With persistent requests, I could persuade the *maṭha*-authorities to remove the cloth for a few minutes on one night. The well-preserved image (about 46 cm wide) of blackish (or blackish grey) stone represents the eighteen-armed Chundā[21] in *vajra-paryaṅkāsana* on a lotus with two rows of broad petals incised with a donative inscription. Unfortunately, the few minutes permitted to me to have a look at the image with the help of the dim light of a torch were not sufficient to identify the attributes as well as to decipher the inscription fully. I could barely make out that it is a dedicatory inscription of a *bhikshu*, a resident of Apa(?)bha(or ha)yagiri (*Apa?bha(ha)yagirivāsina*). It is likely that the engraver or the composer, due to carelessness, wrote Apa(?)bha(or ha)yagiri instead of Abhaygiri. In this connection it may be noted that the variant names (perhaps colloquial use) for Abhayagiri-vihāra or Abhayagiri are Apahayagara-vahara, Apayagara and Apahagara given in inscriptions (of some obscure individuals who lived about the seventh century A.D.), found on the steps of a ruined shrine in the Abhayagiri-vihāra complex.[22] In that case the donor of the image of Chundā came from Siṁhala, the Abhayagiri-vihāra of which was a large Buddhist establishment. In fact, the Abhayagirivāsin is one of the Siṁhalese sects.[23] According to the *Mahāvaṁsa* Vaṭṭagāmani-Abhaya founded the Abhayagiri-vihāra outside the north gate of Anurādhapura in the first century B.C. Afterwards, the *bhikshus* of the Abhayagiri-vihāra, forming a faction, seceded from the orthodox Theravāde upheld by the monks of the celebrated Mahāvihāra.[24] They sponsored new ideas from abroad (particularly India), not favoured by the orthodox. Among the Buddhist establishments of Laṅkā, the community of the Abhayagiri-vihāra was particularly noted for their Mahāyānic views and ultimately Vajrayāna leanings. Stone tablets with Tantric mystic formulae, in north Indian characters of about the ninth century, were found to the south-east of the main *stūpa* of Abhayagiri. These finds support 'the statement in the chronicles that the residents of Abhayagiri were sympathetic towards heterodox teachings introduced from time to time from India'.[25] It is, therefore, not unnatural for an Abhayagirivāsin *bhikshu* to dedicate an image of Chundā at Bodh-Gaya. The spread of this heterodox sect in Java (Indonesia) is attested by an inscription, found on the Ratubaka plateau (in Central Java) and dated Śaka 714 (A.D. 792 or 793), which mentions the construction of the Abhayagiri-vihāra (of the Siṁhalese monks), consecrated to Padmapāṇi, perhaps for the sake of the Siṁhalese monks on the Ratubaka plateau in the kingdom of the Śailendra king Samaratuṅga.[26]

Another inscribed image, fixed against the west wall of the so-called Pañcha-Paṇḍva temple within the enclosure of the Mahābodhi temple at Bodh-Gaya, bears an interesting record of the pious donations of a monk from Siṁhala. This image of blackish stone (schist ?), 143 cm high, represents in relief the eight major events (*ashṭa-mahāpratihāryas*) of the life of Śākya-muni Buddha. The central figure of Buddha in *bhūmisparśa-mudrā* (signifying Māra-*vijaya* and assertion of his right to the seat under the *aśvattha* tree on the eve of his attainment of the *bodhi*) is large, the other seven principal life-scenes (birth at Lumbinī, first sermon at Mṛigadāva, taming of Nālāgiri at Rājagṛiha, descent at Sāṅkāśya, miracle at Śrāvastī, offering of honey to Buddha by a monkey at Vaiśālī and *mahāparinirvāṇa* at Kuśinagara) in smaller dimensions being arrayed by the sides and top of this imposing figure. The donative inscription, in Sanskrit, starts by the sides of the halo of the central figure and continues in three lines, on the pedestal. While the three lines (six or seven letters at the beginning of these lines are broken off and some of the letters of the third one could not be deciphered meaningfully) are taken note of in some publications,[28] it appears that a part of the inscription (on the sinister of the halo) which furnishes the name of and some information (although meagre) about the donor has not been noticed. The donor Buddhasena (or Buddhasevaka) was a venerable Buddhist monk (*Śākya-bhikshu*) and a follower of the excellent Mahāyāna (*pravara-mahāyānaḥ*) and he hailed from the island of Siṁhala (Siṁhala-dvīpa-vinirgata).[29] His pious gift included at least the image bearing the inscription and two *gandhakūṭīs* or temples, one of which might have enshrined this very image. The religious merit accrued from this gift was intended for the attainment of the supreme knowledge by all sentient beings including above all the *āchārya, upādhyāya* and parents of the donor. The gift was made in the eleventh regnal year of Mahārājādhirāja *parama*-Saugata Mahīpāladeva (I) of the Pāla dynasty. According to D.C. Sircar, Mahīpāla I ruled in A.D. 977-1027.[30] From the inscription it could not be determined if the monk Buddhasena (?) came to Bodh-Gaya on a pilgrimage or was a resident of the Siṁhalese monastery, mentioned by Hiuen Tsang, flourishing at Bodh-Gaya. As the residents of this particular monastery belonged to the Sthavira school, it is doubtful if Buddhasena (?), a staunch Mahāyānist, could have secured a place in this monastery. In any case, this monk from Siṁhala stayed for some time at Bodh-Gaya to see the construction of at least two *gandhakūṭīs*.

The name of another Siṁhalese *bhikshu* is found inscribed on a black stone slab attached to the gate of the *maṭha* where it served the purpose of a fulcrum for the gate-hinge. This slab, recovered from the Mahanth of Bodh-Gaya, is now in the Indian Museum (Reg. no. 2610), Calcutta. The long Sanskrit inscription of twenty-one lines, is in characters of about the eleventh century A.D. Incised in the fifteenth regnal year of the Rāshṭrakūṭa king Tuṅga-Dharmāvaloka, the inscription records the dedication of a *gandhakūṭī* for the service of Buddha by King Tuṅga,[31] son of Kīrtirāja and grandson of Nanna-Guṇāvaloka of the Rāshṭrakūṭa lineage. Near the end of the inscription in line 20 is written *Siṁhala-dvīpa-janmanā paṇḍita-ratna śrījana*[32] (most probably *śrījñāna*) *bhikshuṇā)*. The last two letters after this in line 20 and 5 letters of line 21 could not be meaningfully deciphered. It is also not certain that the word *ratna* is connected with *paṇḍita* or a part of *śrījñāna*. In the latter alternative, the name of *bhikshu* is Ratnaśrījñāna; born in the island of Siṁhala, the monk (*bhikshu*) was a learned (*paṇḍita*) scholar. Otherwise we have to take the name as Śrījñāna, a jewel (*ratna*) among *paṇḍitas*. Due to non-decipherment of the seven letters following *bhikshuṇā* the part played by this monk in this donative record could not be determined. 'The composer of the document', according to Rajendralala Mitra, 'was a Sinhalese mendicant of the name of Jana Bhikshu'.[33]

Another instance in the installation of an image of Buddha by a pilgrim named Udayśrī from Siṁhala (*Saiṁhalen-Odayaśriyā*) at Bodh-Gaya is recorded in an inscription on the pedestal of a missing image. This pedestal from Bodh-Gaya, which had been presented to the Patna Museum in 1918 and given Acc. no. 146, was stolen in 1939. Its description in the Patna Museum Register is: 'Sandstone pedestal of a statue, 2' x 9$^1/_2$", with devotees, horse, elephant and probably Jambhala, inscribed.' According to T. Bloch, this inscribed pedestal 'contains small rilievo figures, representing from right to left the following: (*a*) two small kneeling devotees, mother and son; (*b*) a horse; (*c*) a wheel; (*d*) a swordsman; (*e*) a conch-shell (śaṅkha); (*f*) a diademed male figure seated; (*g*) perhaps a wheel; (*h*) a seated female figure; (*i*) a lotus flower with some indistinct object over it; (*j*) an elephant; (*k*) a kneeling male figure holding a garland'. Bloch took 'the figure of a male (*k*) as a portrait of the donor of the statue, Udayaśrī from Ceylon, and the female with boy as a portrait of his wife and son. The intermediate symbols (*b* to *k*) evidently represent the nine jewels (*navaratnāni*) so often referred to in Buddhist scriptures'.[34] Bloch furnished the transcript and edited the translation of the two-lined inscription, in Sanskrit. The translation given by N.G. Majumdar who re-edited the inscription,[35] and assigned it to the twelfth century A.D., is as follow: 'This [image of the] Lord was caused to be made by Udayaśrī, from Ceylon, with a desire to deliver the world submerged in an ocean of woe.' None of these two scholars have published the photograph of the pedestal and the facsimile of the inscription. Udayaśvī seems to have been a lay worshipper and came from Siṁhala on a pilgrimage, perhaps with his family. Bloch appears to be right in identifying the male figure holding a garland as Udayaśrī and the female and the boy as his wife and son. Of the remaining figures and symbols, seven depict definitely *ratnas* (elephant, horse, wheel, *maṇi, gṛihapati, pariṇāyaka* and *strī*), the representations of which are found on some *stūpa*-platforms and image-pedestals at Bodh-Gaya. The remaining symbols, presumably, depict ritualistic objects.

The exalted position of the Siṁhalese monks at Bodh-Gaya in the thirteenth century A.D. is testified not only by some inscriptions but by the biography of the Tibetan monk-pilgrim Dharmasvāmin. An inscription on a stone slab from Bodh-Gaya (now in the Indian Museum, Acc. no. A 22389, the old number being 6263), mentioning the name of Aśokavalla, is dated in the year 51 of the *atītarājya* of Lakshmaṇasena. 'It records the erection of a Buddhist shrine (*vīhārī*), with an image of the Buddha, by Bhaṭṭa Dāmodara, etc., with the assent of king Aśokachalladeva at the request of a number of his officials. Provision was also made for offerings (*naivedya*) in three *chaityas* with lamps by certain officials, to be offered to the god daily by members of the Singhalese order at Mahābodhi and others.'[36] D.C. Sircar was of the opinion that the Lakshmaṇasena era was counted originally from the accession of Lakshmaṇasena about A.D. 1179 and suggested equation of the year 51 to 1230.[37]

The Tibetan monk-pilgrim Dharmasvāmin (Chag-lo-tsā-ba Chos-rje-dpal), during his visit to Bodh-Gaya in A.D. 1234, met the king Buddhasena who 'was the ruling Rājā of Magadha, residing at Vajrasena'.[38] According to him, inside the three gates of the enclosure-wall of the Mahābodhi temple 'no one slept except the sacristans. There are three hundred sacristans, natives of Ceylon, who belong to the Śrāvaka school; other (schools) have no such right.'[39] These Śrāvakas, as natural with their orthodox tenets, had a disdain towards Mahāyāna-Vajrayāna doctrines and practices and the keeper, a Śrāvaka of the Vajrāsana-Saṅgha-vihāra, in fact, asked Dharmasvāmin to throw into the river a manuscript of the Mahāyāna *Ashtasāhaśrikā-Prajñāpāramitā* which he was carrying. The Śrāvaka, further, instructed the Tibetan monk-pilgrim not to worship images of deities like Khasarpaṇa (considered by him a householder).[40] From the account of Dharmasvāmin it is evident that the orthodox Theravadin monks from Siṁhala were the privileged, if not the exclusive, priests of the Vajrāsana temple at this time.

Buddhasena, seen by Dharmasvāmin, is known from an undated stone-slab inscription,[41] of the thirteenth century A.D. from Bodh-Gaya, now in the Museum für Indische Kunst (No. I

1141), Berlin. According to this inscription Pīṭhīpati Āchārya Buddhasena (who issued the grant from Vikramapāṭaka) granted permanently 'the *vṛtti* or rent-free property of the entire foundation called Mahābodhi comprising various establishments like the *gandhakuṭī* etc... in favour of *Bhikṣu Paṇḍita* Dharmarakṣita who was the chief among king Aśokavalla's... (probably, teachers) and the *Rājaguru* (royal receptor) of the Kamā (correctly, Kāma) country'.[42] It is enjoined in the grant that the donee Dharmarakshita 'has to arrange for the rehabilitation of those Ceylonese monks who were just then in Ceylon and those monks of the said country who were still in the place (*i.e.* Bodhgayā) in accordance with an arrangement that had been previously made' and 'that the *Mahābodhi-viṣaya*, i.e. property at Mahābodhi, belonging to the Ceylonese should be handed over to them by the donee'.[43]

Buddhasena's son, the king Jayasena, styled Pīṭhīpati and Āchārya like his father, was also favourably disposed towards the Siṁhalese monks, as evident from an inscribed oblong post-like slab (now in the Patna Museum, Acc. no. 104) from Janibigha,[44] about 10 km east of Bodh-Gaya. Dated in the year 83 (A.D. 1261 or 1262, if the Lakshmṇasena era, as suggested by D.C. Sircar, commenced at A.D. 1179) of the *atītarājya* of Lakshmaṇasena according to this Sanskrit inscription, Jayasena made over permanently, without reserve, the village of Koṭṭhalā (possibly Koṭṭalā, in Saptaghaṭṭa) with its land and water and the plough-tax to Vajrāsana for the residence (or monastery) of the Siṁhalese monk Maṅgalasvāmin, versed in the *Tripiṭaka*, in whose hands was placed the charter registering the grant by the king.

This record would suggest that the Vajrāsana establishment was practically under the direct control and supervision of the Siṁhalese monks. Full facts about the way by which they attained such a vested interest in the Mahābodhi establishment are not known. The profound devotion, sincere efforts, zealous offerings and sumptuous contributions of not only the resident Siṁhalese monks but also of the pious pilgrims from Siṁhala no doubt played a significant role in the enhancement of the influence and prestige of the Siṁhalese Buddhists residing at Bodh-Gaya.

NOTES AND REFERENCES

1. The *Mahāvaṃsa or The Great Chronicle of Ceylon*, translated by Wilhelm Geiger, published by the Ceylon Government Information Department (Colombo, 1950), .p. 54.
2. *Ibid.,* p. 80.
3. Sircar, D.C., *Inscriptions of Aśoka,* Third Edition (New Delhi, 1975), p. 52.
4. *Ibid.*, p. 42.
5. *The Mahāvaṃsa* (Colombo, 1950), pp. 89-90.
6. *Ibid.*, pp. 128 ff.
7. *Ibid.,* pp. 193-94.
8. Majumdar, N.G., *A Guide to the Sculptures in the Indian Museum*, Part I (Delhi, 1937), p. 67.
9. Sylvain Lévi, 'Les Missons de Wang Hiuen-ts'e dans l'Inde', *Journal Asiatique*, Neuvieme Série, Tome XV, No. 2 (Mars-Avril, 1900), pp. 316 and 317. The English translation is mine.
10. Śrī-Meghavarṇa.

11. The Chinese pilgrim Hiuen Tsang (variously written Hiuen Tsiang, Yuan Chwang, Hsüan-Chuang, Xuanzang and Hsüan-tsang), who after visiting numerous Buddhist places for fourteen years left India in A.D. 644, tells almost the same story about the foundation of the monastery (at Bodh-Gaya) built by a former king of Siṁhala without mentioning the name of the king of Siṁhala and the name of the monk; Samuel Beal, trans., *Si-Yu-Ki: Buddhist Records of the Western World, Translated from the Chinese of Hiuen Tsiang* (A.D. 629), popular edition (London), Vol. II, pp. 133-35; for details, see below. Samudragupta has been taken as the Indian king of the same name (*c.* A.D. 335-76) of the Gupta dynasty; R.C. Majumdar and A.D. Pusalker, eds., *The Classical Age* (Bombay, 1954), p. 11.

12. Wilhelm Geiger, *The Mahāvaṃsa or The Great Chronicle of Ceylon* (Colombo, 1950), p. xxxix.

13. T. Bloch, 'Notes on Bodh Gaya', *Archaeological Survey of India, Annual Report, 1908-9* (Calcutta, 1912), pp. 156 and 157. H. Panday, 'The Bodh-Gaya Inscription of Prakhyatakirtti', *The Journal of the Bihar and Orissa Research Society*, Vol. IV, 1918, pp. 405-11, Plate between pp. 404 and 405. Bhandarkar's List 1737 in *Appendix to Epigraphia Indica*, Vols. XIX-XXIII.

14. John Faithfull Fleet, 'Bodh-Gaya inscription of Mahānāman—The year 269', *Corpus Inscriptionum Indicarum*, Vol. III, Reprint (Varanasi, 1970), pp. 274-78. In the index (p. 324) Fleet suggested the era being 'Gupta or perhaps Kalachuri' (A.D. 248-49). There is some controversy about the Ceylonese chronology as worked out by W. Geiger.

15. John Faithfull Fleet, 'Bodh-Gaya image inscription of Mahānāman', *Corpus Inscritionum Indicarum*, Vol. III, Reprint (Varanasi, 1970), pp. 278 and 279.

16. Vincent A. Smith was inclined to identify him with Mahānāman I, *The Indian Antiquary*, Vol. XXXI, 1902, p. 193.

17. *Corpus Inscriptionum Indicarum*, Vol. III, pp. 281 and 282.

18. Thomas Watters has rendered this part in following words: 'Its buildings formed six courts, with terraces and halls of three storeys, enclosed by walls between 30 and forty feet high'; *On Yuan Chwang's Travels in India*, Vol. II (London, 1905), p. 136.

19. As regards the use of this term by Hiuen Tsang, Watters' observations are: 'It will be noticed that Yuan-chuang describes the monks of this establishment as Mahāyānists of the Sthavira School, and he applies the same terms to the Brethren of Ceylon in his account of that island. As the Sthavira School is generally represented as belonging to the early and Hīnayana form of Buddhism it would seem that in these and other passages Yuan-chuang uses the term Mahāyāna in a peculiar sense', Thomas Watters, *op. cit.*, p. 138. Vidya Dehejia states that, 'The Chinese pilgrim chose to describe the Sinhalese Buddhists as Mahayanists of the Sthavira school. This is a term he used to describe those Buddhists who were not orthodox Hinayanists, but incorporated certain Mahayanist features into a basic Hinayana tradition based on the Pali *Tripitaka'*, *Bodhgaya, the site of enlightenment*, ed. Janice Leoshko, Marg Publications (Bombay, 1988), p. 96.

20. Samuel Beal, *op. cit.*, pp. 133-35.

21. Debala Mitra, 'Images of Chundā at Bodh-Gaya', Amita Ray & Samir Mukherjee, eds., *Historical Archaeology of India: A Dialogue between Archaeologists and Historians* (New Delhi, 1990), pp. 300-302, & III. 40.

22. G.P. Malasekera, ed., *Encyclopaedia of Buddhism*, Vol. 1, Facicle 1: A-Acala, published by Government of Ceylon, 1961 (reprinted in 1984), p. 23; *Epigraphia Zeylanica*, IV, pp. 139f.

23. Nalinakaha Lutt, *Buddhist Sects in India* (Delhi, 1978), pp. 49 and 284 n. The name of Abhayagiravāsins 'is given to the monks residing in or connected with the Abhayagiri-vihāra in Anurādhapura, Ceylon, with special reference to their doctrinal and other differences with the orthodox monks of the Mahāvihāra, from the first century B.C. till the 12th century', *Encyclopaedia of Buddhism*, Vol. 1, p. 25.

24. *The Mahāvaṃsa*, pp. 236 and 237; *Encyclopaedia of Buddhism*, Vol. 1, p. 22.

25. *Encyclopaedia of Buddhism*, Vol. 1, p. 23. There are some references to India's influence on Sri Lanka in respect of the doctrines of Abhayagirivāsins. 'In the reign of Vohārika Tissa (209-301 A.C.,) this faction, which had earlier received a body of Vajjiputta monks from Pallārāma in India led by their teacher

Dhammaruci, is reported to have adopted some views belonging to the Vetulya-vāda, although there is nothing on record indicating essential doctrinal differences between them and the Mahāvihārvāsins' (*ibid.*, p. 25). 'In the time of Silākāla (518-31) a Vaipulya Sutta (Mahāyāna text) known as *Dhammadhāt* was brought from India by a merchant of Kāsī, named Pūrṇa. This text was readily accepted by Abhayagiri and was honoured in the place' (p. 26). 'In the 9th century a member of the Vajraparvata sect in India came to reside in Abhayagiri from where he spread his teaching which is described as "secret teachings and popular with the foolish and ignorant." Some granite slabs with Tantric formulae (see foregoing article supports the statement in the chronicles that Abhayagiri was friendly towards heterodox teachings periodically introduced from India' (*ibid.*, p. 26).

26. J.G. de Casparis, 'New Evidence on Cultural Relations between Java and Ceylon in Ancient Times', *Artibus Asiae*, Vol. XXIV, 1961, p. 241-48; Lokesh Chandra, 'Cultural Contacts of Indonesia and Sri Lanka in the Eighth Century and their bearing on the Barahudur', to be published shortly in his forthcoming book, *Cultural Horizons of India*, Vol. 4 (New Delhi, Aditya Prakashan, 1994).

27. A drawing of this image, got prepared by Francis Buchanan (later on Buchanan-Hamilton), has been illustrated by Montgomery Martin on Pl. X (Fig. 6) of his *History, Antiquities, Topography and Statistics of Eastern India, comprising the Districts of Behar, Shahabad, Bhagulpoor, Goruckpoor, Dinajepoor, Purania, Rungpoor & Assam*, Vol. I (London, 1838), p. 74. Rajendralala Mitra, *Buddha Gayā* (Calcutta, 1878), pp. 133, 197 and 198, Pl. XX, Fig. 3 (also a drawing). Susan L. Huntington, *"Pala-Sena" Schools of Sculpture* (Leiden, 1984), p. 57, Fig. 54. Janice Leoshko, ed., *Bodhgaya, the site of enlightenment*, Marg Publications, (Bombay, 1988), p. 40, Fig. 14 on p. 42.

28. *Archaeological Survey Report*, Vol. III (Calcutta, 1873), p. 122, Pl. XXXVII, No. 5. Rajendralala Mitra, *op. cit.*, pp. 197 and 198. *The Indian Antiquary*, Vol. IX, 1880, p. 114. A. Cunningham, *Mahābodhi* (London, 1892), p. 65. R.D. Banerji, 'The Pālas of Bengal', *Memoirs of the Asiatic Society of Bengal*, Vol. V, No. 3 (Calcutta, 1915), p. 75, Pl. XXX. Susan L. Huntington, *op. cit.*, pp. 221 and 222.

29. Debala Mitra, 'Image of Buddha of the 11th regnal year of King Mahīpāla', *Indian Museum Bulletin*, Vol. XXVI, 1991, pp. 7-12 (particularly p. 8) and Fig. 2.

30. *Pāl-Sen Yuger Vaṁśānucharit* (in Bengali) (Calcutta, 1982), pp. 15, 81 and 179. The recent discovery of a copperplate charter of the Pāla king Mahendrapāla at Jagajjibanpur (District Malda, West Bengal), will change to some extent the Pāla chronology worked out by D.C. Sircar. Gouriswar Bhattacharya, 'The New Pāla Ruler Mahendrapāla: Discovery of a Valuable Charter', *South Asian Studies*, Vol. 4, 1988, pp. 71-73; K.V. Ramesh and S. Subramonia Iyer, 'Māldā District Museum Copper-plate Charter of Mahendrapāladeva, year 7', *Epigraphia Indica*, Vol. XLII, 1977-78 (New Delhi, 1992), pp. 6-29.

31. Rajendralala Mitra, *op. cit.*, pp. 194-97, Pl. XL. *The Indian Antiquary*, Vol. IX, 1880, p. 143. A. Cunningham, *Mahābodhi or the Great Buddhist Temple under the Bodhi tree at Buddha-Gaya* (London, 1892), p. 66. Bhandarkar's List, no. 1668, p. 233 of the Appendix to *Epigraphia Indica*, Vols. XIX-XXIII. Shyamalkanti Chakravarti, *A Descriptive Catalogue of the Prakrit and Sanskrit Inscriptions in the Epigraphy Gallery, Indian Museum* (Calcutta, 1977), p. 8.

32. "Rajendralala Mitra read", *Śrījana*, *op. cit.*, p. 195.

33. *Ibid.*, p. 194.

34. *Archaeological Survey of India, Annual Report 1908-9* (Calcutta, 1912), p. 157.

35. N.G. Majumdar, 'Inscription of Udayaśrī (Patna Museum)', *The Journal of the Bihar and Orissa Research Society*, Vol. V, 1919, pp. 143 and 144.

36. Vinoda Vihari Vidyavinoda, 'Two inscriptions from Bodh-Gaya', *Epigraphia Indica*, Vol. XII, 1913-14, Reprint 1982, p. 28, Plate facing p. 29. Bhagvanlal Indraji's version appears in the *Journal of the Bombay Branch of the Royal Asiatic Society*, Vol. XVI, 1883-85, pp. 357-60. Bhandarkar's List no. 1467.

37. *Journal of Ancient Indian History*, Vol. VI, 1972-73, p. 50.

38. George Roerich, *Biography of Dharmasvāmin* (Patna, 1959), p. 64.

39. *Ibid.*, p. 73.

40. *Ibid.*, pp. 73 and 74.

41. D.C. Sircar, 'Bodhgayā Stone Slab Inscription of Buddha-sena in the Berlin Museum', *Journal of Ancient Indian History*, Vol. VI, 1972-73 (Calcutta, 1973), pp. 47-53. Bhandarkar's List no. 1749.

42. *Ibid.*, p. 50. From an inscription found in a temple of Sūrya at Gaya, dated in the year 1813 (probably A.D. 1270 according to D.C. Sircar) of Buddha's *nirvāṇa* (*The Indian Antiquary*, Vol. X, December, 1881, pp. 341ff. and Pl. Bhandarkar's List no. 1459) it is gathered that Dharmarakshita was the spiritual teacher of Purushottamasiṁha, the latter having been a ruler of Kāma (usually identified with Kumaun) and a feudatory of Aśokavalla (read as Aśokachalla by some, 'the crest jewel of the kings of the Sapādalaksha mountains'). From this inscription it is also known that Dharmarakshita supervised the construction of a *grandhakūṭī* of Buddha established by Purshattamasiṁha.

43. D.C. Sircar, *op. cit.*, p. 51.

44. H. Panday, 'The Janibigha Inscription', *The Journal of the Bihar and Orissa Research Society*, Vol. IV, 1918, pp. 273-80; a note by K.P. Jayaswal, *ibid.*, Vol. IV, pp. 266ff. and Pl. and Vol. V, p. 145. N.G. Majumdar, 'Patna Museum Inscription of Jayasena', *The Indian Antiquary*, Vol. XLVIII, 1919, pp. 43-48, Bhandarkar's List no. 1469. Parmeshwari Lal Gupta, ed., *Patna Museum Catalogue of Antiquities* (Patna, 1965), p. 82.

76
EARLY CONTACTS BETWEEN INDIA AND INDONESIA

KALYAN KUMAR SARKAR

The study of the extent of Indian influence on the religious art of ancient Java in Indonesia eventually leads one to the examination of an important aspect, namely, transformation of Hindu and Buddhist iconographic traditions in Indonesia. It may, however, be pointed out that iconographic study of some of the important members of the Hindu and Buddhist pantheon is still in its infancy. Sculptural representations of some Hindu deities and their mounts clearly point to the fact that the Javanese sculptors took the liberty of introducing certain elements that are not to be found in the Indian textual prescriptions that were behind their creation, and consequently, in their Indian counterparts.

To illustrate our point, let us look into the iconography of the Hindu goddess Durgā Mahishāsuramardinī. My conclusions are based on a personal examination of some Javanese stone images of Mahishāsuramardinī now kept in the Rijksmuseum voor Volkenkunde, Leiden, The Netherlands, National Museum, Jakarta and Radyapustaka Museum, Surakarta, Java, Indonesia.

In Hindu mythology the goddess who was created by the gods to destroy the buffalo demon (Mahishāsura) finally killed the demon after a prolonged battle and came to be known as Mahishāsuramardinī. In early medieval period Indian sculptors tried to depict the dynamic energy of the goddess by showing her in the act of killing the buffalo demon. Sometimes she is shown in actual combat as in the full-fledged battle scene in Mamallapuram. Regarding the attributes and number of arms of the goddess, the representation of the demon and the very depiction of the combat, the iconography of Mahishāsuramardinī in India shows wide variations depending on regions and periods, and points to a considerable freedom from textual prescriptions. In an early Indian example from Vidiśā, central India, the goddess is shown killing the demon in animal form by thrusting a trident into his back, pressing its head with her right leg and lifting its hind part by catching its tail. This relief sculpture which is found at proper left of the entrance of the cave temple has been generally dated in the early fifth century. I have been able to find a Javanese image of the goddess which bears close resemblance to the previous Indian example. The image, now kept in National Museum, Jakarta, originally came from Tenjolaya, Cicalengka, about 30 kms east of Bandung. The jewellery this eight-armed goddess is wearing, including the chain girdle with short ends indicates an early date like seventh century A.D. The dagger she is holding in one of her left hands is put into the hind part of the buffalo, while her lowest left hand holds the tail of the buffalo, thus trying to lift the animal from the hind part. This is exactly the same manner in which she is shown in the Indian example. The identity of the person sitting on the right side of the goddess is not clear. Thus it appears that in earlier Javanese images the extent of Indian influence was preponderant.

A close examination of some of the images of the goddess from central Java brings out two significant points, namely, first: whereas in the Indian representation the goddess usually has lion as her mount, in central Javanese images it is the buffalo which is invariably shown as the mount of the goddess; besides, in the central Javanese images both of her feet are resting on its back in the *samapāda sthānaka* pose. Secondly, the buffalo is not decapitated; the demon is actually emerging from the neck of the buffalo, carrying a dagger and a shield. In one of the earliest images from central Java, dated about A.D. 600 found at Magelang, north-west of Yogyakarta, the goddess has got eight hands as usual; in the left hands she is holding *śaṅkha*, shield, bow and the lowest hand holding the locks of the demon's hair. The right hands are holding *chakra*, dagger, trident and the buffalo's tail. Another image now kept in the Radyapustaka Museum in Surakarta is not dated and differs very little stylistically from similar images from central Java of A.D. 800. Most probably it belongs to the same period. Here the goddess is leaning her lowest left hand on the shield of the demon giving us the impression of blessing him. As usual, the buffalo is shown as the mount. The image of the goddess now kept in the National Museum, New Delhi, India, is shown ten-armed, holding the elongated tail of the buffalo in one of her right hands, while one of her left hands rests on the head of the demon emerging from behind the buffalo's head. It seems that she is holding locks of his hair. He appears to touch the sword which is in the sheath fastened to his waist. Like most of the central Javanese images, this one also shows buffalo as her mount and she is standing in a somewhat static *samapāda sthānaka* pose. In view of her standing pose and the manner in which she is dressed, that is to say, the waistband and other ornaments, I am inclined to think that the image in question is a product of central Java and that it should be assigned to about ninth century.

When we consider images of the goddess from east Java, a remarkable departure from the Indian iconographic tradition is further noticeable in the fact that there is no trace of combat and it appears that there is hardly any connection between the buffalo and the demon. It may also be noted that instead of holding the hair of the demon as it appears in earlier examples, in most of the east Javanese specimens she is shown touching the head of the so-called demon as if she is blessing him. Let us consider the well-known image of Mahishāsuramardinī from Singasari temple, east Java, dated in the thirteenth century, and now kept in the Museum voor Volkenkunde, Leiden, The Netherlands.[1] Unfortunately most of the arms of the goddess are broken. Yet it is possible to notice the general iconographic features. We do not fail to notice that in this case the so-called demon is shown separate from the buffalo. Significantly he is not shown brandishing his sword; on the contrary, he seems to hold his right hand in the *abhaya mudrā*, as if he is receiving blessings from the goddess. Like most of the images from east Java, the goddess is shown here standing on the buffalo with her legs widely apart—a device which seems to have grown out of the original *tribhaṅga* pose found in some of the central Javanese images. It is important to note that one of the left hands of the goddess is touching the head of the so-called demon as if she is blessing him. Thus an examination of certain images from central Java of the ninth and tenth centuries and most of the images from east Java of the thirteenth century tends to show that the Javanese sculptor was trying to evolve a way of depicting the episode which substantially differs from the corresponding Indian convention. In this rather stereotyped Javanese version, the combat aspect is reduced to the minimum and the benevolent and benign aspects of the goddess are emphasized. Incidentally it may be mentioned that in view of the spiritual expression present in the face of the goddess, this particular image has been praised for its sublime quality. In the words of H. Zimmer, "In the features of the great victress there is no trace of wrathful emotion; she is steeped in the serenity of eternal calm. The dramatic, climatic element is sublimated into a serene grandeur; sensuality is made subtle into a spiritual charm and gracefulness."[2] Another fine example of the image of Durgā Mahishāsuramardinī comes from Candi Jawi, east Java, assigned to the fourteenth century, and is now kept in Museum Tantular, Surabaya, east Java, Indonesia.[3] This statue displays many characteristics typical of the sublime east Javanese interpretation of the classical theme.

We may recall that this is the period (13th-14th centuries) which is considered to have been the last phase of the process of Indianization in ancient Java, and as such it is not altogether impossible that what is reflected in this particular representation of the goddess could have been the result of some sort of mingling of Indian iconographic tradition of Durgā Mahishāsuramardinī with an episode of Javanese origin connected with her. While searching for corroboration of such an episode in Old Javanese literary sources, I came across a passage in one of the major *kakawins* or Old Javanese poetical works, which refers to a visit to goddess Durgā by Abhimanyu, son of Arjuna. The literary work called *Ghaṭotkachāśraya* (Ghaṭotkacha as an ally) was a poem composed by Panuluh and was a product of Kaḍiri which flourished as a centre of culture and literature between the eleventh and thirteenth centuries. Late Professor R.M. Sutjipto Wirjosuparto who made a special study of this work (unpublished Ph.D. thesis in 1960, Universitas Indonesia, Jakarta), suggests that the poem was composed during the twelfth century. The story deals with the romance of Abhimanyu who fell in love with Kshitisundarī, the daughter of King Kṛshṇa. In section 30, verse 1 to section 32, verse 6, we are told that Abhimanyu went to the abode of goddess Durgā. "She appears, her hands outstretched to seize him, but halts when she hears his *mantras*. She listens to him worshipping her and praising her as the goddess who is one with the Supreme Being, and is merciful and generous to her devotees, but terrifying to her enemies, and she becomes so kindly disposed towards him that she favours him with her advice."[4] It is highly likely that the east Javanese sculptural representation of the goddess might have resulted from an adaptation of the original Indian iconographic tradition to this east Javanese episode of Abhimanyu's visit to Durgā as recorded in the *Ghaṭotkachāśraya*. If this literary evidence has any bearing upon the interpretation of the sculptural representation of the goddess in question, then the person portrayed by the proper left side of the goddess is certainly not the demon but Abhimanyu, who pleased her through worship for her advice. If this interpretation is accepted, then it would be much easier to explain the spiritual element in Durgā's representation.

Let us now pass on to the iconography of Gaṇeśa, the Hindu god of auspiciousness and remover of all obstacles, in ancient Java. The most distinctive feature of his sculptural representation is the manner in which he is shown seated. One of the magnificent specimens comes from the site of Candi Banon, central Java, assigned to ninth century, now kept in the National Museum, Jakarta. On a double-petalled lotus cushion, he sits with the soles of his feet facing each other. This particular posture was totally unknown in India and seems to have been a local Javanese innovation. It is possible that the Javanese sculptor was not very sure about the anthropomorphic aspect of the body of the elephant-headed god.

Another significant feature of the iconography of Gaṇeśa is this : Whereas in all the early images of Gaṇeśa the elephant-head is remarkably true to life, in later images there is an attempt to give it a human aspect; we notice unusually elongated trunk, and his eyes are human in shape with prominent eyebrows.

A significant departure from the Indian tradition is noticed when we examine some images of the Singasari period (thirteenth century) in east Java. The stone image from Bara near Blitar in east Java, dated A.D. 1239, has a skull bowl in Gaṇeśa's lower left hand and his seat is decorated with a row of skulls. To the same category belongs the well-known image of Gaṇeśa from the Singasari temple, now kept in the Rijksmuseum voor Volkenkunde, Leiden, dating from the end of the thirteenth century. Here skulls form an important and unique feature of the god's dress and ornaments—again a purely Javanese innovation. It is this feature which endows these images with a terrifying aspect.

Interestingly enough, this terrifying aspect of Gaṇeśa finds an echo in an Old Javanese literary work entitled *Smaradahana* by mpu Dharmaja (Kaḍiri period, second half of the twelfth century).[5] The son of Śiva and Umā is called Sang Hyang Gaṇa "who will by nature be a remover of obstacles and will destroy the enemies of the gods." A fierce battle has been referred to between the demon king Nīlarudraka and Sang Hyang Gaṇa (Gaṇeśa), and the battle finally led to the defeat of the demons. (Sections 24.1 to 37.14).[6] I am inclined to suggest that it is this terrifying aspect of Gaṇeśa found in *Smaradahana*, which might have inspired the iconography of Gaṇeśa images from east Java. Incidentally, according to *Smaradahana*, Gaṇeśa was born with an elephant's head. Javanese Gaṇeśa is invariably shown with four arms and there is no specimen of *nrtta* Gaṇapati. Also Gaṇeśa's mount, mouse, is conspicuous by its absence.

Needless to say, as we pursue a further study of images of Hindu pantheon, we come across more instances of such iconographic innovations. Indeed this is a fascinating aspect of the process of the spread of Indian cultural influence in early Java.

NOTES AND REFERENCES

1. *The Sculpture of Indonesia*, Catalogue of an Exhibition held at the National Gallery of Art, Washington, D.C., 1990, pp. 158-59.
2. H. Zimmer, *Myths and Symbols in Indian Art and Civilization*, p. 196.

3. *The Sculpture of Indonesia*, Catalogue of an Exhibition held at the National Gallery of Art, Washington, D.C., 1990, pp. 156-57.
4. P.J. Zoetmulder, *Kalangwan : A Survey of Old Javanese Literature,* 1974, p. 266.
5. *Bibliotheca Javanica*, edited by Dr. Poerbatjaraka, 1931.
6. P.J. Zoetmulder, *Kalangwan : A Survey of Old Javanese Literature,* 1974 p. 294.

77

NṚTTA–GAṆAPATI IN INDIA AND BEYOND ITS FRONTIERS*

SUDHA MALAIYA

Dance has always constituted the life breath of the culture of the world and especially of India, where not only mortals but immortals also dance. Galaxy of major gods and goddesses of Hindu pantheon dance. The elephant-headed Gaṇesha, the son of Śiva has also not remained a whit behind.

The mythology surrounding the origin and development of the iconography of Gajānana, as a deity to be worshipped, is steeped in a complete and inexplicable oblivion. There are frequent references in the early literature to Gaṇapati as a creator of obstacles—Vighnesha—and later as remover of obstacles—Vighnavināśaka. His origin has been traced by different scholars as early as to *Baudhāyana-Dharmasūtra, Yājñavalkya* and *Mānava-Gṛhasūtra*. However, without delving into the deep-rooted controversy over his origin, elephant head, single tusk, derivation of name, it is sufficient to state that by the time of Guptas his identity, as an independent deity to be worshipped was established. He has frequently been mentioned in *Matsya-Purāṇa* and *Varāha-Purāṇa*, and creative literature like *Kādamabrī, Malatīmādhava* and others.[1]

Gaṇesha achieved a very exalted position in the hierarchy of gods in a very short span of time. The general opinion is that his worship as an independent deity began in sixth century A.D. and by tenth century we come across an independent sect of his followers known as Gāṇapatya. Gaṇesha was also borrowed by other religious systems such as Buddhism and his worship spread almost all over Asia where Buddhism and other sects of Hindusim became living faiths. Gaṇesha travelled to distant lands along with Buddhism. In South-east Asia he was worshipped as a Hindu deity, whereas in Far East he was adored as a Buddhist deity. It is true that on either side of Bengal, in Buddhist as well as Brahmanic texts one deals with Indian ideas.

* This study is with special reference to central India.

No study of the different kinds of arts and culture of India is complete without the notice of the salient features of its important facets in countries far away across the sea where Indian religion and culture travelled. The texts of the famous Sanskrit inscriptions in Cambodia, Java and Bali which have parallels from the *Kāvya* literature, the popularity of the stories of *Mahābhārata* and *Rāmāyaṇa* as favourite themes in Javanese literature, dance, drama and musical orchestra and names of early rulers of Java, Thailand and Cambodia are all closely influenced by Indian culture. There survive the Indian traditions which have some times disappeared from India centuries ago. In harp of Burma is alive in the *vīṇā* of the Buddha period. The palaeography of the early inscriptions, the influence of Śaṅkarāchārya who achieved a synthesis of cults in India in the distinct lands as Funan all speak volumes of Indian influence on the art, religion and culture of these lands.

Gaṇesha's striking figure won all the Eastern countries in turn. In spite of his uncouth looks he was universally accepted. He got linked with thickset, stout and dwarf goblins and imps of Māra or *yakshas* or *rākshasas* or *gaṇas* on one hand, being given the rank of the chieftain of *gaṇas* as Gaṇesha, the 'Lord of Gaṇas' and on the other he became associated with Naṭarāja, the 'Lord of Dancers' as his son.

Unlike his father who is directly associated with the dance as its creator, Gaṇapati's association with dance is uncertain and obscure. While we have numerous references to the dance of Śiva in mythology, his adopted son lacks any episode to his credit. We do not come across any legend where Gaṇesha has actually danced. Yet his dance has fancifully been described in literature and epigraphic records and picturesquely been portrayed in art. Perhaps the universally accepted truth that *abhaṅgī, tribhaṅgī* and *atibhaṅgī* dance movements and fascinating poses look more attractive as compared to the simple standing postures, accounts for the abundance of the dancing images of almost all the gods and goddesses irrespective of his/her connection with dance. All the more Vināyaka has double reasons to be connected with dance. The inheritance of family traits from the parents who are the greatest exponents of *tāṇḍava* and *lāsya,* could be one and being the head of the dancing *gaṇas* of Bhūtesha, could be another. The genesis of Gaṇapati's dance can be traced in *Mahābhārata* where elephant-headed dancing gaṇa, along with others, is mentioned.[2]

Gaṇapati's relation with dance can also be traced in his obscure origins. Many believe that he was the village god-*Asfribaldie* worshipped by lower classes, the first one to be pacified and propitiated. At a very early date he was connected with the harvest ceremonies as the "Lord of the Harvest". As we know through the evidences, the rites and ceremonies as well as the deities associated with the harvest festival, mostly included dancing and were full of symbolic meaning. Was it that Gaṇesha in his dancing form became part of the ritual dancing? The elephant head suggesting his animal origin can also be traced back to the old superstitious totem worship and agrarian rites. The elephant holds an important place in Indian folklore through its height, unequalled strength, surprising docility and intelligence. Getty has suggested that his single tusk symbolically stands for the most important implement of the harvest, the plough, especially *Ekadanta* may be translated as ploughshare. However, his relation with Śiva and his ghost retainers *gaṇas* who also dance accounts for his association with dance more than anything.

In the literary texts and southern Śaiva literature, the symbolic, spiritual and aesthetic significance given to the dance of Gaṇesha is no less than his father's. Nṛtta Gaṇapati either represents the cosmic dance of Śiva—the supreme and indivisible one or the dance of *gaṇas* who are said to be the representations of *bhūtas* and *bhūtāṁshas* or *tattva* and *tattvaṁshas*. It is worth mentioning that name Gaṇesha in *Mahābhārata* is related to 'Śiva' and 'Gaṇapati' found in *Ṛgveda* to *Brahmaṇaspati* (Father of Gods).[3] Is it for this reason that we do not find any independent dancing episodes related to Gaṇesha? It is to be noted that some scholars consider Śiva and Gaṇesha originally one and the same god. Although Gaṇesha does not figure in the *Mahābhārata* as distinct from Śiva, he was none-the-less an aspect of Śiva and might, therefore, have been considered identical with Rudra Śiva, even if he was introduced into the Indian pantheon as Gaṇesha—'Lord of the Gaṇas'. In *Yājñavalkya,* the group of 4 *Vināyakas,* addressed as one god and son of Ambikā, according to Getty, may be considered as the earliest form of Gaṇapati whom Rudra appointed as the leader of Gaṇas or Gaṇapati Vināyaka, to create difficulties and obstacles if not properly propitiated. *Mahābhārata* lists 9 classes of benevolent deities, *i.e.* gaṇas who are to be called Gaṇeshas. Highlighting the symbolic significance, Someśwara and Vāsukalpa have graphically described in *Kathāsaritsāgara* and *Subhāṣita Ratnakoṣa,*[4] Gaṇeśvara's dance in which, showing the mirror to his father, he meticulously follows Śiva. Dancing in twilight like raising his trunk in rhythmic and measured fashion, the 'Victor of obstacles' threatens and swallows the obstacles and eliminates them, also assuring *tāla* and *laya.*[5] His delightful dance is imitated by the elephants of the quarters who spring up as the earth trembles at the stamping of his feet, says Vāsukalpa in *Subhāshitaratnakosha.*[6] He has also drawn a parallel of *ardhanārīśvara* in Śankara's son to bring him closer to his father. His single tusk— *skadanta*—provides him the hermaphroditic form—the tusk representing the masculine and the tuskless half, the feminine form. Gaṇesha is an expert of both. He assumes this guise in his anxiety to imitate his parents—Gaurī and Girīśa.[7] Another beautiful picture of dancing Gaṇesha represents his vermilion stained trunk upraised (*uḍdaṇḍitah karah*) like a coral handle for the moon close to the *ūrdhvatāṇḍava* of Śiva where his leg is thrown up as *daṇḍapāda.*[8]

The praises of the dance of the Naṭarāja's son have also been sung in inscriptions. In the fourth verse of the Koni inscription of Prithivīdeva II of Ratanpur,[9] the poet invokes blessings of Vighnavināśaka, the son of two mothers or *dvaimātura* who destroys obstacles by the humming of bees intoxicated by the drinking of sweet juice that gushes forth with force at the commencement of his dance. Another beautiful picture of the dancing Pārvatīnandana is given in the Ratanpur stone inscription of Prithivīdeva II[10] (year 1207) where not only the large forehead or his frontal globes, *i.e.* the *kumbhasthala* of Vighneshvara are described as stained with brilliant vermilion and the *ugra tāṇḍava* of his trunk also colours the pavilion of the sky of the whole universe.

According to the *Āgamas,* the image of nṛtta-Gaṇapati should have eight hands and one head. But examples of four, six, eight, ten, twelve, sixteen and eighteen-armed images with two, three, four or five heads also occur frequently. In Bombay, a two-headed image called Gaṇesha-Jayantī is locally being worshipped at festivals.[11] Gaṇesha with three or four heads[12] (Japan and Indo-China) and four or five heads[13] (Nepal) is found only outside India. He is ornamented with *sarpayajñopavīta,* overhead snake, *keyūra, kaṅkaṇa, karaṇḍamukūṭa, prabhāmaṇḍala* and *ekamuktāvalīhāra,* with arms carrying his usual attributes—axe, *modaka,*[14] *kuṭhāra, jambu* (wood apple), radish, stylus, a bowl of capes, *sūla* (lasse), *aṅkusha* (gourd), book, sword, pot, snake, one tusk, etc. The radish found in Nepal, Tibet and Japan might be the misinterpretation of tusk.[15] It is noteworthy that in Bengal Ganesha is known as the one with ears like fan and teeth like radish. Pomegranate,[16] the emblem of fertility and *chintāmaṇi*[17] in Nepal and Tibet are also found in esoteric forms. Sometimes instead of *yajñopavīta* he wears snake girdle. Alongwith the iconographic details the *nṛtta* Gaṇapati images have been analysed in terms of vocabulary of dance as discussed in the Nāṭyaśāstra.[18] The latter not only played a dominant role in the realm of theatre but also exercised an indispensable influence on other arts in India.

The evolution of the image of Gaṇesha can the traced in the form of Gajānana-Yakshamūrti. An elephant-headed image on the Amarāvatī railings is considered to be the prototype of Gaṇesha by the scholars,[19] though with reservations by some. It cannot be said with certainty that without the transitional stage there had, out of no where, came the completed form of Gaṇesha. Though elephant-headed divinities of lesser rank were known in south and north India, Indo-China and Chinese Turkestan, but without Gaṇesha's attributes.[20] By the time of the Guptas his iconography was fully developed. His independent images are found at Mathura,[21] Bhumra[22] and Udaigiri. The earliest representation of the dance of Gaṇapati started appearing only in Gupta period which proliferated in medieval period.

Out of the three Gaṇesha images mentioned by Getty the dancing Gaṇesha image No. 1064, preserved at Mathura Museum, is the first example of its kind. The two-armed elephant-headed *gaṇa* like dancing figure (Pl. 77.1) from Bhumra might as well be taken as the *nṛtta*-Gaṇapati image. Yet, the possibility of its merely a *gaṇa* cannot be ruled out. The most important early example is from Rājīvalochana temple, Rajim (Pl. 77.2). It has an eight-armed *nṛtta*-Gaṇapati with its fully developed iconography and implements. At Bādamī[23] and Aihole he is depicted smaller in size standing in a slightly dancing pose in attendance on dancing Śiva in *sama-tryaśra* feet position which is very near to *vaishṇavasthānaka*[24] as well as the initial position of so many *karaṇas*. In few examples he is quite close to *kaṭisama-karaṇa*[25] where he is shown with one hand on *udvahita kati*.[26] Many Naṭarāja and *gaṇa* figures are also shown in the same pose.

In a number of examples one foot is in *kuñchita* (only toes touching the ground and heel raised) and other in *samapāda* (normal foot position) as seen in the four-armed Paramāra example from Hinglajgarh (Pl. 77.3) whose broken left hand must have been on *Raṭi* (hip). The *aṅguliprṣhthaga*[27] foot, kept on the toe back is the characteristic feature of the contemporary dancing sculptures of India. The presence of third eye is significant which does not occur that frequently as in the images of Śiva.

Another example from Hinglajgarh also has it where he is dancing in the accompaniment of a *paṇavavādika* on his right. The right hand is held in *allapallava*[28] near the shoulder and left is kept on the *kaṭi*. The presence of Māheśvarī and Sarasvatī in upper *parikara* are peculiar Paramāra characteristics. In an example of dancing Gaṇesha in Indore Museum there is Naṭarāja in the upper *parikara* flanked with Māheśvarī and Sarasvatī on the sides, a feature not to be regularly seen. Among its Chandela contemporary from Khajuraho is the example from the Kandariya Mahādeva temple, with the only difference that here the right hand is held on the right knee in *kaṭakāmukha.*[29] The *mārdaṅgika* on his left and the snake in his left hand are noteworthy. The Chandela and Kalachuri parallels from Bandakapur and Damoh are no different from these.

One of the outstanding examples is the dancing Vināyaka figure in a gaṇeshapaṭṭa of 9 Vināyakas now preserved at Vikram Museum, Ujjain (Pl. 77.4). Its exact identification remains to be made. They could be the same 9-class of benevolent deities, mentioned in the *Mahābhārata* to be called Gaṇesha's. The eight-armed *nṛtta*-Gaṇapati from Malhar portrays the typical dance pose of this period (Pl. 77.5). It is *lalita karaṇa*[30] with right *vivartita* and left *katihasta* and a *kuṭṭita pāda*. Occurring very frequently throughout in the art of India from 5th to 13th centuries A.D., this pose is being represented by Naṭarājas and *gaṇas* as well. Except for the difference in the conventional attributes of Gaṇesha, Naṭarājas and *gaṇas*, the treatment of the body is just the same. The Gajavaktra from Ujjain (Pl. 77.6) depicted with one leg uplifted and the knee facing side ways represents the *pārśvajānu karaṇa*,[31] holding the ears like Śiva holds the snake over his head. However, the eight-armed Gaṇapati from Hinglajgarh can also be seen representing *ūrdhvajānu*[32] with overhead snake and one tusk in his right hand (Pl. 77.7). This reminds us of the tempestuous *tāṇḍava* of Gaṇapati trampling the earth by his tread as fancied by poet Vāsukalpa. The *ūrdhvajanu* is ideally represented by the *gaṇas* and Naṭarājas of central India. There are examples of a clear *daṇḍapaksha karaṇa*[33] also with the knee facing upwards in *ūrdhvajānu* and one arm extended staff-like in *daṇḍapakṣa hasta.*[34]

While there are many scenes of Śiva dancing in the company of goddesses acting as accompanists, there are few such examples of dancing Gaṇesha where he dances with accompanists represented in the same size (Pl. 77.8). The four-armed Gaṇapati from Sagar district, dancing in the company of female flautist and drummer, is one of its own kind. The examples of Gaṇapati dancing amidst Vīrabhadra and *saptamātṛkās* who are the feminine counterparts of seven great Brāhmaṇa gods created in Andhakāsura battle and Vīrabhadra are many and found at various places. The large panel preserved at Allahabad Museum from Gurgī,[35] is a masterpiece sculpture. But the one found carved at the *siradala* of Toraṇa-Mandira at Gyaraspur is unique in many respects (Pl. 77.9). Gaṇesha is seen here representing the well known bronze Naṭarāja pose. The earliest dancing Śiva image in this pose, predating its southern counterpart, is found in north India at Bhumra and has also been represented by *gaṇas*. Surprisingly this pose vanished altogether from north India after Gupta period, which became so popular in south India. We have not yet come across any further examples of either Naṭarāja or *gaṇa* or Gaṇapati in late period other than these. The pose has not been represented even by any other dance sculpture, barring the sole example from Lakshmaṇa temple, Khajuraho, where in a panel of few *gaṇa*-like figures, one is shown in the same pose. One more striking feature of this panel is that here Vīrabhadra is multi-armed and he is seen dancing on a trampled human figure. Is it *apasmāra*? As there are no other examples of *apasmara's* presence in north India which is totally a south Indian feature, its exact identification remains to be done and calls for an independent research. The examples of Vighnāntaka dancing in the company of *navagrahas* as seen in southern and eastern art, are conspicuously absent in north and central India. Inheriting the other musical traits of his father Gaṇesha is also an adept in all the musical instruments and is taken to be the *rasas* personified. Tradition has it that Gaṇesha almost brought into being the drum as an accompaniment for dance.[36] A sculptural representation of Gaṇesha playing on flute is found at Mallikārjuna temple, Srisailam. But in central India no such example has so far been seen barring the very few examples where he is acting as an accompanist to his father's dance.

The *svastika-pāda* or cross-legged feet position, represented frequently in Gupta period through the Naṭarājas is not seen in *gaṇa* and Gaṇapati figures. The *vṛśchika-pāda*[37] and *lalāṭatilaka*[38] or *ūrdhvatāṇḍava*, a pose so frequently depicted in the art of south India and represented by only the *gaṇas* of Gupta period in north India, remained unrepresented by *nṛtta*-Gaṇapati images and Naṭarājas of central India. The twisted waist and posterior views portrayed in Paramāra and Chandela Naṭarājas, are also significantly absent, but for the above-mentioned Gyaraspur example. Perhaps the artists did not take the risk of depicting the pot-bellied and elephant-headed god with twisted waist!

The vehicle of Gaṇesha is also depicted in a manner similar to Śiva, usually on the right side and at times below the *pādapīṭha*. The tradition of Śiva dancing on bull is also imitated by Gaṇesha who can be seen dancing on the rat in a small temple of Rehli (Sagar) though occasionally. Ekadanta has also adopted Chandraśekhara's *ardhachandra* on his head, justifying his name Bhālachandra. There is, however, a striking dissimilarity in the vehicles of father and son. If Śiva's Nandī takes equal delight in his Master's dance, either by himself sharing the pleasure of dancing or faithfully watching the performance, Gaṇapati's *mūshaka* is always seen busy having his share of the *prasāda* instead of observing his Lord's performance as a keen spectator. *Karaṇḍamukuṭa* is strikingly absent in many examples. He does wear a skull head like his father but only in Java examples and not in Indian ones. Similarly the conch-shell which is seen in the examples from Indochina is also absent here.

Khotan, Mongolia and Afghanistan

In Khotan, Ganesha images are found with Indian as well as typical features of Chinese Turkestan but *nṛtta*-Gaṇapati is altogether absent. In Mongolia Hinduism reached with Buddhism via Tibet in 13th century. The dancing form of Gaṇesha is even listed among the 'Five Hundred gods of Nar-than', with left foot kept on rat and the right leg bent and the four hands holding axe, radish, sweets and trident (seldom carried by him). Nevertheless, no Gaṇesha in dancing attitude can be seen. None of the examples (5th-6th century) available from Afghanistan, is in dancing attitude. However, it is interesting to note such an early representation of Gaṇesha in the land of 'Ariana' which was of course made a part of India at one time.

Nepal

Introduction of Gaṇesha in Nepal is difficult to date but existing sculptural evidence shows that he became quite popular by 10th century and was adored by both Hindus and Buddhists. In Buddhism he is 'Siddhidātā', 'Bestower of success' and a mystic *mantra Gaṇapatihṛdaya*[39] revealed to Ānanda by Buddha is associated to him by tradition. A large number of Gaṇesha images have been found in Nepal, yet independent dancing Gaṇesha sculptures are absent. However, in Buddhist art of Nepal and Tibet Gaṇesha is represented as a Hindu demon called Vināyaka, crouching under the feet of lotus throne of Buddhist goddess *Bhrkuṭi-Tāra*.[40] At the same time as Buddhist god Vināyaka, he had to be depicted in his dancing attitude but is rarely met with except in paintings.[41] In India *nṛtta*-Gaṇapati, if painted, had to be conceived in yellow with bent right leg and left one raised up in *ūrdhvajānu* and with four to 16 arms carrying the conventional attributes. But in Nepal he is conceived in red with 12 arms, third eye, ornamented crown, standing on rat and with one uplifted leg in extreme position.[42] His 10 arms carry usual *tāntrika* symbols and rest of the two carry radish and *chintāmaṇi* in place of tusk and *modaka* as seen in Indian examples. He is also surrounded by four Vināyakas—*Rakta, Chandra, Siddhi* and *Ashoka*—all in dancing attitude, thus making an assembly of five deities. It indicates the group of Buddhist gods with central figure known as Sūrya Vināyaka. It is to be noted that in Nepal along with other temples of Gaṇesha,[43] a Buddhist temple dedicated to five Gaṇapatis is found. Nepalese tradition traces his origin not from any of the Hindu legends in which Śiva and Pārvati created him but he became visible in a sunray, hence his name Sūrya-Vināyaka.

In stone or bronze Gaṇesha is found dancing only in attendance to his parents in many examples. In a number of Umā-Maheśvara images found in Nepal he is represented as four-armed dancing Gaṇesha in the lower tier with the *gaṇas*. The earliest of the typical, well preserved steles[44] showing Umā-Maheśvara with Gaṅgādhara aspect in the usual setting and composition and full component of family members and attendants, (*circa* 9th century), is from the Kumbheśvara tank, Patan. It shows Śiva and Pārvatī seated on Kailāsa in *padmāsana* and *sukhāsana* respectively. Gaṅgā is shown on the top as descending headlong. On the pedestal forming the lowest tier is represented four-armed Gaṇesha dancing together with *gaṇas*: the seated Uluka-mukha playing flute, dancing Kumbhāṇḍa on his left and dancing Ghanṭākarṇa, Bhṛṅgī, Siṁhamukha playing on drum and seated Vānaramukha playing on cymbals. Gaṇesha is dancing in *ardhamaṇḍalī* position with both the *tryasra* feet apart in *maṇḍalasthānaka*. His left main hand is broken and right is perhaps in *varadapatāka hasta*.

Another stele[45] from Gairidhara, Patan, in Gaṅgādhara aspect is with typical Nepalese faces representing Śiva and Pārvatī in *ardhaparyṅkāsana*. In the lower tier four-armed Gaṅesha is seen dancing together with Bhṛṅgī and Kumbhāṇḍa on either sides and other *gaṇas* playing on instruments. In another stele from Giridhara, Patan (12th century) Gaṇesha is represented in the initial position of *pārśvajānu* with uplifted leg facing side ways (Pl. 77.10). The main right arm is spread out staff-like that brings him closer to the *daṇḍapaksha-karaṇa*. Other hands carry usual attributes. Another example[46] of the same category from Patan, also has four-armed Gaṇesha in lower tier dancing similarly though with different leg this time. The depiction of the Himalayan hill-scape by conical configuration is noteworthy.

Ten-armed and five-headed Gaṇesha mounted on lion and known as 'Heramba' is the most popular form of Gaṇesha in Nepal. Though non-dancing, mention can be made of the two or three Heramba images or which show a rat or rat and lion under each foot of the god and a five-hooded *nāga* over the head.[47] The pose can be identified in dance terminology with *ālīḍha-sthānaka*. According to Dhavalikar this appears to have been borrowed from one of the dancing forms of Śiva and Naṭarāja and shows Gaṇesha's connection with Śiva. That the Nepalese were acquainted with Naṭarājas as well as *nṛtta*-Gaṇapati images of north India, is also clear from the examples in Nepal of *nṛtta*-Gaṇesha holding snake overhead which is very common in India. Though no panel of Gaṇesha dancing with seven mothers is discovered from Nepal but in a temple at Kirtipur, eight *devīs* are represented. The eighth possibly is looked upon as the Śakti of Gaṇesha. The *ashṭamātṛkā* panel does not exist in India.

Tibet

Gaṇesha never became popular in Tibetan pantheon of Mahāyāna Buddhism where he is either accorded the role of *dvārapāla* or was degraded to the point of being trodden under the foot of Mahākāla, Aparājitā, Vighnāntaka or Mañjuśrī. No dancing image of Gaṇesha has so far been traced in Tibet.

Burma, Siam and Indo-China

Alongwith the trader colonists from India to Burma, Thailand (Siam) and Indo-China (Cambodia and Vietnam) started the process of Indianization of these countries with the adoption of Buddhism and the worship of Indian gods. Indeed the finds of sculptures, in the style of 'Later Āndhras' in Java and Celebes indicate the spread of Indian Buddhism all over South-eastern Asia. The Indian origins are evident on pre-Khmer civilization of 5th, 6th and 7th centuries. Names of the kings after natural regions of India and Śiva reveal close Indian contacts. Brick ornamentation of the temple of Sambor (Cambodia) suggests Indian precedent of Sirpur and Bhitargaon. The Śiva Temple of Bayang (Burma) reminds us of the shrine at Bhīma's *rath* at Mamallapuram. Sculptures of pre-Khmer period reveal an indebtedness to Indian models and are so closely related to Gupta sculptures that the possibility of their having been carved by Indian craftsmen cannot be disregarded. There had been a continuous alternation between Buddhism and Hinduism throughout the history of Cambodia.

A professedly Buddhist country, Hinduism penetrated into Burma long before Buddhism, which is evident from the large number of Hindu gods found in the country. Traders looking forward to the success in trade carried the "Remover of Obstacles" with them. Statues of Gaṇesha have been found in lower Burma especially in the deltaic region, but none of them is of our interest. Siam also came into contact with India at a very early period and the influence of the Amarāvatī school and then Gupta, Pallava and Pāla elements are noticeable in Siamese art. Mons were devout Hindus. Gaṇesha became popular with the Buddhists as with the Brahmins. But again no dancing Gaṇesha image is found in Ayuthian (Ayodhya) art of Central Siam. The cult of Śiva penetrated into Cambodia from Funan, where Brahmanism was practised at a very early date. There are many temples of Śiva and Gaṇesha dedicated to them (Prasat Bak, 10th century temple). However, Khmer representations of Gaṇesha, also known as Prah Kenes, contain rare independent dancing examples. The dancing Gaṇesha accompanying the 'Lord of Dancers' is available in the temples of Shri Vijaya, Benteaisrei (9th century A.D.), Phnom Chisor, and Baset. In a lintel[48] from Prah Pithu representing ten-armed Śiva dancing with Brahmā and Vishṇu keeping time for him, depicts Gaṇesha as one of the spectators in slightly dancing attitude. In Champa also, the principal Brahmanic cult was of Śiva. Cham dynasty held Śaivism in such a high esteem that it claimed direct descent from Śiva. Epigraphical evidences show that temples were dedicated to Gaṇesha and images of Gaṇesha found, prove the popularity of Gaṇesha cult. The depiction of *ushṇīsha*, similar to Buddha's, on Gaṇesha's head speaks of the Buddhist influence on Hindu images. However, no dancing Gaṇesha is seen in Champa. At Ben-Mala and Banteai Samre are other dancing Śiva[49] flanked by Umā and Gaṇesha (9th century A.D.). Prof. Coedas has described a few dancing figures of Śiva from Angkor Vat and Ben Mealea where Naṭarāja is accompanied by Gaṇesha along with other gods and celestials joining his dance in great glee.

Indonesia

Brahmanism flourished in Malay Archepelago as early as 5th century when Fahien visited Java (Yava-dvīpa) and reported many sanctuaries dedicated to the Lord of the Trident up-till 8th century AD. Images of Gaṇesha also started appearing in great number. But there is no existing evidence of Gaṇesha temples or prevalence of ancient Gaṇesha cult. No images have so far been recovered in Indonesia of our interest except for one exception from Ardmelijo, near Singasari reported by Dhaky, in which a triad of three deities (Java), Gaṇesha is in a slightly dancing pose. He is standing to the right of Nepalese goddess Guhyeśvarī, to the left of whom is Chakrachakra.

In Bālī, Gaṇesha was worshipped amongst the group of five deities, Śiva, Durgā, Vishṇu, Sūrya and Gaṇesha. But no evidence of an actual Gaṇesha cult has been found which justifies the great number of Gaṇesha images in Bali where he is worshipped as 'Protector against Evil Spirit' especially in tjandi niches. In another form he is invariably present to the extreme right of Balinese groups of deified personages in which form he must have been worshipped as "Remover of obstacles". But again no dancing Gaṇesha image exists in Bali.

China and Japan

Despite the fact that the earliest dated image of Gaṇesha is found in China referring to him as the "Spirit King of Elephants" there exists no *nṛtta*-Gaṇapati image. One of the two forms of Gaṇesha known in China and Japan, the single form is known as Vināyaka, the other double one called Kāngiten, is connected with dance.

Conclusion

Notwithstanding Gaṇapati's ungainly elephant head, cunning little eyes and uncouth looks, short arms, bulging girth overhanging his stunted legs and huge trunk swayed on both the sides, these images convey a certain sense of dynamism and rhythm together with humour as the essence of art. As regards India, wherever the artists used their creative genius, the results were astounding. The lack of imagination had, however, often resulted in stereotyped mass production. The stylisation of the iconography of Gaṇapati also accounts perhaps for the lesser variety. As regards *nṛtta*-Gaṇapati beyond Indian frontiers, the above analysis reveals that although Gaṇesha was equally popular in distant lands, his dance form, except in Nepal, did not enjoy similar popularity as did his father. Surprisingly, there is no lack of evidence of other non-secular and secular music and dance sculptures especially in Burma (Śrīkshetra and Pagan), Indonesia (Lara-djjongrang, Prambanan, Borobudur), Thailand, Champa and Cambodia. They followed more or less a dance style, identical in principles of movement, proving thereby an active dialogue that was not copying or influence but an interaction of form and technique, with regional distinctiveness. The stylization in sculpture and dance in India and beyond its frontier emerges from basic *ardhamaṇḍalī* position. It is, therefore, amazing to note the conspicuous absence of independent dancing Gaṇesha images in these countries when his father's dancing form proliferates.

NOTES AND REFERENCES

1. See, Alice Getty, *Ganeṣa*, Delhi, 2nd Ed., 1971, pp. 1-9.
2. See, Sudha Malaiya, "Dancing Gaṇas in Early Art of Madhya Pradesh", *Bājpeya*, Delhi, 1987, pp. 177-81.
3. *Ibid.*, pp. 2-5.
4. See, C. Sivaramamurti, *Naṭarāja in Art, Thought and Literature*, Delhi, 1965, pp. 70, 71.
5. *Kathāsaritsāgara* of Someśvara, 27.1.
6. *Subhāshitaratnakośa* of Vāsukalpa, 5.13.
7. *Kathāsarit sāgara*, 105, 2 and 51.1.
8. *Subhāshitaratnakośa*, 5.24.
9. *Corpus Inscriptionum Indicarum*, 4, p. 465.
10. *Corpus Inscriptionum Indicarum*, 4, p. 485.
11. Getty, *ibid.*, p. 14, Fig. 1.
12. *Ibid.*, pl. 27 (c), in Indo-China, in a private collection, a small bronze image with four heads.
13. Five-headed form of Gaṇesha was most popular in Nepal with four heads pointing to each cardinal points and fifth on top; see, Getty, *ibid.*, pp. 15 & 7 from Dacca also, in an example, the five heads are on the same tier, i.e. two heads on the either side of the central head. See, Getty, *ibid.*, pl. 4(b).
14. *Modaka, jambu*, radish, stylus and bowl of cakes are held by no other deity. *Modaka* is looked upon by certain sects as representing Mahā-Buddhi and others as germ of life.
15. It is never carried by Gaṇesha at the same time as the broken tusk; Getty, *ibid.*, p. 18.
16. Goblet d' Alviella, *La Migration des Symboles*, p. 184.
17. *Modaka* is replaced by *chintāmaṇi* in Tibetan paintings.
18. The *Nātyaśāstra* composed by Bharata Muni is the largest and ancient available text on the art of histrionics which deals largely with the art of theatre, dance and music put together.
19. Coomaraswamy and Jouveau-Dubreuil. See *Amarāvatī*, Burgess, pl. 30, no. 1.
20. Getty, *ibid.*, p. 26, is of the opinion that though earliest terracotta image of Gaṇesha was found at the ancient site of Akra, N.W.F.P., where pre-Gupta objects of as early as the second century have been discovered, yet it is not earlier than the fifth century.
21. Getty, *ibid.*, pl. 2(a), from Sankisa mound, Mathura.
22. *Ibid.*, pl. 3(b).
23. See, Sivaramamurti, *op. cit.*, p. 179, Fig. 17.
24. *N.S.*, Vaishṇava sthānaka.
25. *N.S.*, *Katisama karaṇa. Karaṇa* is basic unit of dance composition, composed of hand and feet movements.
26. *N.S.*, 9. 249(b).
27. *Nṛtta-Ratnāvalī* of *Jāyasenāpati*, 2. 336(b).
28. *N.S.*, 9.91, 9th chapter deals with gestures of hands.
29. *N.S.*, 9.61.
30. *N.S.*, 4.93, one hand stretched across the body, one foot kept on toes and the other hand held near the ear in *allapallava-hasta* is *lalita karaṇa.*

31. *N.S.*, 4.133 (73rd *karaṇa*).
32. *N.S.*, 4.85 (25th *karaṇa*).
33. *N.S.*, 4.94 (34th *karaṇa*).
34. *N.S.*, 9.203.
35. Now preserved at Allahabad Museum, this is one of the most beautiful examples.
36. *Epigraphica Indica*, 5, p. 144.
37. One leg raised backward like a scorpion's tail, is *vṛshchikapāda*.
38. Where the *vṛshchikapāda* touches the forehead it is *lalāṭatilaka*. But in the sculpture it is represented most of the time, erect without any bend in which position it is identified by scholars as *ūrdhvatāṇdava*. Technically, however, this pose is close to *vidutbhrānta karaṇa* (64), *N.S.*, 4.125.
39. *The Sanskrit Buddhist Literature of Nepal*, R. Mitra, Calcutta 1882, quoted by Getty, *op. cit.*, p. 37.
40. *Iconography of Buddhist and Brahmanical Sculptures in the Dacca Museum*, N.K. Bhattasali, Dacca, 1929, Pl. xix.
41. Getty, *Gaṇesha*, p. 38.
42. Getty, *Gaṇesha*, p. 38, pl. 20(a).
43. Sylvain Levi, *Le Nepal*, Vol. II, p. 345. Near Zimpi-Tandu an ancient temple is dedicated to Gaṇesha, dating roughly from 8th to 10th centuries.
44. See, Dhaky, "Śiva images from Nepal", *Discourses on Śiva*, pp. 32 to 37, Pl. 47.
45. *Ibid.*, Pl. 48.
46. K. Deva, "Images of Nepal", *Discourses on Shiva*, Pl. 49.
47. Getty, *Gaṇesha*, p. 38.
48. Sivaramamurti, *op. cit.*, p. 357, Fig. 14.
49. *Ibid.*, p. 357, Fig. 15.

78

CONTRIBUTIONS OF INDIAN BUDDHIST MONKS TO CHINESE PAINTING

UPENDRA THAKUR

I

Painting as an independent art was practised in China since early times, but our knowledge about the earliest forms of this art is too meagre to arrive at definite conclusions as to its beginnings and initial significance. From the account given in the old chronicles we learn that in the beginning painting was done mainly for moral and ceremonial purposes rather than for purely decorative or aesthetic ends. It was during the time of Yu, i.e., the reign of Emperor Shun (B.C. 2317-2208) that painting became quite explicit, and variegated colours came to be gradually applied with the result that 'the pictures became more like the objects.'[1] This period witnessed great expansion of ritual and music which in turn promoted the development of culture.

Speaking of the early wall paintings in China we are reminded of the Buddhist wall paintings at Tun-huang, on the westernmost border of China proper. Situated very close to the Tun-huang oasis is the so-called Chi'en-fo tung (Caves of the Thousand Buddhas) which forms 'the largest agglomeration of Buddhist cave-temples'[2] that grew up at various places along the trade-routes between China, Central Asia and India during the fourth-twelfth centuries A.D. Though most of these foundations are now in dilapidated conditions, some of them have become known through illustrated publications such as *Wan fo-tung, Tung Chi'en-fo tung, Hsi Chi'en-fotung*, and *Ping-ling Ssü*. In this part of China, artistic activities flourished abundantly in the service of Buddhist devotion and some of the remains at these cave-temples are fine examples of paintings and sculptures of the Northern and Eastern Wei periods as well as from the T'ang dynasty which no doubt occupy a prominent place in the history of Chinese art. The scenes depicted in these caves represent invariably the legends associated with the life-story of the Buddha as well as episodes narrated in the *Jātakas* which constitute excellent examples of the earliest style.

It is interesting to note that most of the motifs are inspired from the *Lalita-vistara* or some corresponding account of the life of the last human Buddha. We notice here the scenes depicting the birth of Prince Siddhārtha, the events of his early life and other familiar events such as horses and wagons, hunters chasing deer, a ploughman with his ox, etc. Judging by the formal characteristics of the Sui art it may be said that the artists followed 'the general line of some picture chronicles which had been elaborated somewhere in Central Asia before they became known in China'.[3] The well-established inter-communications between Tun-huang and the oasis along the roads further west were evidently maintained in the Sui period as illustrated by paintings in several caves.

As we know, Bāmiyan Valley was one of the important halting places in Central Asia for nearly a thousand years. Situated midway between Bactria (Balkh) and Purushapura (Peshawar) upon the highway that linked Central Asia with India, caravans halted there to refit after the strenuous exertion involved in crossing the passes of the Hindukush mountains. It was here that religious foundations developed rapidly under the impetus given by sovereigns who favoured Buddhism such as Kanishka and his successors (first to third century A.D.).[4] The relentless pressure of Islam in the second half of the seventh century A.D., however, weakened the political prestige of Iran which greatly affected the peaceful valley. The monks of Bāmiyan fled, out of fear, abandoning their work, turned towards India and received new inspiration from there—unquestionably the influence of Gupta art to which they literally succumbed.

It was in the course of excavating ruins of Buddhist sanctuaries at Miran, to the south of Lop-nor, that Aurel Stein discovered mural paintings, executed in tempera, representing certain episodes in *Vessantara Jātaka*,[5] whose author was certain Titus by name who might have been 'a sort of Roman Eurasian, largely Oriental by blood, but brought up in Hellennistic traditions... whom his calling had carried, no doubt, through the regions of Eastern Iran, impregnated with Buddhism to the very confines of China'.[6] The paintings in the rock sanctuaries at Kizil show compositions that are very Chinese in appearance, scrolls of foliage, elegantly treated, closely resembling the goldsmith's work of the T'ang period (7th-8th century A.D.); some Buddhist divinities presage the excessive gesticulation of the Japanese Foudo. It is striking to observe how strongly Indian influences are displayed in the forgotten sanctuary in eastern Kashgaria, in surroundings so favourable to the development of influences from China which lay closely.[7]

II

A study of the animal sculptures of China would show that the main sources of inspiration for the motifs (Buddhist motifs) were of Indian origin, though they were more or less modified in accordance with local traditions as they passed through intermediary regions before they reached China. As we know, the distance between India and the Middle Kingdom was long, and the journey difficult. The travellers had therefore to choose between the southern sea-route along the Indo-Chinese coast and the northern caravan-routes across the Gobi desert and Central Asia. As Buddhist art had taken deep roots in these areas earlier than in China, it is natural that 'it sometimes reached China in a form which was no longer purely Indian'.[8] However, the fundamental conceptions and iconographic formulae remained the same, though their artistic interpretation varied considerably in different countries. But, on the whole, the Chinese seem to have been 'less interested in the iconographic meaning of Buddhist imagery than in its artistic formulation'.[9]

Very little is known about the earliest beginnings of Buddhist art in China. From the annals of the Eastern Han dynasty we learn that Buddhist sculptures and paintings were made in the beginning of the third century (A.D. 190-220).[10] Though there is evidence to prove that there existed in the fifth century A.D. a Southern School of Buddhist art based on south Indian influences, said to have reached China by the sea-route, the representation of the Buddha in *abhaya* and *varada mudrās* certainly reminds us of Indian sculptures from Mathurā of the late Kushāṇa and early Gupta periods.[11] As regards sculptures and paintings, the formal treatment as well as the types so closely resemble the Gupta style that we may be justified in supposing that 'a direct influence from India had reached the artists who were active at T'ien-lung Shan. Indian monks may have come to this place, which was not very distant from Wu-tai Shan, a place of pilgrimage famous also in the homeland of Buddhism'.[12] This Indian influence subsisted at T'ien-lung Shan also in the T'ang period, as is evident from many artistic specimens of the period.

It is interesting to note that northern China received influences from northern India during the fifth and sixth centuries A.D. through southern or northern transcontinental route. In earlier times these influences came through various Buddhist centres from Tumchuk to Tun-huang; in later times, however, 'they were transmitted in a purer form by Indian and Chinese pilgrims who served as messengers of religions and art'.[13] Besides these, some influences from southern India or Indo-China found their way into China proper by the sea-route. The historical records of the period clearly tell us that the religious and political emissaries who travelled between China and Cambodia, the then kingdom of Funan, used this route very frequently.[14] Several kings of Funan were devoted Buddhists and they kept up inter-communications with India and took a keen interest in the propagation of Buddhist faith and art. They also sent several embassies and missionaries to China with gifts including statues of the Buddha and sacred writings. When the kingdom of Funan was conquered by Chen-la (*c.* A.D. 627), this country continued to send envoys and gifts to the court of T'ang with the result that the artistic traditions of Funan found their way into Central China, though it is very difficult to trace the influence because all the art under the Liang and their predecessors has perished.

It may however be safely presumed that some influences from the southern regions reached Northern Chi dynasty and there are yet certain specimens of painting and sculpture which may possibly be taken as indications of such direct or indirect influences from southern India.[15] For instance, the two large reliefs in the Freer Gallery in Washington representing a 'Buddha Paradise' and scenes of 'Adoration of Buddha' as seen in the cave-temples of Nan-hsiang T'ang, reproduce pictorial compositions more or less of the kind we know from the Tun-huang paintings. Though the resemblance is remote, the artistic expression is more distinctly Indian than in any of those paintings.[16] 'The types of the figures, their comparatively free and varied postures and the draping of the Buddha's mantle over one shoulder (in the Paradise scene) and rather south Indian features. Indian reliefs of quite corresponding character may not be so easily found, nor is it likely that such would have been known to the artists who worked at Nan-hsiang T'ang, but if we turn to the sculptures from Nāgārjunikoṇḍā... we may observe in them essential features of style and composition which correspond to those pointed out in the reliefs from Nan-hsiang T'ang'.[17] It seems that this south Indian style of the third-fourth century presumably exercised a decisive influence on the Buddhist art of Funan, from where it may have been transmitted to China in a somewhat modified form.

The renewed Indian influences which caused these modifications reached China by the overland route rather than by the sea-route; it was the one followed by most of the pilgrims and envoys who at the beginning of the T'ang period greatly strengthened the links of art and religion between China and India which brought about certain modifications also in the field of painting.

III

The paintings decorating the sanctuaries of Chi'en-fo tung do not bear the painter's signature or name and the names that we actually come across in some of the inscriptions do not refer to the painters, but to the donors. In other words, we have no documentary evidence about the artists at all. For instance, the inscription on the memorial tablet set up in A.D. 698 informs us that the first chapel dedicated to the Buddha at Chi'en-fo tung was made in A.D. 366 by the Indian monk Lotsun, which was followed by another chapel by another Indian monk Fa-liang, and then gradually similar foundations came to be established by private donors.

As in India, the artists in ancient China and Central Asia worked, so to speak, *ad majorem gloriam dei*. They belonged to two distinct categories: (*i*) lay brothers of monastic orders with their centres at Tun-huang and (*ii*) itinerant artists who had specialised in certain kinds of religious paintings. They came to Tun-huang only on local demand for votive paintings. The predominating characteristics of the artistic creations of these painters clearly point to their close association with the kind of religious art that flourished then at Turfan, Khotan and Kutch which in turn were in close touch with the religious art of India during this period. Surprisingly, they betray ignorance of the traditional indigenous type of painting which was then popular in the capitals of China.

The Western or Central Asian influence that we come across in the wall-paintings at Chi'en-fo tung gives us a definite clue to the activities of some of the foreign (including Indian) painters in China during the sixth-seventh century A.D. Yao Tsui, Chang Yen-yüan and Chu Ching-hsüan are some of the early Chinese writers who have recorded the activities of these foreign painters in their accounts, which though mainly based on hearsay or learned from early writers, give us an approximate appreciation of these artists, and a discussion of their individual characteristics, if not of their historical position.[18]

The earliest foreign painters mentioned by Yao Tsui[19] followed by Chang Yen-yüan were the three monks who came to China during the Liang dynasty (A.D. 502-36). They came by sea, but we have absolutely no information about where or what they painted. But, judging by their land of origin it cannot be doubted that the dominating influence in their art was India.[20] According to Yao Tsui, 'the monk Chi-ti-chü, a foreigner, middle class; the monk, Mo-lo-pu-ti also a foreigner, middle class; the monk, Chia-to-fo, middle class, a Ch'an monk from India. He was a man of superior conduct and performed many miracles. At the beginning he was with the Wei and the Wei emperor esteemed him highly. When the Sui came to power, the Sui emperor built the Shaolin temple for him. There may still be seen on the door of one of the cells a picture of a spirit by Chia-fo-t'o'.[21] Several pictures by this monk are referred to which represent people from Fu-li, besides other strange things. It seems, this monk-painter (Chia-fo-to) was no other than the Dhyāna master Fo-t'o who lived at the beginning of the sixth century in Shao-lin ssü in Honan.[22] Later Chinese writers have combined and merged this monk-painter of the Liang dynasty (c. A.D. 400-525) with Bodhidharma (in Chinese: Ta-mo), the semi-mythical figure from south India who acquired the greatest distinction not only in China, but also in Japan.[23] His arrival in China during the reign of Wu-ti was one of the most memorable events in the religious history of China (*c.* A.D. 520 or 526). He gave the impulse to a trend of thought and an attitude towards nature and art which bore rich fruits in the field of painting in later times.[24] His teachings 'imparted a special tone and character to a section (though not the whole) of Far-Eastern Buddhism',[25] known in China as *Ch'an* (*i.e.*, Dzyna=Dhyāna) and in Japan as *Zen*. Thus, Buddhist religion and philosophy served as a great source of inspiration to further artistic development. The cultural prosperity of Nanking during the heyday of Liang Wu-ti was practically wiped out in the time of his sons (A.D. 550-55) by the rebel, Hou Ching. 'Millions of people were captured and enslaved, a thousand cart loads of books went up in smoke. Nothing like this has ever been known in history when all learning and literature came to be destroyed without a trace.'[26] None-the-less, it came to be revered to a great extent in northern China under the Northern Wei dynasty (*c.* A.D. 398-552). Most of the rulers were devoted Buddhists and quite active in propagating this religion by 'establishing institutions of learning, where teachers from India and Central Asia were welcomed, and great centres of worship for the crowd'.[27]

In fact, Indian art was increasingly influencing Chinese art traditions from the T'ang period onward. The influence was so great that in the course of time the faces of all Buddhist deities became almost Chinese in appearance. Traditions of the art of the Wei period are so closely connected with Indian traditions that we can easily see how the distinct Indian figures of the Wei period went through physiognomical changes to become Chinese by the Śuṅga period. There were Indian artists, both painters and sculptors, in this period in China, and works of some of the painters of this and subsequent periods were much esteemed there. We have names of three Indian painters—Śākyabuddha, Buddhakīrti and Kumārabodhi[27a]—who seem to have been widely respected in China, but unfortunately we have no details either about their works or about their personal life.

The Chinese aesthetic traditions can be traced back to the fifth century A.D., when Buddhism was well established in China. The oldest of these traditions strongly remind us of the Indian principles of aesthetics as seen in the paintings of Sei-Ho—a great artist living under the Ts'i dynasty of the South (A.D. 479-501) who is credited with having formulated the following six principles of painting for the first time:

(i) Mental revolution gives birth to the life motion.

(ii) To bring out the anatomical structure with the help of the brush.

(iii) To draw forms in conformity with nature.

(iv) To make the colours correspond to the nature of the objects.

(v) To distribute the lines in their proper places.

(vi) To propagate the forms by passing them on into the pictures.

These six principles are more or less the same as the *shaḍaṅga* (six essential components) relating to painting so elaborately discussed in ancient Indian literature such as *rūpa* (form), *pramāṇa* (proportion), *bhāva* (idea), *lāvaṇya* (beauty or finish), *sādṛśya* (conformity with the object) and *varṇikābhaṅga* (distribution of colours). Though the order is somewhat different, the principles are the same.[27b] We come across these Indian influences in the T'ang ideal of feminine beauty also in a more pointed face and rounded figure, hair collected around and above the head, and an air of cheerful health. The most splendid paintings of this period are those by Wei-Chih-Ising, Yen Li-pen and Wu Tao-tzu who was unquestionably the greatest of all the Chinese painters.

Chin-Kang-San-tsang was yet another Indian monk who has been mentioned (by Chang Yen-yuan) among the T'ang painters. He was an inhabitant of the "Country of Lions" (Siṁha or Ceylon or Śrī Laṅkā) who had 'specialised in painting Buddhist images of the Western countries, grave and dignified, not like ordinary paintings. In the pagoda of Kuang-fu-ssü in Loyang we have some simple images sketched by Santsang'.[28]

Of all the foreign painters Ts'ao Chung-ta was the most important painter who 'has left deeper traces in the history of Chinese painting'. Though he has been widely mentioned by writers of various epocs, yet we have no more definite information about him as historical personality than the monk-painters noted above. According to Chang Yen-yüan, he came from Sogdiana (Ts'ao) and attained great fame under the Northern Ch'i dynasty (A.D. 550-77). His skill in painting Hindu images who bore 'a supernatural effect' was remarkable. These images, we are told, were made after 'the manner of foreign countries; there was no one equal to him at the time'. Chang Yen-yüan is all praise for this great painter who created new kinds of Buddha motifs. According to him, 'there are three manners of painting Buddhas: one is the manner of the Ts'ao School, another the manner of the Chang (Sēng-yu) School and the third, the manner of the Wu (Tao-tzü) School'.[29]

The above statement by Chang Yen-yüan as well as some passage in his descriptive note have given rise to controversies regarding the origin of Ts'ao Chung-ta and his place in the history of Chinese painting. Pelliot believes that he was born in China and honoured with a high position at the court of Northern Ch'i and the Sui emperors in Ch'ang-an (A.D. 590).[30] But, according to Waley[31] he was a man from the west who represented a foreign mode of painting in contradistinction to the Chinese. Though we are not in a position to determine his exact place of birth, there is no doubt about his artistic education which included contacts with Indian art. His wall paintings in K'ai-yuan ssü and other Buddhist temples in the capital contained features of style and iconography 'which seemed new and strange to the Chinese and gave birth to the statement that T'sao started a special school of religious painting different from that of his predecessor Chang Sēng-yu and his still more famous successor Wu Tao-tzü'.[32]

As no paintings of T'sao have survived we cannot say anything about his artistic innovations. Some T'ang and Sung critics have, however, described certain characteristic features in his paintings which give some idea about his paintings in general. We are told that the figures painted by T'sao were 'clad in garments which clung to the body: they looked as if they had been drenched in water, whereas the mantles of Wu's figures were draped in billowing folds and looked as if they had been caught by the wind'.[33] Exactly the same distinction existed in Ts'ao and Wu schools of sculpture. In other words, Ts'ao style was the early Indian mode of representing thin garments as clinging closely to the body as seen in the Gupta sculptures and their offshoots in Central Asia and China. Wu, on the other hand, introduced a bolder individual style of draping better fitted for the representation of bodily form, muscular tension and movement.[34] We should, however, remember here that Ts'ao flourished at least one hundred years earlier than Wu, and as such the juxtaposition of the two masters seems arbitrary. Ts'ao was no doubt unanimously recognised as the main representative of the Indian mode in the religious painting of the period and he exercised tremendous influence during the latter half of the sixth century A.D. It was Chin Ch'h-i, a pupil of Ts'ao, who later 'changed the harmonies and transformed the foreign manner into Chinese. He was the originator of the Change'.[35]

IV

Chin Chih-i was later followed by several painters at the beginning of the T'ang period who tried to harmonise some of the new elements of style by Indian (foreign) artists with indigenous traditions. It was the age of national renaissance strong enough to absorb important elements of foreign extraction and give them the stamp of the full blown T'ang mode. Some of these foreign (Indian) painters were greatly honoured during this period for their technical innovations by which they contributed to the great patrimony of Chinese art.[36]

Two of the best known foreign painters of this period in Ch'ang-an were from a noble Khotanese family called Wei-Ch'ih (*Vijayā* in Sanskrit). The older of the two, Wei-Ch'ih Po-Chih-no, also known as the "Greater Wei-Ch'ih" became famous for his pictures of Buddhist themes as well as paintings of 'strange objects from foreign lands of flowers which were remarkably life-like and painted in a bold and free manner'. His son I-Seng came to be renowned as "Lesser Wei-Ch'ih".[37] He is said to have been sent to the Chinese court with a recommendation by the ruler of his native country 'because of his great skill in paintings'.[38] He executed his famous wall-paintings in the Buddhist temples in Ch'ang-an, the capital of China. He did a votive picture on the front of the Pagoda of Tz'u-en ssŭ and also a composition of flowers rendered in relief and in their mist 'a thousand-armed and thousand-eyed Great compassionate one (*i.e.* Kuanyin) of a more wonderful appearance than can be described in words. Besides the terrace of the Seven Precious things (*Sapta-Ratna*) he painted the conquering of Māra, a truly wonderful picture, full of strange and extraordinary things'.[39]

Though none of the contemporary records contain any definite information about the date of I-Sēng's activities in China, it seems most probable that it extended over the second half of the seventh century and possibly a few years longer. We have, however, an informative description of his paintings in the *T'ang-Ch'ao ming-hua lu* which says that 'his paintings whether votive images, human figures or flowers and birds, were always foreign-looking and not like Chinese things', and his 'brush-work was tight and strong like bending iron on coiling (resilient) wire'.[40] Writing about him T'ang Hou, one of the best informed later art-historians, says that 'Wei-Ch'ih I-sēng, a man from a foreign country also painted Buddhist images. He used deep colours which he piled up in raised layers on the silk and did not leave any obscure traces'.[41]

These paintings of the school of Wei-Ch'ih I-sēng form just a minor group among the numerous Central Asian art products in the Far East. I-sēng was no doubt the most important among the painters from India, Khotan, Turfan or Kutch who came to seek their fortune in China at the beginning of the T'ang period. But, during the Sui and early part of the T'ang dynasty we have some specimens of decorative art no less important as evidences which were probably imported from the above centres, — possibly to a larger extent— made in China and Japan by artists most of whom had come from India (western countries) because of their skill in certain arts. The most extraordinary 'store of such works of art may today be seen in the imperial treasure-house, in Nara, known as Shōso-in (Japan) which has remained practically intact since the eighth century'.[42]

It would suffice to say that these paintings give us a clear idea of the element of rustic vivacity which can be seen in some of the minor illustrative scenes in the Tun-huang wall paintings. The painters originated mostly from India, Khotan or other places in Central Asia and were much esteemed in China because of their "unconventional realism" which served them well as illustrators.

The T'ang period witnessed the great expansion of art and culture. And, during this period more important than the commercial exports were the cultural, *i.e.* religious and artistic, influences radiating from China to the neighbouring countries like Japan, Korea, Tibet and Indo-China. The diffusion of Chinese art in Japan and Korea which had received it from India became most considerable in the seventh and eighth centuries, and 'hand in hand with this went the transmission of the Chinese forms of Mahāyāna Buddhism'.

Just as in other departments of life, so also in painting, it is to the T'ang age that the Chinese have always looked back as their period of classic achievement, partly because of its foreign origin, partly because of its popular contacts. In China, Buddhist painting has followed a course rather apart from the rest. The first two hundred years of the T'ang dynasty witnessed the most flourishing period and Wu Tao-tzü (*c.* A.D. 680-740) was the greatest artist of this age who was first and foremost a Buddhist painter. He is said to have painted more than three hundred frescoes in the palaces of Ch'ang-an and Loyang. But, unfortunately, all these paintings seem to have perished 'with much of the rest of the great T'ang Buddhist during the persecution of A.D. 841-45 and nothing now remains of his work. He is said to have used a violent, sweeping style, his draperies blown out, as if caught in the wind'.[43]

The number of artistically trained monks who carried on the tradition of Ch'an painting at the end of the Sung and the beginning of the Yuan dynasty in China was no doubt considerable, though relatively few of them have been recorded, and it also included men from foreign lands,[44] specially from Central Asia and India.

Yin-t'o-lo, known in Japan as Indara (Indra in Sanskrit), was one of these foreign painters, who though completely unknown in the Chinese literature, is mentioned in the *Kundaikan* and more than a dozen of his works are preserved in Japanese collections, several of them being signed and provided with inscriptions (by himself or contemporary Ch'an priests). These inscriptions clearly show that he was born in Magadha (in the Bihar State, India), but he lived in the T'ien-chen temple near Hangchou (in the second half of the thirteenth century), and possibly also in the Shang-fang Yukuo temple in K'aifeng.[45] But, we do not know when and by what route this monk painter came to China and settled down there. We have also no information about his parentage and early education. But, as regards his talent as a teacher and monk painter, there is no doubt that he enjoyed a great reputation as a Ch'an teacher as well as an artist. All his pictures bear poetic comments by prominent monks of the period. They were apparently admired for their symbolic or illustrative significance. They represent 'some of those extraordinary pictures from the history of Ch'an Buddhism who by their eccentric behaviour stirred the students and made them realise that there is a realm unreachable by the senses and logic based on them'.[46] His pictures include the dancing Pu-tai, the Bodhidharma 'crossing the river on a reed-leaf', the pair of lunatic poets 'with broom and a writing brush known as Han-shan and Shih-tae and several of the famous Ch'an masters of T'ang times such as Yao-shan and Tan-hsia who burned the Buddha-statue in order to demonstrate the uselessness of idolatry. Such fantastic pictures were no doubt meant to illustrate the difference between Ch'an masters and ordinary people who are chained by moral and intellectual conventionalism'.[47]

P'u-Kuang was another monk-painter who made ink-drawings of Bodhidharma and other Buddhist patriarch in somewhat the same fashion as Yin-t'o-lo. He did not belong to the Ch'an school. He was the head of a religious sect, known as *Dhuta*, in the reign of Kublai Khan and was active still in A.D. 1312. But, the only paintings by him known nowadays are a series of nineteen album leaves representing Bodhidharma, Putai and seventeen others.[48] A study of his pictures shows that he was more of a calligraphist who translated forms into conventional styles. Though he was also of Indian origin, unfortunately we have no information about his parentage and place of birth in India.

Chang-Fang-ju was yet another Buddhist monk-painter of China of Indian origin who is unrecorded in China, but mentioned in the *Kundaikan*. He is credited with having painted pictures representing buffaloes with herd-boys containing an undercurrent of Ch'an ideas. They form a pair representing the buffaloes grazing at some distance from a boy who is sitting on the river-bank, with his back turned towards the animal, and is busy with a fishing rod—apparently unconscious of his Buddha nature—while the other picture represents the boy riding on the buffalo and carrying a large bag on a rod over his shoulder.

A remarkable school of painting directly connected with Indian thought was inspired by Dhyāna Buddhism, although it did not follow Indian artistic traditions. This school gained popularity during twelfth and thirteenth centuries, and had a much closer approach to nature than any other school. Though landscape painting had become quite popular during the T'ang period, 'the landscape works of the Sung artists inspired by Chan (Zen - Dhyāna) Buddhism are the best'. As we know, the painters of this school transformed the elements of nature into abstract ideas, because the Chan doctrine holds that the spiritual essence of things may be found everywhere, say, in man, animal, plant, flower, mountain, stream, and so on. The outstanding artists of this school were Liang Kai and Muchi whose work is now mostly preserved in Japan. In one of Muchi's paintings, entitled "The Ch'an Master in Meditation", we come across a serpent curling around an ascetic or a holy man, completely unconcerned, which reminds us of a familiar scene in Indian art. But, in China it is particularly characteristic of the Ch'an school.

The influence of this school can also be seen in the painting of flowers. The Ch'an artist saw in flowers a reflection of the Buddha essence and he sought to capture its spiritual significance 'by identifying himself with the object through intense mental concentration'. The favourite objects were plum blossoms, vines, orchids and narcissi—messengers of spring. Another favourite theme was the bamboo 'which by its uprightness, and the inner emptiness of its hollow stem, symbolised the Buddhist ideal. Hence to paint bamboo with devotion was deemed to be an ascetic exercise leading to a state of spirituality'.[49]

Indian influence on painting gradually started waning by the thirteenth century although the artists prepared the images of the Buddha in the traditional manner. The Buddhist art, however, declined in China with the decline of Buddhism there.

NOTES AND REFERENCES

1. Osvald Siren, *Chinese Painting,* Pt. I, Vol. I, Introduction, p. 1.
2. *Ibid.*, p. 62.
3. *Ibid.*, p. 68.
4. J. Hackin, Siren, L. Warner & P. Pelliot, *Studies in Chinese Art and some Indian Influences*, London, 1938, p. 3.
5. F.H. Andrews, *Indian Art & Letters*, Vol. VIII, No. 1.
6. Sir Aurel Stein, *Serindia*, Vol. I, p. 531.
7. *Studies in Chinese Art*, p. 14.
8. Osvald Siren, *Studies in Chinese Art*, p. 23.
9. *Ibid.*, p. 23.
10. O. Siren, *Chinese Sculpture from the Fifth to the Fourteenth Century*, p. xxxiii, note.
11. J. Ph. Vogel, "La Sculpture de Mathura" in *Arts Asiatica*, Vol. XV, pp. 26-28.
12. O. Siren, *Studies in Chinese Art*, p. 31.
13. *Ibid.*, p. 32.
14. Paul Pelliot, *Bulletin de l'E'cole Francaise d'Extreme Orient*, Vol. III.
15. O. Siren, *Studies in Chinese Art*, p. 32.
16. For details, see *ibid.*, pp. 32-33.
17. *Ibid.*, p. 33, fn. 20.
18. *Ibid.*, p. 68.
19. Cf. his work *Hsü hua p'in*.
20. Osvald Siren, *op. cit.*, p. 69.
21. Cf. his work *Hsü hua p'in*.
22. Pelliot, "Notes sur quelques...et des T'ang" in *T'oung Pao*, Vol. XXII, 1923.
23. For details about Bodhidharma, see the author's book *Aspects of Asian History*, Chapter XV.
24. For details, Osvald Sren, *Op. cit.*, pp. 38-39.
25. Charles Eliot, *Hinduism and Buddhism*, Vol. III, London, 1921, pp. 255 ff.

26. Osvald Siren, *op. cit.*, p. 41.
27. *Ibid.*
27a. P.C. Bagchi, *India & China*, p. 163.
27b. *Ibid.*, p. 163.
28. Quoted, Osvald Siren, *op. cit.*, p. 69, fn. 1. For a detailed discussion about the foreign artists during the Six Dynasties and the early T'ang period, see Alexander C. Soper, "Literary Evidence for Early Buddhist Art in China" in *Oriental Art,* Vol. II, 1949, and in *Artibus Asiae,* Vol. XVI, 1953; Omura Seigal's *History of Chinese Sculpture.*
29. Quoted, Osvald Siren, *op. cit.*, p. 70.
30. Pelliot, "Les Fresques de Touen-houang... de M. Eumorfopoulos" in *Revue des Arts Asiatiques,* 1928, Vols. III, IV; Hirth, *Fremde Einflusse in der Chinesischen Kunst,* 1896 and *Scraps from an Art Collector's Note-Book;* H.A. Giles, *An Introduction to the History of Chinese Pictorial Art,* 1918.
31. A. Waly, *An Introduction to the History of Chinese Painting,* 1923.
32. Osvald Siren, *op. cit.*, p. 70.
33. Kuo Jo-hsu in *Tu-hua Chi'en-W'en Chih,* Vol. I, Chap. 9.
34. Osvald Siren, *op. cit.*, p. 70.
35. Chang Yen-yuan, *Ming-hua Chi,* Chap. IX.
36. Osvald Siren, *op. cit.*, p. 71.
37. Cf. Waley, *op. cit.*, p. 107.
38. For other details see Acker's trans. in *Some Tang and Pre T'ang Texts,* Leiden, 1954, p. 290; Nagahiro's article "On the Painter Wei-Ch'ih I-Seng" in the *Silver Jubilee Volume of the Jimbun Kagaku Kenk Ysuhō,* 1954.
39. Cf. *The T'ang Cha'o ming-hua lu.*
40. Cf. *Li-tai minghua Chi,* Chap. IX.
41. T'ang Hoa, *Kuchin hua Chien* (*The Mirror of Old and Modern Painting*). For other details, see Osvald Siren, *op. cit.*, pp. 72-77.
42. Osvald Siren, *op. cit.*, pp. 76-77.
43. Leigh Ashton & Basil Gray, *Chinese Art* (London, Memliu), pp. 113-15.
44. Osvald Siren, *Chinese Painting,* Pt. I, Vol. II, London, 1956, p. 146.
45. *Ibid.*, p. 146.
46. Suzuku, "The Zen Life in Pictures" in *Essays in Zen Buddhism* (Third Series), Kyoto, 1934.
47. O. Siren, *op. cit.*, p.146.
48. *Ibid.*, pp. 146-47.
49. D.P. Singhal, *op. cit.*, p. 128.

79
INDIAN ARCHAEOLOGICAL EXPEDITIONS ABROAD

JAGAT PATI JOSHI

Archaeological Survey of India (ASI) was founded in 1861 with the primary objective of exploring, preserving, conserving monuments of national importance and studying archaeological remains in the country and also undertaking excavation, exploration, conservation of monuments and studies of different aspects of archaeology in foreign countries. Besides, individual eminent archaeologists and institutions have been also collaborating in archaeological expeditions abroad.

Afghanistan

After the epoch-making expeditions to Central Asia under the leadership of Sir Aurial Stein, the last one which took place in 1913-14, it was only after independence that India's archaeological expeditions abroad received a new life. However, a small cultural mission with Sir Mortimer Wheeler, the then Director General, ASI as its leader visited Afghanistan in 1946. Wheeler's contribution to Indian archaeology is manifold. In respect of archaeological expeditions abroad he suggested, 'Such missions were to secure an enduring cooperation; they must be followed by action'. Somehow, due to financial considerations and other difficulties, expedition to Afghanistan could not take place till the Central Advisory Board of Archaeology in 1954 recommended to organise and despatch an archaeological mission to Afghanistan to work there for archaeological expedition and search of sculptures, inscriptions and caves and archaeological sites of interest to India. In pursuance, the ASI sent a delegation to Afghanistan on 15th May 1956 which worked under T.N. Ramachandran and Y.D. Sharma for a period of two and a half months and returned at the end of July 1956.

The main objective was a rapid reconnaissance and get a first-hand knowledge of archaeological wealth of Afghanistan. During the expedition, a large number of sites were visited

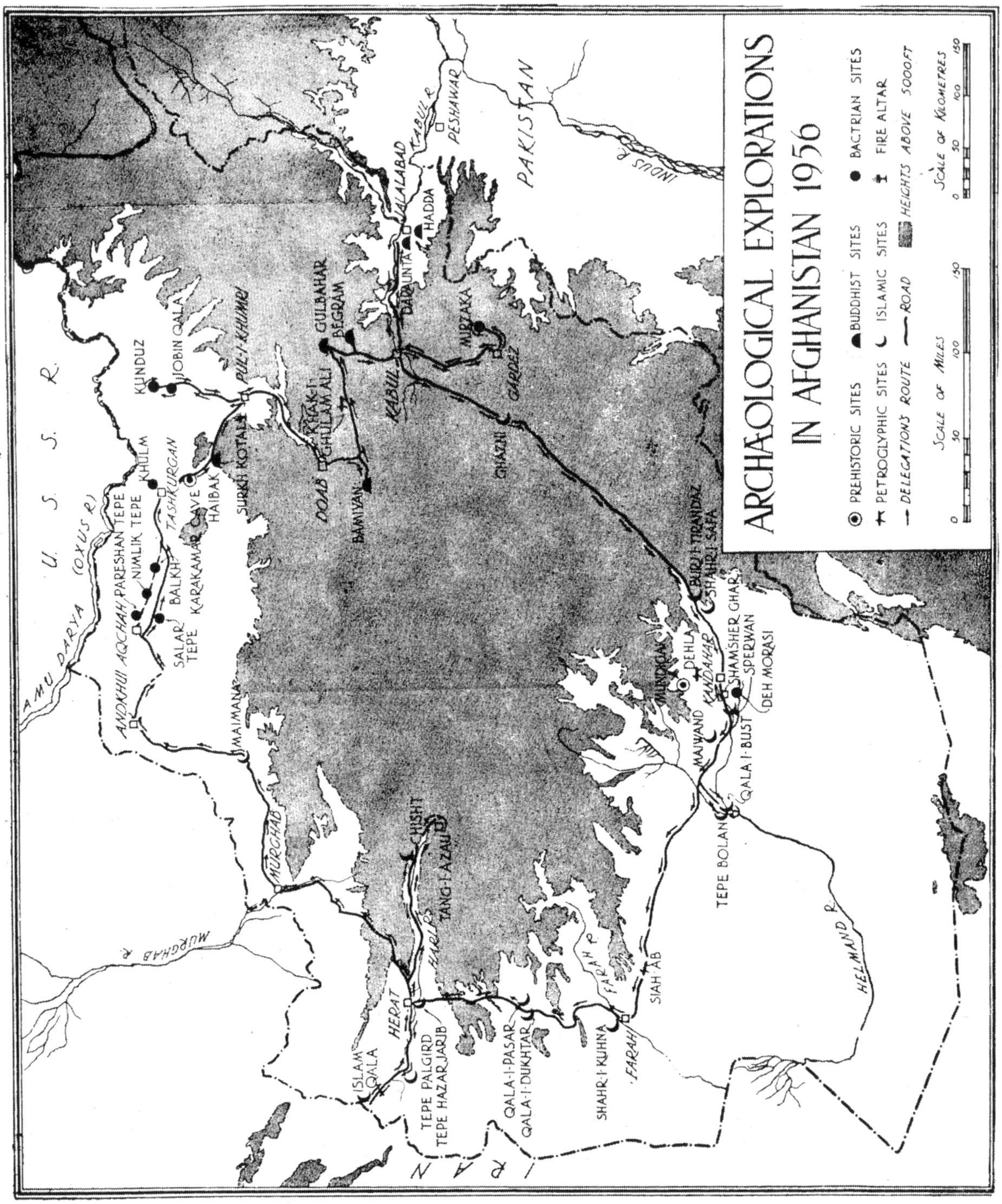
ARCHÆOLOGICAL EXPLORATIONS
IN AFGHANISTAN 1956
PREHISTORIC SITES
PETROGLYPHIC SITES
DELEGATION'S ROUTE
BUDDHIST SITES
ISLAMIC SITES
ROAD
BACTRIAN SITES
FIRE ALTAR
HEIGHTS ABOVE 5000FT
SCALE OF MILES
SCALE OF KILOMETRES
U. S. S. R.
AMU DARYA (OXUS R)
PAKISTAN
IRAN
INDUS R.
KABUL R.
PESHAWAR
JALALABAD
HADDA
DARUNTA
KABUL
GULBAHAR
BEGRAM
MURTAKA
GARDEZ
GHAZNI
KUNDUZ
JOBIN QALA
PUL-I-KHUMRI
KHULM
TASHKURGAN
HAIBAK
CAVE
SURKH KOTAL
BAMIYAN
DOAB
PARESHAN TEPE
NIMLIK TEPE
BALKH
KARAKAMAR
SALAR TEPE
AQCHAH
ANDKHUI
MAIMANA
MURGHAB
MURGHAB R.
CHISHT
TANG-I-AZAU
HARI R.
HERAT
ISLAM QALA
TEPE PALGIRD
TEPE HAZARJARIB
QALA-I-PASAR
QALA-I-DUKHTAR
SHAHR-I-KUHNA
FARAH
FARAH R.
SIAH AB
TEPE BOLAN
HELMAND R.
QALA-I-BUST
MAIWAND
KANDAHAR
DEHLA
SHAMSHER GHAR
SPERWAN
DEH MORASI
SHAHR-I-SAFA
BURJ-I-TRANDAZ

Fig. 1.

and a study of objects in the museums at Kabul, Herat, Begram, Kandhar and Majar-i-Sherif was made. The map of the expedition explains the expedition's work.

Borobudur

In the meantime, a delegation led by N.P. Chakravarti and Sivaramamurti was sent to study the grand monument at Borobudur. This expedition did a good photo-documentation of architectural marvel within the limited time.

In 1961-62 in the sphere of archaeological expedition abroad, ASI took a significant leap and three teams of Indian archaeologists were sent out, one to Egypt led by B.B. Lal and two to Nepal, one led by R.V. Joshi and another by D. Mitra.

Egypt

A team visited Nubia in Egypt in response to a worldwide appeal by UNESCO to salvage the antiquities from the submersible area of Aswan Dam. The team, for the first time, discovered middle and late Stone Age tools from the two upper and lower terraces of the Nile respectively near Afyeh.

The excavation of the site at Afyeh in an occupational deposit of 50 cm. revealed two structural phases of stone rubble set in Nile mud of A Group people. In one case a house having six rooms had been found besides quite sizable houses there. Door sockets to right hand side have been found. Crops were ground in saddle querns. The inhabitants had a rural economy. They domesticated animals and were agriculturists. Pots with a light red to creamy surface were painted in deep colour with a variety of linear designs; the other pottery was a buff ware with painted designs in chocolate on black pigment. On the score of C14 dates, the site is datable to *circa* 2600 B.C. to 2400 B.C.

Finally the team also excavated cemetery of C-Group people, consisting of 109 graves. In these graves body was found placed in a crouched position in an 'oblong but round ended pit', 1.50 to 2 m in length and 1 m wide and 1 to 1.50 m deep. The body was oriented north-west to north-south, head being on the latter side in the tibn pillow or a headrest. Decomposed mat suggests the body was wrapped in it. The body was found wearing ornaments made of beads, e.g. anklet, bracelet and necklaces, of steatite, faience and shell. The funerary furniture consists of pots, bowls of all black or black and red ware with incised designs filled in white, red ware and kench ware. A dancing design on a row of human figures is very interesting, dish with kohl mark and a wooden mirror handle are the other finds. The grave used to be capped by tumulus of mud and rubbles with, at times, some variations. In this cemetery some graves where the body was laid in supine extended position and leaned towards north-west belonging to New Kingdom have been found. The black and red ware has some resemblance to the south Indian megalithic pottery. The date of C-Group graves is 1500 B.C.

Nepal (Pls. 79.1-79.2)

Exploration was carried out in the districts of Bhairawa and Taulihawa and 36 sites were visited. Out of these 15 were discovered earlier and rest were found by the present expedition. The sites belong to *circa* third century B.C. to the beginning of the Muslim conquest.

Excavation at Kudan revealed the existence of a beautiful well surrounded by 7 m square brick platform with remarkable ornamental treatment of its facade. The area has yielded exquisite remains of two temples called Temple-1 and Temple-2. Temple-1 admeasures 42x31x4.50 m. The platform was made by constructing four brick walls having an average width of 2.50 m within which was enclosed some area surrounding the plinth of the sanctuary and the porch. The facade was most beautiful treated with mouldings carved in the best tradition of terracotta architectural art. (Pl. 79.1) Later on, a new sanctuary was built on the earlier octagonal plinth. Temple-1 has a *linga* and *arghyapatta* around it in the sanctum. Two fragmentary images of the Mahisasuramardini and Kartikeya have also been found from the ruins of Temple-1.

Temple-2 had a filled up mud platform. The plinths of temple was square at base. It was *triratha* and near the top *panch-ratha*. The debris has yielded some exquisitely carved bricks comparable to Temple-1 of the earlier phase. The date of temple at Kudan was not later than 9th century A.D.

The excavation at Tilaurakot in the trench across fortification in a cultural deposit of 3.80 m revealed the existence of pre-defence Period-I having two phases, the earlier Phase-A yielding Northern Black Polished Ware and the ring-wells and the Phase-B yielding two brick structures and a ring well having 53 rings. In both phases grey ware, a red ware painted in black is available along with NBP associated antiquities, i.e. terracotta beads, iron and copper objects etc., and footed saddle querns. Period-I is heralded after a burnt layer and is characterized by the building of a mud rampart. The rampart filling has yielded Maurya and Sunga terracottas from earth dug in the surrounding area and thus making room for a good moat around the fortification. The outer face of the rampart had a fortification wall of bricks and brickbats. The average width of the wall was 4 m. The brick wall was capped by an enormous debris representing its fall. The site has yielded in a small trench five gold objects, sixty-five coins, twenty-seven terracotta human figurines of 3rd-1st B.C. century, fifty-seven animal figurines, two terracotta sealings, beads, bangles, large number of objects of iron and red sandstone head of Mathura school.

Another expedition working from Kathmandu valley collected important geomorphological data of the Pleistocene period. However, no palaeolithic tools could be found.

In 1963, Krishna Deva collaborated with Deptt. of Archaeology and Culture, H.M. Govt. of Nepal and carried out an iconographical survey of the icons of Nepal and results of the expedition are published in a book, *Images of Nepal* by ASI and it is a rich collection of iconographic wealth of Nepal. During this survey, some rare iconographic types have been found, e.g. Siva as Ekpada-Trimurti, Chandra (the Moon god) riding on a chariot of geese, (Pl. 79.2), Mahisha-Samhara and Vishnu in Ardhanari (androgynous) etc. The Brahmanical and Buddhist images prior to tenth century have striking affinity with Indian image in theme and

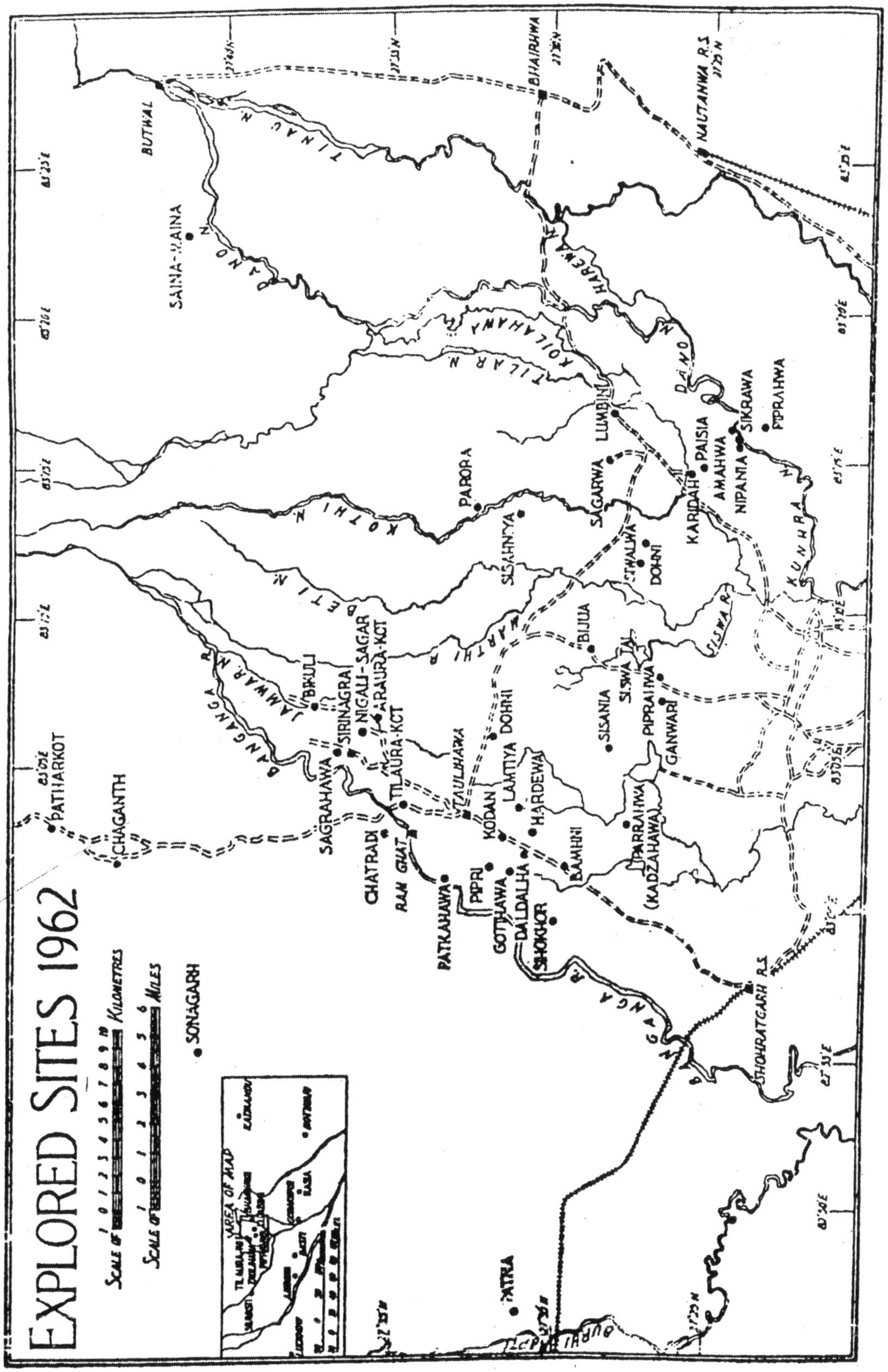
EXPLORED SITES 1962
SCALE OF KILOMETRES
SCALE OF MILES
BUTWAL
SAINA-MAINA
BHAIRHWA
NAUTANWA R.S.
LUMBINI
PIPRAHWA
SIKRAWA
PAISIA
AMAHWA
NIPANIA
KARIDAH
SAGARWA
PARORA
SISAHNIYA
DOHNI
BIJUA
SISANIA
GANWARI
SAGRAHAWA
SIRINAGRA
NIGALI-SAGAR
ARAURA-KOT
TILAURA-KOT
TAULIHAWA
CHATRADI
RAM GHAT
PATKAHAWA
PIPRI
KODAN
GOTIHAWA
DALDALHA
SHOKHOR
LAMTIYA
HARDEWA
BAMHNI
CHAGANTH
SONAGARH
SHOHRATGARH R.S.
KOTHI N.
BETIN N.
DANO N.
TINAU N.
TILAR N.
KOILAHAWA
KUNHRA
SISWA R.
JAMWAR N.
BANGANGA R.

Fig. 2.

treatment. "But from tenth century, the art idioms and conventions of Nepal increasingly assert themselves and icons show unmistakable traits of local physiognomy and facial features which together with the distinctive art convention of Nepal tend towards greater stylization and complexity in course of centuries".

Prof. S.B. Deo of Deccan College, the then Colombo Professor of Ancient Indian Culture, Tribhuwan University under the employ of Indian Cooperation, Nepal and in collaboration with Deptt. of Archaeology, H.M. Govt. of Nepal and Tribhuwan Universty and Technical Assistants from the ASI carried out excavations in 1965 at two sites in the Kathmandu valley namely Lajimpat and Madigaon and brought to light the earliest traces of human culture which began some time in the early centuries of Christian era in the valley on the basis of icons and inscriptions. However, Lajimpat might not have had any early historical deposits.

Again in 1965, the same team carried out excavations at Banjarahi, south of Lumbini and brought to light a sequence of two periods with two sub-periods in Period-I. The sequence is as below:

(a) Period-I A : Grey ware overlapping with NBP datable to *circa* 7-6th cent. B.C.

(b) Period-I B : NBP and Red Ware-terracottas betrayed Sunga characteristics.

(c) Period II : Red Ware-post Gupta to early medieval.

Excavation at Paisa, having a group of three mounds north-east of Barjarahi yielded remains of four temples and two platforms. "The association of medieval sculptures like the Siva-Parvati panel showing also Nandi and Ganas, the torso of a female figure, fragmentary sculpture showing a male figure wearing a *dhoti* and the use of moulded and decorated bricks as at Kudan, tend to assign the Temples Nos. 4 and 5 to medieval period and rest to a still later period."

Exploration in the area from Bhairahawa to Triveni Ghat yielded the following sites:

1) Dhak Lahi yielded sherds of red ware; 2) Chhipa Ghar has a Ganesh temple and a sculpture of Bhagawati; 3) Badegaon yielded red slipped ware; 4) Katahawa was full of red ware; 5) Barad Gọria yielded several sculptures including Ganga, Jamuna and Kartikeya and architectural members; 6) Derawa has a huge stupa mound 30 ft. high, 70 ft. in diameter; 7) Triveni Ghat has a high section having two grave deposits; 8) Jatashankar has a medieval temple.

Afghanistan

In 1965, a reconnaissance caused by Dr. B.B. Lal and R. Sengupta prepared a project report for the execution of work at Bamiyan.

In July 1969, a team consisting of B.B. Lal and R. Sengupta had reconnaissance tour of Bamiyan and Kabul with a view to assess the feasibility of entering into a bilateral cultural agreement for the preservation of Buddhist shrine at Bamiyan.

Under the Indo-Afghan joint project, ASI worked at Bamiyan from 1969 to 1978 to conserve and preserve the Big and Small Buddha and caves around, besides two seasons' work at Khwaja Parsa's Mosque at Balkh. (Pls. 79.3 & 79.4) This was a very important project carried out by the ASI under the leadership of R. Sengupta and Dr. B.B. Lal. During these years, the big Buddha and Small Buddha caves around were conserved and preserved. All the cracks were filled androck-bolted. Necessary structural repairs at the floor level were completed. The damaged east wall of the Buddha shrine was repaired by constructing a masonry wall. This facilitated to approach stucco decoration at higher levels. The paintings on the walls and ceilings of the shrines were cleaned and preserved. Broken edges of painted surface were also filled. Paintings on the ceiling of the Buddha shrine were cleaned. Restoration to the folds of the upper garment of the Big Buddha to a limited portion 'where it was absolutely necessary' was done. The horizontal cracks on the high ceiling were repaired and plastered and steps were reconditioned. The hanging loose block of stone around the passage in the right facade was rock-bolted and restored to original position. A ledge in cement concrete reinforced with M.S. rods was provided with drip course to arrest the snow melt water affecting the paintings.

The arched portion and the side walls of the Big Buddha having paintings and other caves representing flora designs, Buddha and Jataka stories executed over fine mud plaster were preserved. Minute cracks, detachment of painted surface from rock and mud streaks were found. Paintings were made free from superficial accretions, loose pigments were firmly fixed to the ground and painted area cleaned by organic solvents. Bulging portions were pressed back to original ground carefully after consolidation of carrier by injecting plaster of Paris. Broken edges of paintings were secured by filleting process. The ceiling of the cave at the ground level also contained beautiful flora designs in relief with bird motifs in stucco. The interior surface had thick oily surface. It was removed and preservative applied. After repairs, the entire look of the surroundings of the Small Buddha has immensely improved. The image of the Buddha properly preserved now looks far better. The walls and ceilings have paintings. After chemical treatment, R. Sengupta has identified one painting having depiction of miracle of Sravasti and another huge face of Sun God painted on the ceiling of the main shrine of Small Buddha.

The remains of wooden legs on the face establish the fact that the face portion of the both Big Buddha and Small Buddha had been modelled over wooden armature.

Both the Buddha shrines were formally handed over to the Govt. of Afghanistan after successfully completing the task of conservation and preservation in 1977 by the Ministry of External Affairs, Govt. of India.

Extensive repairs were also carried out by ASI at the shrine of famous Sufi saint Khwaja Abu Nasar who died in *circa* 1460 A.D. at Balkh, Afghanistan. (Pl. 79.5) The cost of structural conservation was paid by Govt. of India. The work, although slated for three working seasons, was completed during two seasons at the request of the local people and Afghan Govt. The cracks and fissures on the ceiling of the front vestibule were repaired. The facade and two minars on its either side which have ornamental tiles have been built giving bondage in old work and plastered with gutch. The dome which had developed vertical cracks was strengthened by giving additional support from inside. For this, three arches were erected from inside along the introdos of the dome suitably bounding them with the dome. The two bastions at the rear were repaired and made watertight. The terrace of the high cylindrical drum of the dome was made watertight by resetting the loose bricks with an outward slope to drain off rain and snow water. The minarets which were bereft of the covering were provided with flat roof at the lower level using timber with mud and layer of bricks in gypsum mixed with lime mortar. Brick flooring of the underground cellar and the front aisle were provided with a closed underground drain. The ribbed main dome was originally covered by blue tiles which had mostly fallen down. For this, tiles of the same type were manufactured at Mazar-i-Sharif in the traditional way. Fluted ribs of the main dome built in typical Timurid style with ribs following the original indication and curvature were restored. The hollow portion underneath was filled in by brickbats and gutch after fixing of these panels. After cleaning of patches, chemical preservative was applied. The work was completed and monument was handed over to Afghan authorities in 1977.

A team of archaeologists under Sri B.K. Thapar of ASI visited the Farah region in Afghanistan in 1975 and during the course of exploration two sites, Kafir Qila or Kaki Kahzand, located about 20 km south-west of Farah town and Qila Faridan on the outskirts of Farah were found to have medieval fortification and Qila Faridan had pre-Islamic levels also.

The party also explored some areas along the Arghandab river besides revisiting earlier sites. While examining the pottery of various sites, Northern Black Polished Ware was observed at Shah-i-Kuhna in Kandhar, a fortified settlement supposed to be founded by Alexander. At Shahr-i-Kuhna and Begram the sites had an upper and lower city and also at Qila-i-Bost. Here the commanding fort was found encircled by a moat, and glazed pottery of 10-13th century was found at the site besides ribbed ware. Harappan potter was identified from Shoturghai, a site explored by the French archaeologists on the Oxus. Blades of late Stone Age were picked up about 35 km from Kandhar on way to Mundigak.

Cambodia

From 1980 to 1992, ASI had sent four preparatory expeditions and six expeditions for conservation of Angkorvat. (Pls. 79.6-79.8)

The famous monumental complex at Angkorvat in Cambodia was built during the early part of the 12th century by King Suryavarman II under whose inspiration this great temple was constructed. During this period a number of edifices were built out of which the temple at Angkorvat is the most outstanding one. Angkorvat is an ultimate expression both in massiveness and ornamental details after centuries of architectural experiment in the Khemer art. The temple's greatest sculptural treasure is exemplified by its alternative reliefs depicting episodes from Ramayana, Mahabharata and Puranas as well as the Khemer expeditions.

The temples are built of a coarse grained sandstone. The temple rises in three successive stages culminating in its central cluster of five towers. The complex besides the main temple consists of six large structures popularly known as libraries. A wide moat encircles the temple. A stone causeway to the west of the temple across the moat provides access to the main entrance represented by an imposing gateway.

Nothing was known to the outside world about Angkorvat till 1850 when a French missionary visited the site. Henry Manhot published about Angkorvat in 1863. Conservation was carried out by the French at this great monument complex from 1954 to 1970. The last French conservator Grosshlier had to leave the country and abandon the conservation in 1974.

In July, 1980 immediately after recognizing the new government under Heng Samrin, India offered assistance to Kampuchea (now Cambodia) including restoration of Angkorvat in order to revive age old cultural relationship of the two countries and accordingly:

1. In October, 1980 a team consisting of R. Sengupta (Leader), B.N. Tandon and R. Duttagupta was sent to assess the damage and the status of the temple in respect of its structural and chemical needs. In pursuance to their recommendations, three persons from Cambodia were given training in conservation and photography. Some equipment and instruments were also made available to them to start documentation and preliminary works on protection of the site.
2. In February 1982, a team of experts under the leadership of K.M. Srivastava was deputed to prepare a project feasibility report as well as to carry out some experimental work in the temple. The team stayed for a period of four months. This report later became the basis for future expeditions.
3. In April 1986, a five-member team under M.S. Nagaraja Rao went to Angkorvat and on return submitted a report accompanied with some modification based on Srivastava's report.

   From 1986 to 1992, six teams of ASI worked at Angkorvat led by K.P. Gupta, B.S. Nayal, C.L. Suri and Narasimhaiah. The teams consisted of 14 to 18 members. In 1988, a high level team consisting of A.K. Banerjee, R.K. Rai of Min. of External Affairs, R.C. Tripathi, Deptt. of Culture and Jagat Pati Joshi, ASI inspected the monuments, jointly submitted a report on four years of expedition's work and recommended the financial and technical needs.

   The work of conservation and preservation of the embankment of the moat causeway Esplanade, four enclosure libraries, various galleries, particularly restoration of the Samudra Manthan Gallery, a most challenging task, and towers was completed.

   Before completion of the work, the site was visited by a team consisting of Dr. (Smt.) Kapila Vatsyayana of IGNCA and Sri M.C. Joshi of ASI who expressed satisfaction on the work carried out by ASI, in their report.

After Bamiyan, this was a major conservation and preservation project which could be jointly completed by India and Govt. of Cambodia.

Bahrain

In response to the request of Govt. of Bahrain in 1983 for sending a team of archaeologists, on the report submitted by Jagat Pati Joshi, the Govt. of India, in November 1984, sent a 13-member team under K.M. Srivastava to Bahrain.

Half of the area in Bahrain is occupied by ancient graves. For the expansion, development of the township and laying of wide roads, it was only appropriate to document, after excavation, each and every grave so that account is preserved for the posterity. The Indian team excavated seventy graves out of which two were low lying natural formation. The graves were of the following types:

1. Cairn with filled up circular burial chamber.
2. Tumulus with filled up oblong burial chamber made of undressed stone.
3. Tumulus with oblong burial chamber without filling made of semi-dressed stone.
4. Tumulus with flattened and triangular chamber.

These burials are further classified by the orientation of alcove burial chamber and position of the skeleton. The Indian team in their excavations of allotted graves in Hamad town did not find any evidence which could suggest that those particular graves were made in advance. There was no evidence of a central authority of grave burials and there does not seem to be a uniformity in construction between two graves in this area.

On the basis of pottery and other finds, the chronology of burials is as below:

Type I : Locally dated to Jamdat Nasr. Indian archaeologists did not get any such evidence.

Type II : 2200-2000 B.C.—Find of Indus seal–Barbar Culture I; –2000 B.C. - 1800 B.C.

Type III : Barbar Culture II.

Type IV : Later than 1800 B.C.-1600 B.C.–Kassite Period.

Six Indus seals, two of steatite and four of shell and one of Bahrain (Dilmun type) besides one unfinished seal have been found. A circular steatite seal with typical Indus script was discovered from grave 1757. The evidence confirms the trade links of Indus with West Asia and Bahrain being a halfway house in the third millenium B.C.

Maltai (Sri Lanka)

B.K. Thapar, John Carlswell of Chicago University and Siran Deraniygala of the Deptt. of Archaeology, Govt. of Sri Lanka collaborated along with their supporting teams and excavated at Maltai in Sri Lanka in 1984 for a period of three months and brought to light a double fortified port at Maltai. The occupation was datable from pre-Christian era to 13-14th century A.D.

Maldives

Under the aegis of SAARC Technical Assistance Programme, a two-member team of ASI led by B.P. Bopardikar along with M.I. Loutfi of National Centre of Linguistic and Historical Research, Male, carried out investigation of the pre-Islamic remains in the Maldives. A survey of the Buddhist structures had been carried out earlier by M.I. Loutfi. Among the pre-Islamic remains, only Buddhist structures were noticed under coral stones in different atolls. The present work was restricted to excavation/clearance of debris of some of the Buddhist remains. Small scale excavations were carried out in the islands of Ariadu, Kudahuvadu and Kurumathi in middle Maldives. Besides, traits to Buddhist remains at Toddu and North Nilandu were also noticed.

1. The island of Landu is situated north of Male. A seven-metre high mound was found indicating a stupa. It measures 30x30 m and is totally covered with corals.

   A Buddhist establishment consisting of a stupa and other structures around it were noticed covered with coral stones in dilapidated condition. Five to six other stupas covered with coral and marshy vegetation in an area of about 0.5 km have been noticed. The area has yielded a red ware and celadon ware.

   Excavations here revealed an entrance consisting of the basement decorated with mouldings. The basement is characterized by retaining stone casing in a line which is an abutment to the unexposed square platforms of the stupa. Both the walls of entrance contain offsets of tiles and dressed stones running north-south. In order to trace the moonstone, digging was extended to southern side where two broken stone slabs were found placed at right angle to the basement on either side.

   The staircase is sunken due to overlying debris. The pathway leading to the stupa measures 6 m in length and 2 m in width. The thickness of the wall is 40 cm having seven courses with moulded base with crescentic stone as stepping stone to the entrance. The pathway joins an unexposed square platform.

   The noteworthy finding was a fragment of a bow with flora design on its lip in celadon collected during the clearance of the lowermost part of the basement.

2. Arindu island is located to the south-west of Male. It is said to have had several Buddhist structures. But at present only two ruined structures measuring 3 m in height and 9 m and 8 m respectively in diameter were noticed. The larger structure, a stupa which had been disturbed earlier by digging was taken up for further excavation. Four courses of dressed stones facing north were noticed. The excavated structure measures 1.60 m in length, 0.35 m in breadth and 0.37 m in height above the platform.

3. At Kurumathi island, north-west of Male, the mound measuring 70x40x2 m approximately having coral packing on the top was noticed. Excavations in a trench lying at the top of the mound revealed an alignment of dressed stones in two courses at a depth of 50 cm. The ashlar stonewalls are not of uniform size. These walls are running east-west and north-east direction measuring 27 cm to 48 cm in length, 38 cm to 45 cm in width and 10 cm to 25 cm in thickness. A few broken dressed stones carved with geometrical designs and offset and vertical mouldings were recovered during excavations. A few sherds of red ware were found scattered nearby the site. A number of contextual antiquities including different types of beads of agate, carnelian, coral, crystal and silver and gold ring foil and cowries, conch and a terracotta ram figurine were found encased in a squarish relic chamber of sandstone during earlier clearance. These antiquities are now kept in National Museum, Male.

4. Toddu is situated in the north-west of Male. Here the Buddhist stupa site lies to the north-west of the island. The stupa is in a better state of preservation in comparison to the other Buddhist remains of the island. It is built up of dressed stones of beach rock which retain lime plaster covered over it. The stupa is raised over a circular drum in tiers. The drum of

stupa is characterized by vertical moulding. It measures 5.25 m in diameter. Dome of the stupa is partially missing. The stupa is enclosed by a square platform which in turn is upraised by a number of tiers in tapering fahion. The stupa faces east. The lower portion of the stupa has inset stone railing around the entire drum which has lime plaster. The Buddha head in the National Museum is reported to have been brought from this place.

5. Besides, a number of potsherds of red ware, glazed ware and celadon ware were collected from Kurumathi, Kudahuvadu and Landu islands during explorations and excavations. The shapes of ceramics include carinated bowl, jars, handis and lids. The red ware sherds are devoid of any slip of wash or any other colour designs. However, sherds of glazed ware and celadon ware show floral decorations.

Hukum Mosque, Male

A team headed by O.P. Agrawal carried out various types of studies on the coral stones and biological growths inside and outside the mosque. The fungus identified was Memnoneilla, Eclionurata, Paricillum, Fumchlosum and Chaetomium, Globosum. It was successfully treated with a fungicide.

Bhutan

Between 1987-88 and 1988-89, two expeditions were sent to Bhutan by ASI under the leadership of N. Venkateswarn and Jayaramsundaram respectively for the preservation of murals of Nekhang-Lhakhange, Mithrugpe-Lhakhang of Tongza D Zong and Do-De-Drak monasteries in Bhutan and for the chemical preservation of murals which suffered longitudinal cracks in the wall due to earthquakes, dust and dirt deposition of soot of butter oil lamp deposited on the lower portion of the paintings. In the earlier repairs, cement was used in filling the cracks which obliterated many of the paintings. After documentation of the paintings, the filling in of the cracks was done and bulged portions were set right with plaster of Paris. Removal and cleaning of the dirt, dust and soot were done and thereafter preservatives were applied.

Similarly, chemical cleaning and application of preservatives were carried out in the paintings of Mithrugpe-Lhakhang having major problems, e.g. detachment of pigments, discolouration of dust and dirt and presence of discoloured varnish. In Do-De-Draks monastery, the paintings were cleaned and preserved. Preservation of mural paintings was carried out in the shrine of Chuk Chi Shey in Sunthoka Dzung in the Thimpu Valley, Bhutan.

Angola

Consequent upon a visit of Rajiv Gandhi, the then Prime Minister of India in May 1986, restoration and reorganisation of the Central Armed Forces Museum housed in the old fortress of Sao Miguel in Luanda, the capital city of Angola was undertaken by ASI as a gesture of goodwill and friendship towards the people of the Republic of Angola. The work was entrusted to the ASI and a three-member delegation of experts headed by L.K. Srinivasan from ASI and G.N. Pant from National Museum visited Luanda in October, 1986 to identify the quantum of work involved in the proposed project and to prepare a prepatory report for the reorganisation of the Museum and restoration of that part of the fortress where it was housed.

The fortress of Sao Miguel overlooking the Atlantic Ocean built by the Portuguese in 1648 was found to be in a very bad state of preservation being constantly exposed to the effects of humidity, seepage of water and salt action. The Museum was set up by the Portuguese colonisers in the first half of the 20th century with a collection of sculptures, architectural pieces, arms and armaments, various Christian icons and silver ritual church objects besides other miscellaneous items. However, this Museum was dismantled and the collections were kept in storage by the Angolans after their independence.

The project of restoration and reorganisation was executed by two teams consisting of technical personnel.

The first team headed by Shri D.K. Sinha started the work in July, 1988. His work comprised structural conservation, chemical treatment, accessioning and photo-documentation of objects and electrification of galleries. The second team headed by Smt. M. Khatun arrived at Luanda in December, 1989 and completed the project which entailed extensive repair of all the galleries, refixing of detached and dislocated glazed tiles in their proper places, classification of exhibits after studying the old records, accessioning and documentation of newly acquired objects, laying out of the galleries, planning of the display, preparation of show-cases and finally organising the galleries with proper display and labelling of objects. The following four galleries were organised:

I. Prehistory and Portuguese Gallery

Three main categories of objects were displayed in this gallery, *viz.* (a) Prehistoric tools found from Luanda and its neighbourhood; (b) arms and armaments, military badges, medals and other miscellaneous objects of Portuguese colonial period; and (c) Angolan martial heritage.

II. The Chapel

The altar was renovated and an ivory figure of Jesus Christ besides three other wooden figures and a banner were displayed. Attempt was made to restore the original character of the Chapel as far as possible.

III. Comrade Agostinho Neto Gallery

This gallery was organised to commemorate the life and activities of the Angolan National Hero and the first President of the People's Republic of Angola, Dr. Antonio Agostinho Neto (1922-1979). Various objects belonging to and associated with Comrade Neto and photographs showing his eventful life were displayed here.

IV. Struggle for Independence Gallery

The history of the struggle for freedom (1956-1975) divided into four phases, was presented through relics of war, various documents and photographs.

The reorganised Museum was handed over to the Government of Angola on the occasion of Gandhi Jayanti on 2nd October, 1990.

Acknowledgement

The article is based on (1) *Indian Archaeological–A Review*, 1955-56 and 1987-88; (2) Mrs. D. Mitra, "*Excavations at Tilaurakot*"; (3) Dr. S.B. Deo, "*Excavations in Kathmandu*" and "*Excavations in Nepal Tarai*"; (4) Personal communication from B.K. Thapar for Excavations at Maltai; (5) Personal communication from Smt. Monira Khatun for Museum at Luanda, Angola which is acknowledged with gratitude. The courtesy of the Archaeological Survey of India for the illustrations and His Majesty's Govt. of Nepal for the map of explored sites is acknowledged.

Pl. 34.1: Excavated site, Barabati Fort, Cuttack.

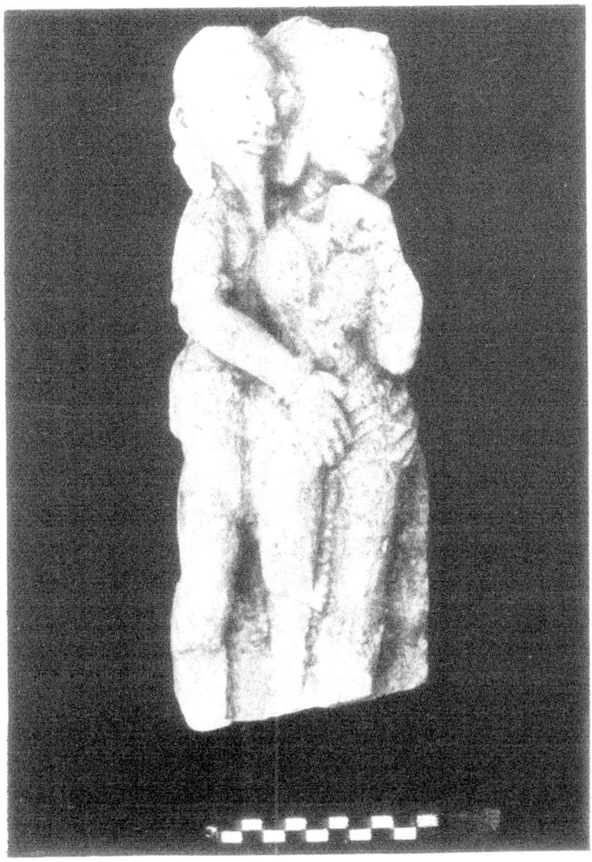

Pl. 34.2: Mithuna Couple, Barabati Fort, Cuttack.

Pl. 34.3: Mutilated figure of male musician, Barabati Fort, Cuttack.

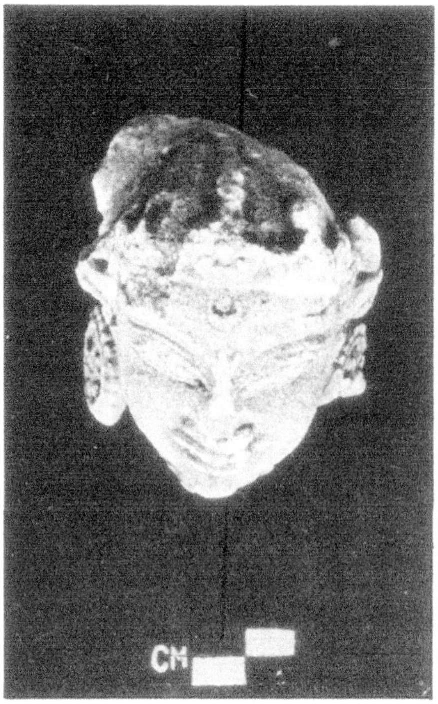

Pl. 34.4: Female head showing ornaments, Barabati Fort, Cuttack.

Pl. 34.5: Two female *Chawrī* bearers, Barabati Fort, Cuttack.

Pl. 35.1: General view of the mound from the North-East showing river Betwa in the background and also the remains of a bastion of the fortification-wall (Erich, Jhansi).

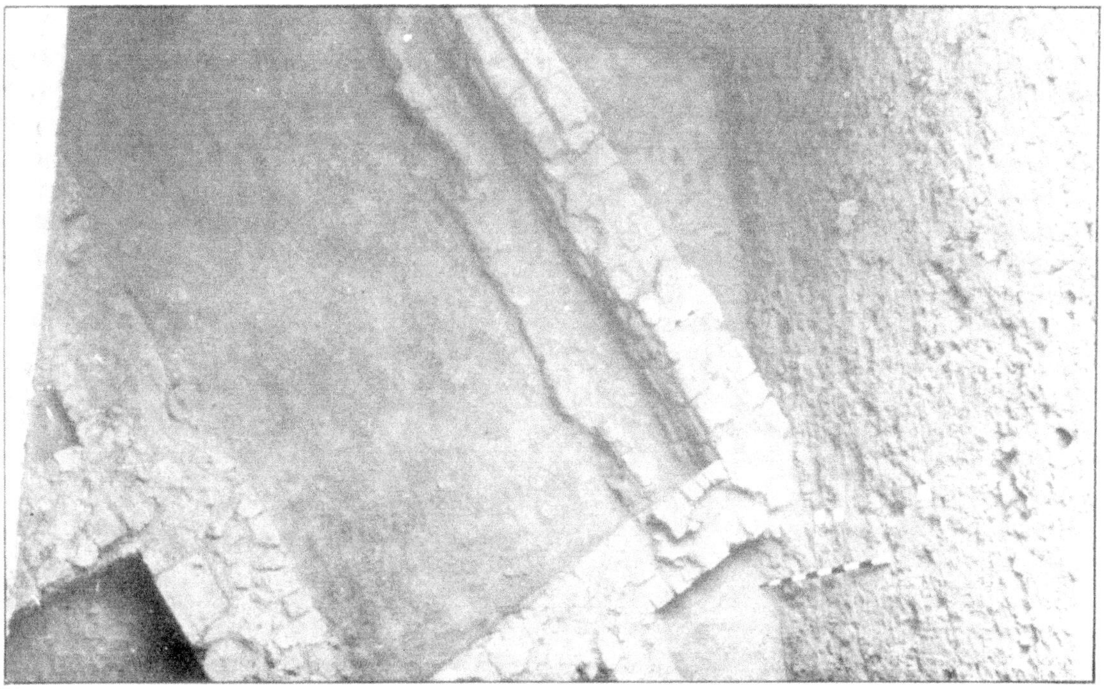

Pl. 35.2: View showing the excavated brick structure of the Gupta period in Tr. Bz3 Qd.4; view from N.W., Period IV (Erich, Jhansi).

Pl. 35.3: View showing a brick structure in Tr. XF 1 assignable to Kushan Period III (Erich, Jhansi).

Pl. 35.4: View showing a drain of burnt-bricks assignable to Sub-Period II-B. (Erich, Jhansi).

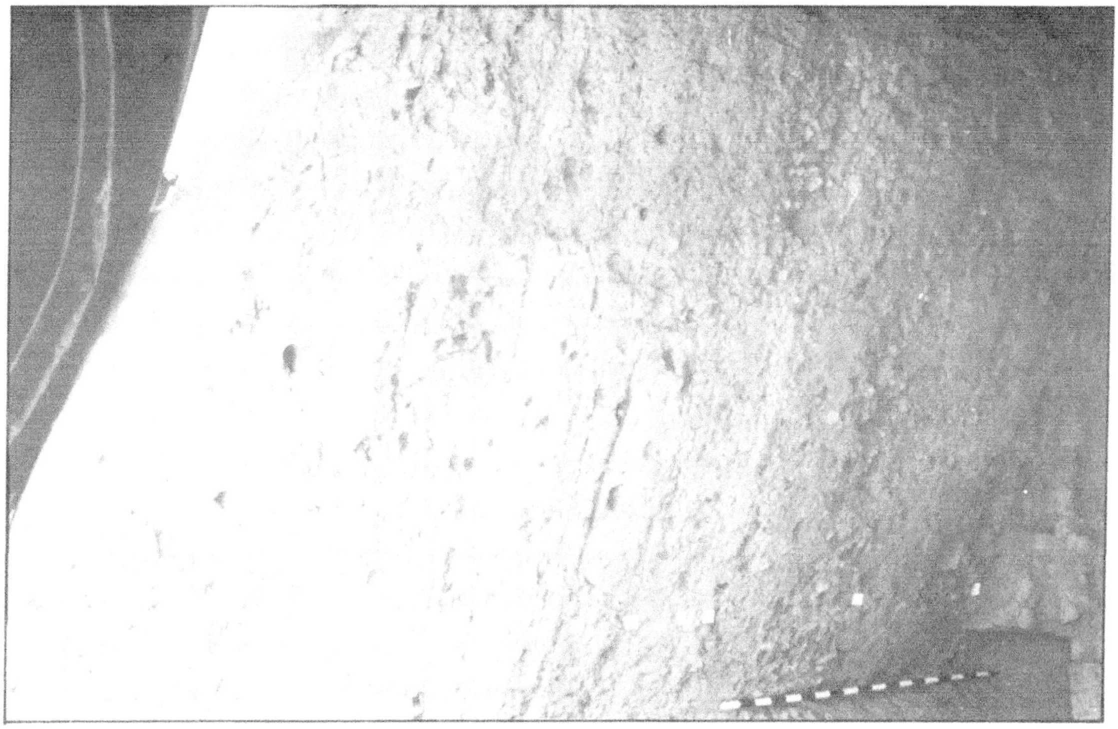

Pl. 35.5: View showing the section running E-W facing south, Tr. B3 Qd.4 (Erich, Jhansi).

Pl. 35.6: View showing the section running IV-S facing east, Tr. B3 Qd.4 (Erich, Jhansi).

Pl. 40.1: Satdhara : General view of Stupa No. 1, view from west.

Pl. 40.2 Satdhara : Stupa No. 8, during conservation.

Pl. 40.3: Satdhara : Showing stupa with inscription painted in rock-shelter near the site.

Pl. 40.4: Satdhara : Tree in railing.

INSCRIPTION

TRANSLITERATION

RATHAKAS DĀNAM

TRANSLATION

GIFT OF RATHAKA?

Pl. 40.5: Satdhara : Inscription.

Pl. 41.1: Sanghol PDI : Mud walls with remains of floor (two phases).

Pl. 41.2: Sanghol PD III : Two houses separated by a lane; the walls are of large sized mud and burnt bricks.

Pl. 41.3: Sanghol PD III : Hathiwara, house plan of mud and burnt bricks with a floor hearth in the room.

Pl. 41.4: Sanghol PD IV : Hathiwara, Palatial building in burnt brick, floors and post holes (Assembly Hall ?), Kushana Period.

Pl. 41.5: Sanghol PD IV : Hathiwara, Palatial Building-Details of brick walls and floor (Kushana Period).

Pl. 41.6: Sanghol PD IV : Hathiwara, Brick Platform or seat with post holes for a roof or canopy (Kushana Period).

Pl. 41.7: Sanghol PD IV : Hathiwara, Walls of the building identified as administrative block.

Pl. 41.8: Sanghol: Hathiwara, Brick building close to the palatial complex (?), Kushana Period.

Pl. 41.9: Sanghol: Hathiwara, General view of the religious complex, Kushana Period.

Pl. 41.10: Sanghol : Hathiwara, Burnt brick floor and an entrance close to the fort wall.

Pl. 41.11: Sanghol : Hathiwara, Fort wall of mud rivetted with burnt bricks.

Pl. 41.12: Sanghol : Hathiwara, Plan of house built of burnt bricks.

Pl. 41.13: Sanghol : Hearths or furnaces on a mud and brick floor, possibly a workshop.

Pl. 43.1: Bannikoppa : Śrī Rāma (Locally known as Arjuna).

Pl. 43.2: Bannikoppa : Śrī Rāma bearing Chakra on the right shoulder (1) and holding Śankha in the left hand along with bows.

Pl. 43.3: Bannikoppa : Late Rashtrakuta pillar (1) and Chandvaśita (2) in the locally called Kṛshṇa (Sūrya) temple.

Pl. 43.4: Bannikoppa : (1) The Sūrya (locally called Kṛshṇa) image in the "Kṛshṇa" temple (2) Close view of the upper indicating the lotus designed nimbus.

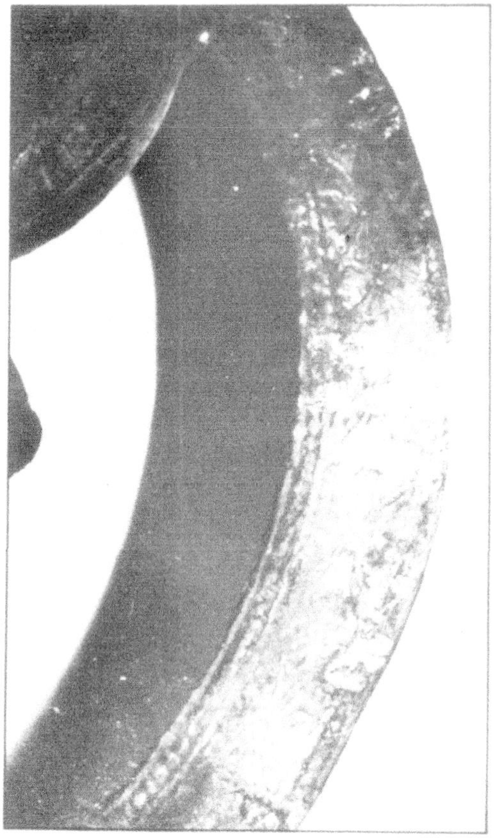

Pl. 43.5: Bannikoppa : (1) Sūrya image, lower part displaying Uṣā and Pratyaṣā and wheeled chariot drawn by seven houses. (2) Flower design on the prabhavali.

Pl. 43.6: Bannikoppa : (1) An 8th Cent. Badami Chalukyan inscription stating about the construction of a temple for Arjunīśvara by an individual from Uttarāpatha (2) The sculpture of Dūrga.

Pl. 44.1: Temple No. 1, General view from north-west, Ramgarh, Distt. Vidisha.

Pl. 44.2: Temple No. 1, (Door jamb), Ramgarh, Distt. Vidisha.

Pl. 44.3: Mahishasuramardini, Rock cut image, Ramgarh, Distt. Vidisha.

Pl. 44.4: Cave No. 6, Rock-cut images of Vishnu, Mahishasuramardini and Triviklama, Ramgarh, Distt. Vidisha.

Pl. 44.5: Rock-out image of Mahishasuramardini at the fort of the hill, Ramgarh, Distt. Vidisha.

Pl. 47.1: The Jackal at the Ram-fight.

Pl. 47.2: The Geese and the Tortoise.

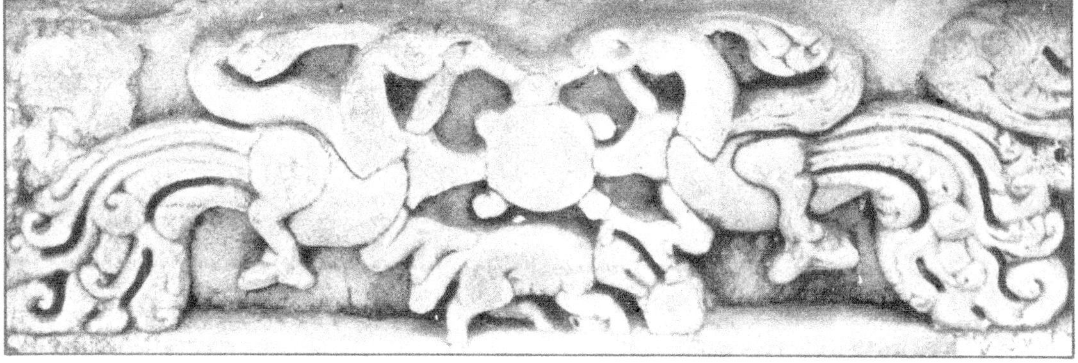

Pl. 47.3: The Geese and the Tortoise.

Pl. 47.4: Self defeating Forethought.

Pl. 47.5: The Brahman and the Crab.

Pl. 47.6: The Brahman, the Thief and the Ghost.

Pl. 47.7: The Monkey and the Crocodile.

Pl. 47.8: The Loyal Mongoose.

Pl. 48.1: Dharaṇendra, Badli (Haryana), 10th century A.D.

Pl. 52.1: Descent of Buddha, Kirtail, West Bengal, Stone, 11th Century A.D.

Pl. 52.2: Buddha in *bhumisparśamudrā*, Bareya, West Bengal, Stone, 11th century A.D.

Pl. 52.3: Buddha's life scene, Nepal, wood, 16th century A.D.

Pl. 54.1: A Harihara Sculpture from Khajuraho.

Pl. 55.1: Andhāsura Temple, General View.

Pl. 55.2: Andhāsura Temple, *Mahamandapa*.

Pl. 55.3: Andhāsura Temple, *Makara torana*.

Pl. 55.4: *Makara torana*, close up of *Makara* & Brahma.

Pl. 55.5: *Makara torana*, close up of Trinity.

Pl. 55.6: *Makara torana*, Close up of Vaikuntha & *Makara*.

Pl. 55.7: *Makara torana*, close up of Siva *tandava*.

Pl. 55.8: *Makara torana*, closer view of Brahma.

Pl. 55.9: *Makara torana*, closer view of Vaikuntha Vishnu.

Pl. 55.10: Lakshmi-*sahita* Vaikuntha Vishnu, Banashankari temple, Basava Kalyana, Dist-Bijapur.

Pl. 57.1: Jina Ṛsabhanātha (with figs. of navagrahas, and Gomukha-Chakreśvari) Khajurāho.

Pl. 57.2: Gomukha and Brahmaśanti yakṣas and Ambikā yakṣī, Aisle Ceiling, Mahāvīra Temple Kumbhāriā, 11th cent. A.D.

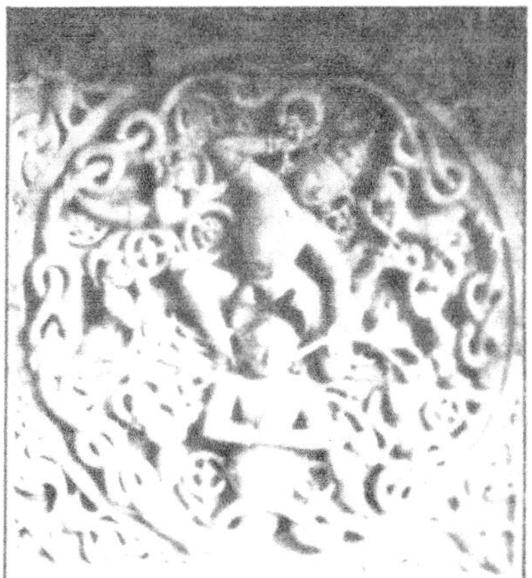

Pl. 57.3: Kṛshṇa Subduing Kāliya, Bhramīkā ceiling, Vimalavasahī (Mt. Abu).

Pl. 57.4: Āliṅgana-mūrti of Rāma-Sītā accompanied by Hanumān, north facade, Pārśvanātha Temple, Khajurāho, c. 950-70 A.D.

Pl. 57.5: Gaṇeśa, Neminātha Temple, Kumbhāriā, 12th cent. A.D.

Pl. 57.6: Brahmaśānti Yakṣa, ceiling near *raṅgamaṇḍapa*, Vimalavasahī, c. 11th century A.D.

Pl. 57.7: Kṣetrapāla, Temple No. 1, Deogarh, c. 11th century A.D.

Pl. 58.1: Śiva Temple, Panaheda, Rajasthan, General view.

Pl. 58.2: Śiva Temple, Panaheda, Rajasthan, Main Temple.

Pl. 58.3: Śiva Temple, Panaheda, Rajasthan, Door frame.

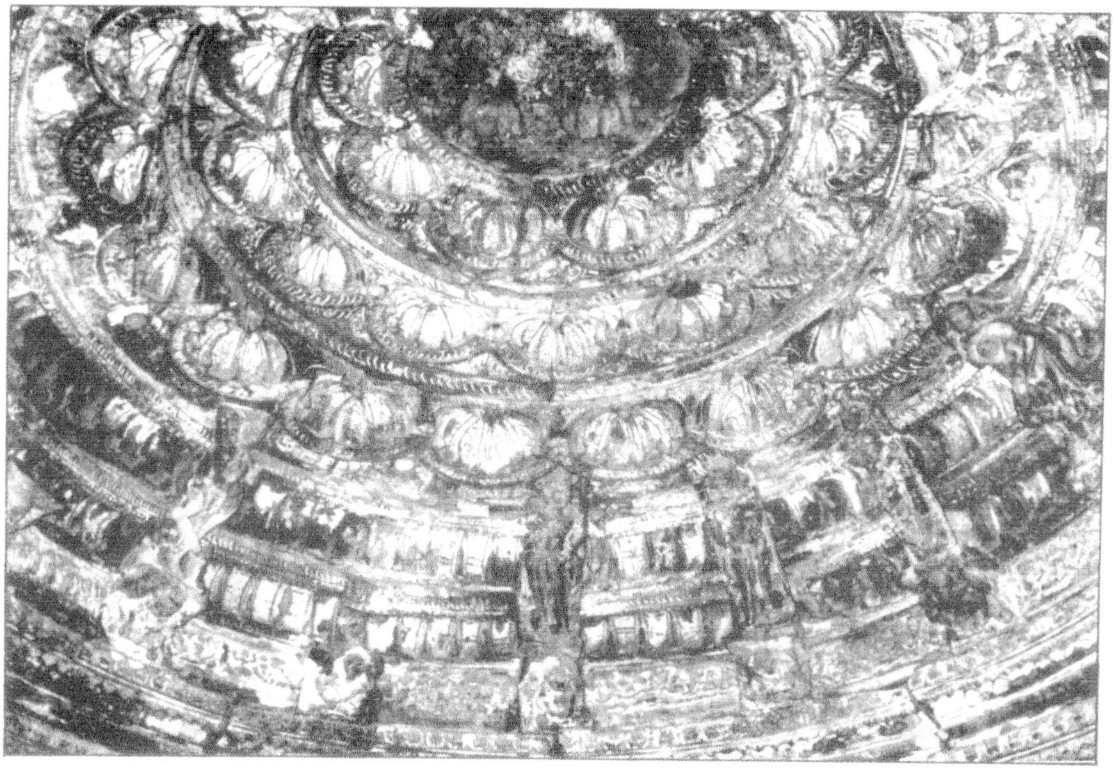

Pl. 58.4: Śiva Temple, Panaheda, Rajasthan, Central ceiling of *Sabhāmaṇḍapa*.

Pl. 58.5: Śiva Temple, Panaheda, Rajasthan : Śaivāchāryas.

Pl. 58.6: Śiva Temple, Panaheda, Rajasthan : Vaikuṇṭha.

Pl. 58.7: Śiva Temple, Panaheda, Rajasthan : Andhakāntaka Śiva, western *bhadra* niche.

Pl. 60.1: Seated Kubera, from Pabhosa, Allahabad. (Now in Lucknow Museum, No. G 56 c. 700 A.D.).

Pl. 60.2: Seated Kubera, from Mathura (Now in Mathura Museum, No. C 4. c. 600 A.D.).

Pl. 60.3: Seated Kubera from Mathura (Now in Mathura Museum, No. C 5, c. 600 A.D.).

Pl. 60.4: Kubera with his consort, from Badoh, Madhya Pradesh (Now in Central Museum, Gwalior, No. 11/4, c 9th cent. A.D.).

Pl. 63.1: Twin Vārāhi as Mothers, exterior of Jarai Mātā Temple, Baruā Sāgar (Jhansi).

Pl. 63.2: Twin Vārāhi, Indian Art Museum, Berlin (No. I. 5922).

Pl. 65.1: Karsha Monastery, Zanskar.

Pl. 65.2: Karsha Monastery, Zanskar.

Pl. 65.3: Sani Gonpa : Kanika *chorten*.

Pl. 65.4: Sani Gonpa : Sākyamuni Buddha.

Pl. 65.5: Karstekhar : Maitreya.

Pl. 65.6: Padam : Five Dhyānī Buddhas.

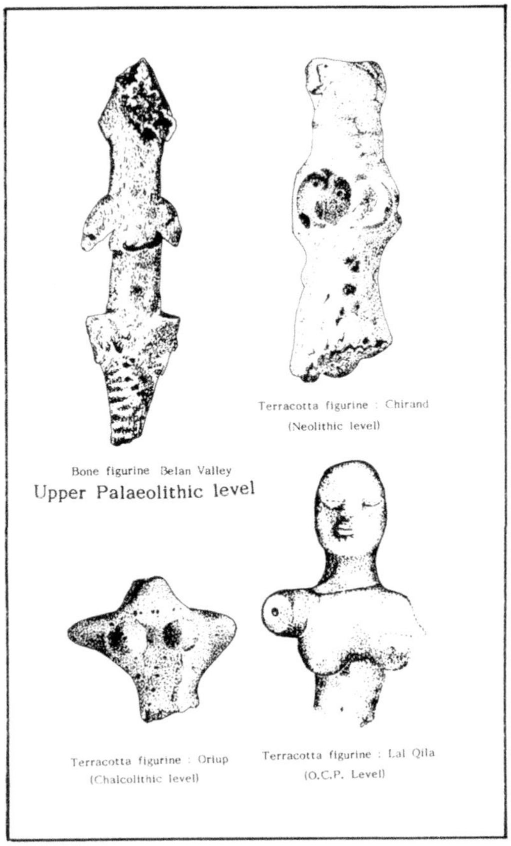

Pl. 66.1: Terracotta figurines.

Pl. 66.2: Terracotta figurines, Buxer (Pre N.B. Lend).

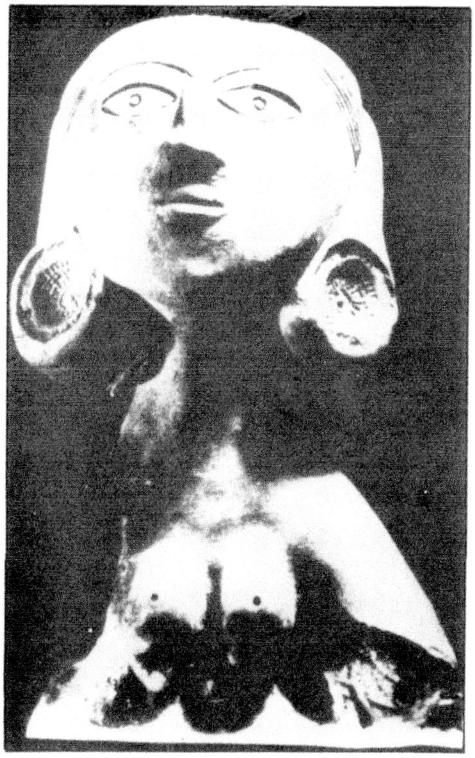

Pl. 66.3: Terracotta figurine, Buxer.

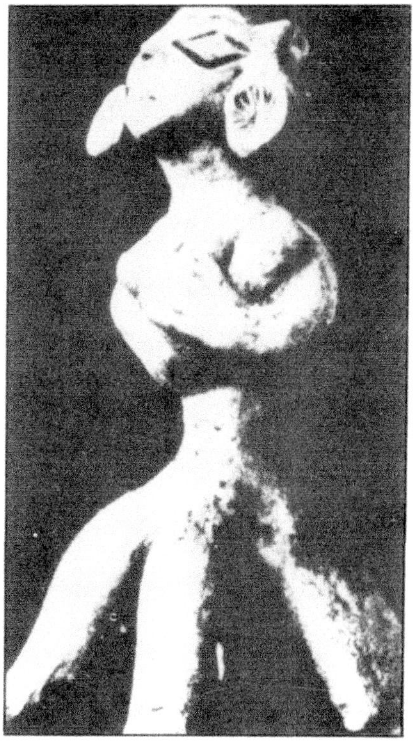

Pl. 66.4: Terracotta figurine, Buxer.

Pl. 66.5: Terracotta head, Buxer.

Pl. 66.6: Terracotta Sakti-Goddess : Champa (Sunga Period).

Pl. 67.1: A Gandharan stele depicting a standing scene from Jataka.

Pl. 68.1: Lakśmī-Nārāyaṇa, Kawardha.

Pl. 68.2: Lakśmī-Nārāyaṇa, Kawardha.

Pl. 68.3: Lakśmī-Nārāyaṇa, Kawardha.

Pl. 68.4: Lakśmi-Nārāyaṇa, Kawardha.

Pl. 68.5: Vāmana from Khatutola, Distt Rajnandgaon (M.P.).

Pl. 68.6: Four-armed Viṣṇu from Birkha-Bilahari, Distt. Rajnandgaon (M.P.).

Pl. 68.7: Four-armed Viṣṇu from Birkha-Bilahari, Distt. Rajanandgaon (M.P.).

Pl. 71.1: Lajjā Gaurī plague from Tarsang.

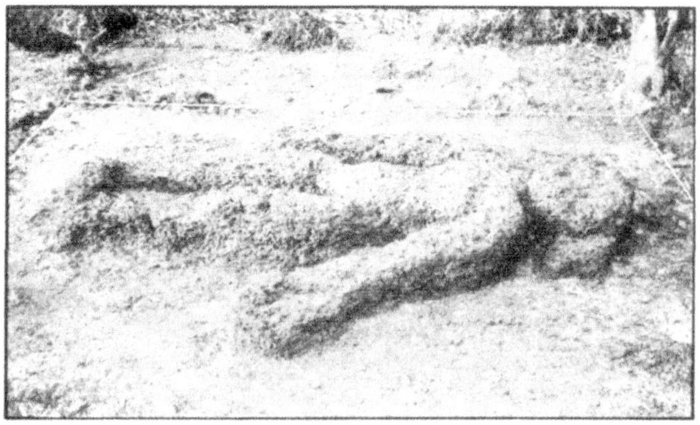

Pl. 72.1: Mother-goddess from Curdi-Goa.

Pl. 72.2: Stone disc from Ropar depicting mother-goddess.

Pl. 72.3: Mother-goddess on gold plague from Lauriya, Nandangarh, Bihar.

Pl. 77.1: Dancing Gaṇesha, Bhumra.

Pl. 77.2: Gajanana dancing, Rājīva lochana temple, Rajim (Raipur).

Pl. 77.3: Dancing Viglinavināśhaka, Hinglajgarh (Mandsore).

Pl. 77.4: Gaṇeshapaṭṭa with nine vināyakas.

Pl. 77.5: Nṛtta Gaṇapati in *lalita Karaṇa*, Malhar (Bilaspur).

Pl. 77.6: Gajavaktra dancing in *pārshvajānu*, Ujjain.

Pl. 77.7: Gaṇapati dancing in *ūrdhvajānu* Hinglajgarh (Mandsore).

Pl. 77.8: Gaṇesha dancing with the goddess accompanists, Sagar.

Pl. 77.9: *Ekadanta* dancing amidst *Saptamātṛkās* and *Vīrabhadra*, Toraṇa Mandira, Gyaraspur (Vidisha).

Pl. 77.10: Gaṇesha dancing with *gaṇas* in lower tier of a stele, Patan, Nepal.

Pl. 79.1: Kudan, Nepal : Moulding in Temple.

Pl. 79.2: Nepal : Moon god riding on a chariot of geese.

Pl. 79.3: (A) Bamiyan : Big Buddha during repairs.
(B) Bamiyan : Big Buddha after repairs

Pl. 79.4: (A) Bamiyan : Small Buddha during repairs.
(B) Bamiyan : Small Buddha after repairs.

Pl. 79.5: Balkh : Shrine of Khwaja Abu Nasar.

Pl. 79.6: Angkorvat : General view of temples.

Pl. 79.7: Angkorvat : Repairs on Embankment.

Pl. 79.8: Angkorvat : Apsara.